Productivity in Higher Education

National Bureau of
Economic Research
Conference Report

Productivity in Higher Education

Edited by **Caroline M. Hoxby and Kevin Stange**

The University of Chicago Press

Chicago and London

The University of Chicago Press, Chicago 60637
The University of Chicago Press, Ltd., London
© 2019 by the National Bureau of Economic Research, Inc.
Published 2019
Printed in the United States of America

28 27 26 25 24 23 22 21 20 19   1 2 3 4 5

ISBN-13: 978-0-226-57458-5   (cloth)
ISBN-13: 978-0-226-57461-5   (e-book)
DOI: https://doi.org/10.7208/chicago/9780226574615.001.0001

Library of Congress Cataloging-in-Publication Data

Names: Stange, Kevin M., author. | Hoxby, Caroline Minter, author.
Title: Productivity in higher education / Caroline M. Hoxby and Kevin
    Stange, editors.
Other titles: National Bureau of Economic Research conference report.
Description: Chicago : University of Chicago Press, 2019. | Series:
    National Bureau of Economic Research conference report | Includes
    bibliographical references and index.
Identifiers: LCCN 2019016543 | ISBN 9780226574585 (cloth) |
    ISBN 9780226574615 (ebook)
Subjects: LCSH: Educational productivity—United States. |
    Education, Higher—United States—Costs. | Educational
    accountability—United States.
Classification: LCC LB2806.24 .S73 2019 | DDC 378.73—dc23
LC record available at https://lccn.loc.gov/2019016543

♾ This paper meets the requirements of ANSI/NISO Z39.48-1992
(Permanence of Paper).

Relation of the Directors to the
Work and Publications of the
National Bureau of Economic Research

1. The object of the NBER is to ascertain and present to the economics profession, and to the public more generally, important economic facts and their interpretation in a scientific manner without policy recommendations. The Board of Directors is charged with the responsibility of ensuring that the work of the NBER is carried on in strict conformity with this object.

2. The President shall establish an internal review process to ensure that book manuscripts proposed for publication DO NOT contain policy recommendations. This shall apply both to the proceedings of conferences and to manuscripts by a single author or by one or more co-authors but shall not apply to authors of comments at NBER conferences who are not NBER affiliates.

3. No book manuscript reporting research shall be published by the NBER until the President has sent to each member of the Board a notice that a manuscript is recommended for publication and that in the President's opinion it is suitable for publication in accordance with the above principles of the NBER. Such notification will include a table of contents and an abstract or summary of the manuscript's content, a list of contributors if applicable, and a response form for use by Directors who desire a copy of the manuscript for review. Each manuscript shall contain a summary drawing attention to the nature and treatment of the problem studied and the main conclusions reached.

4. No volume shall be published until forty-five days have elapsed from the above notification of intention to publish it. During this period a copy shall be sent to any Director requesting it, and if any Director objects to publication on the grounds that the manuscript contains policy recommendations, the objection will be presented to the author(s) or editor(s). In case of dispute, all members of the Board shall be notified, and the President shall appoint an ad hoc committee of the Board to decide the matter; thirty days additional shall be granted for this purpose.

5. The President shall present annually to the Board a report describing the internal manuscript review process, any objections made by Directors before publication or by anyone after publication, any disputes about such matters, and how they were handled.

6. Publications of the NBER issued for informational purposes concerning the work of the Bureau, or issued to inform the public of the activities at the Bureau, including but not limited to the NBER Digest and Reporter, shall be consistent with the object stated in paragraph 1. They shall contain a specific disclaimer noting that they have not passed through the review procedures required in this resolution. The Executive Committee of the Board is charged with the review of all such publications from time to time.

7. NBER working papers and manuscripts distributed on the Bureau's web site are not deemed to be publications for the purpose of this resolution, but they shall be consistent with the object stated in paragraph 1. Working papers shall contain a specific disclaimer noting that they have not passed through the review procedures required in this resolution. The NBER's web site shall contain a similar disclaimer. The President shall establish an internal review process to ensure that the working papers and the web site do not contain policy recommendations, and shall report annually to the Board on this process and any concerns raised in connection with it.

8. Unless otherwise determined by the Board or exempted by the terms of paragraphs 6 and 7, a copy of this resolution shall be printed in each NBER publication as described in paragraph 2 above.

Contents

Acknowledgments

This project, *Productivity in Higher Education*, came out of long discussions among National Bureau of Economic Research (NBER) economists, especially those who study colleges and universities. We, as a group, believe that our understanding of how productive these institutions are has been recently transformed by much better data, to which we can apply much better analysis. As a group, we believe we can be much more helpful to higher education policy makers than in previous years. We believe we can provide them with the evidence and tools they need in order to engage in meaningful self-evaluation and evidence-based planning. Our main concern, as economists who work in this area, is that we are getting far out in advance of leaders in higher education—that is, while these leaders believe that many questions cannot be answered or analyzed, we economists are confident that they are wrong in this regard. Specifically, although their intentions are excellent, they do not recognize the pace of advance in the economics of higher education. We economists are determined to give them the full advantage of our data and tools, even if we have to argue them into the idea that it is possible to be much better informed.

When we, as a group of NBER economists, took our arguments to NBER president James Poterba, he enthusiastically set us on the path toward writing this book and hosting the two conferences related to it. We thank him for his insight and support.

In addition, we wish especially to thank two people, and their associated foundations, who understood the promise—better evidence, better analysis—that we had to offer. These two people are Daniel Goroff of the Alfred P. Sloan Foundation and Michael McPherson, then of the Spencer Foundation. (McPherson has recently retired from Spencer but remains active in higher education policy.) Goroff and McPherson contributed to this project with their thoughts, their advice, and their participation in our enterprise. We are also deeply grateful for the generous funding that we received from the Sloan Foundation and the Spencer Foundation, which made this volume and its associated conferences possible.

This volume benefited greatly from the feedback that we, the editors, and the authors received from participants in two conferences we held. Specifically, we wish to thank, for their comments and insights, Lawrence Bacow, Jeffrey Brown, Charles Clotfelter, Will Dobbie, Glenn Ellison, John Friedman, Joshua Goodman, Catharine Hill, Marguerite Joutz, David Lee, Bridget Long, Jed Marsh, Patrick Methvin, Philip Oreopoulos, Martha Pollack, Francesca Purcell, and Jeffrey Smith. We are also grateful for the thoughtful questions of Nick Anderson, Goldie Blumenstyk, Zachary Goldfarb, Neil Irwin, Doug Lederman, David Leonhardt, Dylan Matthews, Joshua Mitchell, Paul Tough, and Joshua Zumbrun.

Volumes like this depend on the generosity and hard work of many people. We are very grateful to the anonymous reviewers who gave us thoughtful and constructive feedback on all the chapters in the volume, greatly improving the quality of its scholarly contribution. We wish that we could thank you by name for this selfless service. We are extremely appreciative of Helena Fitz-Patrick, of the NBER Publications Department, who has shepherded this volume through to completion. We could not have done it without her. We also thank Charles Radin of the NBER and the extraordinarily conscientious NBER conference staff, all of whom provided invaluable support to our conferences.

Finally and most importantly, we acknowledge each of the authors whose work is represented in this volume. Their thought and rigorous analysis have advanced our collective understanding of productivity in higher education.

Introduction

Caroline M. Hoxby and Kevin Stange

Our Enterprise

One of us (Hoxby) recalls a meeting, not so long ago, in which university leaders and faculty were discussing a vast project that cost at least nine figures. The costs were discussed in great detail. As the discussion neared its end, Hoxby finally asked, "But what are the benefits of the project? Is its ratio of benefits to costs high, or would it be better to allocate the funds to more productive uses?" These questions startled the group for two reasons. First, those assembled had fallen into the habit of associating the merit of a project with its costs, not its ratio of benefits to costs (its productivity). Second, most thought it absurd even to consider measuring benefits. These two reasons were related: because most believed that it was impossible to measure benefits, they routinely focused on costs. Indeed, these habits are not limited to university staff. When higher education experts were asked which was the best institution, they tended to suggest a costly one and cite its high spending as evidence of its quality.

To economists at least, it seems unnatural to think so much about costs but so little about the productivity of a sector, higher education, that plays such a crucial role in the economy and society. For any society-wide question that involves allocating resources between some other sector, such as health

Caroline M. Hoxby is the Scott and Donya Bommer Professor in Economics at Stanford University, a senior fellow of the Hoover Institution and the Stanford Institute for Economic Policy Research, and a research associate and director of the Economics of Education Program at the National Bureau of Economic Research.

Kevin Stange is associate professor of public policy at the University of Michigan and a research associate of the National Bureau of Economic Research.

For acknowledgments, sources of research support, and disclosure of the authors' material financial relationships, if any, please see http://www.nber.org/chapters/c13874.ack.

care, and higher education, we need to know the sectors' relative productivity. When judging whether the market for higher education generates good incentives or, rather, is plagued by market failures that allow institutions to be grossly inefficient, we need to know productivity. When assessing government policies, such as grants or loans, that subsidize students, we need to know the productivity of the investments these policies facilitate. To allocate a budget efficiently among their institution's many activities, higher education leaders need to understand productivity. When students decide whether and where to attend college, they need to know whether those investments will be productive. Thus, at every level of decision-making (social, institutional, individual), the productivity of higher education investments is crucial.

This volume, *Productivity in Higher Education*, is the result of a concerted effort by National Bureau of Economic Research scholars to advance the frontier of knowledge about productivity in higher education. The timing of this push is not accidental. Rather, it is the result of newly available data that allow us to assess benefits *much* better and analyze costs better as well. The new data come from administrative sources and therefore tend to be accurate. They also tend to be population data, not a sample. These attributes of the data are crucial for many of the studies in this volume. It is not merely that the better data make the findings more precise or permit otherwise infeasible empirical strategies, though they do both of these. Crucially, they allow researchers to ask questions that simply could not have been asked previously. This expansion of the frontier of questions we can credibly answer meets a heightened demand for these answers from students, parents, and policy makers. We think it is fair to say that the productivity of higher education institutions—from large elite research universities to small for-profit colleges—has never been under greater scrutiny than right now. In short, this is an exciting and opportune time for research on productivity in higher education.

This is not to say that the enterprise is without challenges. Some of these challenges recur so often among the studies in this volume that it is worthwhile enumerating them now. The first challenge is multiple outcomes. Higher education potentially affects skills, earnings, invention, altruism, employment, occupations, marriage, and many other outcomes. Even if we have data on all such outcomes, how are researchers to prioritize them for analysis? A related difficulty is the "multiproduct" nature of institutions of higher education. Even the simplest institutions usually have several degree programs, and large research universities conduct a bewildering array of activities across numerous major domains: undergraduate teaching, professional programs, doctoral advising, research, medical experimentation, and so on. Any study of higher education must prioritize which activities to analyze and make thoughtful decisions about how to allocate costs associated with resources, such as infrastructure, that are shared by several activities.

The third recurrent challenge, which can be formidable, is selection on students' aptitude and prior achievement. By the time they arrive at the door of a postsecondary institution, students are already greatly differentiated. Indeed, students who attend the most-selective universities have arguably learned as much by the end of the eighth grade as have the high school graduates who attend the least selective institutions. Any study that credits the most-selective institutions with the incoming preparation of its students will greatly exaggerate the productivity of those institutions. Similarly, a study might exaggerate the productivity of an institution if it draws students from richer backgrounds and these backgrounds have an independent effect on future outcomes. A fourth recurrent challenge is attribution. Students who attend nonselective institutions often initially enroll at one school, take some classes at another, and finally finish at a third. Students who attend highly selective colleges do not "roam" so much as undergraduates, but they often pursue graduate education. All these layers of education affect a person's outcomes, making attribution to any one institution difficult. A fifth recurrent challenge is the public nature of some potential benefits of higher education. Public benefits range from students learning from one another (at the micro end) to research findings that benefit all mankind (at the macro end). While these benefits may be measurable, it is often difficult to trace them to their source. A final recurrent issue is that there are always at least a few perspectives from which to assess productivity. There is the view of society as a whole, personified as the social planner who takes into account all the benefits of higher education, including public ones, but also takes into account all the costs, regardless of who pays for them or how. Then there is the view of a government: Will its current spending on higher education generate sufficient future tax revenue to balance the books? Finally, there is the view of students. They may care little about public benefits and will surely focus on costs they pay themselves versus those funded by taxpayers or philanthropists.

In common, the studies in this volume confront these challenges. Each study deals with them differently, and that is part of what makes the collection interesting. Together, the studies constitute a concise course in approaches to overcoming these challenges. But is there anything that these approaches share?

First, all the studies in this volume are resolutely practical when approaching the challenges mentioned above. The authors refuse to give up on measuring benefits or costs simply because the measures are imperfect. They make smart choices or, when the choice is not obvious, adopt a pluralistic attitude and offer several reasonable measures as alternatives. When the authors choose which outcomes to prioritize, they pay attention to those that appear to matter most to those who finance higher education. The authors are also practical in consistently focusing on institutions' "core business," the activities that are most important to the schools they are studying. (These are not necessarily the same activities for, say, a for-profit online institution versus a selective research university.)

Second, the studies in this volume are scrupulous about differentiating between evidence that is credibly causal and evidence that is only correlational. Each study devotes great effort to developing an empirical strategy that can produce results that can confidently be identified as causal. Some of the studies use the equivalent of randomized controlled trials. Others rely on natural experiments. Others must rely on nonexperimental and descriptive analysis. Regardless, all the studies are frank about which results can confidently be given a causal interpretation and which should be read more cautiously.

Finally and most importantly, all the studies draw deeply on economic reasoning. Prior work on productivity in higher education has not used economics to structure hypotheses and evidence. But at least in the United States, economics does apply to the higher education sector. Institutions do function in markets. They encounter prices set by others and set prices themselves. They face incentives, and their workers act in accord with incentives. Institutions cannot set faculty salaries or tuition arbitrarily but are constrained by supply and demand. Their nontuition sources of revenue (grants, gifts, appropriations, patent revenues) also depend, in a fairly systematic way, on their producing certain outcomes. Students may be less informed investors than is optimal, but they do make choices among institutions and decide whether to stay enrolled or leave. In short, higher education has its own labor markets, its own investors, and its own industrial organization. By drawing systematically on insights from labor economics, finance, and industrial organization, researchers make much more progress than would otherwise seem possible. (Admittedly, the analysis would be easier if all institutions of higher education shared a straightforward objective function such as maximizing profits.)

The Challenges Are Not Unique to Higher Education

We enumerated five major challenges to understanding productivity in higher education: multiple outcomes, the multiproduct nature of institutions, selection, attribution, and the public nature of some potential benefits. In a very insightful follow-up to this introduction, in chapter 1, "What Health Care Teaches Us about Measuring Productivity in Higher Education," Douglas Staiger explains how the *same* challenges plague the study of productivity in health care. By showing us the parallels, he clarifies each challenge and allows us to see it at a 1,000-foot view, not a view too close for acumen. Moreover, he lays out how health care research has addressed each challenge, thereby giving us highly practical guidance. We encourage readers to read Staiger's contribution as a second introduction that will organize their thinking on all subsequent chapters.

What We Learned

In chapter 2, "The Productivity of US Postsecondary Institutions," Caroline Hoxby attempts to compute the productivity of the vast majority of undergraduate programs in the United States. In the process, she addresses several of the key issues that plague studies of productivity in higher education. For instance, she argues that the multiple outcomes problem cannot be evaded but can be addressed by presenting results based on a variety of outcomes. The study emphasizes productivity results based on earnings (because these matter disproportionately for the financial stability of the postsecondary sector) but also shows productivity results based on public service and innovative contributions.

The study's most important advance is a proposed remedy for the selection problem that is based on comparing the outcomes of students who are extremely similar on incoming achievement (test scores, grades) and who, crucially, apply to the same postsecondary institutions, thus demonstrating similar interests and motivation. This approach employs all the possible quasi experiments in which a student "flips a coin" between schools that have nearly identical selectivity or in which admission staff "flip a coin" between students with nearly identical achievement. This quasi-experimental remedy is intuitive and credible, but it also generates extraordinary data requirements. Thus this study gives us our first example of how having better data allows us to pursue empirical and econometric strategies that would otherwise be out of bounds.

The longitudinal data in this study allow Hoxby to compute *lifetime* educational costs (private and social) and predict *lifetime* benefits.

The study's most important finding is that when earnings are used to measure benefits, the productivity of a dollar is fairly similar across a wide array of selective postsecondary institutions. This result is striking because the most-selective schools spend several times as much per pupil as schools that are only modestly selective. That is, educational resources and students' capacity to use those educational resources are rising in a sufficiently parallel way that productivity is roughly flat—even though selectivity and resources both rise fairly dramatically. This result indicates that there are no easy gains to society from, say, taking a dollar away from the most-selective institutions and giving it to somewhat less-selective ones. Also, this result suggests that market forces compel some amount of efficiency among selective institutions. However, Hoxby also finds that compared to selective institutions, nonselective postsecondary institutions are less productive on average and vary greatly in their productivity. This result implies that market forces exert little discipline on such schools, allowing nonproductive institutions to attract students even when they are located side by side with much more productive ones.

Interestingly, the study also concludes that market forces do not discipline postsecondary institutions if public service is used as the measure of institutional output: selective schools that enroll very similar students and cost very similar amounts differ substantially on their contributions to public service.

The multiple outcomes problem is also tackled by Veronica Minaya and Judith Scott-Clayton in chapter 3, "Labor Market Outcomes and Postsecondary Accountability: Are Imperfect Metrics Better Than None?" This chapter exemplifies the relentless practicality described as a prime virtue of studies in this volume. Minaya and Scott-Clayton put themselves in the shoes of policy makers who want to assess their state's institutions but who can access only the data that could likely be made available. They use an impressive database that contains demographics (race, ethnicity, sex, age), zip code at initial enrollment, and full postsecondary transcripts for all students who enrolled in a public institution in one of the most populous US states over an 8-year period. They then follow the students for 10 years in the state's employment, unemployment, and earnings records. They face realistic constraints, such as students being "lost" if they transfer to private colleges or move out of state.

What could a policy maker learn about institutions' productivity from such data? Minaya and Scott-Clayton's first key finding is that transcript data are insufficient. While transcript data allow them to construct productivity measures based on credits earned and degree attainment, schools' rankings change substantially when outcomes based on labor market data are added. This indicates that the skills students learn are not fully summarized by what their transcripts say, especially if we weigh skills by how employers value them. Moreover, Minaya and Scott-Clayton find that there are important improvements in knowledge about productivity if we do not merely rely on *early* labor market–based measures (earnings and employment in initial jobs) but observe the whole first decade of a student's career.

The authors' other key finding is that productivity measures are problematic if they do not adjust for students' demographics and the sociodemographics of the zip code from which they come. Unadjusted measures overstate the productivity of institutions that draw students whose incoming demographics likely give them advantages in college and in finding initial jobs. Tellingly, *adjusted* short-term measures are more correlated with long-term labor market outcomes. This is a classic test of whether a measure truly records value added or whether it reflects incoming differences (selection). The reason this test works is that incoming differences, such as whether a student grew up in a richer family, are valued less by the labor market over time, whereas skills are valued as much or more over time (Altonji and Pierret 2001).

A similar test is used by Evan Riehl, Juan E. Saavedra, and Miguel Urquiola, who analyze administrative data that includes, remarkably, learning outcomes. For chapter 4, "Learning and Earning: An Approximation to College

Value Added in Two Dimensions," they draw on data from Colombia, a country with a vigorous market for higher education that is not dissimilar to that of the United States. Importantly, Colombian students' learning is assessed by standardized examinations not only before they enter universities but also when they exit. Although the exit examinations are partially field-specific, parts of the preentry and exit examinations are designed to measure progress on a core set of skills. Thus the exams generate natural, learning-based measures of institutional value added. As a result, Riehl, Saavedra, and Urquiola assemble a uniquely comprehensive set of outcomes: outcomes based on transcripts (which provide important outcomes such as degree completion but are hard to compare across institutions); outcomes based on earnings and employment; and outcomes based on measures of learning that are standardized across institutions. We cannot overemphasize how singular this situation is. It is not merely that other researchers lack data like these: measures of standardized learning gains do not exist in other contexts.

Riehl, Saavedra, and Urquiola demonstrate that college productivity based on learning measures produces something quite different from productivity based on earnings, especially initial earnings. Learning-based measures are more highly correlated with long-term earnings than they are with initial earnings. As in Minaya and Scott-Clayton, this suggests that learning reflects long-term value added, while initial earnings more heavily reflect students' precollege characteristics. The authors confirm this by showing that productivity measures based on initial earnings favor schools that recruit students from affluent backgrounds and whose curricula stress business and vocational fields. Productivity measures based on learning favor schools that enroll high-aptitude students (regardless of their income background) and that stress the sciences, social sciences, and arts (the traditional liberal curriculum). Riehl, Saavedra, and Urquiola's analysis thus provides a cautionary tale for performance systems based entirely on graduation rates or initial earnings—the metrics that are currently popular (see Minaya and Scott-Clayton).

So far, we have only discussed how productivity differs among institutions. However, it could potentially differ substantially by field or program within each institution. Joseph G. Altonji and Seth D. Zimmerman, in chapter 5, "The Costs of and Net Returns to College Major," analyze whether productivity within an institution differs by college major. They begin by noting that people have often thought that they have answered this question when they have simply examined the initial earnings of graduates by college major. There are a few reasons why such a simplistic exercise does not suffice. For instance, there is substantial selection into majors: students with higher college aptitude tend to major in certain fields, and their higher earnings cannot be attributed entirely to their field. Also, the relationship between initial earnings and lifetime earnings varies by major. Engineering majors, for instance, have high initial earnings but subsequently experience unusually slow earnings growth.[1] However, Altonji and Zimmerman investigate a third and completely different explanation as to why initial earnings by college major are not a reliable guide to *productivity* by major: different majors cost different amounts, and costs are the denominator in any calculation of productivity.

The reason why cost differences between majors have rarely, if ever, been systematically analyzed is because even administrators often lack information on how much their school spends educating a history major, say, as opposed to a chemistry major. For want of data, administrators and researchers alike have therefore assumed costs are the same across majors. However, using uniquely detailed administrative data for all Florida public institutions, Altonji and Zimmerman show that this assumption is false: majors that are intensive in equipment, space, or faculty (especially highly paid faculty) can be dramatically more costly on a per-student basis. Examples are engineering and health sciences. The least-expensive majors require no equipment, need no dedicated space, have large classes, and have modestly paid faculty. An example is psychology. The authors show that if we consider costs, the productivity findings are very different from what we might conclude from a naive look at initial earnings. Strikingly, the ratio of initial earnings to costs is similar in majors with high earnings and high costs (such as engineering) and modest earnings and modest costs (such as public administration). The majors with the highest ratios of initial earnings to costs are ones such as business that have relatively high earnings but relatively low costs.

Few if any higher education leaders use data like that of Altonji and Zimmerman to make similarly sophisticated calculations of how productivity varies across majors. But perhaps they use less-formal, quantitative means to reach similar conclusions? If so, we might expect that they reallocate resources toward more-productive majors and away from less-productive ones. This is one of the important questions addressed Paul N. Courant and Sarah Turner in chapter 6, "Faculty Deployment in Research Universities."

In addition to the US Department of Education's administrative database that covers all research universities, Courant and Turner use internal data from two important public research universities.[2] The latter data, the likes of which are rarely available to researchers, allow them to study the productivity of individual faculty in an incredibly detailed way. For instance, they know how many students are in each class and whether it is taught by a faculty member alone or with the help of nonfaculty instructors, graduate students, and so on. Their measure of teaching productivity is novel: essentially, how

---

1. For evidence on these points, see Hoxby (2018).
2. The database is the Integrated Postsecondary Education Data System. It is, in fact, used to some extent by every study in this volume, a demonstration of its ubiquitous value.

many students are produced by each dollar of faculty pay. This measure makes sense if each student generates about the same amount of revenue.[3]

Courant and Turner first demonstrate that faculty differ greatly in both their research productivity and their teaching productivity. These differences occur across universities, across fields within a university, and across faculty within a field within a university.

This is a fascinating finding, but what explains it? Here, Courant and Turner demonstrate how economic reasoning can guide hypotheses. They argue that faculty in different fields must be paid different amounts because their *outside* labor market opportunities differ. For instance, an economics or business professor's pay outside of academia would be high relative to that of a classics professor's. Moreover, the authors argue, it is very difficult for universities to reallocate either students or faculty across fields to equalize productivity. Given that universities compete for students in a market and students choose their fields based on factors that include later remuneration, universities cannot plausibly force students to major in undersubscribed fields simply to raise faculty productivity there. Universities cannot reallocate faculty easily for reasons that are both more mechanical and more economically subtle. As a mechanical matter, a professor who is expert in chemistry is not prepared to conduct research or teach courses that require expertise in history or vice versa. (Of course, a university can gradually reallocate its faculty by slowing hiring in some fields and accelerating it in others. Courant and Turner show that universities do this to some extent.) But even if a university could easily reallocate its faculty to equalize productivity fully, it has incentives not to do so but rather to protect a critical mass of expertise in all fields. A research university that failed to comprehend all fields of knowledge would have difficulty attracting philanthropic and government support.

Constrained by the labor market, the market for students, and the market for support, how can universities align faculty pay and faculty productivity? Courant and Turner show that they do this (perhaps as much as they can) by allowing larger class sizes and more nonfaculty teaching in fields where faculty are expensive. Faculty who are more productive researchers are allocated less undergraduate teaching and more time for research—compensating differentials for their not taking jobs outside of academia. On the whole, one comes away from the study with the impression that, though constrained in many and complex ways, universities maximize productivity more than one might think based on their reluctance to conduct formal analyses.

---

3. This measure of teaching productivity applies less well to the most selective private institutions for two reasons. First, revenue differs greatly across students because they pay more differentiated tuition, because gifts are associated much more with some students than others, and because no revenue comes from state appropriations (which tend to be made on a flat per-student basis). Second, a faculty member's influence on the world is less likely to run through mass teaching than through instructing relatively few but stellar students.

Pieter De Vlieger, Brian Jacob, and Kevin Stange, in chapter 7, "Measuring Instructor Effectiveness in Higher Education," examine similar issues, but in a very different part of the postsecondary market: the for-profit sector where online course-taking is prevalent and institutions focus almost entirely on teaching, especially the teaching of elemental college courses. This sector also differs greatly from the research university and selective college sectors because the for-profit institutions' objectives are fairly unidimensional (profits) and because 100 percent of their revenue comes from tuition (as opposed to philanthropy or government appropriations). For-profit institutions therefore only have incentives to operate programs that attract students and that can be taught at a low-enough cost to turn a profit. Furthermore, their students tend to be intent on receiving educational credentials in order to raise their earnings as opposed to having more-complex goals, such as becoming liberally educated, earning a top professional degree (medical, for instance), or learning to conduct research. In short, we should think of the University of Phoenix, the institution the authors study, as facing very different economic incentives and constraints than research universities and selective colleges.

De Vlieger, Jacob, and Stange estimate instructor productivity in college algebra, a course required of all students in the University of Phoenix's baccalaureate programs. They observe more than 300,000 students and 2,000 instructors, a testament to the size of the institution. Using internal administrative data, the authors show that the assignment of students to teachers is virtually random once they condition on the identity of the course, section, level, and student characteristics. Thus they analyze what is essentially a randomized controlled trial and, as a result, produce highly credible results.

De Vlieger, Jacob, and Stange show that the algebra instructors vary greatly in their productivity. A 1 standard-deviation increase in their value added translates into a 0.3 standard-deviation increase in students' math skills. Variation is also great when instructors' productivity is measured by students' taking follow-up courses or earning subsequent credits. Interestingly, instructors' productivity varies more for in-person than online courses. Put another way, if students want to obtain instruction that has maximum value added, they must do it in person because the online experience suppresses variation in instructional value added.[4] This result has important implications, to which we return below.

De Vlieger, Jacob, and Stange's most striking result, from the economics perspective, is that the University of Phoenix pays these highly variant instructors exactly the same amount. Thus performance differences translate directly to large productivity differences across instructors. This is not because the institution is constrained to do so: its instructors are on short-term con-

---

4. Of course, if students wanted to experience unusually low instructional quality, they might also seek out in-person settings.

tracts and are not unionized. Of course, it is possible that the institution, having learned from the study, will henceforth make pay more differentiated. Alternatively, the result suggests that the institution's profits are more purely a function of its total enrollment than they are a function of its students' success in acquiring skills or attaining credentials. If the sort of students who consider nonselective for-profit institutions do not make their enrollment choices based on the schools' record of skill production, it might make sense for the University of Phoenix to pay all instructors the same amount.

In 2006, the US Department of Education eliminated a rule that constrained postsecondary institutions to offer no more than 50 percent of their courses online. This rule had forced institutions such as the University of Phoenix to locate instructional space in metropolitan areas with sufficient population density that each space could attain minimum efficient scale. (Minimum efficient scale requires enough students taking each class and enough total classes to justify renting and managing the space.) Moreover, the rule change occurred at a time when broadband service had become available almost everywhere, even in areas of low population density.

In chapter 8, "The Competitive Effects of Online Education," David J. Deming, Michael Lovenheim, and Richard Patterson show that the 2006 rule change allowed online enrollment to expand greatly and, more specifically, into markets that had previously supported only a few postsecondary institutions. For the brick-and-mortar institutions in those markets, the change potentially constituted a major and rather sudden increase in competition. For the students in those markets, online enrollment constituted an increase in their educational options, especially with regard to price and timing flexibility. (It is not obvious that online enrollment constituted a major increase in curricular options. This is because online postsecondary programs remain, probably for technical and cost reasons, focused on fairly standard courses and credentials that were likely already available locally, even in markets with only a few brick-and-mortar institutions. The availability of online education has not yet much affected the ease with which a person can earn, say, a degree that is equivalent to one from a major research university or selective college.)

Deming, Lovenheim, and Patterson show that the increase in competition reduced enrollment at private, nonselective brick-and-mortar institutions located in areas where they had previously been one of only a few such choices. This makes sense because they are the closest substitutes for online institutions that also tend to be nonselective and that offer similar curricula.

A superficial economic analysis might then suggest that the private, nonselective brick-and-mortar schools would respond to the competition by reducing tuition. But they need not compete purely on price. Indeed, when we recall that instructors' productivity varies more for in-person classes, economics helps us anticipate what actually happened: private brick-and-mortar schools reduced class size and raised tuition. Such a response could only be a market equilibrium if the brick-and-mortar and online institutions were becoming increasingly differentiated on grounds *other* than price. What seems most likely (and in accord with models from industrial organizations) is that the brick-and-mortar schools began to specialize in students who valued a fairly intimate in-person experience where, as previously shown, instructors can exercise their talent more than they can in online classes. The online institutions probably specialized in students who put greater weight on price or the flexibility of the timing of their classes.

These results remind us that as the market for (brick-and-mortar) higher education became dramatically more geographically integrated and competitive during the 20th century, institutions did not merely compete on price (tuition) but instead became differentiated on student aptitude, curriculum, and many other dimensions (Hoxby 2009). The market for postsecondary education has never been a simple market for an undifferentiated good where pure price competition prevails. It is interesting that such a statement applies to nonselective institutions focused on teaching elemental courses, not only to research universities and selective colleges.

In the most recent Beginning Postsecondary Students study, 94 percent of students who commenced their postsecondary education at a two-year public institution (community college) stated, in their first year, that their degree goal was a baccalaureate degree.[5] This would suggest that such schools' productivity ought to be evaluated, at least in part, on whether they allow students to achieve that nearly universal goal. Interestingly, almost no studies prior to Carrell and Kurlaender's, in this volume, attempt such an evaluation. This is largely because prior studies often depend on data sources that do not reliably track students as they transfer from two- to four-year colleges. Carrell and Kurlaender, instead, use remarkable administrative data that allow them to follow all California students from their high schools, to community colleges, and on to the California State University campuses (which are the destination of the vast majority of students transferring from two- to four-year colleges).

In chapter 9, "Estimating the Productivity of Community Colleges in Paving the Road to Four-Year College Success," Scott E. Carrell and Michal Kurlaender estimate each community college's productivity, where the outcomes of interest are the probability of students making a successful transfer to a four-year college (the "extensive margin") and the achievement of those students once at four-year colleges (the "intensive margin"). The data are so rich that the authors can adjust for several measures of students' incoming preparation and high school quality. They can effectively control for students' unobserved motivation and interests, normally unobservable, by controlling for the identity of each four-year college.[6] That is, they can

---

5. Authors' calculations based on National Center for Education Statistics (2016).
6. Of course, this strategy works only for the intensive margin estimates.

compare two students who not only had the same high school achievement but also both transferred to Cal State-Chico having previously attended different community colleges.

Carrell and Kurlaender find that community colleges' productivity, in terms of successful transfers, differs substantially. Despite enrolling approximately the same students and relying on the same set of destination (four-year) schools, some community colleges are significantly more likely to induce a student to attain baccalaureate education. Moreover, more- and less-productive community colleges are often located fairly close together, and the less-productive ones continue to attract students.

This final result suggests that students who make up the bulk of demand for community colleges either (1) choose programs without having very much information about the program's likelihood of helping them achieve their goals or (2) (despite being informed) choose programs based on attributes that are only weakly correlated with the program's productivity. For instance, they might choose a less-productive program simply because of its proximity or the timing of its class schedule. Carrell and Kurlaender's analysis thus lends support to Hoxby's conclusion that market forces are not disciplining the productivity of nonselective institutions.

Some Immediate Takeaways

This brings us to a few takeaways for university leaders, policy makers, and researchers.

First, although our findings suggest that economics delivers powerful insights about all institutions of higher education, the market forces that drive nonselective, selective, and research institutions differ. It is not that these institutions function in disjoint markets. Rather, the market is sufficiently differentiated that, as we move around within it, the circumstances that schools face change. Students' enrollment choices appear to weigh different factors. The sources of revenue differ. The outputs valued by funders differ. There are changes in the relevant production function—whether it includes research, for example. Thus, although we are confident that economic reasoning is crucial for strong analysis of higher education, we are mindful that deep institutional knowledge is required if we are to apply economics well. It would be specious simply to transfer thinking from, say, the analysis of for-profit industries to the analysis of postsecondary education.

Accounting for selection and measuring costs in higher education are serious problems for analysis. However, there are also serious remedies available if researchers have the right data. We have been repeatedly struck by the fact that the remedies employed by the studies in this volume would have been impossible without data only recently made available. This suggests that if higher education is to learn about itself and improve, it must allow and even expand access to data for well-grounded research.

We recognize the problems inherent in measuring the outcomes produced by higher education, but we do not believe that they are so insurmountable that it is better to abandon the effort to measure them. Although there is a great deal to be learned by studying outcomes not measured by studies in this volume, we believe that we gained valuable knowledge from the outcomes we were able to evaluate. Moreover, we believe that many of the findings in this volume would help policy makers, postsecondary leaders, and students make more informed decisions.

Changing the Conversation

We began this introduction by describing a conversation that not only really occurred but that is fairly typical of the conversations that take place within institutions of higher education. We find that sort of conversation—in which some (but only some) costs were discussed and no benefits were discussed—frustrating. If all the participants in that conversation had read this book, would it have been more insightful?

We would argue "yes" in the following sense. Many are the proposals for improving the productivity of institutions of higher education. These range from proposals to direct most students to community colleges, to proposals to funnel students into certain majors, to proposals to move most learning online, to proposals to put all instructors on one-year contracts, and so on. Most of these proposals are based on little more than speculation. We believe that studies such as the ones in this volume show how discussions of these proposals could become reasonably grounded in evidence. In other words, the purpose of the studies in this book is *not* to prescribe productivity-enhancing policies for institutions. (Such prescribing would, in any case, violate the NBER's mission.) Rather, the studies in this volume make the case that future conversations can be informed by evidence both about benefits and about the full array of costs. In medicine, better diagnoses lead to better solutions. We believe that similar logic applies to higher education.

However, we observe that we still face formidable challenges in changing some parts—very important parts—of conversations like the one with which we began this introduction. In particular, it remains very difficult to assess the public benefits of higher education for civil society, the macro benefits for the economy, and the benefits for individuals' well-being (the "nourishment of the soul"). These benefits do not lend themselves to modern empirical research in which experimental methods feature prominently. Nevertheless, from the ancients onward, commentators have argued for the importance of such benefits of higher education. Providing empirical grounding so that these considerations can be included in conversations is a challenge for the next generation of studies.

References

Altonji, J., and C. R. Pierret. 2001. "Employer Learning and Statistical Discrimination." *Quarterly Journal of Economics* 116 (1): 315–50.

Hoxby C. 2009. "The Changing Selectivity of American Colleges." *Journal of Economic Perspectives* 23 (4): 95–118.

———. 2018. "It Is the Student Who Matters, Not the Student's Major: Towards Credibly Causal Returns to College Majors." Stanford Institute for Economic Policy Research Discussion Paper.

National Center for Education Statistics. 2016. *2012/14 Beginning Postsecondary Students Longitudinal Study*. Restricted-Use Data File, NCES 2016404. May.

1

What Health Care Teaches Us about Measuring Productivity in Higher Education

Douglas Staiger

1.1 Parallel Problems, Parallel Lessons

As discussed in the introduction to this volume, any study that attempts to measure productivity in higher education faces numerous challenges. Knowing these challenges and laden with institutional knowledge, higher education experts may be tempted to "go it alone" in studying productivity. They may even, feeling that the challenges are insurmountable, refrain from studying productivity in higher education at all. However, many of the same issues arise when studying productivity in the health care industry, and there is a rich history of researchers confronting and overcoming these issues. It would be wasteful not to distill the lessons learned in health care and suggest how they apply to higher education. Thus, in this chapter, I identify parallels between the health care and higher education sectors. I suggest lessons from health care that might translate to the study of productivity in higher education.

1.2 Measuring Productivity in Health Care: A Central Example

To help make the discussion that follows concrete, especially for a higher education audience less familiar with health care, let us begin with a typical

Douglas Staiger is the John French Professor in Economics at Dartmouth College and a research associate of the National Bureau of Economic Research.

I thank the editors, Caroline Hoxby and Kevin Stange, for their substantial help with drafting this chapter. I also acknowledge that I am a founder of, have an equity interest in, and consult for ArborMetrix, a company that provides software and services for profiling hospital quality and episode cost efficiency.

For acknowledgments, sources of research support, and disclosure of the author's material financial relationships, if any, please see http://www.nber.org/chapters/c13956.ack.

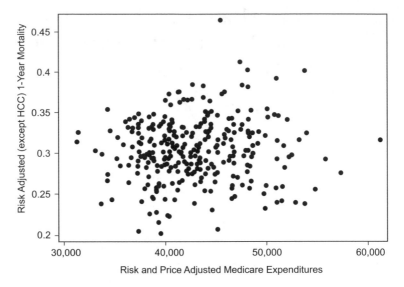

Fig. 1.1   An illustrative example from health care. Risk- and price-adjusted one-year expenditures and mortality by hospital
Note: Sample limited to hospitals with at least 200 AMI patients age 65+; 2007–9.
Source: Author's analysis of Medicare claims data.

exercise in measuring hospital productivity. To do this, researchers typically choose a "target outcome"—the mortality of a patient, say—and compare it to the inputs (expenditures) associated with treating a certain condition. Figure 1.1 presents what is probably the modal example: one-year mortality outcomes for patients who suffer an acute myocardial infarction (AMI), popularly known as a heart attack. For each US hospital that treated at least 200 AMI patients aged 65 or older between 2007 and 2009, the figure plots one-year mortality versus expenditures (Skinner et al. 2013).

There are a few features of this example that are noteworthy and to which I return. First, AMI is the condition most studied not only because cardiovascular disease is a leading cause of death but also because patients are nearly always treated for AMI at the same hospital where they are taken to an emergency room. This makes it easy to assign patients—and the costs their treatment incurs—to particular hospitals. Patients who suffer from other conditions might be treated at multiple hospitals. Second, short-term mortality is often the target outcome because data are available, it is very accurately measured, and reducing it is clearly a goal of AMI treatment. Third, both mortality and expenditures are *risk adjusted*. This means that the researcher has controlled for characteristics of patients that were present when they arrived at the hospital. For instance, a patient might be a smoker, be obese, or have concurrent diabetes. Since these conditions might make treating AMI harder and might affect mortality regardless of AMI, the researcher would not want to attribute their effects to the hospital. Otherwise, productivity would be overstated for hospitals that draw upon an unusually healthy population and vice versa.

The figure shows that there is a large variation in risk-adjusted expenditure across hospitals. Hospitals in the highest decile spend more than $50,000 per AMI patient, while those in the bottom decile spend only $35,000. There is also a large variation in mortality across hospitals. Risk-adjusted one-year mortality ranges from below 25 percent to above 35 percent for hospitals in the top and bottom decile. Interestingly, mortality and spending are not highly correlated, implying substantial differences in *productivity* of hospitals in treating AMI patients. Some hospitals—those in the lower left quadrant—appear to be very productive. Their patients were given low-cost treatment but nevertheless have low mortality rates. Other hospitals—those in the upper right quadrant—have low productivity, with high costs and high mortality. If the risk adjustments work as intended, these productivity differences are real and do not simply reflect the hospitals' different patient populations.

What have policy makers taken away from evidence such as that shown in figure 1.1? They have become deeply curious about hospital and physician practices that might explain such a large variation in productivity. They hope that researchers will be able to identify practices that, if adopted, would improve the low-productivity hospitals. The following statement from former director of the Office of Management and Budget and Congressional Budget Office Peter Orszag exemplifies this curiosity: "If we can move our nation toward the proven and successful practices adopted by lower-cost areas and hospitals, some economists believe health-care costs could be reduced by 30%—or about $700 billion a year—without compromising the quality of care" (Orszag 2009).

1.3   Parallels between Health Care and Higher Education

Several of the key challenges to measuring productivity in health care also prevail in higher education. These include multiple outcomes, selection, the multiproduct nature of health care providers, and the attribution problem.

1.3.1   Multiple Outcomes

In the example, the outcome studied was one-year mortality: the fraction of patients treated for AMI who survived the first year after treatment. We might easily get health practitioners and policy makers to agree that it was reasonable to focus on this outcome rather than on, say, long-term mortality, morbidity, functional mobility, or various measures of quality of life. The ease of agreement for AMI does not imply, however, that it would *generally* be easy to obtain such widespread agreement. Rather, AMI is the modal example in part *because* agreement is easy. For other conditions, different people would put different weights on the multiple outcomes affected by treatment.

The key point is that even for AMI, there is no correct target outcome. There is also no correct set of weights that we could use to form an index based on multiple outcomes. Choosing a target outcome or choosing index weights is inherently a value-laden decision: statistics do not help us. Rather, the choice is inevitably a reflection of our preferences and subjective judgments, not an objective truth.

With this in mind, what are some lessons from health care that apply to higher education?

First, if researchers decide to prioritize one outcome as the target or "gold standard" outcome, this choice will drive everything. A target outcome sends a message to patients, providers, and staff about institutional mission and priority. Hospital leadership will guide providers and staff to focus on the target outcome, often to the exclusion of other objectives. In extreme cases or where the target outcome is easily manipulated, there may be unintended consequences, such as altering diagnoses (so that only certain patients count toward the measured outcome) or cherry-picking patients who are healthier than their risk score would suggest (Werner and Asch 2005).

Second, the choice of a target outcome is crucial even if it is not directly used to measure productivity but instead guides how to use other indicators. For instance, in health care, indicators other than mortality are often used because they are available more quickly and are therefore more useful for immediate feedback. These include indicators of hospital use (e.g., patient volume), process (use of "best practices"), and proximate outcomes (e.g., infection rates and one-month hospital readmission rates). However, indicators are often selected or given weights in a composite index based on how highly correlated they are with the target outcome (Staiger et al. 2009). As a result, the target outcome remains a driving force.

Thus the first lesson from medicine for higher education is that the choice of a target outcome is likely to be highly consequential. Policy leaders and researchers ought to think through the decision of whether to choose a target at all. Several chapters in this volume (chapters 2, 3, 4, and 9) demonstrate that while the multiple obvious outcomes in higher education (graduation rates, learning, public service, innovation, short-term earnings and employment, long-term earnings and employment, etc.) *are* correlated, they are not so correlated that privileging one outcome would not have the effect of undercutting other objectives.

1.3.2 Selection

Selection poses a significant challenge to estimating hospital productivity because the sorting of patients to hospitals is not random. Some hospitals, because of their specializations or unusual resources, are destination facilities for patients who are especially ill. The Mayo Clinic and top research

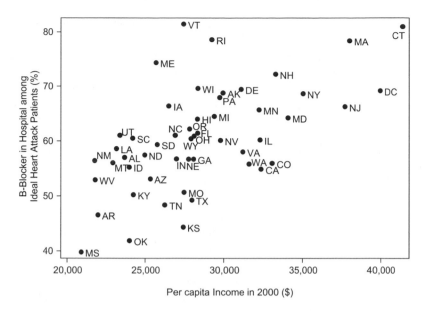

Fig. 1.2   Per capita income and beta-blocker use in the hospital among ideal heart attack patients (correlation = 0.59)

Note: Data on beta-blocker use from Cooperative Cardiovascular Project, 1994–95.

university hospitals are examples. Other hospitals receive unusually healthy or ill patients simply because of their location. A hospital located in a poor area is likely to receive more impoverished patients, for instance.

However, a correlation between mortality and the income or race of the population the hospital serves is not necessarily evidence of a difference in patient selection—it may be that hospitals serving disadvantaged populations are less likely to follow best practices and are truly low productivity. Figure 1.2 suggests that hospitals serving low-income populations may be less likely to follow best practices. As a proxy for whether a hospital is using best practices, the figure uses the probability of beta-blocker treatment among AMI patients in a state. This is a popular proxy for best practices because beta-blockers are widely regarded as a highly effective, low-cost treatment for all patients (and therefore, unlike mortality, their use should not depend on differences across hospitals in patient risk). The figure shows that this best-practice proxy is highly correlated with average income in the state, suggesting that hospitals serving low-income populations may in fact be low productivity. Therefore, measuring hospitals' productivity is difficult because we need to separate the contribution of hospitals to outcomes from the contribution of patients' own characteristics to their outcomes. Recall our motivating AMI example (figure 1.1). Do the hospitals in the lower left quadrant appear to be especially productive because they use effective, inexpensive beta-blockers? Or are they in the lower left quadrant because their patients have higher incomes? The raw data cannot answer these questions.

Fortunately, in health care, it appears that by applying risk-adjustment procedures to raw data, we can remedy much of the potential selection bias. In theory, any condition with which a patient arrives at the hospital door should be categorized for use in risk adjustment. In fact, the coding of hundreds of risks by the Centers for Medicare and Medicaid Services (CMS) is well regarded and widely used. An example of a risk is "F10.20 Alcohol Dependence, uncomplicated." The only obvious risk factors not widely used to address selection are the sociodemographics of a hospital's patient population. CMS discourages their use despite evidence that it is harder to treat poor and minority patients.

How do we know that risk adjustment largely remedies selection in health care? We compare risk-adjusted estimates with those derived from experiments where patients are randomly or quasi-randomly assigned to hospitals so that selection is not an issue.[1] We compare risk-adjusted estimates with direct observation of surgical technical quality.[2] We compare risk-adjusted estimates with estimates where a researcher is able, owing to especially rich and complete data, to control for *comprehensive* clinical information at the patient level.[3] In all these cases, standard risk-adjusted estimates of hospital performance compare favorably to credibly causal estimates.

Can we extrapolate to higher education the finding that risk adjustment largely remedies selection in health care? Not obviously. On the one hand, in both hospitals and colleges, much of selection arises because of geography (people use nearby institutions) or self-selection (better-informed and higher-income people may seek out better institutions). Another similarity is that selection issues are particularly problematic for the most resource-intensive institutions in both health care (the Mayo Clinic, for instance) and higher education (Harvard University, for instance). A difference, though, is in the direction of selection for the most resource-intensive institutions: the most-resourced hospitals generally see the least-healthy patients, while the best-resourced universities serve the most-able students. Consequently, if we fail to account for nonrandom selection, the most-resourced hospitals will appear to be low performing, while the most-resourced universities will appear to be high performing. Another difference between health care and higher education is that hospitals do not explicitly practice selective admission, while many postsecondary institutions do. However, explicitness seems likely to make selection *easier* to remedy in higher education. A researcher may know for certain or at least have a very good idea of the factors a col-

---

1. See Doyle, Ewer, and Wagner (2010); Doyle (2011); and Doyle et al. (2015).
2. See Birkmeyer et al. (2013).
3. See Dimick and Birkmeyer (2008); Dimick et al. (2010); McClellan and Staiger (2000); Morales et al. (2005); and Skinner et al. (2005).

lege is weighing in the admissions process and can use this information to account for the selection generated by the admissions process.

Summing up, the second lesson from medicine for higher education is that researchers ought not to assume that selection is so unremediable that it is pointless to work on developing the best possible adjustment procedures for precollege factors such as high school achievement and family background. In health care, research devoted to risk adjustment has borne fruit. To validate their adjustment procedures, higher education researchers should compare their estimates to estimates generated by policy experiments or quasi experiments such as discontinuities in admission criteria. While experiments and quasi experiments are not common in higher education, they are sufficiently common for such validation exercises, which have proven so useful in health research.

1.3.3   Multiproduct Issues

Hospitals provide multiple service lines delivered by different departments: oncology, cardiology, infectious disease, and so on. Each department also employs an array of procedures: surgery, biopsy, blood testing, radiology, and so on. In the language of economics, hospitals are multiproduct organizations. Hospitals also serve multiple populations, most notably patient populations whose risk profiles differ. If each hospital were equally productive in all its departments, procedures, and patient populations, then it would not matter which we examined when evaluating a hospital.

But in fact, research suggests that hospitals are not equally productive in all their service lines. Consider patients treated in two important service lines: AMI and hip fractures. Figure 1.3 plots the risk-adjusted one-year mortality rate for AMI patients against the one-year mortality rate for hip fracture patients. Both measures are for patients aged 65 or older who were treated at hospitals that saw at least 200 such patients and have been normalized to be mean zero. Hospital performance across these two service lines is only modestly correlated with a correlation coefficient of 0.30. Additional analyses I and coauthors have done using Medicare data indicate that most of the variation in productivity within hospitals across departments comes from variation in patient outcomes (the numerator) rather than patient costs (the denominator). Still further analyses suggest that variation in productivity is mainly *across* departments, not mainly (1) within departments across procedures or (2) within departments across patients' risk profiles. In other words, departments seem to have integrity as service lines and give high- or low-quality service regardless of their hospital's cost structure, procedural units, and patient risk profiles.

For hospitals, this all suggests a need to measure productivity separately by service line (department). It also indicates that evaluating a hospital based on a single service line (oncology, say) is likely to be problematic. Narrow evaluation might encourage a hospital to reallocate fungible resources

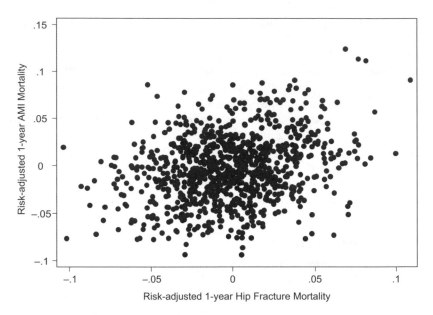

Fig. 1.3   Correlation across departments
Correlation (0.3) in hospital mortality rates for AMI and hip fracture patients
Note: Sample limited to hospitals with at least 200 AMI and hip fracture patients age 65+;
2000–2002.

(nurses, laboratory time, etc.) from departments that are not evaluated to departments that are.

Institutions of higher education are also multiproduct organizations that serve multiple populations. The typical institution supports many different departments and programs and distributes many different types of degrees. Some of the students may be undergraduates of traditional age. Others may be graduate students, professional students, or nontraditional undergraduates. Postsecondary schools also have the equivalent of procedural units that serve many departments—libraries, for instance.

The third lesson that higher education can learn from health care is therefore that there is no reason to assume that the evidence will show that a postsecondary institution is equally productive across all its service lines (departments, programs), student populations, and library-like procedural units. This may seem like a discouraging lesson because it implies that researchers have a formidable task ahead of them: estimating productivity for each activity at each postsecondary institution. However, it is worth pointing out that health care researchers have made great progress by first focusing their attention on service lines that are important and central. By important, I mean that the service line is crucial to a hospital's identity. By central, I mean that the service line deals with a broad swath of the patient population and uses many procedural units. If a service line is central, its productivity is less easily manipulated by the hospital moving resources around (the multitasking problem).

For instance, the fact that the most examined department is cardiology is not an accident. As emphasized above, cardiovascular disease is a leading cause of death, so this area is important to most hospitals. Moreover, cardiovascular disease is not rarified or confined to some minority of the potential patient population. The cardiology department also draws upon many procedural units. Cardiology is therefore central.

By parallel logic, higher education researchers might first focus on undergraduate education because it tends to be important and central—that is, the quality of its undergraduate program is key to most (though not all) institutions' identities, and undergraduates draw upon a wide range of departments and procedural units (libraries, etc.). Researchers might secondarily focus on the high-profile professional and doctoral programs that define research universities.

1.3.4   Attribution

Patients often interact with multiple hospitals as well as other health care providers when they are being treated for a condition. Although we know which procedures and which costs are attributable to each provider, patients' outcomes (e.g., their one-year mortality) cannot so easily be assigned to providers. Their outcomes are presumably due to the entire sequence of care. Moreover, it is not obvious that a provider's responsibility is proportional to its share of costs. Changing the quality of even a single procedure could be consequential if other procedures are endogenous to it. For instance, if cardiac catheterization were poorly performed, all of a patient's subsequent treatment for heart disease might be less effective. Thus, when attempting to measure productivity in health care, we often face the question of how to attribute patients' outcomes to individual hospitals or other providers.

Health care researchers have found two ways to deal with this problem. First, they often focus on conditions, such as AMI, where the attribution problem is minimal for technical reasons. That is, when people suffer heart attacks, they are usually taken to the closest hospital with cardiac capacity, and they are treated there until released. Second, health care researchers often define health "episodes" that begin with a diagnosis or event (such as a stroke) and then attribute all or most care within the episode to the hospital in which treatment began. The logic is that the initial hospital made choices to which all subsequent treatment (in the episode) is endogenous. A person may have multiple health episodes in his life.

The first of these solutions, focusing on situations where the attribution problem is minimal, does not seem helpful for higher education, where the attribution problem occurs because students (1) take classes at various institutions while pursuing the same degree and (2) engage in degree programs serially, with each degree at a different institution. One-third of students transfer institutions at least once within their first six years of college and before receiving a bachelor's degree, and nearly one-sixth transfer more than once (National Student Clearinghouse 2015). Or consider people who earn an associate's degree at a community college, a baccalaureate degree at a (different) four-year college, a master's degree at a third institution, and a professional degree at yet a fourth institution. To which institution should their postprofessional-degree outcomes, such as earnings, be attributed? If researchers were to exclude all students whose education spanned multiple institutions, the exclusion would be highly nonrandom and introduce bias. There is no parallel to AMI.

The second solution is more promising: attribute productivity to the initial institution in an educational episode where an episode is defined by fairly (though not entirely) continuous enrollment. People might still have multiple episodes if they, for instance, attained a baccalaureate degree between age 18 and age 24 and then, after an interval of more than a decade, enrolled in a master's degree program.[4] This approach is exemplified by chapter 2 in this volume.

A fourth lesson that higher education can take from health care is therefore that attribution issues, while important, can be overcome by treating educational episodes that span multiple institutions as the object of interest. It may not be desirable—or feasible—to try to separate the individual contribution of a community college from the four-year institution it feeds. It should be noted that identifying health episodes spanning multiple providers requires patient-centric data that track patients across these providers. Similarly, identifying education episodes spanning multiple institutions requires student-centric data.

1.4   Lessons for Measuring and Using Productivity in Higher Education

The experience of measuring productivity in health care offers four main lessons to similar efforts in higher education. First, the choice of a target outcome is likely to be highly consequential. Policy leaders and researchers

---

4. A third possibility is suggested by value-added research in elementary and secondary education. A few researchers have attempted to identify the long-term value added (to adult earnings, say) of each teacher in a succession of teachers who instruct a student. As an econometric matter, such identification is possible so long as students' teacher successions sufficiently overlap. Chapter 9 in this volume illustrates this approach that works, in their case, because many California students attend overlapping community colleges and California State Universities. However, this solution is often infeasible in higher education because students are not channeled so neatly through a series of institutions as through a series of primary and secondary teachers: the teachers available in a school in a grade are much more limited than the institutions among which students can choose. Postsecondary students are also not channeled so neatly through a series of grades: they can exit, get labor market experience between periods of enrollment, choose multiple degree paths, and so on.

ought to think through the decision of whether to choose a target at all or how multiple targets should be combined. Graduation, alumni earnings and employment, innovation, student learning—these are all plausible objectives of postsecondary institutions and systems, but giving priority to one may generate neglect of the others. Second, although selection issues are important, adjusting for selection may be successful if rich-enough controls are available. In addition, selection adjustment should be validated by experimental or quasi-experimental evidence. Third, institutions are unlikely to be equally productive across all their service lines and populations. Initial productivity measurement should focus on service lines that are important and central, such as undergraduate education. Finally, attribution issues can be overcome by treating educational episodes that span multiple institutions as the object of interest, attributing outcomes to the initial institution.

I conclude with two broad lessons about the use of productivity measures in health care that may also inform how they are used in higher education.

First, productivity measures have multiple uses, and there ought to be a match between the productivity measure and the use made of it. Productivity measures in health care have been used to inform patients who are trying to choose a provider, make providers accountable for health outcomes and costs, and provide timely feedback so that providers continuously improve. These different uses require different measures. For instance, patients may care about how a provider will affect their health and the costs they themselves will pay, but they may be uninterested in costs paid by insurers. Patients may also care more about, say, the treatment experience as a whole, while policy makers care more about mortality or disability. These differences may explain why patients seem to make little use of hospital "report cards," while insurers make considerable use of them to direct patients toward providers that appear to be more productive. If the productivity measures published in the report cards are only those requested by insurers and policy makers, it should be no surprise that patients ignore them. As another example, hospitals trying to adjust their processes to improve treatments require productivity measures that are very timely and will be more interested in direct measures of the processes themselves, even though such process measures are of little direct value to patients. Physicians participating in quality improvement may be willing to sacrifice accuracy and knowledge of long-term benefits so that they can observe and adjust processes in real time. Patients and policy makers presumably weigh accuracy more and timeliness less. Finally, developing broad performance measures that cannot be gamed is most important for high-stakes uses such as pay-for-performance and public reporting (think of how the behavior of universities has been distorted by the weight placed on various factors by highly influential college rankings) but less important if the measures are being used for continuous quality improvement. Increasingly in health care, improvement networks are forming around narrow clinical departments in order to share data, measure variation across hospitals in patient outcomes, identify best practices, and learn from high-productivity hospitals. This approach may be a promising way forward in higher education.

Second, stakeholder buy-in is important if we are to see university leaders (especially) but also students and policy makers take productivity measures to heart. They will not use them to improve decision making if they find them unconvincing. Buy-in is especially important in hospitals and postsecondary institutions because they are inherently decentralized organizations where much expertise resides in departments or even in individual physicians or faculty. Crucial testing, treatment/curriculum, and staffing decisions must inevitably be delegated to those with the expertise. Thus productivity measures will only be used well if they are truly respected by individuals and units throughout the health care / higher education organization. For instance, suppose that university leaders think that initial earnings are beyond their control but agree that learning (as measured by an exit exam, say) is within their control. Suppose furthermore that learning is more correlated with long-term earnings and employment outcomes, which university leaders care about, than are initial earnings. In such a case, productivity measures must include learning-based outcomes if they are to enjoy actual use by leaders. In health care, efforts to measure productivity and have the measures actually inform stakeholders' decisions were only successful when researchers sought input from those same stakeholders. This is a lesson that surely applies to higher education.

References

Birkmeyer, John, Jonathan Finks, Amanda O'Reilly, Mary Oerline, Arthur Carlin, Andre Nunn, Justin Dimick, Mousumi Banerjee, and Nancy Birkmeyer. 2013. "Surgical Skill and Complication Rates after Bariatric Surgery." *New England Journal of Medicine* 369 (15): 1434–42.

Dimick, Justin, and John Birkmeyer. 2008. "Ranking Hospitals on Surgical Quality: Does Risk-Adjustment Always Matter?" *Journal of the American College of Surgeons* 207 (3): 347–51.

Dimick, Justin, Nicholas Osborne, Bruce Hall, Clifford Ko, and John Birkmeyer. 2010. "Risk Adjustment for Comparing Hospital Quality with Surgery: How Many Variables Are Needed?" *Journal of the American College of Surgeons* 210 (4): 503–8.

Doyle, Joseph. 2011. "Returns to Local-Area Healthcare Spending: Using Health Shocks to Patients Far from Home." *American Economic Journal: Applied Economics* 3 (3): 221–43.

Doyle, Joseph, Steven Ewer, and Todd Wagner. 2010. "Returns to Physician Human Capital: Evidence from Patients Randomized to Physician Teams." *Journal of Health Economics* 29 (6): 866–82.

Doyle, Joseph, John Graves, Jonathan Gruber, and Samuel Kleiner. 2015. "Measuring Returns to Hospital Care: Evidence from Ambulance Referral Patterns." *Journal of Political Economy* 123 (1): 170–214.

McClellan, Mark, and Douglas Staiger. 2000. "Comparing the Quality of Health Care Providers." In *Frontiers in Health Policy Research*, vol. 3, edited by Alan Garber. Cambridge, MA: MIT Press.

Morales, Leo, Douglas Staiger, Jeffrey Horbar, Joseph Carpenter, Michael Kenny, Jeffery Geppert, and Jeannette Rogowski. 2005. "Mortality among Very Low Birthweight Infants in Hospitals Serving Minority Populations." *American Journal of Public Health* 95 (12): 2206–12.

National Student Clearinghouse. 2015. *Signature Report: Transfer and Mobility: A National View of Student Movement in Postsecondary Institutions, Fall 2008 Cohort.* https://nscresearchcenter.org/wp-content/uploads/SignatureReport9.pdf.

Orszag, Peter. 2009. "Health Costs Are the Real Deficit Threat." *Wall Street Journal*, May 15.

Skinner, Jonathan, Amitabh Chandra, Douglas Staiger, Julie Lee, and Mark McClellan. 2005. "Mortality after Acute Myocardial Infarction in Hospitals That Disproportionately Treat Black Patients." *Circulation* 112:2634–41.

Skinner, Jonathan, Weiping Zhou, Daniel Gottlieb, and Elliott Fisher. 2013. *Measuring Hospital-Level Healthcare Expenditures and Outcomes with Disease-Specific Cohorts.* Final Report for the Institute of Medicine Committee on Geographic Variation in Health Care Spending, January 10.

Staiger, Douglas, Justin Dimick, Onur Baser, Zhaohui Fan, and John Birkmeyer. 2009. "Empirically Derived Composite Measures of Surgical Performance." *Medical Care* 47 (2): 226–33.

Werner, Rachel, and David Asch. 2005. "The Unintended Consequences of Publicly Reporting Quality Information." *JAMA* 293 (10): 1239–44.

2

The Productivity of US Postsecondary Institutions

Caroline M. Hoxby

2.1 Introduction

This chapter proposes procedures for measuring the productivity of US postsecondary institutions. It also implements these procedures for most undergraduate programs. The evidence has interesting implications. For instance, at least at selective institutions, a dollar spent on a student's education appears to generate multiple dollars of value added based on earnings over her lifetime. Productivity is also stable across a wide range of selective institutions, suggesting that market forces are sufficiently strong to maintain regularity in how these institutions' resources scale up with the capacity of their students to convert educational resources into value added. Compared to selective institutions, nonselective institutions have productivity that is

Caroline M. Hoxby is the Scott and Donya Bommer Professor in Economics at Stanford University, a senior fellow of the Hoover Institution and the Stanford Institute for Economic Policy Research, and a research associate and director of the Economics of Education Program at the National Bureau of Economic Research.

The opinions expressed in this chapter are those of the author alone and do not necessarily represent the views of the Internal Revenue Service or the US Treasury Department. This work is a component of a larger project examining the effects of federal tax and other expenditures that affect higher education. Selected, deidentified data were accessed through contracts TIR-NO-12-P-00378 TIR-NO-15-P-00059 with the Statistics of Income (SOI) Division at the US Internal Revenue Service. The author gratefully acknowledges the help of Barry W. Johnson, Michael Weber, and Brian Raub of the Statistics of Income Division, Internal Revenue Service. James Archsmith and Steven E. Stern provided important help with paired comparison methods. The author is grateful for comments from Joseph Altonji, David Autor, Sandra Black, Scott Carrell, John Cawley, Paul Courant, David Deming, Maria Fitzpatrick, Brian Jacob, Michael Lovenheim, Paco Martorell, Jordan Matsudeira, Jonathan Meer, Douglas Miller, Marianne Page, Juan Saavedra, Judith Scott-Clayton, Douglas Staiger, Kevin Stange, Sarah Turner, Miguel Urquiola, and Seth Zimmerman. For acknowledgments, sources of research support, and disclosure of the author's material financial relationships, if any, please see http://www.nber.org/chapters/c13875.ack.

lower on average but also much more dispersed. This suggests that market forces may be too weak to discipline productivity among these schools.

This study also examines institutions' productivity based on their producing public service and innovation. Public service productivity varies substantially even among selective schools. Innovation productivity is distinctly higher at very selective schools than all other schools.

The study attempts to cover considerable ground and is in a "glass-half-full" mode in the sense that it attempts to answer key questions about productivity in higher education while acknowledging that it cannot answer them all or answer them perfectly. In the first part of the study, I define what is meant by productivity in higher education and explain why measuring it is a useful exercise even if an imperfect one. I outline the key issues that plague measurements of productivity: (1) the multiplicity of outcomes that schools might affect and the difficulty of measuring some of them, (2) the fact that a student may enroll in several schools before her education is complete (the "attribution problem"), and (3) selection.

Since vertical selection (students who differ in aptitude enrolling at different institutions) and horizontal selection (similarly apt students who differ on grounds such as geography enrolling at different institutions) are arguably the most serious issues for measuring productivity, I especially discuss methods for addressing these problems. The proposed remedy for the selection problem is based on comparing the outcomes of students who are the same on measured incoming achievement (test scores, grades) and who also apply to the same postsecondary institutions, thus demonstrating similar interests and motivation. This approach employs all the possible quasi experiments in which a student "flips a coin" between very similar schools or in which admission staff members "flip a coin" between very similar students. Put another way, schools are compared solely on the basis of students who are in the common support (likely to attend either one) and who are quasi-randomly allocated among them. See below for details about the method.

Using this method to account for selection, the study computes productivity for approximately 6,700 undergraduate programs. I show productivity for three outcomes: earnings, a measure of public service based on the earnings a person forgoes by being employed in the nonprofit or public sector (think of a talented attorney employed as a judicial clerk), and a measure of participation in innovation. The first measure is intended to reflect private returns, the second social returns, and the third spillovers to economic growth.

In the next section, I define productivity for the purposes of this chapter. Section 2.3 explains why productivity measures would be useful to policy making but also for numerous other reasons. The key challenges we face in measuring productivity are described in section 2.4. Because selection is so important, Section 2.5 is dedicated to the method used to address it. Other empirical issues are discussed in sections 2.6–2.8, and section 2.9 presents the main productivity results. A discussion of the broad implications of the results closes the chapter in section 2.10.

2.2 Defining Productivity

For the purposes of this study, the productivity of an institution of higher education is the value to society of its *causal* effect on outcomes (value added) divided by the cost to society of educating its students (social investment). Specifically, this is the productivity of the average dollar of social investment in a university's students, and it is this measure of productivity that policy makers usually need to make a returns-on-investment argument (see below). There are, however, certain questions for which the productivity of the *marginal* dollar of social investment is more relevant. This is the point I take up below.[1]

The main causal effects of a postsecondary institution are likely to be on its own students' private outcomes, such as earnings. However, some effects, such as its students' contributions via public service, may not be reflected in private outcomes. Also, some effects, like its students' contributions to innovations that raise economic growth, may spill over onto people who were not the students of the institution.

Social investment is the total cost of a student's education, not just costs funded by tuition. For instance, taxpayers fund some social investment through government appropriations and tax expenditures. Social investment is also funded by current and past donors to postsecondary institutions.

Thus the productivity of an institution is not in general equal to the private return on private investment that an individual could expect if she were to enroll in the school. Such private calculations are interesting for individuals but less so for policy makers. I employ them in related studies (for instance, studies of how students choose colleges), but they are not the object of interest in this study. In any case, private calculations are less different from social calculations than they might seem at first glance.[2]

---

1. For some economic applications, we might instead be interested in marginal productivity: the increase in value added produced by a marginal increase in social investment. Although most of the analysis in this study applies equally to average and marginal productivity, I compute only average productivity because to compute the marginal productivity, one would need a comprehensive set of policy experiments in which each school's spending was raised for an exogenous reason uncoordinated with other schools' spending. This is an extremely demanding requirement. We would not merely require "lightning to strike twice" in the same place; we would need it to strike many times.

2. For instance, if taxpayer funding of a student's education corresponds approximately to funding he will have to contribute to *others'* education through paying higher future taxes (higher as a result of education-driven higher earnings), his private investment may be close to social investment. As a result, the productivity of a dollar of social investment may be close to the productivity of a dollar of private investment.

2.3   Why Measuring Productivity Is Useful

Higher education in the United States has survived and even thrived for many years without reasonably credible or comprehensive measures of institutions' productivity. Why, then, should we attempt to produce measures now? There are at least four reasons.

First, as government intervention in higher education has grown, it is reasonable for the public to ask for productivity measures. Most government interventions are based on returns-on-investment logic that requires the education to be productive. Policy makers, for instance, often argue that appropriations that support higher education institutions pay for themselves by generating benefits that are more than equal to the social investment. They make a similar argument for tax credits, grants and scholarships, and subsidized student loans. Leaders of postsecondary institutions also make the returns-on-investment argument: donations to their school will more than repay themselves by delivering benefits to society.[3]

Second, the United States contains unusual (by international standards) and varied environments for higher education. We cannot know whether these environments promote a productive postsecondary sector if productivity is never measured. For instance, should institutions compete with one another for students and faculty, or should these people be allocated through centralized rules as they are in many countries and a few US public systems? What autonomy (in wage-setting, admissions, etc.) and governance structures (e.g., trustees, legislative budget approval) promote an institution's productivity? Does the information available to students when they are choosing schools affect the productivity of these schools? Is productivity affected by an institution's dependence on tuition-paying students versus students funded by grants or third parties? While this study does not attempt to answer questions such as those posed above, it does attempt to provide the dependent variable (productivity) needed for such analyses.[4]

Third, highly developed economies like that of the United States have a comparative advantage in industries that are intensive in the advanced skills produced by postsecondary education. These industries tend to contribute disproportionately to such countries' economic growth and exports. Advanced-skill-intensive industries also have some appealing features, such as paying high wages and being relatively nonpolluting. However, economic logic indicates that a country cannot maintain a comparative advantage in advanced-skill-intensive industries if it is not unusually productive in generating those skills. A country cannot maintain a comparative advantage in

3. In a related paper, I show how the productivity estimates computed in this chapter can be used to evaluate policies such as the tax deductibility of gifts to nonprofit postsecondary institutions.
4. Some of these questions are addressed in Hoxby (2016).

equilibrium simply by generously funding a low-productivity higher education sector.

Finally, once we have measures of institutions' productivity, we may be better able to understand how advanced human capital is produced. What the "education production function" is is a long-standing and complex question. While productivity measures, by themselves, would not answer that question, it is hard to make progress on it in the absence of productivity measures. For instance, some results presented in this chapter strongly suggest that the production function for selective higher education exhibits single crossing: a higher-aptitude student is likely to derive more value from attending an institution with a higher level of social investment than a lower-aptitude student would derive. While many economists and higher education experts have long suspected the existence of single crossing and assumed it in their analyses, evidence for or against single crossing is scanty. If true, single crossing has important implications, a point to which I return toward the end of the chapter.

2.4 The Key Issues for Measuring Productivity

2.4.1 Selection

As previously stated, vertical selection (students who differ in aptitude enrolling at different institutions) and horizontal selection (similarly apt students who differ on grounds such as geography enrolling at different institutions) are probably the most serious issues for measuring productivity. A naive comparison of, for instance, earnings differences between Harvard University's former students and a nonselective college's former students would be largely uninformative about Harvard's value added. A naive comparison of earnings differences of community college students in San Francisco (where costs of living are high) and rural Mississippi (where costs of living are low) would also be largely uninformative about their relative value added. Addressing selection is sufficiently challenging that I devote the next section entirely to it.

2.4.2 The Attribution Problem

The second problem for evaluating a postsecondary institution's productivity is attribution. Suppose that we have mastered selection and can credibly say that we are comparing outcomes and social investment of students at schools A and B who are as good as randomly assigned. Even under random assignment, we would have the issue that school A might induce students to enroll in more classes (a graduate program at school C, for instance) than school B induces. When we eventually compare the lifetime outcomes of school A students to school B students, therefore, the A students will have more education, and not just at school A. There is no way for us to identify the part of the school A students' outcomes that they would have had if they had attended only school A for as long as they would have attended school B. Part of school A's causal effect on outcomes flows through its inducing students to attend school C.

Another example of the attribution problem arises because even when pursuing a single degree, students may take classes at multiple institutions. For instance, part of the effect of a two-year college flows through its inducing students to transfer to four-year colleges. One-third of students transfer institutions at least once before receiving a bachelor's degree and nearly one-sixth transfer more than once.[5]

Consider two examples. Suppose that one two-year college tends to induce students to finish associates degrees that have a vocational or terminal (not leading to a four-year degree) character. Suppose that another two-year college tends to induce students to transfer to a four-year college and earn their degrees there. If we were not to credit the second college with the further education (and outcomes and social investment) it induced, the second college would appear to be very unproductive compared to the first college. Much of its actual productivity would be attributed to the four-year colleges to which its students transferred. Consider Swarthmore College. It is a liberal arts college and, as such, does not train doctoral students. However, it tends to induce students to attend PhD programs in academic subjects. If they go on to become leading researchers, then Swarthmore is productive in generating research and should be credited with this effect.

In short, part of the outcomes and thus the productivity of any school are due to the educational trajectory it induces. This attribution issue cannot be evaded: it is a reality with which we must deal. I would argue that the best approach is to assess the productivity of a school using lifetime outcomes as the numerator and *all* the social investments induced by it as the denominator.[6]

---

5. This is a quotation from Staiger (chapter 1 in this volume), who is quoting from National Student Clearinghouse (2015).

6. In theory, one could identify the contribution of each institution to a person's lifetime outcomes. To see this, consider teacher value-added research in elementary and secondary education. Some researchers have been able to identify the effect on long-term outcomes of each teacher whom a student encounters in succession. Identification can occur if teacher successions overlap in a way that generates information about their individual contributions. What is ideal is for each possible pair of students to have some teachers in common and some not in common. By combining the results of all pairs of students, one can back out each teacher's contribution. Chapter 9 (Carrell and Kurlaender) in this volume has some of this flavor. Identification works, in their case, because California students who attend community colleges tend to have overlapping experiences as they move into the four-year California State Universities. However, identification is often impossible in higher education because students' experiences do not overlap in a manner that generates sufficient information. Postsecondary students are not channeled neatly through a series of grades: they can exit, get labor market experience between periods of enrollment, choose multiple degree paths, take courses in the summer at school A and then return each fall to school B, and so on. In other words, there are so many factors that

2.4.3   Multiple Outcomes

Postsecondary institutions may causally affect many outcomes: earnings, public service, civic participation, research, innovation, cultural knowledge, tolerance and open-mindedness, marriage, and child-rearing, to name but a few.[7] These outcomes may affect individuals' utility, sometimes in ways that would be invisible to the econometrician. Also, some of these outcomes may have spillover effects or general equilibrium effects. For instance, higher education might generate civic participation, and societies with greater civic participation might have institutions that are less corrupt, and less corrupt institutions might support a better climate for business. Then higher education might affect the economy through this indirect channel. Researchers encounter severe empirical challenges when trying to evaluate such spillover and general equilibrium effects.

Even if we could accurately observe every outcome, there is no correct or scientific way to sum them into a single index that could be used as the universal numerator of productivity. Summing across multiple outcomes is an inherently value-laden exercise in which preferences and subjective judgments matter.[8] It is fundamentally misguided to attach a weight to each outcome, compute some weighted average, and thereafter neglect the underlying, multiple outcomes. To make matters worse, the choice of weights in such exercises is not merely arbitrary but sometimes designed to serve the ends of some interest group.

I would argue that researchers ought to make available credible estimates of all the outcomes for which there appears to be a demand and for which reliable measures can be constructed. This would at least allow an individual student or policy maker to evaluate each postsecondary institution on the grounds that matter to him or her. Accordingly, in this chapter, I show evidence on multiple outcomes that—though far from comprehensive—are intended to represent the three basic types: private (earnings), social (public service), and spillover-inducing through nonsocial means (innovation).

This being said, lifetime earnings have a certain priority as an outcome because they determine whether social investments in higher education are sufficiently productive to generate societal earnings that can support social investments in higher education for the next generation of students. However, even if we accept the priority of earnings, we are left with the problem that many of the outcomes listed above affect societal earnings, but they do

can differ between pairs of students that identifying the contribution of each institution is very challenging outside of somewhat special cases like the California Community College example.

7. All the chapters in this volume deal with the multiple outcomes problem, but see especially those by Staiger (chapter 1); Minaya and Scott-Clayton (chapter 3); and Riehl, Saavedra, and Urquiola (chapter 4).

8. Staiger (chapter 1 in this volume) makes the same point, referring to multiple outcomes affected by health care providers.

so in such an indirect way that the earnings could not plausibly be connected to the institution that produced them. For instance, consider the problem of attributing to specific schools the societal earnings that arise through the indirect civic participation channel described above.

How bad is it to focus on the private earnings of a school's own students as the basis of productivity measures? The answer depends, to some extent, on how the measures are used. If the data are used to evaluate individual institutions, the focus is problematic. Certain institutions are at an obvious disadvantage because they disproportionately produce outcomes whose effects on society run disproportionately through externalities or general equilibrium channels: seminaries, women's colleges, schools that induce students to become future researchers, and so on. However, if we are looking not at individual schools but at more aggregate statistics (schools grouped by selectivity, for instance), these concerns are somewhat reduced. For instance, within the group of very selective schools, some may be more research oriented, others more public service oriented, and yet others more business oriented.

2.5 Selection

For measuring productivity, the problems associated with selection are the "elephant in the room." Vertical selection occurs when students whose ability, preparation, and motivation are stronger enroll in different colleges than students whose ability, preparation, and motivation are weaker. If not addressed, vertical selection will cause us to overestimate the value added of colleges whose students are positively selected and to underestimate the value added of colleges whose students are negatively selected. This leads to the legitimate question that plagues college comparisons: Are the outcomes of students from very selective colleges strong because the colleges add value or because their students are so able that they would attain strong outcomes regardless of the college they attended?

However, colleges' student bodies are not only vertically differentiated; they are also horizontally differentiated—that is, they differ on dimensions like geography and curricular emphasis. For instance, suppose that earnings differ across areas of the country owing, in part, to differences in the cost of living. Then two colleges that enroll equally able students and generate equal value added may have alumni with different earnings. We could easily mistake such earning differences for differences in value added. As another example, consider two colleges that are equally selective but whose students, despite having the same test scores and grades, differ in preferring, on the one hand, a life replete with inexpensive activities (local hikes) and, on the other hand, a life replete with expensive activities (concerts with costly tickets). These incoming differences in preferences are likely to play out in later career and earnings choices regardless of what the colleges do. We do not wish to mistake differences in preferences for differences in value added.

Vertical selection is probably the more serious problem for two reasons. First, social investment at the most- and least-selective colleges differs by about an order of magnitude. Second, some nonselective colleges' median students have a level of achievement that is similar to that attained by the eighth grade (or even earlier) by the median students at the most-selective colleges.[9] One cannot give the most-selective colleges credit for the four or so additional years of education that their incoming students have. Nor can one give them credit for the ability that allowed their students to acquire learning more readily than others. (Ability earns its own return, human capital apart.)

Solving selection problems is all about (1) randomization or something that mimics it and (2) overlap or "common support." Randomization solves selection problems because with a sufficient number of people randomized into each treatment, the law of large numbers ensures that they are similar on unobservable characteristics as well as observable, measurable ones for which we might control.

The point about common support is less obvious and is especially important for selection problems in higher education.

2.5.1   Addressing Selection, Part 1: Common Support

The requirement of common support means that it is highly implausible if not impossible to use comparisons between the outcomes of Harvard University students and students who would be extremely atypical at Harvard to judge Harvard's productivity. We need students who overlap or who are in the common support between Harvard and another institution. There are many such students, but most end up attending another very selective institution, not a nonselective institution or a modestly selective institution. The common support requirement also exists horizontally. Two geographically proximate institutions that are similarly selective are far more likely to have common support than ones located thousands of miles away. Similarly, two similarly selective institutions that have the same curricular emphases (engineering or music) or campuses with similar amenities (opportunities for hiking versus opportunities for concert-going) are more likely to have common support.

We can analyze productivity while never moving outside the common support. In fact, the problem is almost exactly the same, as a statistical matter, as rating tennis players, for example. The top tennis players in the world rarely play matches against players who are much lower rated: the vertical problem. Also, apart from the top players whose matches are international, most players play most of their matches against other players from the same region: the horizontal problem. In tennis (as in many other sports that require ratings), the problem is solved by statistical paired comparison

---

9. Author's calculations based on the National Educational Longitudinal Study, US Department of Education (2003).

methods (PCMs) that rely entirely on players who actually play one another (i.e., players in the common support).

Sticking to the tennis analogy, the rating of a top player is built up by seeing how his outcomes compare with those of other fairly top players whom he plays often. Then their outcomes are compared to those of other slightly less-apt players with whom they play often. And step-by-step, the distance in outcomes between most- and least-apt players is computed even if the most apt never play the least-apt ones. Similarly, the rating of players who are geographically distant is built. A Portuguese player might routinely play Spanish players who routinely play those from Southwest France, who play against Parisians, who play against Belgians, who play against Germans, who play against Danes. What is key is that PCMs never employ mere speculation of how one player would play someone whom in fact he or her never plays. Also, PCMs are designed to incorporate the information generated when a lower-rated player occasionally beats a much higher-rated one. PCMs do not impose any functional form on the rating. There can be abrupt discontinuities: for instance, the distance between players 2 and 3 could be small, but the distance between players 4 and 5 could be very large. There can be ties.

If we compare the outcomes of people who could attend either institution A or institution B but in fact divide fairly randomly between them, then we can measure the relative value added of the two schools. These are the direct A-versus-B "tournaments," but of course there are many other tournaments: A versus C, A versus D, B versus D, B versus D, and so on. Using the same PCMs that one uses to build up a tennis player's ranking, one can build up a school's value added. Step-by-step, the difference in value added between schools with the most- and least-apt students is computed even if the most apt rarely choose among the same portfolio of schools as the least-apt ones. Similarly, the value added of schools that are, say, geographically distant is built. Again, what is key is that PCMs never employ mere speculation of how one student would choose among schools that, in fact, he never considers. An institution that has lower value added on average is allowed to have higher value added for some students. (This is the equivalent of the less-apt player beating the more-apt player sometimes.) PCMs seamlessly incorporate the information generated when a student occasionally chooses a school that is much less selective than the "top" one to which he was admitted. And PCMs do not impose any functional form on how value added relates to students' aptitude. There can be abrupt discontinuities: for instance, the distance in value added between similarly selective schools A and B could be small, but the distance between similarly selective schools B and C could be very large. There can be ties. In short, we derive the same benefits from common support: the measure of value added is never based on mere speculation of how outcomes would compare among students who differ in aptitude or in the colleges they consider. There is no functional form imposed on institutions' value added: institutions can be tied, very close, or very far apart.

Interestingly, PCMs are much easier to apply to value added than to sports because outcomes such as earnings are far more continuous than the score of a tennis match or other game. Also, small score differences that result in a win versus a loss matter in sports but not in the outcomes that matter for schools' productivity. No one would care, for instance, if one school's students earned $50,000 on average and another school's earned $50,001.

So far, this discussion has emphasized that by applying PCMs, I can estimate differences in value added among schools. But all the points just made apply equally to differences in social investment. Attending school A might trigger a social investment of $20,000 in a student, while attending school B might trigger a social investment of $22,000. Just as with value added (the numerator of productivity), social investment is built through PCMs step-by-step so that the difference in social investment between schools with the most- and least-apt students is computed even if the most apt rarely choose among the same portfolio of schools as the least-apt ones. Similarly, PCMs build, step-by-step, the differences in social investment between schools that are, say, geographically distant. We derive all the same benefits from common support: the measure of social investment is never based on mere speculation of how educational spending would compare among students who differ in aptitude or in the colleges they consider. There is no functional form imposed on the social investment triggered by attending an institution: institutions can be tied, very close, or very far apart.

PCMs can be used to build a school's value added (akin to a tennis player's ranking) or its marginal value added relative to another school (akin to the ranking difference between two players). Similarly, it can be used to build the social investment triggered by attending a school or the marginal social investment triggered by attending one school versus another. However, important caveats apply. I take them up after discussing the data because they can be made more clearly at that point.

2.5.2   Addressing Selection, Part 2: Quasi Randomization

Applying PCMs to measuring productivity without the plague of selection is straightforward *if* we can identify students whose attendance at any given pair of institutions is quasi random. I do this with two procedures that correspond, respectively, to the vertical and horizontal selection problems.

The procedure for the horizontal problem is simpler. In it, we identify pairs of students who have equally observable application credentials, who apply to the same schools A and B that are *equally selective*, and who have a high probability of admission at schools A and B. For instance, one might think of students who choose between equally selective branches of a state's university system. If the students knew for certain which school had the higher value added for them, they might always choose it. But in fact, they have an imperfect understanding and still must make a choice. Thus horizontal college choices are often influenced by small factors that only affect the students' lifetime outcomes through the channel of which college they attend. While few students actually flip a coin, they choose among horizontally equal colleges based on the architecture, the weather on the day they visited, the offhand suggestion of an acquaintance, and so on. This is quasi randomization.

Once we have identified students who choose quasi randomly among horizontally equal and proximate schools A and B, we can identify students who choose among horizontally equal and proximate B and C, C and D, and so on. Thus we can derive a measure of school A's productivity relative to D's even if students do not (or rarely) choose between A and D. The horizontal selection problem is solved. While geography is the most obvious source of differentiation among horizontal equals, the logic applies far more broadly. For instance, A and B might both have strong engineering programs, B and C might both have strong natural sciences programs, C and D might both be strong in the biological sciences, and so on.

Now consider the procedure for the vertical selection problem. Here, we identify pairs of students who have equally observable application credentials, who apply to the same schools A and B that are not necessarily equally selective, and who are "on the bubble" for admission at school A. I define students as being on the bubble if admissions staff are essentially flipping coins among them when making admissions decisions.

That is the definition, but why does this range exist, and how can one learn where it is? A typical procedure for selective colleges is to group applicants, after an initial evaluation, into fairly obvious admits, fairly obvious rejects, and students who are on the bubble because they would be perfectly acceptable admits but are not *obvious*. The on-the-bubble group might contain two or three times as many students as the school has room to admit once the obvious admits are accounted for. (For instance, a school that plans to admit 1,000 students might have 800 obvious admits and put 400 in the on-the-bubble group in order to admit 200 more.) The staff then look at the composition of the students whom they intend to admit and note deficiencies in the overall class composition. For instance, the prospective class might be missing students from some geographical area or with some curricular interest. Then the staff conduct a final reevaluation of the on-the-bubble students, keeping themselves attuned to these issues. Thus an on-the-bubble student may be more likely to be admitted if she comes from a geographical area or plans to major in a field that was initially underrepresented. In another year, these same characteristics would not increase her probability of admission. Thus admissions officers make decisions that, while not random, are arbitrary in the sense that they only make sense in the context of that particular school in that year.

How does one find the on-the-bubble range? It is the range where, as a statistical matter, there is a structural break in the relationship between the probability of admission and observable credentials. To clarify, the probability of admission *above* the bubble range is fairly high and fairly predictable. It increases smoothly and predictably in observable credentials such as test scores and grades. The probability of admission *below* the bubble range is low but also increases smoothly and predictably in observable credentials. (Students below the bubble range who gain admission usually have, in addition to their academic qualifications, some other observable characteristic, such as athletic prowess.) In contrast, the probability of admission *in* the bubble range is very difficult to predict using observable credentials. This is because the on-the-bubble students all have perfectly acceptable credentials, and the admissions decision, which occurs in the final reevaluation, depends not on these credentials but on some characteristic that in another year or similar school would not predict a more favorable outcome.

Statistical methods that uncover structural breaks in a relationship are made precisely for situations such as this: a relationship is smooth and predictable in range A; there is another range B in which the relationship is also smooth and predictable. Between ranges A and B, the relationship changes suddenly and cannot be predicted using data from either the A or B range. This is an issue into which I go into more detail in the companion methodological study (Hoxby 2015). The point is, however, that structural break methods are a statistical, objective way to find the on-the-bubble range. While structural break methods will find a strict credentials cutoff if one exists (for instance, if a school admits students who score above some threshold and rejects those who score below it), the methods will also find the on-the-bubble range for schools that practice more holistic admissions. It is worth noting that the on-the-bubble range does not typically coincide with the admits who have the lowest academic credentials. Rather, it contains students whose credentials usually place them only modestly below the median enrollee.[10]

Once one has located each school's on-the-bubble range, one can solve the vertical selection problem using chains of schools. One can compare schools A and B by comparing the outcomes of students who were on the bubble at school A. Some of them end up at school A; others end up at school B. Schools B and C may be compared using students on the bubble at school B, C and D may be compared using students on the bubble at school C, and so on. Thus school A ends up being compared to school D through these connections even if few on-the-bubble students at A actually attend school D.

Summarizing, I identify "horizontal experiments" among students who have equal admissions credentials and who apply to the same equally selective schools where they are obvious admits. They more or less flip coins

10. Note that students who have minimal academic credentials but some offsetting observable characteristic such as athletic prowess are not on the bubble. Their admission is predictable.

among the colleges. I identify "vertical experiments" among students who are on the bubble at some college and who are therefore admitted based on the equivalent of coin flips by the admission staff. I combine all these experiments using PCMs. Notably, these measures comply to the maximum extent possible with the requirements of randomization and common support. More detail on the procedure can be found in Hoxby (2015).

In this chapter, I show the results of applying this procedure to undergraduate students. It could also be applied to graduate and professional schools where test scores (LSAT, GMAT, etc.) and undergraduate grades dominate an admissions process that is run by staff.[11]

2.6 Data

I use administrative data on college assessment scores, score sending, postsecondary enrollment, and 2014 earnings from wages and salaries for people in the high school graduating classes of 1999 through 2003 who were aged 29 through 34 in 2014. That is, I employ data on students who graduated from high school at age 18 and 19, which are the dominant ages at high school graduation in the United States. Earnings are from deidentified Form W-2 data, and these data are available for nonfilers as well as tax filers. A student with no W-2 is assumed to have zero wage and salary earnings. Enrollment data come not from students' self-reports but from institutions' reports to the National Student Clearinghouse and through Form 1098-T. Further details on this part of the data set are in Hoxby (2015).

The data on social investment come from the US Department of Education's Integrated Postsecondary Education Data System (IPEDS), a source derived from institutions' official reports. For the purposes of this study, social investment is equal to the amount spent on a student's education. This is called "core" spending by the US Department of Education and is equal to the per-pupil sum of spending on instruction, academic support[12] (for instance, advising), and student support.[13] In IPEDS data, core spending is the same for all students who attend the same school in the same year at the same level (i.e., undergraduate versus graduate). This is a limitation

---

11. It would work less well for small doctoral programs where faculty meet with or read considerable material from the students with whom they may choose to work and whose admission they greatly influence.

12. Academic support includes expenses for activities that support instruction. For instance, it includes libraries, audiovisual services, and academic administration. The source is National Center for Education Statistics (2015).

13. Student support includes expenses for admissions, registrar activities, and activities whose primary purpose is to contribute to students' emotional and physical well-being and to their intellectual, cultural, and social development outside the context of the formal instructional program. Examples include student activities, cultural events, student newspapers, intramural athletics, student organizations, supplemental instruction outside the normal administration, and student records. The source is National Center for Education Statistics (2015).

of the data. In fact, core spending differs among programs and thus among students within a school year level. For instance, Altonji and Zimmerman (chapter 5 in this volume) demonstrate that some undergraduate majors, such as engineering, are actually more expensive than others, such as philosophy. Also, some graduate programs are more expensive than others.

Another limitation of the core spending measure is that it probably contains a type of error that I call "classification error." Schools may make every effort to allocate each expenditure properly to its IPEDS category, but inevitably *some* judgment is required for certain expenditures. For instance, an administrative staff person in a math department might mainly coordinate instruction but occasionally help with an activity that would best be classified as "public service." For instance, the math department might have its students tutor in local secondary schools, and she might organize that activity. Her salary would probably be classified as core spending, even though part of it could really be classified as public service. Another university, though, might put all its tutoring programs, regardless of field, under one unit with dedicated staff. The salaries of those staff persons would be classified as public service.

Because the classification of many expenditures is unambiguous, classification error is unlikely to dominate the variation in core spending among schools. Nevertheless, small differences in core spending between two schools should be interpreted with caution.

2.7   Three Empirical Issues: A Normalization, Lifetime Measures, and the Productivity of the Average Dollar versus the Marginal Dollar

In this section, I discuss three important empirical issues: (1) normalizing the value added of some schools to zero, (2) constructing lifetime measures of value added and social investment, and (3) measuring the productivity of the average dollar of social investment versus measuring the productivity of the marginal dollar.

2.7.1   A Normalization

I do not believe that there is a method of accounting for selection between *no* and *some* postsecondary education that is both credible and broadly applicable. There are methods that credibly account for this selection at the extensive margin for a particular institution or set of students.[14] However, a method that works fairly ubiquitously does not exist for the simple reason that the decision to attend postsecondary school *at all* is not a decision that most people make lightly or quasi randomly. It is a fairly momentous decision. Thus it does not lend itself to selection control methods that require quasi randomization and common support.

---

14. See the recent review by Oreopoulos and Petronijevic (2013).

Because I cannot find a broadly applicable, credible method of accounting for selection between no and some postsecondary education, I normalize the value added of some institutions to zero. In practice, these will be the least selective institutions, for reasons discussed below. This does not mean that these institutions' value added is *actually* zero. An institution in the lowest selectivity group may have value added near zero, but it might improve earnings or other outcomes substantially relative to no postsecondary education at all. It might also worsen outcomes relative to no postsecondary school if attending an institution keeps the student away from employment at which he would gain valuable skills on the job. In short, I caution readers against interpreting the normalized zeros as a true value added of zero: the true value added could be positive, zero, or negative for those institutions.

2.7.2 Lifetime Measures

Investments in higher education generally take place over a number of years and generate an asset (human capital) that creates benefits for potentially an entire career. Thus I need to have lifetime measures of both social investment and value added. There are two issues that arise as a result: discounting the future and predicting benefits at higher ages than I observe in the data.

Only the first of these issues, discounting, really applies much to the computation of lifetime social investment. This is because I observe actual social investment for people when they are age 18 to age 34, and social investments in higher education are in fact very modest for people aged 17 or under or people aged 35 and over. Thus I do not attempt to project social investment after age 34, and I need only choose a plausible discount rate.[15]

In my main results, I use a *real* discount rate of 2.5 percent. In sensitivity testing (available from the author), I have considered real rates as low as 2 percent and as high as 3 percent. Keep in mind that these are real discount rates that might correspond to nominal discount rates that cover a wider range, depending on the rate of inflation. For instance, with an inflation rate of 3.0 percent, a real discount rate of 2.5 percent would be 5.5 percent.

Computing lifetime value added is more complicated because it is necessary not only to discount but also to project outcomes to higher ages.

For earnings through age 34, I simply take observed earnings from the data and discount them using the same discount rate applied to social investment.

But I do not use a person's actual earnings at ages greater than 34 because it would force me to compute value added based on students who attended

---

15. More precisely, by age 34, most people have completed the postsecondary education that is induced by their initial enrollment. If people return to college after, say, a decade in the labor market, that second enrollment episode is likely triggered by a labor market experience and should be evaluated separately.

postsecondary school too long ago: the results would be unduly dated. For instance, a 65-year-old in 2014 would likely have started attending postsecondary school in 1967 or 1968. On the other hand, I do not attempt to project future earnings based on earnings at an age earlier than 34 because people tend only to "settle down" on an earnings trajectory in their early 30s, not their 20s. That is, studies of US workers tend to establish that their later earnings are substantially more predictable when one uses their earnings through their early 30s as opposed to earnings through, say, their 20s.

To project earnings, I use empirical earnings dynamics. Specifically, I categorize each 34-year-old by his percentile within the income distribution for 34-year-olds. Then I compute a transition matrix between 34-year-olds' and 35-year-olds' income percentiles. For instance, a 34-year-old with income in the 75th percentile might have a 10 percent probability of moving to the 76th percentile when aged 35. I repeat this exercise for subsequent pairs of ages: 35 and 36, 36 and 37, and so on. In this way, I build up all probable income paths, always using observed longitudinal transitions that differ by age. (When a person is younger, she has a higher probability of transitioning to a percentile far from her current one. Incomes stabilize with age, so off-diagonal transition probabilities fall.) I considered alternative projection methods, the more plausible of which generated similar projections.[16]

Note that this method produces earnings for ages 35 and higher than are already in the same dollars of the day as earnings at age 34.

2.7.3   The Productivity of the Average Dollar versus the Marginal Dollar

In a previous section, I described how I build a school's value added using PCMs. This gives me the numerator for a measure of the school's productivity of the average dollar of social investment. I also use PCMs to build the social investment triggered by a student's enrolling in a school. This gives me the denominator for the school's productivity of the average dollar of social investment.

---

16. I investigated alternatives to this procedure. The first set of alternatives used empirical earnings paths that played out for the same person over a longer time span than one year (i.e., the year-to-year transition matrix mentioned in the text). For instance, one could take a time span of 10 years. In this case, one would use the longitudinal pattern for each 34-year-old, following him through age 43. One would use the longitudinal pattern for each 43-year-old, following him through age 52. And so on. The longer the time span, the more one has allowed for patterns in earnings that play out of multiple years. However, a longer time span has the disadvantage that one is forced to use data from calendar years that are farther away from the present (more outdated). For time spans of two to ten years, this set of alternatives produced results similar to those shown. An alternative method that I rejected was keeping a person at the same percentile in the earnings distribution as he was at age 34. For instance, a person at the 99th percentile at age 34 would be assigned 99th percentile earnings for all subsequent ages. I rejected this alternative method because it does not allow for a realistic degree of reversion toward the mean. Thus despite the method's producing reasonable lifetime outcomes for middling percentiles, it produces lifetime earnings distributions that contain too many extremely low and extremely high outcomes compared to reality.

In theory, one could build a measure of school A's productivity of the *marginal* dollar of social investment by focusing exclusively on the vertical and horizontal experiments that involve other schools whose core spending is only a little lower than school A's. However, such calculations—which I call the "marginal PCM exercise" hereafter for conciseness—turn out not to be reliable in practice, owing to classification error. (I do not give up entirely on computing the productivity of the marginal dollar. See below.)

Why does classification error make the marginal PCM exercise described in the previous paragraph unreliable? Although classification error probably has only a minor effect on measures of the *level* of a school's core spending, it may very plausibly have a major effect on measures of the *differences* in core spending among schools whose core spending levels are similar. This is a familiar result in applied econometrics, where measurement error that causes only modest problems in levels regressions often causes dramatic problems in differenced regressions.[17] The problem is, if anything, exacerbated in this application, owing to the fact that IPEDS-based core spending is the same for all students who attend the same school at the same level in the same year.

To see this, suppose that schools A and B are similarly selective and have similar core spending. Suppose that they often compete with one another for the same students so that they generate many horizontal experiments. Suppose that true social investment is the same at schools A and B but that the two schools classify certain spending differently so that school A's *measured* core spending is slightly higher than school B's. Then the difference in the two schools' measured core spending is entirely classification error (measurement error).

If one were to carry out the marginal PCM exercise in an attempt to compute the productivity of the marginal dollar of social investment at school A, then A's horizontal experiments with school B would naturally receive considerable weight because it competes often with school B and because school B's measured core spending is only a little lower than school A's. But each of the A-B horizontal experiments would reveal nothing about the productivity of *true* marginal differences in social investment, since the two schools truly have identical social investment.

Indeed, the A-B comparisons could easily generate an estimate that suggests (wrongly) that the productivity of a marginal dollar of social investment at school A is *negative*. School A would only need to have value added that is slightly lower than school B. Its slightly lower value added would be associated with slightly higher measured core spending.

17. The seminal demonstration of this point is made in Griliches (1979). He is interested in measures of educational attainment where measurement error is a minor problem in levels regressions but becomes a dramatic problem in differenced regressions—for instance, regressions that depend on differences in attainment between siblings. The point applies much more broadly, however.

This problem is exacerbated by the fact that the same classification error affects every A-B comparison. That is, the classification error does not vary among students within a school, as would other types of measurement error—in earnings, say—where error for one student might very plausibly offset error for another student.

It might seem at this point that one can only credibly estimate the productivity of the average, not marginal, dollar at various schools. The reality is less disappointing. Although classification errors do not cancel out across students within a school, they do tend to cancel out *across* otherwise similar schools. Thus a logical way to proceed is to group schools with others that are similar. Then one can estimate the productivity of the marginal dollar for each group by carrying out the marginal PCM exercise at the group level rather than the school level. One obtains only a group-level estimate of the productivity of the marginal dollar, but this is informative for many purposes as shown below.

2.8   Why the Results Are Shown with Institutions Grouped in Selectivity- Based Bins

2.8.1   Group-Based Results

In the sections that follow, I present the productivity findings for schools grouped into "bins," not for individual schools. This is for several reasons.

First, since there are more than 6,000 postsecondary institutions, it would be impractical to show productivity school by school.

Second, small differences among similar schools tend to be interpreted more strongly than is justified by the nature of the estimates. Even in exercises like those carried out in this chapter, which rely on administrative data that are vast and not prone to error, there are reasons why small differences may be misleading and not robust. For instance, structural break methods are a statistically grounded and logical way to identify each school's on-the-bubble region, but they are not a perfect way. Thus some schools' on-the-bubble regions are probably slightly off, and this could affect their results enough to make small estimated differences misleading.

Third, this chapter and other chapters in this volume aim to produce evidence about higher education productivity that addresses consequential, long-standing questions. It is difficult to see how productivity calculations for individual schools would much advance this goal. Indeed, reports on individual schools, such as the US News and World Report rankings, seem to trigger plenty of gossip but few important analyses.

Fourth, as noted in the previous section, it is necessary to group schools in some way to estimate the productivity of the *marginal* dollar of social investment.

2.8.2   Grouping Postsecondary Institutions by Selectivity

There are a variety of ways in which one could group postsecondary institutions, and several could be interesting. The logical place to start is grouping them by selectivity—for a few reasons. First, differences in vertical selection among institutions are a dominant feature of US higher education and a key feature that explains students' college choices and institutions' roles in the market for higher education (Hoxby 2009). Second, vertical selection is the primary threat to accurate calculations of productivity, so by grouping schools by selectivity, I allow readers to judge how remedying the selection problem (as described above) affects the results. Third, productivity by selectivity is *the* crucial statistic for understanding the education production function, especially for assessing single crossing—the degree to which a higher-aptitude student derives more value from attending an institution with a higher level of social investment than a lower-aptitude student would derive.

I present the results using figures in which each institution is assigned to a "selectivity bin" according to the empirical combined math and verbal SAT (or translated ACT) score of its average student.[18] Note that it is *institutions*, rather than individual students, that are binned, since we are interested in showing the productivity of institutions.

Although score-based bins are probably the most objective way to organize the institutions by selectivity, it may help to provide an informal translation between the scores and the "competitiveness" language used in *Barron's Profiles of American Colleges and Universities*, familiar to higher education researchers and policy makers. Roughly, institutions with an average combined score of 800 are noncompetitive. Indeed, they often explicitly practice "open admission," which means that they admit anyone with a high school diploma or passing score on a high school equivalency test. Institutions with an average combined score of 1,000 to 1,050 are "competitive plus"; 1,050 to 1,150 are "very competitive"; 1,150 to 1,250 are "very competitive plus"; 1,250 to 1,350 are "highly competitive" or "highly competitive plus"; and 1,350 and over are "most competitive." These classifications are approximate, and some schools do not fit them well. There is an indeterminate area between nonselective and selective schools that corresponds roughly to the 800 to 1,000 range. Toward the top of this range, schools tend to be selective but more reliant on high school recommendations and grades and less reliant on test scores. Toward the bottom of this range, schools tend to be nonselective. However, schools in this range can be hard to classify because information about them is often only partial. This is a point to which I will return.

18. The empirical average score is not necessarily the same as the SAT/ACT score that appears in college guides. Some schools submit scores to the college guides that reflect "management" of the (subpopulation of) students for whom scores are reported.

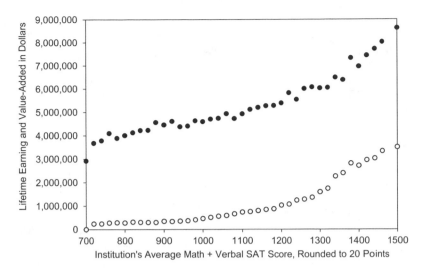

● Present Discounted Value of Earnings from Age 18 through Age 65 ("raw earnings")

○ Value-Added Based on Earnings from Age 18 Through Age 65

Fig. 2.1   Lifetime earnings and value added in dollars, institutions grouped by selectivity

2.9   Results

I show productivity for three key outcomes: wage and salary earnings (including zero earnings for people who have none), a measure of public service, and a measure of innovation produced. The construction of the two latter measures is discussed below. All of these are lifetime measures in which I compute the actual measure for ages 18 through 34 and then project the outcome for ages 35 through 65, the ages for which persons' outcomes cannot be linked to their postsecondary institutions. A real discount rate of 2.5 percent is used throughout for the results shown here. I consistently normalize the productivity of the least-selective institutions to zero.

2.9.1   Productivity Measures Based on Earnings

Figure 2.1 shows lifetime wage and salary earnings and value added for institutions of higher education. The earnings are "raw" because no attempt has been made to account for the effects of selection. Value added, in contrast, is computed using the method described above to account for selection.

The figure shows that both raw earnings and value added are higher for institutions that are more selective. Indeed, both series rise almost monotonically. However, value added rises more slowly than earnings. This is particularly obvious as we reach the most-selective institutions, where the slope of the relationship implies that about two-thirds of the earnings gains

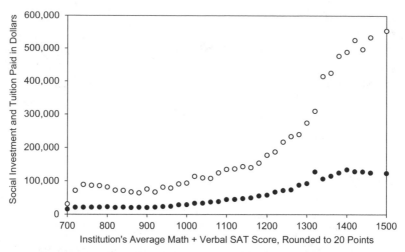

o Present Discounted Value of Social Investment (Educational Expenditure from All Sources) from Age 18 to Age 65

● Present Discounted Value of Tuition Paid (Paid by Individual Him/Herself at Time of Enrollment) from Age 18 to Age 65

Fig. 2.2   Social investment and tuition paid from age 18 to 32 in dollars, institutions grouped by selectivity

do *not* represent value added but instead represent what their very apt students would have earned if they had attended less-selective schools. (Because of the normalization, only the gain in value added relative to the lowest-selectivity schools is meaningful. The level is not.)

Of course, this does not mean that the more selective an institution is, the greater its productivity. Value added rises with selectivity but, as figure 2.2 demonstrates, so does social investment in each student's education. Recall that social investment is the increase in educational spending triggered by attending one institution rather than another. Like value added, this measure accounts for selection using the method described above. Also like value added, it is a lifetime measure and discounted using a real rate of 2.5 percent.[19]

Just for comparison, figure 2.2 also shows the present discounted value of tuition paid. This is always lower than social investment because it does not include spending funded by taxpayers, donors, and so on.

Social investment in each student's education is higher for institutions that are more selective. It rises almost monotonically with the institution's average test score. Note also that social investment rises notably more steeply

19. Recall that I consider social investment only through age 34, since by that age, the vast majority of people have completed the postsecondary education induced by their initial enrollment.

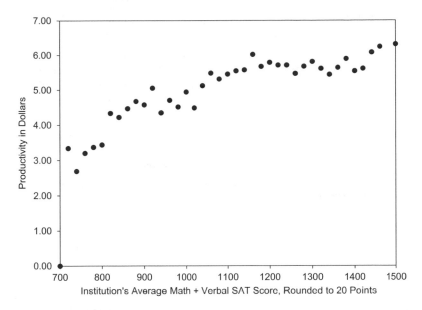

Fig. 2.3 Productivity based on lifetime earnings of a dollar of social investment in higher education, institutions grouped by selectivity

than tuition paid. This is partly because more selective institutions spend considerably more per curricular unit on each student's education. But it is also partly because students who attend more-selective institutions tend to enroll in more curricular units. They are less likely to drop out, more likely to attend full time, more likely to continue onto graduate school, and so on. This is true even when we have accounted for selection.

Figures 2.1 and 2.2 suggest that the pattern of institutions' productivity of an average dollar will be something of a race between value added (the numerator), which is rising in selectivity, and social investment (the denominator), which is also rising in selectivity. Figure 2.3 shows the results of this "race." The pattern is striking: (1) Within the selective institutions (combined SAT scores of 1,000 or above), productivity of the average dollar is quite flat; it rises slightly but not at all dramatically. (2) Within the nonselective institutions, productivity of the average dollar is roughly flat in selectivity. (3) The productivity of the average dollar is lower among non-selective schools than it is among the selective ones.

The first of these results—that among selective schools, the productivity of the average dollar rises only slightly with selectivity—is very striking and has potentially important implications. It is striking because social invest-ment and earnings both rise substantially, not slightly, as selectivity rises. Thus the relative flatness comes from the numerator and denominator rising at a sufficiently similar rate so that the value added of the average dollar is not terribly different between an institution with an average score of 1,000 and one with an average score of 1,400. An implication of this finding is that there would be little change in sector-wide productivity if one were to remove the average dollar from more-selective schools (i.e., make a radial reduction in core spending) and were to use that dollar to make a radial increase in the core spending of less-selective schools.[20] Moving the dollar in the other direction would also generate little change—that is, social investment is scaling up with student aptitude such that higher-aptitude students get resources that are commensurate with their capacity to use them to create value.

This result, with its important implications, seems unlikely to be a matter of pure coincidence. Since students are actively choosing among the institutions throughout this range, this may be the result of market forces: students choosing among schools and schools consequently competing for faculty and other resources. In other words, students who can benefit from greater resources may be willing to pay more for them, inducing an allocation of schools' resources that corresponds roughly to students' ability to benefit from them.

That market forces would have this effect would not be surprising if all students paid for their own education, the financing of such education was efficient, and students were well informed about the value they could expect to derive from educational resources. But clearly, these idealized conditions do not obtain: third-party payers (taxpayers, donors) are the proximate funders of a considerable share of selective higher education, student loan volumes and interest rates are such that students can be liquidity constrained (on the one hand) or offered unduly generous terms (on the other), and many students appear to be poorly informed when they choose a postsecondary school. Thus what the result suggests is that even with all these issues, market forces are sufficiently strong to maintain some regularity in how institutions' resources scale up with the aptitude of their students.

The empirical result does not imply that the educational resources are provided efficiently. It could be that all the institutions provide resources in a similarly inefficient manner. However, unless the productivity of least-productive institutions is substantially negative (so that the normalization to zero overstates their productivity a lot), a dollar spent on educational resources at a selective institution appears to generate multiple dollars of value over a person's lifetime.

The second of these results—that productivity is rather flat in selectivity among nonselective schools—is not terribly surprising. More specifically,

20. A radial change is one that changes all categories within core spending equally. For instance, if 70 percent of core spending were on instruction and 30 percent were on academic support, a radial reduction of a dollar would reduce instructional spending by 70 cents and academic support spending by 30 cents. If decision making at selective institutions is such that spending changes are usually radial, the average and marginal dollar might be spent very similarly.

among institutions whose average student has a combined score of 800 or below, productivity is rather flat. This may be because the institutions do not actually differ much in student aptitude: their average student's score may not be terribly meaningful because some of their students take no college assessment or take an assessment but only for low stakes.[21] Or it could well be that the aptitudes that may matter for their students' success are poorly measured by tests. Finally, being nonselective, these institutions may differ mainly on horizontal grounds (geography, curriculum, how learning is organized) so that showing them vis-à-vis an axis based on the average student's score is just less informative.

The third of these results—that productivity is distinctly lower at nonselective institutions—is interesting and consistent with several possible explanations. First, nonselective institutions enroll students who have struggled in secondary school, and it may simply be harder to turn a dollar of investment into human capital for them. Simply put, they may arrive with learning deficits or study habits that make them harder to teach. Second, many students who enroll in nonselective schools do not choose among them actively or in an informed manner. They simply choose the most proximate or one that becomes salient to them for an arbitrary reason (an advertisement, for instance). Because these schools infrequently participate in national college guides, students may have a difficult time comparing them on objective grounds. For all these reasons, market forces may fail to discipline these institutions' productivity. Third, nonselective institutions disproportionately enroll students who do not pay for their own education but instead have it funded by a government grant, veterans' benefits, or the like. As in other third-party-payer situations, this may make the students less sensitive to the commensurability between cost and benefit than they would be if they were paying the bills themselves.

The patterns discussed so far are robust to several alternatives in computing productivity, such as using discount rates anywhere within the plausible range of 2 to 3 percent real. They are robust to removing institutional support from social investment. (Social investment should certainly include instructional spending, academic support, and student support.) They are robust to excluding extensive research universities whose accounting of how spending is allocated across undergraduates and other uses is most contestable.[22] All of these alternatives change the magnitudes of productivity, but

21. Many American students take a college assessment (or preliminary college assessment) solely to satisfy their state's accountability rules or for diagnosis/placement. Thus many students who do not apply to any selective postsecondary school nevertheless have scores.

22. The 2000 edition of the Carnegie Commission on Higher Education classified postsecondary schools as Extensive Research Universities if they not only offer a full range of baccalaureate programs but also are committed to graduate education through the doctorate, give high priority to research, award 50 or more doctoral degrees each year, and annually receive tens of millions of dollars in federal research funding.

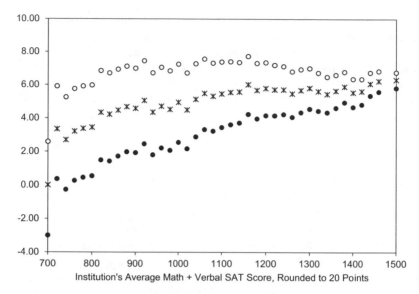

Fig. 2.4   Average, 10th percentile of and 90th percentile of productivity of a dollar of social investment in education, institutions grouped by selectivity

they do not change the three key patterns just discussed. They also do not change the fact that both earnings and social investment rise fairly monotonically in selectivity.

Among institutions of similar selectivity, is productivity similar? In other words, is the average productivity within each bin representative of all institutions, or does it represent an average among schools whose productivity differs widely? This question is clearly important for interpretation, and figure 2.4 provides the answer.

Figure 2.4 shows not just the average productivity in each selectivity bin but also the productivity of the 5th and 95th percentile institutions with each bin. It is immediately obvious that productivity differences among schools are wide among nonselective institutions but narrow as schools become more selective. Indeed, among the very selective schools, productivity differences are relatively small.

Given the results on the average levels of productivity, these results on the dispersion of productivity should not be too surprising. The level results suggest that market forces might be operative among selective institutions. The students who would likely maintain the most market pressure would be students who make active choices among schools (not merely choosing the most proximate), who are best informed, whose families pay for some

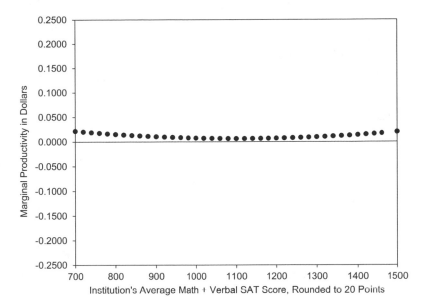

Fig. 2.5   Marginal productivity of a dollar of social investment, institutions grouped by selectivity

or most of their education, and who are the least likely to be liquidity constrained. Such students will disproportionately be apt. Thus the more selective an institution is, the more it is probably exposed to market forces that discipline its productivity—explaining why we see low dispersion.

If market forces weaken as students get less apt, then the pressure for similarly selective schools to be similarly productive would fall as selectivity falls. This would be consistent with the pattern of dispersion in figure 2.4. Market pressure might be very weak for nonselectives if the students who tend to enroll in them choose only among local schools, are poorly informed, and have their tuition paid by third parties. Indeed, for many nonselective schools, there is not much information available about students' outcomes. Thus we should not be surprised that low-productivity, nonselective schools do not get eliminated even though some nonselective schools have much higher productivity.

So far, the discussion in this section has focused on the productivity of the average dollar of social investment. But as discussed previously, we can potentially learn about the productivity of the *marginal* dollar of social investment. One way to do this without imposing much structure is to plot the marginal productivity curve implied by the average productivity curve shown in figure 2.2. (This is analogous to plotting the marginal cost curve associated with an average cost curve.) When I do this, I obtain figure 2.5. It shows that the productivity of the marginal dollar of social investment

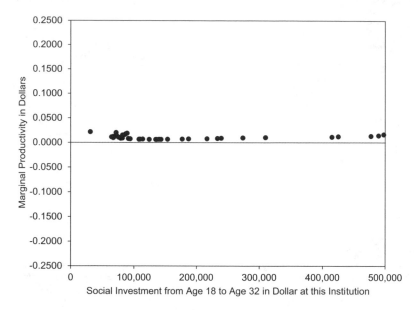

Fig. 2.6   Marginal productivity of a dollar of social investment, horizontal axis in dollars of social investment, institutions grouped by selectivity

is also quite flat but slightly upward sloping in selectivity over the range of selective institutions. In figure 2.6, I switch the scale of the horizontal axis to dollars of social investments, rather than selectivity, while still grouping institutions in selectivity-based bins. The resulting marginal productivity curve is, in some ways, easier to interpret because it reveals the productivity of the marginal dollar and allows us to see what that marginal dollar is. The curve is even flatter.

An implication of this finding is that there would be little change in sector-wide productivity if one were to remove the marginal dollar from more-selective schools and were to use that dollar to make a marginal increase in the core spending of less-selective schools. Moving the marginal dollar in the other direction would also generate little change. That is, social investment is scaling up with student aptitude such that higher-aptitude students get marginal resources that are commensurate with their capacity to use them to create marginal value.

2.9.2   Productivity Measures Based on Public Service

Conceptually, one wants to have a measure of public service that picks up contributions to society that earnings do *not*. This suggests that a good measure of public service is the percentage difference in earnings in a person's occupation if he works in the public or nonprofit sectors versus the for-profit sector. This is a measure of his "donation" to society: the earnings he foregoes by not being in the for-profit sector. Two concrete examples may be helpful. Highly able lawyers usually work for for-profit law firms, but some work as judicial clerks, district attorneys, and public defenders. The latter people earn considerably less than they would in the for-profit sector. Similarly, executives and managers of nonprofit organizations, such as foundations, usually earn considerably less than those in the for-profit sector. While a measure of public service based on "pay foregone" is certainly imperfect (in particular, the different sectors may draw people who have different levels of unobserved ability), it is at least an economics-based measure, not an ad hoc measure. It is also a continuous measure and one that can be specific to the schools in each selectivity bin, limiting the unobserved ability problems just mentioned.

I classify each school's former students by their one-digit occupation at about age 34. Then I compute, for each selectivity bin, the average earnings by occupation for those employed in the for-profit sector. Next, I compute each public or nonprofit employee's contribution to public service as the difference between his occupation-by-selectivity bin's for-profit average earnings and his earnings. To make this akin to a lifetime measure, I multiply it by the person's ratio of projected lifetime earnings to his age 34 earnings. (The last is simply to make magnitudes analogous to those in the previous subsection.) Also, if the contribution calculated is negative, I set it to zero. (I return to this point below.) I assume that the contribution to public service is zero for for-profit employees. Clearly, they may make contributions through volunteering or other means, but most such contributions pale in comparison to those of someone who foregoes 15 percent of pay, for example.

Once this contribution to public service is computed, it can be used to make productivity calculations in a manner that is exactly analogous to how earnings are used in the productivity calculations based on earnings. To be precise, productivity based on public service is value added through public service contributions divided by social investment.

Figure 2.7 shows the results of this exercise. The relationship is fairly noisy and nonmonotonic, although, overall, productivity based on public service rises with selectivity. The bumpy relationship is the net result of two competing relationships. The percentage of former students who take up government employment falls as selectivity rises. This would tend to make public service productivity fall as selectivity rises. However, this fall is offset by the rise in earnings foregone as selectivity rises. A concrete example may help. For most of the selectivity range (above the nonselectives), the tendency of former students to become public school teachers is falling with selectivity. However, in the lower selectivity bins, public school teachers are relatively well paid compared to for-profit employees in their occupational category, so their foregone earnings are little to none. Relatively few former students

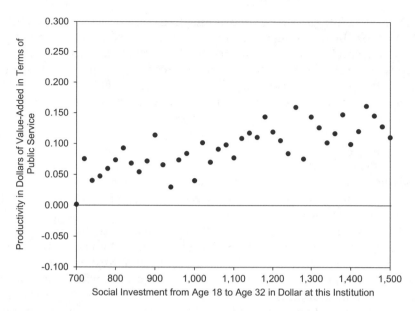

Fig. 2.7 Productivity measured in terms of average value added through public service of a dollar of social investment, horizontal axis in dollars of social investment, institutions grouped by selectivity

from the highest selectivity bins become public school teachers, but those who do forego a large share of their for-profit counterparts' earnings. Similar phenomena hold for other local, state, and federal employees.

Figure 2.8 shows the dispersion of productivity based on public service. The pattern shown contrasts strikingly with that of figure 2.4, which showed that the dispersion of productivity based on earnings fell steady with selectivity. The dispersion of productivity based on public service does not. It is noisy, but it rises with selectivity. This indicates that among very selective schools, some are much more productive in public service contributions than others. Put another way, some very selective schools are much more likely to induce their students to enter public service than are other very selective schools. One might speculate that some schools have more of a service ethos or a greater number of service opportunities available to students on or near campus. In any case, there is little indication that market or any other forces constrain similarly selective schools to have similar productivity based on public service.

2.9.3 Productivity Measures Based on Innovation

Conceptually, one wants to have a measure of contributions to innovation that is broader than, say, a measure based on patenting would be. Many

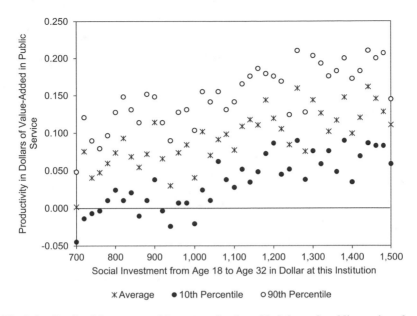

Fig. 2.8   Productivity measured in terms of value added through public service of a dollar of social investment, 10th percentile, average, and 90th percentile, horizontal axis in dollars of social investment, institutions grouped by selectivity

more people contribute to innovation than own patents. Similarly, a measure based on former students themselves becoming researchers seems too narrow. The software industry, for instance, fits the definition of *innovative* that many economists have in mind, and it is certainly a growing industry in which the United States has a comparative advantage.[23] Yet it does not have many employees who would describe themselves as researchers. For these reasons, I computed a measure of contributions to innovation based on the research and development (R&D) spending of each person's employer. Specifically, I took each employer's ratio of R&D spending to total expenses. Nonprofit and public employers, especially universities, were included as much as possible. I then multiplied each employee's earnings at age 34 by this R&D ratio. Finally, I multiplied by the person's ratio of lifetime earnings to her earnings at age 34. (This final multiplication is simply to make the magnitude analogous to those in the previous subsections.)

Thus a person who works for a firm that spends 10 percent of its budget on R&D would have 10 percent of her lifetime pay listed as her contribution to innovation. Of course, this is not meant to be a measure of her direct contributions. Rather, it is a way of forming an index that both reflects value

23. See Hecker (2005).

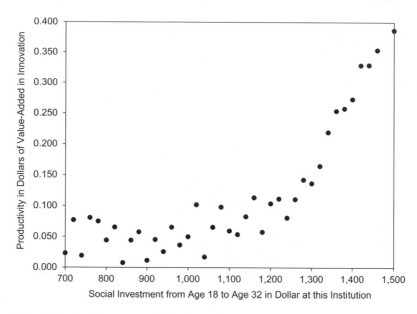

Fig. 2.9   **Productivity measured in terms of average value added through innovation of a dollar of social investment, horizontal axis in dollars of social investment, institutions grouped by selectivity**

(from earnings) and innovation (from the R&D ratio). This index permits people to contribute to innovation even if they do so in a supportive capacity, as most do, rather than as an investigator or patentee. For instance, a secretary or market researcher for a software firm would be counted because she indirectly supports the innovation occurring there.

Once this contribution to innovation is computed, it can be used to make productivity calculations in a manner exactly analogous to how earnings are used in the productivity calculations based on earnings. To be precise, productivity based on innovation is value added through the innovation measure divided by social investment.

Figure 2.9 shows the results of this exercise. The pattern is mildly upward sloping in selectivity until the most-selective institutions are reached. At that point, the relationship becomes steeply upward sloping. This convex relationship indicates that very selective institutions are much more productive in contributions to innovation than all other institutions. There are at least two possible explanations. Most obviously, there is no reason to think that the relationship should be flat as it is for productivity based on earnings. In the latter case, market forces could plausibly generate a flat relationship. But if much of the return to innovation spills over onto others or works through general equilibrium effects, there is no obvious mechanism that would ensure that social investment scales up with contributions to innovation. Alternatively, social investment, the denominator of productivity, could be understated in the most-selective schools. Social investment does not include these schools' spending on research, and this research spending may have benefits for undergraduates. In fact, the channel could be subtle. It may be that research spending has no direct benefits for undergraduates but that it attracts a different type of faculty (research-oriented) who, even when they teach undergraduates, teach in a manner oriented toward developing knowledge at the frontier. Thus the undergraduate program might be almost unintentionally research oriented.

I do not show dispersion in productivity based on research because the focus would be on such a small number of schools.

2.10   Discussion

At selective institutions, a dollar in social investment appears to generate multiple dollars of value added based on earnings over a person's lifetime. This conclusion is only unwarranted if nonselective schools have substantially negative productivity.

This is a simple but important result with broad implications for many government policies. For instance, the estimated productivity of selective institutions appears to be sufficiently high to justify taxpayer support and philanthropic support incentivized by the tax deductibility of gifts. I lay out such calculations in a companion chapter that is in process.

For nonselective schools, it is less clear whether a dollar in social investment generates at least a dollar in value added based on earnings. This is *not* to say that these schools' productivity is near zero. Rather, it is to say that understanding their productivity is difficult because their students tend to be at the no-enrollment versus some-nonselective-enrollment margin, where it is extremely difficult to account for selection. For instance, this study does not attempt to say how the productivity of nonselective schools compares to the productivity of on-the-job training.

The results for productivity based on earnings suggest that market forces are sufficiently strong to maintain some regularity in how institutions' resources scale up with the ability of their students to convert social investment into value added. Without market forces as the explanation, the stability of productivity over a wide range of schools would be too much of a coincidence. This does not necessarily imply that selective institutions provide educational resources with maximum efficiency: market forces might only compel them to provide resources in a similar but inefficient manner. However, selective schools' efficiency is at least such that social investment channeled through them generates multiple dollars of value added.

Given the strong, even dramatic and convex, increases in the social investment that are associated with more and more selective institutions, the result discussed in the foregoing paragraphs are only possible—as a logical matter—if single crossing holds. Moreover, single crossing must not only hold with regard to its positive sign, but the magnitude of the cross partial derivative must be fairly substantial. Put another and less purely mathematical way, education production must be such that students with greater aptitude derive substantially more value added from any marginal dollar of social investment. The implications of this finding are fairly profound for the economics of education. Exploring them fully is beyond the scope of this chapter, but I take them up in my Alfred Marshall Lectures (University of Cambridge).[24]

Productivity based on earnings is much more dispersed among nonselective and less-selective schools than among very selective schools. This is a hint that market forces weaken as selectivity falls, perhaps because students become less informed and/or less responsive to productivity when choosing which school to attend. In any case, a student choosing among nonselective schools can make a much larger "mistake" on productivity than a student choosing among very selective schools.

The results for productivity based on public service suggest that market forces do not maintain regularity in how institutions' resources scale up with the ability of their students to convert social investment into public service. A plausible explanation is the lack of market rewards for public service. Without such market-based rewards, there may be no mechanism by which schools that are that more productive at public service generate more funds to support additional investments.

The results for productivity based on innovation suggest that highly selective schools are much more productive than all other schools. This is not surprising if the rewards for innovation run largely through spillovers or general equilibrium effects on the economy. In such circumstances, there would be no market forces to align social investment with contributions from innovation. Alternatively, social investment (the denominator of productivity) could be understated because it does not include spending on research. Undergraduates may learn to be innovative from research spending or simply by being taught by faculty who spend part of their time on research supported by research spending.

The three outcomes by which productivity is measured in this chapter were chosen to represent private returns (earnings), social returns (public service), and likely sources of economic spillovers (innovation). But there are, of course, many other outcomes by which productivity of postsecondary institutions could be measured.

---

24. These are currently available in video format online and will, in time, be published in written format. See Hoxby (2018).

References

Avery, Christopher, Mark Glickman, Caroline Hoxby, and Andrew Metrick. 2013. "A Revealed Preference Ranking of U.S. Colleges and Universities." *Quarterly Journal of Economics* 128 (1): 1–45.

Barrow, Lisa, and Ofer Malamud. 2015. "Is College a Worthwhile Investment?" *Annual Review of Economics* 7 (August): 519–55.

Bulman, George B., and Caroline M. Hoxby. 2015. "The Returns to the Federal Tax Credits for Higher Education." *Tax Policy and the Economy* 29:1–69.

Cohodes, Sarah, and Joshua Goodman. 2012. "First Degree Earns: The Impact of College Quality on College Completion Rates." HKS Faculty Research Working Paper Series RWP12-033. http://web.hks.harvard.edu/publications/getFile.aspx?Id=836.

Deming, David, Claudia Goldin, and Lawrence Katz. 2011. "The For-Profit Postsecondary School Sector: Nimble Critters or Agile Predators?" NBER Working Paper no. 17710, Cambridge, MA.

Duquette, Nicholas. 2016. "Do Tax Incentives Affect Charitable Contributions? Evidence from Public Charities' Reported Revenue." *Journal of Public Economics* 137:51–69.

Goodman, Joshua, Michael Hurwitz, Jonathan Smith. 2015. "College Access, Initial College Choice and Degree Completion." NBER Working Paper no. 20996, Cambridge, MA. http://www.nber.org/papers/w20996.

Griliches, Zvi. 1979. "Sibling Models and Data in Economics: Beginnings of a Survey." *Journal of Political Economy* 87 (5, part 2): Education and Income Distribution (October): S37–S64.

Hastings, Justine, Christopher Neilson, and Seth Zimmerman. 2012. "Determinants of Causal Returns to Postsecondary Education in Chile: What's Luck Got to Do with It?" NBER conference paper.

Hecker, Daniel. 2005. "High Technology Employment: A NAICS-Based Update." *Monthly Labor Review*, July, 57–72.

Hoekstra, Mark. 2009. "The Effect of Attending the Flagship State University on Earnings: A Discontinuity-Based Approach." *Review of Economics and Statistics* 91 (4): 717–24.

Hoxby, Caroline. 2009. "The Changing Selectivity of American Colleges." *Journal of Economic Perspectives* 23 (4): 95–118.

———. 2015. "Estimating the Value-Added of U.S. Postsecondary Institutions." Internal Revenue Service Statistics of Income Division working paper.

———. 2016. "The Dramatic Economics of the U.S. Market for Higher Education." The 8th Annual Martin Feldstein Lecture, National Bureau of Economic Research. Full lecture available online at http://www.nber.org/feldstein_lecture_2016/feldsteinlecture_2016.html and summarized in *NBER Reporter*, no. 3, 2016.

———. 2018. The Alfred Marshall Lectures, University of Cambridge. http://www.econ.cam.ac.uk/Marshall_Lecture.

Kaufmann, Katja Maria, Matthias Messner, and Alex Solis. 2012. "Returns to Elite Higher Education in the Marriage Market: Evidence from Chile." Working paper, Bocconi University. http://tinyurl.com/kaufmanncollrd.

Langville, Amy N., and Carl D. Meyer. 2012. *Who's #1? The Science of Rating and Ranking*. Princeton: Princeton University Press.

National Center for Education Statistics, Institute for Education Sciences, US

Department of Education. 2003. National Education Longitudinal Study of 1988 (NELS:88/2000 Restricted Use Data Files, NCES 2003-348).

———. 2015. Integrated Postsecondary Education Data System (data as of July 2015, nces.ed.gov website).

National Student Clearinghouse. 2015. "Signature Report: Transfer and Mobility: A National View of Student Movement in Postsecondary Institutions, Fall 2008 Cohort." https://nscresearchcenter.org/wp-content/uploads/SignatureReport 9.pdf.

Oreopoulos, Philip, and Uros Petronijevic. 2013. "Making College Worth It: A Review of Research on the Returns to Higher Education." *The Future of Children: Postsecondary Education in the United States* 23 (1): 41–65.

Saavedra, Juan Estaban. 2009. "The Learning and Early Labor Market Effects of College Quality: A Regression Discontinuity Analysis." Rand Corporation working paper. http://tinyurl.com/saavedracollrd-pdf.

Zimmerman, Seth D. 2014. "The Returns to College Admission for Academically Marginal Students." *Journal of Labor Economics* 32 (4): 711–54.

Labor Market Outcomes and Postsecondary Accountability
Are Imperfect Metrics Better Than None?

Veronica Minaya and Judith Scott-Clayton

3.1 Introduction

The postsecondary accountability movement is motivated by the idea that reporting and rewarding measures of institutional performance can generate both better information and stronger financial incentives to improve the decision-making processes of prospective consumers, policy makers, and institutions (Dougherty and Reddy 2013). In his 2013 State of the Union address, President Obama gave voice to this movement by calling for institutions to be "[held] accountable for cost, value, and quality," eventually by linking measures of institutional performance to federal aid (US Department of Education 2013).

This accountability agenda is even more advanced at the state level. As of 2015, 32 states were already utilizing some form of performance or "outcomes-based" funding, with another 5 in the process of implementing it

Veronica Minaya is a senior research associate at the Community College Research Center at Teachers College, Columbia University.

Judith Scott-Clayton is associate professor of economics and education at Teachers College, Columbia University, a senior research scholar at the Community College Research Center at Teachers College, and a research associate of the National Bureau of Economic Research.

Authors are listed in alphabetical order; both contributed equally to this project. The authors gratefully acknowledge Josh Hawley and Lisa Neilson at the Ohio Education Research Center, who helped facilitate their application for the restricted data utilized herein, and Caroline Hoxby, Kevin Stange, Jeff Smith, Robert Kelchen, and NBER conference participants for valuable suggestions. Funding to obtain and clean the data used herein was provided by the Institute of Education Sciences, US Department of Education, through Grant R305C110011 to Teachers College, Columbia University. The opinions expressed are those of the authors and do not represent views of the Institute, the US Department of Education, or the Ohio Education Research Center. For acknowledgments, sources of research support, and disclosure of the authors' material financial relationships, if any, please see http://www.nber.org/chapters /c13876.ack.

(National Council of State Legislatures [NCSL] 2015). While in most states the portion of state funding that is performance based remains small—typically less than 10 percent—two states (Tennessee and Ohio) now base the majority of institutional funding on performance metrics (Snyder 2015).

These accountability efforts increasingly look beyond just credit and credential completion to what some view as the most important dimension of student outcomes: postcollege labor market success. In September 2015, the Obama administration took a major step toward this goal by releasing an updated version of its College Scorecard, which for the first time provided information not just on college costs and graduation rates but also on median postcollege earnings for more than 4,000 institutions nationwide. Several states now incorporate job placement, employment, and earnings data into their performance funding formulae, at least for portions of their postsecondary sectors. And the Texas State Technical College System uses information on students' postcollege earnings as the *sole* criteria for making funding recommendations to the Texas legislature (Selingo and Van Der Werf 2016; Texas Higher Education Coordinating Board [THECB] 2013).

There is no consensus, however, on how such labor market measures should be constructed, nor is there much evidence regarding how the choice of measure may affect the resulting institutional ratings. While the College Scorecard provides earnings for all entrants 10 years after entry, states using labor market data in performance funding formulae sometimes examine outcomes for graduates less than a year after graduation. Does it matter whether employment/earnings are measured 1, 2, or 10 years postgraduation? Moreover, should schools be held accountable for all students or just those who graduate? What difference does it make whether metrics are adjusted to account for the incoming characteristics of the student population? And can labor market data be used to examine more than just earnings?

In this chapter, using administrative data from one state that links postsecondary transcripts to in-state quarterly earnings and unemployment records over more than a decade, we construct a variety of possible institution-level labor market outcome metrics. Our goal is not to identify the "best" metric but to explore how sensitive institutional ratings may be to the choice of metric, length of follow-up, and inclusion of adjustments for student characteristics, particularly in the context of real-world data limitations. We believe we are the first to use a state-level database to assess labor market outcome metrics beyond earnings, including full-time, full-year employment rates; social service sector employment; and unemployment claims. We also examine how these metrics compare with the academic-outcome-based metrics more commonly incorporated into state accountability systems. This work builds on similar efforts to analyze labor outcome metrics in the postsecondary sector using Internal Revenue Service (IRS) data (Hoxby 2015; also see chapter 2 in this volume), the College Scorecard data (Executive Office of the President [EOP] 2015), and data on four-year colleges in Texas and Canada

(Betts, Ferrall, and Finnie 2013; Cunha and Miller 2014). It also builds on research on institutional performance measurement in sectors with similar features, including job training (Heckman, Heinrich, and Smith 2002) and health care (Staiger et al. 2013).

We conclude that labor market data, even when imperfect, *can* provide valuable information distinct from students' academic outcomes. As has been found in other sectors, however, ratings are highly sensitive to the choice of outcome and length of follow-up (and, to a lesser extent, to the inclusion of compositional adjustments). The most obvious labor market outcomes—graduates' employment and earnings in the year after graduation—are unreliable predictors of institutional performance on the same metrics measured several years later. Earnings and employment alone also fail to capture other aspects of economic well-being that may be valued by both policy makers and students themselves. Consistent with Cunha and Miller (2014), our findings suggest a cautious approach: while a mix of feasible labor market metrics may be better than none, reliance on a single unadjusted earnings metric, especially if measured too early, may undermine policy makers' ongoing efforts to accurately quantify institutional performance.

The remainder of the chapter proceeds as follows. Section 3.2 provides policy context around performance accountability efforts in higher education. Section 3.3 provides a conceptual and practical overview of the challenges of using state-level labor market data for this purpose. Section 3.4 describes our data and methodology. Section 3.5 presents results, and section 3.6 provides a concluding discussion.

3.2   Policy Background

Policy goals in higher education traditionally have been measured and financed primarily using input metrics—such as student enrollment and credit hours—for many decades (SRI International 2012).[1] This stands in contrast to the job training sector, which has a more established tradition of evaluating programs based on participants' labor market outcomes going back at least to the Job Training Partnership Act of 1982 (Barnow and Smith 2015). Over the past three decades, however, there has been a push to align higher education funding with academic outputs, such as credits completed or degrees conferred, rather than inputs. Output-based accountability efforts range from purely informational reporting to higher-stakes performance-based funding (Burke 2001; Dougherty and Reddy 2013; Umbricht, Fernandez, and Ortagus 2015). The idea behind outcomes-based

---

1. A cost-plus approach is a traditional budgeting strategy in which public colleges and universities primarily base their projected budgetary needs on current costs, student enrollments, and inflationary increases.

accountability policies is that they generate both better information and stronger financial incentives to improve the decision-making processes of prospective consumers, policy makers, and institutions (Dougherty et al. 2014; Heckman, Heinrich, and Smith 2002; Muriel and Smith 2011).

The first wave of performance funding (PF) policies, or PF 1.0, used metrics to award bonuses over and above base state funding for higher education (Dougherty and Reddy 2013; Snyder 2011; Dougherty, Natow, and Vega 2012). These early programs eventually lost support, however, due to dissatisfaction with the reliability and validity of the chosen performance metrics, the top-down process by which they were determined, and the small amount of funding at stake (Burke and Serban 1997; Snyder 2015). More than half of PF 1.0 programs were abandoned in the early 2000s (Dougherty, Natow, and Vega 2012).

A new wave of performance funding that "no longer takes the form of a bonus but rather is part and parcel of regular state base funding for higher education" (Dougherty et al. 2014a) began spreading in the late 2000s. Ohio and Indiana both established such PF 2.0 programs in 2009, followed by Tennessee in 2010 (Dougherty et al. 2014b; Dougherty and Reddy 2013). By 2015, 32 states had a policy in place to allocate a portion of funding based on performance indicators, with 5 others in the process of transitioning (NCSL 2015). Although many states continue to use performance funding to allocate relatively small percentages of higher education funding, some states now allocate much larger percentages of funding using performance metrics (Dougherty and Reddy 2013). For example, outcomes-based funding represents about two-thirds of total state support to all higher education institutions in Ohio (Snyder 2015). This high proportion of funding is one reason why Snyder (2015) classifies Ohio and Tennessee as the two most-advanced/high-stakes funding systems, which some are calling PF 3.0 (Kelchen and Stedrak 2016).

With respect to the range of outcomes considered, 28 states currently consider the number of degrees awarded by a university, 16 use some form of course completion, 12 include retention rates, and 12 incorporate graduation rates (NCSL 2015). Many states give extra weight to outcomes for certain subgroups, such as Pell-eligible students (Burke 2002; Dougherty, Hare, and Natow 2009).

Recently, and particularly after the recession, accountability conversations have increasingly focused on the financial costs and benefits of college. Ten states now put weight on postgraduation outcomes such as job placement rates or earnings (EOP 2015; NCSL 2015; see appendix table 3A.1 for additional details). The Texas State Technical College System now uses information on students' postcollege earnings as the *sole* criteria for making funding recommendations to the Texas legislature (THECB 2013). Other states—such as California, Virginia, and Ohio—provide interactive online tools that can be used to explore median earnings after graduation by degree level, field, and/or institution (Nye et al. 2015).

Rigorous evidence regarding the effectiveness of PF policies is limited but discouraging. Two recent quasi-experimental studies compare trends over time in states adopting new policies to states that did not and find evidence of unintended strategic responses. Kelchen and Stedrak (2016) find suggestive evidence that colleges under PF may enroll fewer low-income students as a result, while Hillman, Tandberg, and Fryar (2015) find that two-year colleges in Washington state increased the production of short-term certificates, but not associate's degrees, when completion rates were introduced as a performance metric. A broader review of the literature by Hillman (2016) identifies 12 studies, which find mostly null or even negative results of PF policies.

As indicated by the failure of many early performance funding programs in the late 1990s, the successful design of such programs requires a close examination of the mission of institutions, the type of student body it serves, and the institution's capacity for organizational learning and change (Dougherty et al. 2014; Li 2014). Alignment with state and social priorities for higher education is crucial, as is confidence in the reliability of the chosen metrics. As more states begin to use labor market data for accountability, it is essential to understand the implications of alternative metrics as well as the potential for unintended consequences in order to avoid repeating the mistakes of earlier efforts at reform.

3.3   Conceptual and Practical Challenges to Using State Labor Market Data

As more and more states are able to track students into the labor market via state unemployment insurance (UI) databases, it opens the door to use this information for institutional accountability. Such use presents a number of important practical and conceptual challenges, however. Practical challenges derive from both mundane data limitations—limited length of follow-up, for example, or an inability to track graduates out of state—and the fundamental statistical difficulty of disentangling differences in institutions' true productivity from mere differences in the composition of their respective student populations. Even when stakeholders agree on an outcome they'd like to measure, these challenges can lead to biased estimates in practice.

Moreover, stakeholders may not always agree on what should be measured and when, even if ideal data are available. Conceptual challenges derive from both the multiple objectives that postsecondary institutions serve (e.g., improving not just labor market outcomes but also well-being more broadly; promoting degree completion but also access and persistence at other levels) and the multiple purposes and audiences accountability data may be used for (e.g., informing enrollment decisions by students, short-term funding decisions by the state, and longer-term strategic planning by institutions). This section describes these challenges and helps motivate the variety of metrics that we create and compare in the subsequent analysis.

3.3.1   Productivity versus Student Composition

It is one thing to simply measure student outcomes and another thing entirely to assign all credit (or blame) for those outcomes to the institution. Students at highly selective institutions are likely to have higher graduation rates and better labor market outcomes at least in part because these students come in with stronger academic preparation, better family supports, and greater financial resources. Similarly, student preferences may drive differences in outcomes: students at institutions with strong math and science programs may have better outcomes because math and science majors have better outcomes in general, regardless of the strength of the institution. Finally, students who attend institutions in strong labor markets may have higher earnings than those in weaker labor markets (Hoxby 2015 distinguishes these last two types of selection bias as horizontal selection, while the first represents vertical selection). Failure to account for selection in a PF system can lead to both biased estimates of true productivity as well as adverse incentives for institutions to reduce access, as suggested by Kelchen and Stedrak (2016).

Assessing and addressing the selection or "cream-skimming" problem has been a major focus of performance measurement efforts in other sectors (Heckman, Heinrich, and Smith 2002; Muriel and Smith 2011; Staiger et al. 2013). While randomized control trials (RCTs) have been used to circumvent selection bias in the evaluation of job training programs, they are less feasible in the context of evaluating schools or hospitals. Still, these concerns have motivated a small but growing literature that uses rigorous quasi-experimental methods to measure institutions' true causal effects or "value added." In higher education, some studies have relied on admissions cutoff policies at a limited number of institutions (Hoekstra 2009), while others have compared students with similar qualifications who were admitted to the same set of selective schools (Dale and Krueger 2002, 2011). More recently, Hoxby (2015 and chapter 2 in this volume) uses a vast data set combining college admissions test scores, enrollment data, and income data from the US Treasury to estimate institutional value added, relying on idiosyncrasies both in how schools choose between similar students and in how students choose between similar schools to isolate plausibly causal institutional effects. For a detailed review of the selection challenge and related empirical literature in higher education, see Hoxby (2015) and the Executive Office of the President (2015).

Unfortunately, there is no guarantee that state policy makers will have access to both the right data and the right natural experiment to undertake these types of rigorous causal analysis. The one state system currently using a "value-added" approach, the Texas technical college system, simply deducts a fixed minimum amount from observed earnings (corresponding to full-time, full-year employment at the minimum wage; see THECB 2013). Such a strategy is vulnerable to strategic "cream-skimming" behavior if colleges shift recruitment away from students with the largest potential benefits and toward those with the highest preexisting earnings potential.

A more generally feasible state strategy would be to compute institutional "fixed effects" that use regression analysis to control for any differences in student outcomes that are attributable to observable student characteristics, such as age, race/ethnicity, gender, location of residence at entry, and declared major. These regression adjustments may be less transparent and require more choices to be made by the analyst than simply presenting unadjusted student outcomes. Moreover, differences in *unobserved* student characteristics (such as ability or motivation) are likely to remain even after observed characteristics are taken into account. This may explain why state and federal tools allowing students to browse earnings by institution/ program generally provide simple unadjusted means or medians rather than attempting to control for student characteristics.

In the analysis that follows, we present both unadjusted institutional mean outcomes and adjusted outcomes using an increasingly rich set of controls. Even in our richest model, however, we do not attempt to interpret the resulting institutional fixed effects as causal. Nor are we able to identify the method that most closely approximates a causal analysis. Our modest goal is to evaluate how much these choices actually matter in practice.

3.3.2   Interstate Mobility

A major practical challenge in using state UI databases to measure earnings is that such databases typically include information only for individuals who remain in state (though some states do have data-sharing agreements with border states).[2] Individuals who leave the state are indistinguishable from those who are in state but simply not working.

This complicates the analysis of both employment rates and earnings: without any adjustments, institutions that send many graduates out of state could be seriously disadvantaged on these outcome measures.[3] For

---

2. In addition, UI databases do not include those who are self-employed, some student employees (e.g., work-study students), railroad workers, some agricultural workers, and federal employees. Despite coverage gaps relative to self-reported survey data, prior research has found UI data to provide comparable estimates of program impacts (Kornfeld and Bloom 1999).

3. Note that our subsequent analysis will focus on Ohio's in-state student population, both because such home-state students are of particular interest to state policy makers and because students who migrate to Ohio for college have a particularly high likelihood of leaving the state after college.

example, using data from the National Longitudinal Survey of Youth 1997 (NLSY-97), Scott-Clayton and Wen (2017) show that attending or graduating from a four-year institution is associated with an increased likelihood of living outside of one's home state after college and that four-year students who later live outside their home state earn significantly more than their counterparts who remain in their home state. Prior research further indicates that the effects of education on mobility are causal (Bound and Holzer 2000; Malamud and Wozniak 2012; Wozniak 2010). Moreover, as mobility accumulates over time, this problem worsens the longer the follow-up period. Grogger (2012) discusses this problem in detail in the context of job training program evaluation and finds that it can seriously compromise the validity of program impact estimates. Out-of-state mobility may be less of a concern for evaluating outcomes for two-year colleges, as two-year enrollment and graduation are not associated with the likelihood of leaving the state, nor do two-year students appear to earn substantially different returns if they leave the state (Scott-Clayton and Wen 2017).[4]

In part to minimize this bias, the states that provide information on graduates' employment and earnings often do so within a relatively short period of time postgraduation (e.g., three to six months) and condition earnings metrics on at least some level of observed employment. For example, Ohio examines in-state retention (a combination of employment and subsequent educational enrollment) in the fourth quarter of the year for spring graduates. Earnings are considered only for those who have earnings above a minimum level approximating full-time employment.

Examining earnings conditional on some approximation of full-time employment has the advantage of avoiding confounds not just from out of state mobility but also from individual choices regarding labor force participation (e.g., relating to family formation or continued educational investments). Scott-Clayton and Wen (2017) show that these conditional earnings estimates are much more robust to out-of-state mobility than unconditional earnings estimates: the estimated returns to two- and four-year degrees are quite similar whether analysts condition on employment in any state or on employment only in the home state. On the other hand, these conditional measures will also miss important effects institutions may have on the likelihood of finding and maintaining stable employment.

Our solution to this is to look at graduates in four subsequent quarters in a focal year. If they show up in the data at all, we make the assumption that they are part of the in-state labor force. We then examine our measures

4. Scott-Clayton and Wen (2017) find no relationship between out-of-state mobility and estimated earnings returns to two-year college enrollment. Two-year college graduates who leave the state appear if anything to earn somewhat lower returns than graduates who remain in state, but the differences are not statistically significant.

of full-time, full-year employment; social service sector employment; and unemployment claims only for those who appear in the data in that year. For earnings, we further condition on a proxy measure of full-time, full-year employment (described in more detail in the methodology section below).

3.3.3   Timing of Outcomes Measurement

Measures of employment and earnings from relatively early in the life cycle can be not only noisy but also potentially biased measures of lifetime earnings. As discussed by Heckman, Heinrich, and Smith (2002), "In [the context of human capital programs], the short-run measurements on which performance standards are based will likely be perversely related to long-run benefits" (780). Those with the highest long-term earnings potential may have lower-than-expected earnings if measured soon after graduation if they continue to invest in additional skills/education both on and off the job. Moreover, those with the highest earnings potential may optimally spend more time after graduation searching for a good job match. Evidence suggests that the optimal time to measure individuals' earnings is not until their early 30s to mid-40s (Haider and Solon 2006). Outcomes measured mere months after graduation may reflect mostly noise, or worse, they could be inversely correlated with outcomes over a longer period of time.

From an accountability perspective, however, long time lags also have their own conceptual and practical limitations. To be useful, accountability metrics should reflect institutional performance from a relatively recent period. In addition, the longer the lag between graduation and labor market observation, the more serious the interstate mobility problem becomes. Since the optimal time lag is far from obvious in this context, we measure labor market outcomes four years after graduation but also test variations from one year to seven years postgraduation.

3.3.4   Measuring Outcomes beyond Earnings

Even with ideal data on earnings, a fundamental critique that has been leveled against the use of earnings data for postsecondary accountability is that they fail to capture many other positive impacts of education. For example, institutions that send many graduates into teaching or social service jobs will perform worse on earnings-based metrics than those that send many graduates into finance. Even within a given industry, individuals make trade-offs between wages and other "job amenities" such that wages alone may be a poor summary of overall labor market success. In addition, policy makers (and individuals) may care more about earnings differences at the bottom of the income distribution than in the middle or at the top, but neither average nor median wage metrics will reflect this. Finally, ideally, measures of postsecondary accountability would include not just measures of labor market success but also measures of health and well-being.

State UI databases obviously cannot measure all relevant possible institutional effects. Still, even within UI databases, it is possible to construct a more diverse range of metrics to capture dimensions beyond earnings. For example, UI data can be used to look at the stability of employment over time (such as whether individuals are employed full time for the entire year or how many employers they have had in a given period). Information on industry of employment can also be used to measure employment in "social service" sectors such as teaching or government. Finally, actual unemployment claims can be examined as a measure of job loss (though in practice, UI claims data are typically held separately from quarterly wages and may require additional data permissions to merge). We describe the specific additional measures that we create in section 3.4 below.

3.3.5   Outcomes for Whom? Graduates versus Entrants

Most of the state data tools that provide earnings information by institution and program—such as in California, Florida, Virginia, and Ohio—do so for graduates only rather than looking at outcomes for all students who enter the institution. The conceptual argument for looking only at graduates is twofold: first, institutions may have limited influence over the earnings of students who drop out, and second, given the vast differences in earnings of graduates versus nongraduates, averaging across both groups may be a poor summary of either group's typical outcomes. On the other hand, examining the earnings only of graduates may seriously distort institutions' overall productivity if they graduate only a fraction of entrants. The federal College Scorecard is one data source that provides median earnings for all entrants, not just those who graduate.

Our resolution to this trade-off is to examine labor market outcomes for graduates only but to examine these metrics alongside graduation metrics that *are* measured for all students. This avoids the problem of interpreting labor market metrics that muddle both margins while still holding institutions accountable for both.

One limitation of this strategy is that it will not credit institutions that are particularly effective or ineffective at increasing the earnings of nongraduates relative to graduates. This might occur if an institution has a program that is so effective that students leave to take good jobs even before they graduate or if an institution's degrees have a particularly high "sheepskin effect" component, such that the payoff to completing 99 percent of the degree is far less than 99 percent of the payoff to completing the degree. In general, however, it seems reasonable to assume that whatever the earnings payoff to graduating from a given institution, the payoff to attending but not graduating may be proportional to the fraction of the degree that was completed (indeed, empirical evidence on the returns to credits from Kane and Rouse [1995] supports this proportional-payoff hypothesis).

3.4   Empirical Methodology

3.4.1   Data and Sample

Deidentified data were provided by the Ohio Education Research Center (OERC) under a limited-use, restricted-data agreement. The OERC assembles data from multiple state agencies, including the Ohio Board of Regents (OBR) and the Ohio Department of Job and Family Services (ODFJS), into a repository known as the Ohio Longitudinal Data Archive (OLDA).[5]

From the available data, we requested elements from the Ohio Higher Education Information (HEI) system, including students' demographic characteristics, entrance and enrollment records, major choice, and certificate and degree completion from each of Ohio's higher education institutions (14 universities with 24 regional branch campuses and 23 community colleges, some of which also have multiple campuses). We also requested elements from the UI data, including quarterly earnings and unemployment claims to enable us to examine students' labor market outcomes. While the OLDA data cover more than a decade, for this project we utilize student data from 2000 to 2007 (to enable sufficient follow-up of entrants/graduates) and labor market data from 2000 to 2012. We describe some additional sample restrictions below after providing more detail about our methodology.

The data do not include any measure of students' academic ability upon admission (such as SAT/ACT scores, high school grade point average or test scores, or college entrance or placement exam scores), nor do they include financial aid application data or family income information. The data do include information on financial aid receipt for some years; however, for this project, we chose to prioritize elements that are available for all analytic cohorts. We may incorporate this information into subsequent sensitivity analyses.

3.4.2   Methods and Metrics

This section describes the outcome variables we use, the key analysis groups, and the process we employ to estimate the resulting metrics. After

---

5. The following acknowledgment is required to be stated on any materials produced using workforce or higher education data accessed from the OLDA: This workforce solution was funded by a grant awarded to the US Department of Labor's Employment and Training Administration. The solution was created by the Center for Human Resource Research on behalf of the Ohio Department of Job and Family Services and does not necessarily reflect the official position of the US Department of Labor. The Department of Labor makes no guarantees, warranties, or assurances of any kind, express or implied, with respect to such information, including any information on linked sites and including, but not limited to, accuracy of the information or its completeness, timeliness, usefulness, adequacy, continued availability, or ownership. This solution is copyrighted by the institution that created it. Internal use, by an organization and/or personal use by an individual for noncommercial purposes, is permissible. All other uses require the prior authorization of the copyright owner.

computing regression-adjusted "institutional fixed effects" to account for compositional differences across institutions, we standardize group-level means / fixed effects in order to be able to compare metrics that have different natural scales and then assess the resulting metrics using correlation matrices and graphical analysis.

Outcomes. We construct four labor market accountability metrics based on cohorts of bachelor of arts (BA) / bachelor of science (BS) graduates for four-year institutions and cohorts of certificate/degree completers and transfer students for two-year institutions (i.e., two-year students who transferred to a public four-year institution are grouped with those who earned a credential in the same year/institution). We focus on spring graduates only to simplify our analysis and examine outcomes in the fourth full calendar year postgraduation (so, for a spring 2002 graduate, this would be calendar year 2006). We test sensitivity to examining these outcomes earlier or later, from one year to seven years postgraduation.

To avoid contaminating our estimates with out-of-state mobility (those who move out of state are indistinguishable from those in state but not working), we limit all labor market measures to individuals who have at least some in-state earnings during the focal year. We also limit our labor market measures to those who are not enrolled during the focal year.

While our chapter is primarily focused on the potential use of labor market outcomes, we also wanted to compare these to academic outcomes that are more commonly used for accountability purposes. We created several measures, including degree completion and transfer rates, cumulative credits attempted and completed, and the ratio of credits completed to credits attempted. But because all of these measures were very highly correlated, we chose to focus on degree completion rates (or completion/transfer for the two-year sector) as a summary academic measure. Additional details on each outcome and its rationale are below:

1. *Full-time, full-year employment (proxy).* This measure is intended to capture the stable employment margin: what percentage of graduates are substantially and consistently engaged in the labor market? We do not have any measure of full-time status or hours worked, so we approximate this as employment in all four quarters of the year, with real earnings in each quarter above an amount roughly corresponding to 35 hours per week at minimum wage.[6] As noted above, this is computed only for individuals who show up in the employment data and are not enrolled in the focal year.

2. *Annual earnings conditional on full-time, full-year employment.* This is intended to capture the intensive employment margin. This is the sum of real quarterly earnings, adjusted to constant 2013 US dollars. In practice,

6. The minimum wage for Ohio in 2013 was $7.85 according to the US Department of Labor. Therefore, the average quarterly minimum wage for full-time employees in 2013 was approximately $4,396.

since we cannot observe hours of work, this measure captures both variation in wages as well as variation in hours. Earnings are top-coded at the 95th percentile and only for individuals who are not enrolled in the focal year.[7]

3. *Employment in "social service" sectors.* The rationale for this measure is to address the critique that earnings are not the only positive outcome of education. This measure gives credit for potential positive social externalities of public/social sector employment and could also be a way of acknowledging that some sectors offer benefits and job protections not captured by wages alone. Since we only have industry codes in the employment data, this is only a rough proxy: we include those working in educational services (NAICS 661, including private, state, and local government schools), and the federal, state, and local government excluding state and local schools and hospitals (NAICS 999). For those who show up in the employment data (and are not enrolled) at some point within the focal year, we count them as employed in this sector if they worked at least one quarter during that year in one of these selected industries.

4. *Percent ever claiming unemployment since graduating.* This is intended to capture particularly negative employment outcomes that might carry additional weight in policy makers' social welfare function and might not be captured by average earnings. This is computed only for those who show up in the employment data at some point within the focal year.[8] UI claims data are only available from 2004 to 2012; therefore, this metric has only been estimated for two cohorts of graduates. As opposed to the other outcomes, this is a cumulative metric and thus is not restricted by enrollment status within the focal year.

5. *Degree completion (or transfer) rates.* For four-year first-time degree-seeking entrants, we examine BA/BS completion within six years of entry. For two-year first-time degree-seeking entrants, we include completion of any credential, including short-term certificates (less than one year), long-term certificates (more than one year), and associate's degrees, as well as students who transferred to a four-year institution within three years of entry. We count students as completers regardless of whether they completed at their entry institution. Note, however, that the data only track students in

---

7. We considered using median earnings instead of average earnings to diminish the role of outliers. However, medians are more cumbersome to work with in our regression-adjusted models. In sensitivity testing not shown, we found that average earnings after top coding are very similar to medians, so we stick with averages for simplicity.

8. In addition to helping address concerns about out-of-state mobility, this also helps address another concern: individuals cannot claim UI unless they have worked enough in the past year to meet minimum eligibility criteria. This could introduce some ambiguity about whether claiming UI might actually be considered a good outcome, particularly among marginally attached workers. Our extract of the data do not contain the details necessary to precisely determine UI eligibility; however, in our data, about two thirds of those who worked at all during the year have earnings suggesting they are likely to be eligible. (In Ohio, individuals must have at least 20 weeks of work in the past year with average weekly earnings of at least $243.)

public Ohio institutions, so students who transfer to a private institution or out of state will not be counted here.

Key analysis groups. For the labor market metrics, we use six cohorts of baccalaureate and subbaccalaureate graduates/transfers who earned their first degree or certificate (or transferred, for two-year students) between the 2000 and 2005 school years. We examine baccalaureate and subbaccalaureate institutions separately in all analyses.

For our academic metric, we use eight cohorts of first-time college students in 2000–2007, admitted as first-time undergraduates between ages 15 and 60. Students enrolled in a four-year institution whose academic intentions at first entry were to obtain a certificate or associate in arts (AA) / associate in science (AS) were excluded from this sample.

Given that in the HEI system, baccalaureate degrees awarded are recorded at the institution level and our analysis is at the *campus* level, we use the last campus of enrollment before earning the first BA/BS degree.[9] We restrict our sample to Ohio residents.[10] We further exclude students in the BA/BS sample who were enrolled in a two-year institution during their last semester of enrolment (this is not many students and simplifies our analysis).

This sample consists of 172,541 baccalaureate students from 39 four-year main and regional branch campuses and 79,255 subbaccalaureate students from 32 two-year colleges and campuses (which include community colleges, technical colleges, and state community colleges). Finally, however, we exclude from our analysis two medical institutions and some small campuses that had fewer than 100 students in the analysis sample for all outcomes. This brings the number of campuses to 30 at the BA/BS level and 28 for the two-year sample.

Computing mean outcomes. The first and simplest thing to do once outcomes are constructed is to compute mean outcomes by campus. It is also straightforward to compute them by program or program-campus; for simplicity, we focus on campus. An obvious concern, however, is that differences in outcomes across campus will reflect many factors other than institutional performance: they could reflect differences in students' fields of study, background characteristics (age, race, gender), or differences in local labor markets. This suggests the need to adjust these observed means for compositional differences, a process we describe below.

Computing regression-adjusted institutional fixed effects. The institutional "fixed effect" is simply the estimated contribution of the institution to students' outcomes after accounting for other factors via regression analysis. If no other factors are included in the regression, the fixed effect is equivalent

9. In the remainder of the analysis, we use *institution* and *campus* interchangeably to refer to campus-level estimates, unless specifically noted.
10. In the event the zip code at entry is missing, we assume individuals are residents as long as they are not otherwise identified as international students.

to the unadjusted institutional mean. Our most complete regression model (run separately for two-year and four-year institutions) is the following, run on the individual-level data (we run this without a constant in order to estimate a full set of institutional fixed effects):

$$(1) \qquad y_i = instFE + majorFE + \delta X_i + ZLchrs + \gamma_c + \varepsilon_i,$$

where i indexes individuals; y_i is a labor market or academic outcome; $instFE$ is a vector of institutional fixed effects (FEs; entered as a set of dummy variables indicating the institution initially attended); $majorFE$ is a vector of discipline areas (measured upon college entry) using the two-digit Classification of Instructional Programs (CIP) major category,[11] X_i is a vector of individual background characteristics, including gender, race/ethnicity, age, and dummy variables for missing values in student characteristics; and $ZLchrs$ is a vector of five-digit zip code characteristics taken from the 2007–11 American Community Survey (ACS) five-year estimates that include economic and demographic characteristics.[12] Cohort fixed effects, γ_c, are also included to ensure that institutions' graduates (or entrants) are compared against others graduating (or entering) in the same year. We add these covariates in groups to help understand which appear most important. Because college major is not necessarily a fixed student characteristic but is potentially endogenously influenced by institutions, we add majors last. We note, however, that majors declared at entry are potentially less influenced by institutions than degree fields measured at graduation.

Controlling for zip-code-level characteristics is a way to account for both regional differences in family wealth / socioeconomic status (SES), which we have no other way to capture, as well as differences in local labor markets.[13] Note that zip codes are measured at initial enrollment, not the time of actual employment. This is preferable because controlling for location at employment (which we do not have, in any case) could potentially absorb some of

11. We use the 2010 CIP list to create discipline areas. Based on the CIP list, we have the following discipline areas: arts and humanities, business, education, engineering, health, law, natural science and mathematics, services, social and behavioral sciences, and other, which includes trades and repair technicians and undeclared/interdisciplinary. Note that we exclude individuals with missing majors at entry, which are less than 2 percent of the sample.

12. Five-digit zip codes were reported on the admissions application and merged with census data. These zip code characteristics include percent unemployment; percent in labor force; median household income; per capita income; percent of people below the poverty line; median age; percent of white, African American, and other ethnicities; total population of Hispanics; total population 18 to 24 years old; total population 25 years and older; percent population with less than 9 years of schooling; percent population with 9 to 12 years of schooling; percent population with high school education; percent population with some college education; percent population with associate's degree; percent population with less than 9 years of schooling; and percent population with less than 9 years of schooling.

13. Alternatively, we could control for zip code fixed effects (and we did so in a prior version, with broadly similar results). A potential concern with zip code fixed effects, however, is that this may absorb some of the true institutional effects, particularly for institutions that attract a predominantly local population.

the real impacts of a successful education if graduates migrate to stronger labor markets in state.

For first-time college students enrolled in a two-year institution, we also add fixed effects for different categories of students' declared intent at entry (e.g., upgrade skills, train for a new career, transfer before completing, obtain an AA/AS degree). Note that for the academic metrics, we are using age at entry, while for labor market metrics we use age as reported at graduation.

Standardizing institutional means / fixed effects. Once the institutional fixed effects are estimated, an entirely separate challenge is what to do with them. It can be particularly difficult to detect patterns across metrics when the metrics are all in different natural scales. While the simplest solution might be to simply rank the institutions on each metric and compare the ranks, this is also limiting because the ranks eliminate valuable information on how far apart institutions are from each other—a small difference in ranks could represent a huge difference in institutional outcomes for some measures but not others or could represent large differences in the tails of the distribution but not in the middle.

We thus take the middle path of standardizing the institution-level fixed effects by subtracting the overall mean and dividing by the standard deviation. The result is a standardized rating metric that expresses how far above or below the mean the institution is in standard deviation units for that outcome. This allows us to more easily compare across our different metrics, but note that it produces inherently relative ratings. If policy makers were to use this standardization process in practice, it might make sense to standardize using the mean and standard deviation for an earlier cohort so that institutions could show improvement over time. Note that this standardization is performed separately for four-year and two-year institutions.

3.5 Results

3.5.1 Baccalaureate Institutions

Role of adjustments. To first explore the role of compositional adjustments, tables 3.1–3.4 present, for each of our four labor market metrics, unadjusted institution means side by side with institution fixed effects measured with increasingly rich student-level controls. For ease of comparability across models and outcomes, the institutional fixed effects are standardized to mean zero and a standard deviation of one. Note that since model 1 contains no controls, the standardized fixed effects in this column are identical to the standardized raw means. Each table also shows, near the bottom, how each set of metrics correlates with our most fully adjusted model. The pattern of correlations indicates which analytic choices are particularly consequential for the resulting ratings and which are not.

Several interesting findings emerge from these tables. In general, adjusted

Table 3.1		**Institutional fixed effects: Conditional earnings, year 4 postgraduation**			
		Baccalaureate institutions			
Institution code	Raw mean ($)	Model 1 *No adjustments*	Model 2 *Adjusted for student characteristics*	Model 3 *Adjusted for 2 plus zip-level controls*	Model 4 *Adjusted for 3 plus majors at entry*
camp_17	52,988	1.03	1.50	1.44	1.97
camp_06	55,183	1.68	2.16	2.19	1.44
camp_04	55,099	1.66	1.83	1.89	1.38
camp_12	52,755	0.96	0.54	0.64	1.34
camp_16	51,642	0.63	0.84	0.84	1.20
camp_14	53,747	1.26	0.24	0.27	0.90
camp_27	53,547	1.20	1.39	1.45	0.87
camp_19	52,127	0.78	1.05	0.99	0.73
camp_07	51,747	0.66	0.73	0.67	0.55
camp_18	50,318	0.24	0.32	0.25	0.52
camp_23	49,489	−0.01	0.26	0.18	0.48
camp_20	49,787	0.08	−0.22	−0.09	0.44
camp_15	51,335	0.54	−0.45	−0.39	0.11
camp_01	51,061	0.46	0.53	0.47	0.08
camp_29	49,699	0.05	0.29	0.30	−0.08
camp_03	50,384	0.26	0.31	0.19	−0.11
camp_10	49,126	−0.12	−0.25	−0.25	−0.27
camp_22	46,913	−0.77	−0.62	−0.65	−0.34
camp_24	44,895	−1.37	−1.34	−1.09	−0.39
camp_02	47,383	−0.63	−0.35	−0.52	−0.44
camp_28	47,174	−0.70	−0.60	−0.73	−0.45
camp_05	49,853	0.10	−0.19	−0.31	−0.53
camp_25	48,159	−0.40	−0.57	−0.47	−0.60
camp_11	47,424	−0.62	−0.34	−0.33	−0.63
camp_26	47,899	−0.48	−0.58	−0.26	−0.83
camp_30	48,056	−0.43	−0.52	−0.51	−0.88
camp_09	48,276	−0.37	−0.96	−1.00	−0.97
camp_21	44,113	−1.60	−1.39	−1.51	−1.32
camp_13	45,029	−1.33	−1.62	−1.67	−1.80
camp_08	40,293	−2.74	−1.98	−1.98	−2.37
Institution-level mean	49,517	0.00	0.00	0.00	0.00
Institution-level SD	3,367	1.00	1.00	1.00	1.00
Correlations between] metrics					
Model 1		1.00			
Model 2		0.92	1.00		
Model 3		0.93	0.99	1.00	
Model 4		0.91	0.90	0.91	1.00
Observations	66,695	66,695	66,695	66,695	66,695

Notes: Institutions sorted by model 4 effects. Earnings are measured for nonenrolled graduates in four consecutive quarters in the fourth full year postgraduation and are measured conditional on our proxy of full-time, full-year employment (see text for additional details), so the overall average of $49,517 is among those employed full-time, full-year in state and not still enrolled in that year.

Table 3.2 **Institutional fixed effects: Full-time, full-year employment (proxy), year 4 postgraduation**

			Baccalaureate institutions		
Institution code	Raw mean	Model 1 *No adjustments*	Model 2 *Adjusted for student characteristics*	Model 3 *Adjusted for 2 plus zip-level controls*	Model 4 *Adjusted for 3 plus majors at entry*
camp_12	0.80	1.97	2.01	2.28	2.48
camp_10	0.77	1.25	1.30	1.67	1.47
camp_20	0.76	0.94	1.21	0.95	1.47
camp_18	0.77	1.38	1.41	1.21	1.21
camp_17	0.75	0.76	0.61	0.63	0.73
camp_07	0.73	0.35	0.56	0.63	0.64
camp_29	0.75	0.71	0.76	0.78	0.64
camp_02	0.75	0.74	0.61	0.52	0.53
camp_11	0.73	0.25	0.13	0.52	0.50
camp_28	0.77	1.28	1.38	0.78	0.47
camp_01	0.74	0.61	0.61	0.58	0.47
camp_06	0.73	0.30	0.61	0.66	0.44
camp_15	0.74	0.53	0.18	0.52	0.32
camp_23	0.73	0.17	−0.04	−0.03	0.26
camp_22	0.71	−0.11	0.01	−0.17	0.11
camp_04	0.73	0.40	0.36	0.37	0.11
camp_16	0.72	0.12	−0.04	−0.09	−0.01
camp_19	0.72	−0.09	−0.24	−0.17	−0.09
camp_27	0.73	0.33	0.27	0.29	−0.09
camp_21	0.70	−0.40	−0.39	−0.84	−0.36
camp_25	0.70	−0.52	−0.47	−0.72	−0.45
camp_08	0.64	−2.10	−0.73	−0.61	−0.89
camp_26	0.70	−0.45	−0.61	−0.64	−0.89
camp_13	0.67	−1.17	−1.44	−1.07	−0.92
camp_05	0.69	−0.63	−0.79	−0.92	−1.04
camp_14	0.68	−1.04	−1.18	−0.87	−1.07
camp_24	0.66	−1.40	−1.44	−1.59	−1.25
camp_30	0.68	−0.91	−1.13	−1.15	−1.31
camp_03	0.66	−1.40	−1.36	−1.67	−1.66
camp_09	0.65	−1.89	−2.15	−1.85	−1.81
Institution-level mean	0.72	0.00	0.00	0.00	0.00
Institution-level SD	0.04	1.00	1.00	1.00	1.00
Correlations between metrics					
Model 1		1.00			
Model 2		0.95	1.00		
Model 3		0.93	0.97	1.00	
Model 4		0.93	0.96	0.97	1.00
Observations	91,600	91,600	91,600	91,600	91,600

Notes: Full-time, full-year employment is estimated by examining four consecutive quarters in the fourth full year postgraduation and requires a graduate to earn above a minimum amount in each quarter corresponding to 35 hours per week at minimum wage. The sample is restricted to graduates who are not still enrolled and have positive earnings in at least one quarter of the focal year.

Table 3.3   **Institutional fixed effects: Social sector employment (proxy), year 4 postgraduation**

			Baccalaureate institutions		
Institution code	Raw mean	Model 1 No adjustments	Model 2 Adjusted for student characteristics	Model 3 Adjusted for 2 plus zip-level controls	Model 4 Adjusted for 3 plus majors at entry
camp_20	0.44	1.62	1.60	1.56	1.55
camp_25	0.46	1.82	1.70	1.63	1.47
camp_05	0.35	0.76	0.82	1.05	1.29
camp_24	0.49	2.09	2.07	1.88	1.13
camp_26	0.35	0.77	0.81	0.51	0.97
camp_08	0.36	0.81	0.82	0.90	0.86
camp_22	0.33	0.53	0.43	0.39	0.74
camp_19	0.20	−0.60	−0.40	−0.31	0.45
camp_17	0.27	−0.01	0.22	0.38	0.42
camp_23	0.25	−0.16	0.08	0.13	0.42
camp_21	0.35	0.78	0.63	0.41	0.40
camp_29	0.26	−0.06	0.03	0.04	0.39
camp_07	0.24	−0.28	−0.24	−0.10	0.30
camp_28	0.47	1.91	1.77	1.83	0.06
camp_18	0.35	0.72	0.73	0.85	0.05
camp_01	0.23	−0.38	−0.33	−0.31	0.05
camp_04	0.17	−0.97	−0.84	−0.83	−0.01
camp_02	0.26	−0.07	0.11	0.22	−0.02
camp_11	0.21	−0.51	−0.44	−0.33	−0.07
camp_30	0.25	−0.16	−0.13	−0.24	−0.14
camp_27	0.18	−0.81	−0.65	−0.69	−0.19
camp_06	0.17	−0.94	−1.19	−1.18	−0.32
camp_03	0.29	0.19	−0.08	0.11	−0.32
camp_13	0.19	−0.75	−0.74	−0.70	−0.43
camp_16	0.20	−0.67	−0.53	−0.53	−0.47
camp_09	0.23	−0.40	−0.61	−0.57	−0.75
camp_10	0.13	−1.28	−1.28	−1.26	−1.06
camp_12	0.11	−1.48	−1.66	−1.80	−1.91
camp_15	0.18	−0.81	−0.76	−0.77	−1.93
camp_14	0.09	−1.65	−1.93	−2.04	−2.93
Institution-level mean	0.27	0.00	0.00	0.00	0.00
Institution-level SD	0.11	1.00	1.00	1.00	1.00
Correlations between metrics					
Model 1		1.00			
Model 2		0.99	1.00		
Model 3		0.98	0.99	1.00	
Model 4		0.77	0.82	0.83	1.00
Observations	91,600	91,600	91,600	91,600	91,600

Notes: Social sector employment is estimated by examining four consecutive quarters in the fourth full year postgraduation and requires a graduate to have been employed in educational services or government in at least one of these quarters. Sample is limited to graduates who are not still enrolled and who have positive earnings in at least one quarter of the focal year.

Table 3.4   **Institutional fixed effects: Cumulative UI receipt, year 4 postgraduation**

			Baccalaureate institutions		
Institution code	Raw mean	Model 1 *No adjustments*	Model 2 *Adjusted for student characteristics*	Model 3 *Adjusted for 2 plus zip-level controls*	Model 4 *Adjusted for 3 plus majors at entry*
camp_17	0.06	1.03	1.01	1.04	1.09
camp_19	0.08	0.70	0.81	0.83	0.91
camp_23	0.07	0.74	0.72	0.77	0.84
camp_22	0.08	0.57	0.58	0.54	0.68
camp_20	0.09	0.49	0.60	0.65	0.68
camp_26	0.09	0.49	0.56	0.74	0.68
camp_04	0.09	0.42	0.51	0.58	0.66
camp_21	0.08	0.68	0.69	0.56	0.57
camp_28	0.06	1.03	0.96	0.72	0.54
camp_29	0.09	0.44	0.45	0.56	0.54
camp_18	0.08	0.64	0.58	0.58	0.52
camp_13	0.10	0.33	0.36	0.29	0.45
camp_12	0.09	0.42	0.51	0.40	0.41
camp_16	0.10	0.21	0.18	0.20	0.27
camp_24	0.10	0.25	0.22	0.27	0.27
camp_07	0.12	−0.08	0.09	0.20	0.25
camp_01	0.10	0.21	0.22	0.22	0.22
camp_02	0.10	0.33	0.20	0.22	0.13
camp_05	0.10	0.23	0.13	0.18	0.11
camp_09	0.12	−0.05	0.13	0.09	0.09
camp_11	0.10	0.18	0.07	0.02	0.02
camp_27	0.11	0.01	0.00	0.09	0.02
camp_30	0.12	−0.03	0.00	−0.03	−0.12
camp_25	0.11	−0.01	−0.02	−0.05	−0.12
camp_06	0.13	−0.34	−0.49	−0.44	−0.41
camp_15	0.16	−0.87	−0.78	−0.89	−0.89
camp_10	0.16	−0.81	−1.01	−1.09	−1.05
camp_03	0.16	−0.77	−0.92	−1.00	−1.26
camp_08	0.30	−3.49	−3.07	−2.81	−2.67
camp_14	0.27	−2.97	−3.29	−3.45	−3.44
Institution-level mean	0.11	0.00	0.00	0.00	0.00
Institution-level SD	0.05	1.00	1.00	1.00	1.00
Correlations between metrics					
Model 1		1.00			
Model 2		0.99	1.00		
Model 3		0.98	0.99	1.00	
Model 4		0.97	0.99	1.00	1.00
Observations	35,317	35,317	35,317	35,317	35,317

Notes: Institutional fixed effects (FE) from models 1–4 are reverse coded so that lower rates of UI receipt correspond to more positive standardized FE. Cumulative UI receipt is measured as the percent ever receiving UI or other unemployment compensation by the end of the fourth full year postgraduation. To limit bias from out-of-state mobility, sample is limited to those with positive earnings in at least one quarter of the focal year.

Table 3.5   **Correlations of adjusted institution-level metrics**

		Baccalaureate institutions			
Correlations	ba6yr	Ftemp 4yrs	Earn 4yrs	SS sec 4yrs	UI 4yrs
ba6yr	1.000	—	—	—	—
Ftemp 4yrs	0.176	1.000	—	—	—
Earn 4yrs	0.215	0.497***	1.000	—	—
SS sec 4yrs	0.226	−0.117	−0.277	1.000	—
UI 4yrs	0.325*	0.316*	0.202	0.492***	1.000
Avg. diff. vs. BA metric (SDs)	0.00	1.01	1.00	0.97	0.93
Avg. diff. vs. earnings metric (SDs)	1.00	0.86	0.00	1.24	0.94

Note: *** $p < .01$, ** $p < .05$, * $p < .10$.

and unadjusted metrics are very highly positively correlated. Across our four metrics, the correlation between the unadjusted effects and fully adjusted effects ranges from 0.77 (for our social service employment metric) to 0.97 (for our full-time, full-year employment proxy and for our UI receipt metric). For earnings, the correlation is 0.91. Zip-code-level controls appear the least important controls across all outcomes: the correlations between models 2 and 3 are 0.97 or higher across the board. Controlling for field of study makes a particularly large difference for social sector employment.

Even high correlations, however, can mask substantial movement in institutions' ratings and rankings. For our earnings metric, for example, the average institution swung by about half of a standard deviation across the four models (i.e., from its most favorable rating to its least favorable rating), or by 5 positions in the rankings of these 30 institutions.[14] One institution's rank swung by 11 positions depending on which controls were added. Rankings and ratings based on social sector employment rates were similarly volatile. Adjustments matter less for the full-time, full-year employment proxy and UI receipt metric: the average swings were only about 0.39 and 0.20 of a standard deviation, respectively (or about 3 positions in the rankings in both cases).

Correlations across metrics. Table 3.5 and figure 3.1 examine the relationship among our five different metrics using estimates from the fully adjusted model. In figure 3.1, each vertically aligned set of points represents an institution's rating on one of our five measures (standardized to mean zero and SD of one to enable comparisons across metrics). If a point lies above zero, that indicates the institution rates above average on that metric. A point at −2, on the other hand, would indicate an institution fell two standard deviations below the institutional mean for that metric. To the extent all points

14. Even just considering the first three models, which are all correlated at 0.93 or above for the earnings outcome, the average institution swung by 0.32 standard deviations or 3 positions in the rankings of these 30 institutions.

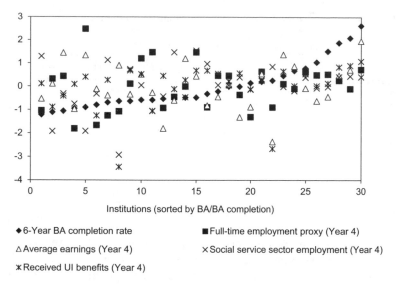

Fig. 3.1   Adjusted institution-level metrics (standardized)

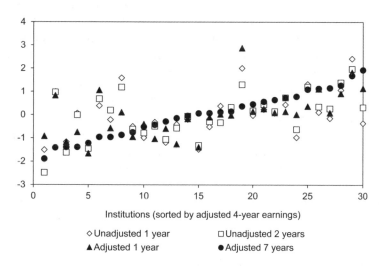

Fig. 3.2   Alternative earnings metrics (standardized)

for a given institution are very tightly clustered, that indicates consistency in the institution's rating across metrics. If the points are very far apart vertically (i.e., for a given institution), it means that an institution's rating could be dramatically different depending on the measure used. To help reveal patterns in the data, the graph is sorted by the degree completion metric, with the lowest-ranking institution on this metric on the left and the highest-ranking on the right. This makes it easy to identify how top institutions on this metric fare on the labor market metrics and vice versa.

Most metrics are positively correlated with each other, though not often not significantly so; they do seem to capture different information. Degree completion rates correlate positively with all other metrics, but the correlation is only significant for our (reverse-coded) UI metric, at 0.33 (the other correlations hover around 0.2). Social sector employment is negatively correlated with both employment and earnings (though not significantly so). Interestingly, the correlation between social sector employment and rates of UI receipt is almost as high as the correlation between employment and earnings (both around 0.49).

In practice, the average difference between an institution's rating on the degree completion metric and its rating on a given labor market metric ranges from 0.93 to 1.01 standard deviations; the average swing across all five metrics is a full 2 standard deviations (or 17 positions in rank). Even just among the four labor market metrics, the average swing is 1.6 standard deviations.

This seemingly large variation in ratings for a single institution is depicted visually in figure 3.1. Each institution's ratings (in standard deviation units) are plotted along a vertical line, and the institutions are sorted from left to right by degree completion rates. The graph illustrates both the general positive correlation among the metrics as well as the dispersion for each institution. The graph also highlights that the dispersion of the labor market metrics is much greater for institutions with low degree completion rates than for those with high degree completion rates.[15]

Correlations of metrics over time. How sensitive are these labor market metrics to different lengths of follow-up? Tables 3.6 and 3.7 explore this question from different angles. First, we examine the correlation of the same metric measured at different points in time. Table 3.6 shows that our adjusted measures are generally positively and significantly correlated over time, with the social sector employment metric having the greatest stability and the full-time employment proxy having the least. In the case of the full-time employment proxy, the one-year and seven-year metrics are barely significantly correlated ($\rho = 0.33$), suggesting these measures may be quite misleading if measured too soon after graduation.[16] The full-time employment proxy also may be particularly sensitive to out-of-state mobility: the sample for which this statistic is computed (those present in the earnings data in a given year) shrinks on average by about 25 percent between the one-year and seven-year follow-up, while in contrast the sample size for our earnings metric (which is conditional on the full-time employment proxy) remains fairly stable over time.

Table 3.7 and figure 3.3 suggest that at least for the conditional earnings

15. We also examined versions of table 3.5 and figure 3.1 using the raw (unadjusted) versions of our five metrics. Overall, whether or not controls are included does not make much difference to the cross-metric correlations. The exception to this is the social sector employment measure, likely because of its sensitivity to field-of-study controls. When no controls are included, this measure is significantly negatively correlated with earnings and no longer significantly correlated with our UI metric (though the positive direction remains the same).

16. We find broadly similar patterns when we perform the same analysis with the unadjusted metrics.

Table 3.6   **Correlations of adjusted LM metrics over time**

	Year 1	Year 2	Year 4	Year 7
	A. Full-time employment proxy			
Year 1	1.000			
Year 2	0.713***	1.000		
Year 4	0.592***	0.730***	1.000	
Year 7	0.331*	0.266	0.337*	1.000
	B. Conditional earnings			
Year 1	1.000	—	—	—
Year 2	0.933***	1.000	—	—
Year 4	0.765***	0.881***	1.000	—
Year 7	0.553***	0.672***	0.874***	1.000
	C. Social sector employment			
Year 1	1.000	—	—	—
Year 2	0.982***	1.000	—	—
Year 4	0.965***	0.955***	1.000	—
Year 7	0.957***	0.948***	0.963***	1.000
	D. UI receipt (inverse)			
Year 1	1.000	—	—	—
Year 2	0.828***	1.000	—	—
Year 4	0.864***	0.886***	1.000	—
Year 7	0.550***	0.745***	0.769***	1.000

Note: *** $p < 0.01$, ** $p < 0.05$, * $p < 0.10$.

Table 3.7   **Correlations between adjusted and unadjusted metrics**

Metric (standardized)	Year 1	Year 2	Year 4	Year 7
Full-time employment proxy	0.920	0.956	0.931	0.941
Conditional earnings	0.778	0.828	0.905	0.905
Social sector employment	0.679	0.701	0.770	0.693
UI receipt	0.989	0.978	0.967	0.965

Note: $p < 0.01$ for all correlations in this table.

metric, analysts may be able to choose between performing statistical adjustments and following graduates for a longer period of time, depending on which is more feasible. Just between year 1 and year 2, the correlation between the adjusted and unadjusted earnings metric grows from 0.78 to 0.83 and then to 0.91 by year 4. Figure 3.3 further illustrates this. The figure shows that unadjusted earnings after one year (the most common and feasible way to measure earnings) are only modestly correlated ($r = 0.38$) with a fully adjusted metric after seven years (which might be the most preferred measure except for the inconvenience of waiting that long). However, adjusting the earnings measure after one year is just as good as using an unadjusted measure after two years: both improve the correlation with seven-year earnings to 0.54.

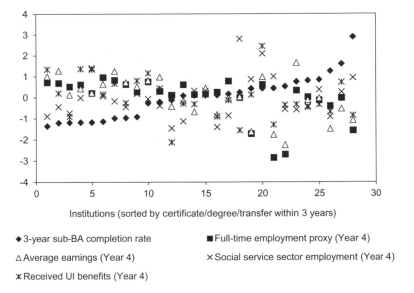

Institutions (sorted by certificate/degree/transfer within 3 years)

◆ 3-year sub-BA completion rate   ■ Full-time employment proxy (Year 4)

△ Average earnings (Year 4)   × Social service sector employment (Year 4)

✳ Received UI benefits (Year 4)

Fig. 3.3   Adjusted metrics for sub-BA institutions

3.5.2   Subbaccalaureate Institutions

Role of adjustments. We repeat the same set of analyses, but this time for subbaccalaureate institutions. Tables 3.8–3.11 present unadjusted and adjusted versions of each of our four labor market metrics, measured four years postgraduation. Again, adjusted and unadjusted versions are always positively correlated, ranging from 0.84 (for our earnings metric) to 0.95 (for our social service employment and UI metrics). The typical ratings swing across model adjustments ranges from about one-third of a standard deviation for the full-time employment proxy, UI, and social sector employment metrics to about half of a standard deviation for the earnings metric. In general, this is quite similar to what we found in the four-year sector.

Correlations across metrics. Table 3.12 and figure 3.3 examine the relationships among our five metrics using estimates from our fully adjusted model.[17] In notable contrast to the four-year sector, we see here that institution-level earnings and employment are both strongly *negatively* correlated with our completion metric (around –0.53 for both metrics), while our measure of social sector employment is positively but not significantly correlated (0.18).[18] The average ratings swing across these five metrics is 2.2 standard deviations.

17. We find broadly similar patterns if we use unadjusted versions of these metrics.
18. Another notable finding is that the UI metric is not as strongly correlated with the other labor market metrics in the two-year sector as compared with the four-year sector. This may be because of the issue raised earlier, that to claim UI, graduates have to have held a job for at least 20 weeks with average earnings above $243 per week. An institution could thus do "well" on this measure either because its graduates are rarely unemployed or because they rarely work long enough to qualify for unemployment benefits. We thank Lawrence Katz for raising this point.

Table 3.8   **Institutional fixed effects: Conditional earnings, year 4 postgraduation**

			Subbaccalaureate institutions		
Institution code	Raw mean ($)	Model 1 No adjustments	Model 2 Adjusted for student characteristics	Model 3 Adjusted for 2 plus zip-level controls	Model 4 Adjusted for 3 plus majors at entry
camp_23	46,940	0.37	0.65	0.92	1.65
camp_08	49,261	1.07	1.02	0.94	1.27
camp_06	49,592	1.17	1.21	1.08	1.26
camp_07	49,985	1.29	1.48	1.52	1.00
camp_21	46,722	0.30	0.61	0.94	0.98
camp_13	49,200	1.05	0.86	0.69	0.97
camp_03	48,919	0.97	0.98	0.89	0.81
camp_20	48,518	0.85	0.80	0.85	0.71
camp_22	48,642	0.88	0.78	0.76	0.64
camp_02	47,651	0.58	0.55	0.62	0.52
camp_04	47,800	0.63	0.93	0.92	0.44
camp_12	47,827	0.64	0.85	0.77	0.42
camp_05	47,354	0.49	0.43	0.20	0.22
camp_19	47,086	0.41	0.22	0.17	0.12
camp_24	42,631	−0.94	−0.90	−0.86	0.02
camp_26	47,103	0.42	0.26	0.27	−0.03
camp_16	46,797	0.32	0.27	0.24	−0.04
camp_14	45,953	0.07	0.24	0.32	−0.13
camp_09	44,329	−0.42	−0.65	−0.73	−0.16
camp_27	45,173	−0.17	−0.81	−0.88	−0.42
camp_25	38,307	−2.25	−1.81	−1.74	−0.54
camp_17	45,554	−0.05	−0.18	−0.13	−0.68
camp_18	42,365	−1.02	−0.97	−1.00	−0.81
camp_10	43,665	−0.63	−0.76	−0.70	−1.08
camp_15	40,392	−1.62	−1.65	−1.65	−1.49
camp_28	40,049	−1.72	−1.58	−1.59	−1.63
camp_01	42,902	−0.86	−1.04	−1.00	−1.77
camp_11	39,743	−1.82	−1.79	−1.84	−2.25
Institution-level mean	45,731	0.00	0.00	0.00	0.00
Institution-level SD	3,297	1.00	1.00	1.00	1.00
Correlations between metrics					
Model 1		1.00			
Model 2		0.98	1.00		
Model 3		0.96	0.99	1.00	
Model 4		0.84	0.88	0.89	1.00
Observations	36,596	36,596	36,596	36,596	36,596

Notes: Institutional fixed effects from models 1–4 are standardized to mean 0 and SD 1. Institutions sorted by model 4 effects. Earnings are measured for four consecutive quarters in the fourth full year postgraduation and are measured conditional on our proxy of full-time, full-year employment (see text for additional details), so the overall average of $45,731 is among those employed full-time, full-year in state in that year. Sample also restricted to those not enrolled within the focal year.

Table 3.9   **Institutional fixed effects: Full-time full-year employment (proxy), year 4 postgraduation**

Institution code	Raw mean	Model 1 No adjustments	Model 2 Adjusted for student characteristics	Model 3 Adjusted for 2 plus zip-level controls	Model 4 Adjusted for 3 plus majors at entry
			Subbaccalaureate institutions		
camp_01	0.53	−2.22	−2.29	−2.36	−2.85
camp_02	0.69	0.26	0.27	0.31	0.27
camp_03	0.72	0.76	0.85	0.96	0.74
camp_04	0.71	0.66	0.69	0.54	0.19
camp_05	0.68	0.13	0.19	0.28	0.20
camp_06	0.67	−0.11	0.33	0.71	0.82
camp_07	0.69	0.21	0.63	0.97	0.71
camp_08	0.70	0.42	0.35	0.53	0.68
camp_09	0.72	0.71	0.55	0.25	0.61
camp_10	0.59	−1.26	−1.41	−1.31	−1.57
camp_11	0.50	−2.77	−2.73	−2.69	−2.70
camp_12	0.71	0.61	0.69	0.71	0.61
camp_13	0.68	0.11	0.00	0.13	0.30
camp 14	0.71	0.58	0.58	0.31	0.02
camp_15	0.65	−0.31	−0.37	−0.45	−0.41
camp_16	0.70	0.40	0.35	0.18	−0.14
camp_17	0.72	0.71	0.62	0.51	0.14
camp_18	0.70	0.39	0.35	0.11	0.25
camp_19	0.74	1.06	0.96	0.65	0.51
camp_20	0.72	0.69	0.66	0.73	0.62
camp_21	0.70	0.39	0.44	0.54	0.61
camp_22	0.73	0.97	0.91	1.09	0.96
camp_23	0.66	−0.23	−0.22	−0.19	0.33
camp_24	0.64	−0.53	−0.56	−0.62	−0.01
camp_25	0.60	−1.10	−0.99	−0.86	−0.03
camp_26	0.74	1.13	1.02	1.02	0.78
camp_27	0.69	0.31	0.03	−0.18	0.11
camp_28	0.55	−1.93	−1.92	−1.87	−1.73
Institution-level mean	0.67	0.00	0.00	0.00	0.00
Institution-level SD	0.06	1.00	1.00	1.00	1.00
Correlations between metrics					
Model 1		1.00			
Model 2		0.99	1.00		
Model 3		0.96	0.98	1.00	
Model 4		0.90	0.93	0.95	1.00
Observations	53,353	53,353	53,353	53,353	53,353

Notes: Institutional fixed effects from models 1–4 are standardized to mean 0 and SD 1. Institutions sorted by model 4 effects. Full-time, full-year employment is estimated by examining four consecutive quarters in the fourth full year postgraduation and requires a graduate to earn above a minimum amount in each quarter corresponding to 35 hours per week at minimum wage. The sample is restricted to graduates who are not still enrolled and have positive earnings in at least one quarter of the focal year.

Table 3.10		Institutional fixed effects: Social sector employment (proxy), year 4 postgraduation			

			Subbaccalaureate institutions		
Institution code	Raw mean	Model 1 No adjustments	Model 2 Adjusted for student characteristics	Model 3 Adjusted for 2 plus zip-level controls	Model 4 Adjusted for 3 plus majors at entry
camp_01	0.15	0.58	0.59	0.59	0.99
camp_02	0.14	0.47	0.41	0.31	0.18
camp_03	0.11	−0.29	−0.40	−0.51	−0.07
camp_04	0.11	−0.29	−0.17	−0.08	0.31
camp_05	0.18	1.55	1.39	1.34	1.40
camp_06	0.15	0.63	0.04	−0.28	−0.18
camp_07	0.10	−0.64	−1.10	−1.23	−0.89
camp_08	0.11	−0.34	−0.38	−0.31	−0.45
camp_09	0.08	−1.07	−1.03	−0.98	−1.14
camp_10	0.17	1.26	1.26	1.26	0.94
camp_11	0.11	−0.42	−0.27	−0.28	−0.56
camp_12	0.12	−0.04	−0.01	−0.11	−0.02
camp_13	0.11	−0.26	−0.30	−0.23	−0.40
camp_14	0.09	−0.80	−0.66	−0.68	−0.43
camp_15	0.10	−0.72	−0.61	−0.53	−0.92
camp_16	0.12	0.01	0.01	0.11	0.37
camp_17	0.13	0.09	0.07	0.09	0.31
camp_18	0.08	−1.32	−1.13	−1.13	−1.41
camp_19	0.09	−0.91	−0.92	−0.83	−0.75
camp_20	0.11	−0.40	−0.38	−0.46	−0.45
camp_21	0.19	1.72	1.71	1.84	2.09
camp_22	0.13	0.06	−0.04	−0.13	0.07
camp_23	0.11	−0.40	−0.22	−0.13	−0.59
camp_24	0.24	3.02	3.09	3.01	2.80
camp_25	0.14	0.39	0.77	0.91	0.26
camp_26	0.07	−1.51	−1.49	−1.38	−0.86
camp_27	0.09	−1.02	−1.05	−1.06	−1.46
camp_28	0.15	0.63	0.82	0.91	0.86
Institution-level mean	0.12	0.00	0.00	0.00	0.00
Institution-level SD	0.04	1.00	1.00	1.00	1.00
Correlations between metrics					
Model 1		1.00			
Model 2		0.98	1.00		
Model 3		0.96	0.99	1.00	
Model 4		0.95	0.95	0.95	1.00
Observations	53,353	53,353	53,353	53,353	53,353

Notes: Institutional fixed effects from models 1–4 are standardized to mean 0 and SD 1. Institutions sorted by model 4 effects. Social sector employment is estimated by examining four consecutive quarters in the fourth full year postgraduation and requires a graduate to have been employed in educational services or government in at least one of these quarters. Sample is limited to graduates who are not still enrolled and who have positive earnings in at least one quarter of the focal year.

Table 3.11 **Institutional fixed effects: Cumulative UI receipt, year 4 postgraduation**

			Subbaccalaureate institutions		
Institution code	Raw mean	Model 1 No adjustments	Model 2 Adjusted for student characteristics	Model 3 Adjusted for 2 plus zip-level controls	Model 4 Adjusted for 3 plus majors at entry
camp_01	0.21	−0.82	−0.86	−0.78	−1.30
camp_02	0.13	0.99	0.96	0.95	0.80
camp_03	0.15	0.62	1.01	0.88	1.16
camp_04	0.15	0.62	0.40	0.37	0.12
camp_05	0.12	1.28	1.44	1.19	1.34
camp_06	0.17	0.05	0.72	0.60	0.67
camp_07	0.12	1.11	1.55	1.58	1.34
camp_08	0.15	0.45	0.47	0.18	0.20
camp_09	0.20	−0.65	−0.66	−0.73	−0.29
camp_10	0.20	−0.75	−0.62	−0.47	−0.86
camp_11	0.19	−0.33	−0.41	−0.19	−0.37
camp_12	0.11	1.51	1.37	1.30	1.36
camp_13	0.13	0.99	0.94	0.58	0.43
camp_14	0.18	−0.21	−0.34	−0.24	−0.47
camp_15	0.22	−1.05	−1.11	−0.94	−0.68
camp_16	0.18	−0.18	−0.21	−0.22	−0.34
camp_17	0.17	−0.07	−0.14	−0.12	−0.32
camp_18	0.22	−1.13	−1.20	−1.22	−0.91
camp_19	0.21	−0.98	−0.93	−1.01	−0.91
camp_20	0.19	−0.37	−0.25	−0.33	−0.26
camp_21	0.08	2.08	1.82	2.17	2.45
camp_22	0.16	0.22	0.35	0.07	0.15
camp_23	0.18	−0.11	−0.46	−0.22	−0.34
camp_24	0.22	−1.13	−1.32	−1.24	−1.56
camp_25	0.14	0.80	0.38	0.77	0.72
camp_26	0.19	−0.35	−0.30	−0.45	−0.13
camp_27	0.29	−2.68	−2.40	−2.60	−2.13
camp_28	0.17	0.10	−0.19	0.11	0.12
Institution-level mean	0.17	0.00	0.00	0.00	0.00
Institution-level SD	0.04	1.00	1.00	1.00	1.00
Correlations between metrics					
Model 1		1.00			
Model 2		0.97	1.00		
Model 3		0.98	0.98	1.00	
Model 4		0.95	0.96	0.97	1.00
Observations	22,467	22,467	22,467	22,467	22,467

Notes: Institutional fixed effects from models 1–4 are reverse-coded so that lower rates of UI receipt correspond to more positive standardized FE. Cumulative UI receipt is measured as the percent ever receiving UI or other unemployment compensation by the end of the fourth full year postgraduation. To limit bias from out-of-state mobility, sample is limited to those with positive earnings in at least one quarter of the focal year.

Table 3.12   Correlations of Adjusted Institution-level Metrics

	Subbaccalaureate institutions				
Correlations	Subba 3yrs	Ftemp 4yrs	Earn 4yrs	SS sec 4yrs	UI 4yrs
Subba 3yrs	1.000	—	—	—	—
AA 3yrs	0.646***	—	—	—	—
LTC 3yrs	0.467**	—	—	—	—
STC 3yrs	0.744***	—	—	—	—
Trans 3yrs	0.376**	—	—	—	—
Ftemp 4yrs	−0.527***	1.000	—	—	—
Earn 4yrs	−0.533***	0.818***	1.000	—	—
SS sec 4yrs	0.183	−0.231	−0.026	1.000	—
UI 4yrs	−0.330*	0.378**	0.488***	0.222	1.000
Avg. diff. vs. BA metric (SDs)	0.00	1.35	1.45	1.06	1.35
Avg. diff. vs. earnings metric (SDs)	1.45	0.47	0.00	1.20	0.80

Note: *** $p < 0.01$, ** $p < 0.05$, * $p < 0.10$.

This vast difference in institutional ratings dependent on the measure is reflected graphically in figure 3.3. As shown, institutions with the highest completion/transfer rates typically have some of the lowest employment and earnings. This striking negative correlation may reflect two issues. First, our completion measure combines certificate completion, AA/AS completion, and transfer to a four-year institution within three years. If we separate these out (not shown), long certificate completion (for programs 1–2 years in length) is the most negatively correlated with subsequent employment and earnings, though associate's degree completion is also significantly negatively correlated with earnings. Transfer rates are only slightly positively correlated with earnings four years after transfer (though these correlations are not significant). Second, although our labor market measures exclude students who are currently enrolled in the focal year, these patterns may nonetheless reflect the fact that students who graduate or transfer may still have spent significant time engaged in school in the intervening periods and thus may have accumulated less work experience than students who drop out. Yet we find that these negative correlations are still strong if we look seven years postgraduation (not shown). Overall, the negative correlations between subbaccalaureate completion rates and subsequent labor market outcomes is puzzling and provides strong motivation for considering measures beyond graduation/transfer for this sector.

Correlation of metrics over time. Table 3.13 examines the sensitivity of these metrics to the length of follow-up. It appears that labor market outcomes are much less sensitive to the length of follow-up for the two-year sector than we found for the four-year sector.[19] Reasons for this could

19. This holds regardless of whether we use adjusted or unadjusted measures.

Table 3.13   **Correlations of adjusted LM metrics over time**

	Subbaccalaureate institutions			
	Year 1	Year 2	Year 4	Year 7
A. Full-time employment proxy				
Year 1	1.000	—	—	—
Year 2	0.977***	1.000	—	—
Year 4	0.920***	0.930***	1.000	—
Year 7	0.887***	0.873***	0.890***	1.000
B. Conditional earnings				
Year 1	1.000	—	—	—
Year 2	0.971***	1.000	—	—
Year 4	0.960***	0.975***	1.000	—
Year 7	0.883***	0.923***	0.933***	1.000
C. Social sector employment				
Year 1	1.000	—	—	—
Year 2	0.937***	1.000	—	—
Year 4	0.918***	0.955***	1.000	—
Year 7	0.841***	0.856***	0.940***	1.000
D. UI Receipt (inverse)				
Year 1	1.000	—	—	—
Year 2	0.894***	1.000	—	—
Year 4	0.798***	0.853***	1.000	—
Year 7	0.712***	0.779***	0.942***	1.000

Note: *** $p < .01$, ** $p < .05$, * $p < .10$.

include lower rates of out-of-state mobility as well as lower rates of further educational enrollment. Table 3.14 further shows that unlike in the four-year sector, it is not obvious that the role of statistical adjustments diminishes over time for this sector. The correlation between adjusted and unadjusted versions of the same metric appears more stable, sometimes even declining over time.

3.6   Discussion

While newly accessible state UI databases present great opportunities for enhancing states' ongoing efforts to measure college student outcomes, it is no straightforward task to figure out how to use these data most effectively. We draw the following conclusions from our analyses.

First, state UI databases can provide richer measures of graduates' labor market experiences beyond just earnings. While three of the four labor market metrics are positively correlated (with social sector employment the exception), they do appear to capture different aspects of postcollege labor market success, and institutions could receive markedly different ratings or rankings depending on which measure is used.

Second, metrics based on labor market outcomes result in substantially

Table 3.14   Correlations between adjusted and unadjusted metrics

	Subbaccalaureate institutions			
Metric (standardized)	Year 1	Year 2	Year 4	Year 7
Full-time employment proxy	0.941	0.931	0.904	0.913
Conditional earnings	0.912	0.898	0.840	0.815
Social sector employment	0.928	0.955	0.947	0.922
UI receipt	0.950	0.947	0.947	0.939

Note: $p < 0.01$ for all correlations in this table.

different institutional ratings and rankings than those based on degree completion (or completion/transfer) alone, particularly in the two-year sector. Indeed, for two-year institutions, degree completion/transfer rates are negatively correlated with three of our four labor market outcome metrics, highlighting the risk involved in relying on academic outcomes alone.

Third, statistical adjustments generally have less consequence for ratings/rankings than the choice of outcome metric and length of follow-up. Moreover, field of study controls appear particularly important. Research in the Canadian context by Betts, Ferrall, and Finnie (2013) similarly highlights the role of field-of-study controls, and it is worth noting that data on major field of study are one of the comparative advantages of state administrative databases compared to alternative national data sources (such as IRS data). Still, overall, the effect of adjustments appears modest compared to other analytic choices. It is possible that even our fully adjusted model omits important factors that if incorporated, could more substantially change institutions' ratings. But our finding echoes a similar pattern in hospital performance measurement, in which the choice of outcome generally matters more than which patient-level controls are included (Staiger 2016).

Fourth, for earnings-based metrics in the four-year sector, statistical adjustments appear more important when outcomes are measured early. Compared against seventh-year adjusted earnings, an adjusted one-year measure performed about as well as an unadjusted two-year measure. This suggests states may be able to choose between using an adjusted measure soon after graduation or an unadjusted measure after a longer period of time, depending on which is more feasible. This trade-off is not evident for every outcome metric, however, or for the two-year sector.

Finally, when we examine the correlation of our metrics over different lengths of follow-up, we find that our conditional earnings metric is much less stable over time for the four-year sector than for the two-year sector. In the four-year sector, the correlation of seven-year earnings with earnings measured earlier ranges from 0.55 to 0.87, while in the two-year sector, the equivalent correlations range from 0.88 to 0.93. The full-time, full-year employment metric is even more unstable for four-year graduates: the correlation between employment measured at one year versus seven years post-graduation is only 0.331 and only marginally significant.

Limitations. Currently we use several cohorts of entrants/graduates to estimate each institution's fixed effect. We have not examined what would happen if these effects were estimated with only one or two cohorts at a time. We have not incorporated any controls for student ability or family income, which have been used in other studies of accountability metrics. Finally, we have not examined any input-based measures of institutional quality/selectivity, such as constructed in Dillon and Smith (2015). It would be very valuable to further investigate the correlation between input- and output-based institutional ratings, as done by Betts, Ferrall, and Finnie (2013) in the Canadian context.

Conclusion. Overall, our preliminary conclusion is that labor market data, even when imperfect, can provide valuable information distinct from students' academic outcomes, particularly for the two-year sector. Institutional ratings based on labor market outcomes, however, are quite sensitive to the specific metric constructed. The simplest labor market metrics at policy makers' disposal—unadjusted employment rates and average earnings within a year after graduation—both prove to be quite unreliable compared to the same outcomes measured later. Moreover, earnings and employment on their own may fail to capture other aspects of economic well-being of value to both policy makers and students themselves. Consistent with similar types of studies conducted in other contexts (such as outcomes-based evaluations of hospital quality), the choice of metric and length of follow-up appear to matter more than compositional adjustments.

Of course, while Ohio is a large and diverse state, there is no guarantee that our results will generalize to other states or contexts. For example, Ohio has a relatively low rate of out-of-state mobility: census data show that approximately 86 percent of Ohio's 26- to 35-year-olds with at least some college education still lived in the state five years later, compared to a median of about 80 percent across all states. In states with high rates of out-of-state mobility, it's possible that compositional adjustments might be particularly important and that outcome measurements might be more sensitive to the timing of follow-up than we estimate here. In addition, it is important to note that our entire analysis is limited to public state institutions (a limitation common to most state administrative databases). Overall, our findings suggest a cautious approach: while a mix of feasible labor market metrics may be better than none, reliance on any one metric—particularly one measured early—may unintentionally undermine policy makers' ongoing efforts to accurately quantify institutional performance.

Appendix

Table 3A.1   Labor market outcome (LMO) metrics used for performance-based funding

State	Sector using LMOs	Mandatory vs. optional	Funding linked to overall performance and role of LMOs	Employment data source	Sample for LMO metrics	LMO metrics
FL	Two- and four-year institutions	Mandatory	$200 million linked to PBF in 2016, half new funds, half reallocated from base fund. Both universities and colleges have mandatory metrics based on LMOs, though specific metrics vary by sector, and LMOs are among several outcomes considered.	Unemployment insurance (UI) data	Graduates	Percent of bachelor's graduates employed and/or continuing their education further one year after graduation; median average full-time wages one year after graduation; job placement; average full-time wages compared to entry-level wages in local service area.
TX	State technical colleges	Mandatory	One hundred percent of state funding recommendations (from THECB to state legislature) are based on LMO.	UI data	Graduates and those who leave TSTCS for at least two years and show up in state workforce	THECB "value-added" measure is based on five years of postenrollment earnings minus the minimum wage.
KS	Two-year institutions	Optional	New state funds; LMOs are options but not mandatory and vary by institution (at least eight are currently using).	UI data	Graduates	Percent of students employed; percent employed in field; wages of students hired; starting wages.
AK	Two-year institutions	Optional	Five percent of funding in the 2012–13 school year, increasing by 5 percent increments until capped at 25 percent during the 2017–18 school year. The remaining 75 percent of funding will be based on enrollment and institutional needs. LMO metric is optional, not mandatory; unclear if any campus is using.	UI data	Graduates	Number of completers that obtain employment (time frame unclear).

LA	Two- and four-year institutions	Optional	Fifteen percent of base appropriations; institutions can also receive permission to raise tuition by 10 percent without legislative approval. LMOs are options but not mandatory and not clear that any institutions are currently using.	Not specified	Graduates	Employment of degree and certificate earners.
MN	Two-year institutions	Mandatory	Five percent of base funding is reserved until institutions meet three out of five performance goals.	Graduate follow-up survey data	Graduates	Percent employed in program-related job during the year after graduation.
UT	In place at two-year and four-year institutions		For fiscal year (FY) 2015, $1.5 million in one-time funding was allocated based on performance.	UI data	Graduates from two-year institutions	Job placement rates following graduation.
WI	Technical colleges	Mandatory	Ten percent of base funding were at stake during FY2014–15. The amount of performance funding increased by 10 percent increments until reaching 30 percent in FY2016–17.	Graduate follow-up survey data	Graduates	Placement rate of students in jobs related to students' programs of study.
TN	Two-year institutions	Mandatory	After a base amount is set aside for operational support, 100 percent of state funding is allocated based on institutional outcomes.	Not specified	Graduates	Job placement within a related field through June 30 of the year following graduation.

Source: NCSL (2015), THECB (2013), FLBOG (2016), and state agency websites.

References

Barnow, Burt S., and Jeffrey Smith. 2015. "Employment and Training Programs." NBER Working Paper no. 21659, Cambridge, MA.

Betts, Julian, Christopher Ferrall, and Ross Finnie. 2013. "The Role of University Characteristics in Determining Post-graduation Outcomes: Panel Evidence from Three Canadian Cohorts." *Canadian Public Policy* 39:S81–S106.

Bogue, E. G., and B. D. Johnson. 2010. "Performance Incentives and Public College Accountability in the United States: A Quarter Century Policy Audit." *Higher Education Management and Policy* 22 (2): 9–30.

Bound, J., and H. J. Holzer. 2000. "Demand Shifts, Population Adjustments, and Labor Market Outcomes during the 1980s." *Journal of Labor Economics* 18 (1): 20–54.

Burke, J. C. 2001. *Accountability, Reporting, and Performance: Why Haven't They Made More Difference?* New York: Ford Foundation.

———, ed. 2002. *Funding Public Colleges and Universities for Performance: Popularity, Problems, and Prospects.* Albany, NY: Rockefeller Institute Press.

Burke, J. C., and A. M. Serban. 1997. *Performance Funding and Budgeting for Public Higher Education: Current Status and Future Prospects.* Albany, NY: Rockefeller Institute Press.

Burke, J., and S. Modarresi. 2001. "Performance Funding Programs: Assessing Their Stability." *Research in Higher Education* 42 (1): 51–71. http://link.springer.com/article/10.1023/A:1018764511093.

Cunha, Jesse M., and Trey Miller. 2014. "Measuring Value-Added in Higher Education: Possibilities and Limitations in the Use of Administrative Data." *Economics of Education Review* 42:64–77.

Dale, Stacy Berg, and Alan B. Krueger. 2002. "Estimating the Payoff to Attending a More Selective College: An Application of Selection on Observables and Unobservables." *Quarterly Journal of Economics* 107 (4): 1491–1527.

———. 2011. "Estimating the Return to College Selectivity over the Career Using Administrative Earnings Data." NBER Working Paper no. 17159, Cambridge, MA.

Dillon, Eleanor W., and Jeffery A. Smith. 2015. "Determinants of the Match between Student Ability and College Quality." Working paper, Arizona State University. http://www.public.asu.edu/~edillon2/Dillon_Smith_Determinants.pdf.

Dougherty, Kevin J., R. J. Hare, and Rebecca S. Natow. 2009. *Performance Accountability Systems for Community Colleges: Lessons for the Voluntary Framework of Accountability for Community Colleges.* New York: Columbia University, Teachers College, Community College Research Center. http://ccrc.tc.columbia.edu/publications/performance-accountability-systems.html.

Dougherty, Kevin J., Sosanya S. Jones, Hana Lahr, Rebecca S. Natow, Lara Pheatt, and Vikash Reddy. 2014a. "Implementing Performance Funding in Three Leading States: Instruments, Outcomes, Obstacles, and Unintended Impacts." Community College Research Center Working Paper no. 74. New York: Community College Research Center.

———. 2014b. "The Political Origins of Performance Funding 2.0 in Indiana, Ohio, and Tennessee: Theoretical Perspectives and Comparisons with Performance Funding 1.0." Community College Research Center Working Paper no. 68. New York: Community College Research Center.

Dougherty, Kevin J., and Rebecca Natow. 2010. "Change in Long-Lasting State Performance Funding Systems for Higher Education: The Cases of Tennessee and Florida." Working Paper no. 18. New York: Community College Research Center, Teachers College, Columbia University.

Dougherty, Kevin J., Rebecca Natow, and B. Vega. 2012. "Popular but Unstable: Explaining Why State Performance Funding Systems in the United States Often Do Not Persist." *Teachers College Record* 114 (030301): 1–41.

Dougherty, Kevin J., and V. Reddy. 2011. *The Impacts of State Performance Funding Systems on Higher Education Institutions: Research Literature Review and Policy Recommendations.* New York: Community College Research Center, Teachers College, Columbia University. http://ccrc.tc.columbia.edu/publications/impacts -state-performance-funding.html.

———. 2013. *Performance Funding for Higher Education: What Are the Mechanisms? What Are the Impacts?* ASHE Higher Education Report. San Francisco, CA: Jossey-Bass.

Executive Office of the President (EOP). 2015. *Using Federal Data to Measure and Improve the Performance of U.S. Institutions of Higher Education.* https://college scorecard.ed.gov/assets/UsingFederalDataToMeasureAndImprovePerformance .pdf.

Florida State University System Board of Governors (FLBOG). 2016. *Board of Governors Performance Funding Model Overview.* Tallahassee: FLBOG. Accessed May 26, 2016. http://www.flbog.edu/about/budget/docs/performance_funding /Overview-Doc-Performance-Funding-10-Metric-Model-Condensed-Version.pdf.

Grogger, Jeffrey. 2012. "Bounding the Effects of Social Experiments: Accounting for Attrition in Administrative Data." *Evaluation Review* 36 (6): 449–74.

Haider, Steven, and Gary Solon. 2006. "Life-Cycle Variation in the Association between Current and Lifetime Earnings." *American Economic Review* 96 (4): 1308–20.

Hastings, Justine S., Christopher A. Neilson, Anely Ramirez, and Seth D. Zimmerman. 2015. "(Un)informed College and Major Choice: Evidence from Linked Survey and Administrative Data." NBER Working Paper no. 21330, Cambridge, MA.

Heckman, James J., Carolyn Heinrich, and Jeffrey Smith. 2002. "The Performance of Performance Standards." *Journal of Human Resources* 37 (4): 778–811.

Heckman, James J., Lance J. Lochner, and Petra E. Todd. 2006. "Earnings Functions, Rates of Return and Treatment Effects: The Mincer Equation and Beyond." *Handbook of the Economics of Education* 1:307–458.

Hillman, Nicholas. 2016. *Why Performance-Based College Funding Doesn't Work.* New York: Century Foundation.

Hillman, Nicholas W., David A. Tandberg, and Alisa H. Fryar. 2015. "Evaluating the Impacts of 'New' Performance Funding in Higher Education." *Educational Evaluation and Policy Analysis* 37 (4): 501–19.

Hoekstra, Mark. 2009. "The Effect of Attending the Flagship State University on Earnings: A Discontinuity-Based Approach." *Review of Economics and Statistics* 91 (4): 717–24.

Hoxby, Caroline M. 2015. *Computing the Value-Added of American Postsecondary Institutions.* Internal Revenue Service. https://www.irs.gov/pub/irs-soi/15rpcomp valueaddpostsecondary.pdf.

Jacobson, Louis, and Robert LaLonde. 2013. *Using Data to Improve the Performance of Workforce Training.* The Hamilton Project and Results for America.

Kane, Thomas J., and Cecilia Elena Rouse. 1995. "Labor-Market Returns to Two- and Four-Year College." *American Economic Review* 85 (3): 600–614.

Kelchen, R., and L. J. Stedrak. 2016. "Does Performance-Based Funding Affect Colleges' Financial Priorities?" *Journal of Education Finance* 41 (3): 302–21.

Kornfeld, Robert, and Howard S. Bloom. 1999. "Measuring Program Impacts on Earnings and Employment: Do Unemployment Insurance Wage Reports from Employers Agree with Surveys of Individuals?" *Journal of Labor Economics* 17 (1): 168–97.

Layzell, D. T. 1999. "Linking Performance to Funding Outcomes at the State Level for Public Institutions of Higher Education: Past, Present and Future." *Research in Higher Education* 40 (2): 233–46.

Li, A. Y. 2014. "Performance Funding in the States: An Increasingly Ubiquitous Public Policy for Higher Education." *Higher Education in Review* 11:1–29.

Malamud, O., and A. Wozniak. 2012. "The Impact of College on Migration: Evidence from the Vietnam Generation." *Journal of Human Resources* 47 (4): 913–50.

Muriel, Alastair, and Jeffrey Smith. 2011. "On Educational Performance Measures." *Fiscal Studies* 32 (2): 187–206.

National Conference of State Legislatures (NCSL). 2015. *Performance Funding for Higher Education*. Denver: NCSL. http://www.ncsl.org/issues-research/educ/performance-funding.asp.

Nye, J., Isaac Rowlett, Gordon Sonnenschein, Anika Van Eaton, and Sarah Wissel. 2015. *Connecting Community College Funding to Workforce Outcomes: An Assessment of the National Landscape*. Workforce Data Quality Campaign, George Washington University. May 1.

Ohio Association of Community Colleges. 2013. SSI Allocation Recommendations. Columbus: Author.

Scott-Clayton, Judith, and Qiao Wen. 2017. "Estimating Returns to College Attainment: Comparing Survey and State Administrative Data Based Estimates." A CAPSEE Working Paper.

Selingo, Jeffrey, and Martin Van Der Werf. 2016. *Linking Appropriations for the Texas State Technical College System to Student Employment Outcomes*. Indianapolis: Lumina Foundation.

Snyder, Martha. 2011. *Performance Funding in Indiana: An Analysis of Lessons from the Research and Other State Models*. Washington, DC: HCM Strategists.

———. 2015. *Driving Better Outcomes: Typology and Principles to Inform Outcomes-Based Funding Models*. Washington, DC: HCM Strategists.

SRI International. 2012. *States' Methods of Funding Higher Education*. Menlo Park, CA.

Staiger, Douglas O. 2016. "What Healthcare Teaches Us about Measuring Productivity in Higher Education." Presentation given at NBER Productivity in Higher Education Conference, Cambridge, MA, June 1.

Staiger, Douglas O., Lena Chen, John Birkmeyer, Andrew Ryan, Wenying Zhang, and Justin Dimick. 2013. "Composite Quality Measures for Common Inpatient Medical Conditions." *Medical Care* 51 (9): 832–37.

Texas Higher Education Coordinating Board (THECB). 2013. *The Texas State Technical College System Returned Value Funding Model Methodology*. Austin: Texas Higher Education Coordinating Board. July.

Umbricht, Mark R., Frank Fernandez, and Justin C. Ortagus. 2015. "An Examination of the (Un)intended Consequences of Performance Funding in Higher Education." *Educational Policy*, December, 1–31. doi: 10.1177/0895904815614398.

US Department of Education. 2013. "Education Department Releases College Scorecard to Help Students Choose Best College for Them." http://www.ed.gov/news/press-releases/education-department-releases-college-scorecard-help-students-choose-best-college-them.

Wiswall, Matthew, and Basit Zafar. 2015. "How Do College Students Respond to Public Information about Earnings?" *Journal of Human Capital* 9 (2): 117–69.

Wozniak, A. 2010. "Are College Graduates More Responsive to Distant Labor Market Opportunities?" *Journal of Human Resources* 45 (4): 944–70.

Learning and Earning
An Approximation to College Value Added in Two Dimensions

Evan Riehl, Juan E. Saavedra, and Miguel Urquiola

4.1 Introduction

Colleges produce outputs in various dimensions. Parents and students, for instance, care about colleges' ability to place graduates on good career trajectories. As a result, the United States and other countries now provide information on the labor market *earnings* of graduates from various colleges and majors.[1] A drawback of such measures is that they typically do not adjust for ability; some colleges might perform better, for instance, simply because they attract more able students.

The earnings dimension, however, is not the only one that parents, students, and especially policy makers care about. A second dimension of interest is *learning*—namely, the ability of colleges to enhance human capital and skills. System-wide measures of learning are uncommon, in part because most countries lack nationwide college graduation exams. Questions remain, therefore, about the extent to which these two dimensions of

Evan Riehl is assistant professor of economics at Cornell University.

Juan E. Saavedra is a research economist at the Dornsife Center for Economic and Social Research at the University of Southern California and a faculty research fellow of the National Bureau of Economic Research.

Miguel Urquiola is professor of economics and international affairs at Columbia University and a research associate of the National Bureau of Economic Research.

For useful comments, we thank Joseph Altonji, Caroline Hoxby, Kevin Stange, and participants of the NBER Conference on Productivity in Higher Education. All remaining errors are our own. For acknowledgments, sources of research support, and disclosure of the authors' material financial relationships, if any, please see http://www.nber.org/chapters/c13877.ack.

1. Other countries, such as Chile and Colombia, have similar initiatives. These are relevant in view of evidence that, at least in some cases, college identity can have a causal impact on graduates' earnings (e.g., Hoekstra 2009; Saavedra 2009; Dale and Krueger 2014; and MacLeod et al. 2015). This finding is not universal; see Stange (2012) for contrasting findings among community colleges.

college productivity relate to each other—whether colleges that improve student earning also improve their learning.

This is the first study to simultaneously analyze system-wide measures of the earning and learning productivity of colleges. We use data from the country of Colombia to arguably improve on the measures in the literature to date. Our detailed administrative records provide the earnings of nearly all graduates in the country upon labor market entry. With these data, we can control for a measure of ability—performance on a national standardized admission exam—and for characteristics related to students' socioeconomic backgrounds. Further, the Colombian setting allows us to propose and implement measures of college productivity in the learning dimension, as all graduates are required to take a national college exit exam. In measuring learning performance, we can similarly control for individual characteristics and precollege ability. In particular, some components of the college exit exam are also assessed in the entrance exam, enabling us to implement an approach akin to those commonly used in the teacher value-added literature.[2] In short, our earning and learning measures may not fully isolate college value added, but they have advantages relative to measures previously used in the context of measuring college productivity.

We then show how these measures of college productivity relate to each other and to characteristics of colleges' entering classes. This yields three findings. First, we find that measures of college productivity on earning and learning are far from perfectly correlated. This implies that college rankings based on earnings differ from those based on learning; in other words, the colleges that seem to add most to students' postgraduation earnings are not necessarily the ones that add most to their measured learning.[3] For instance, we find that on average the top private schools seem to do relatively better on earning, whereas the top public institutions perform better on learning.

Second, the measures of earnings productivity are significantly more correlated with students' socioeconomic status (SES) than the learning measures; not surprisingly, earnings are also more correlated with colleges' tuition levels. This leaves open the possibility that learning measures do a better job of isolating a college's contribution to students' human capital even when one focuses on early career earnings, as we do. For example, learning may be more easily influenced by factors that colleges can control

---

2. See, for instance, Chetty, Friedman, and Rockoff (2014). Our empirical approach is also closely related to the one in Saavedra and Saavedra (2011), discussed below.

3. With learning measures, a concern often arises regarding whether these capture anything that the market and therefore students actually value. In the Colombian setting, student performance on the field-specific component of the exit exam is predictive of student wages, even after controlling for students' performance on the admission exam, college reputation, and socioeconomic status.

directly, such as teaching, as opposed to factors such as parental connections and signaling. Consistent with this, we show that a college's measured performance can vary substantially depending on whether earnings are measured right after graduation or later in workers' careers. This illustrates that colleges have only partial control over the earnings paths of their graduates.

Our third finding is that a college's ranking under the earning and learning measures can differ depending on its mix of majors. We show that the earning measures tend to favor majors related to engineering, business, and law; more specialized majors, such as those in fine arts, education, and social/natural sciences, are relatively higher ranked under learning metrics. Thus if measures such as the ones we calculate became salient, they could lead colleges to make strategic choices on which majors they offer.

Taken together, our findings imply that the design of accountability systems may influence colleges' relative performance—and therefore applicants' school choices—as well as colleges' responses. Policy makers may wish to keep these implications in mind as they begin to release more college performance information to the public.

Our study relates to two strands of work on college productivity: those related to earning and learning. In terms of learning, a variety of standardized tests exist in the United States that could in principle be used to measure student-learning outcomes. These tests include the Measure of Academic Proficiency and Progress (MAPP), the Collegiate Assessment of Academic Proficiency (CAAP), the Collegiate Learning Assessment (CLA), the California Critical Thinking Skills Test (CCTST), the Watson-Glaser Critical Thinking Appraisal, and the Cornell Critical Thinking Tests (Pascarella and Terenzini 2005; Sullivan et al. 2012). However, these tests are not systematically used across the country.

Few studies investigate the extent to which variation in learning value added relates to institutional characteristics. In general, these studies find little systematic relationship between learning growth and institutional characteristics. Arum and Roksa (2011) use longitudinal CLA data from students at 23 US colleges and find no systematic relationship between critical thinking value added and institutional characteristics. The Council for Aid to Education (2013) uses cross-sectional CLA data from students at 158 US colleges to document how colleges exhibit similar growth of critical thinking skills regardless of ownership status, institution size, Carnegie Classifications, or selectivity. Hagedorn et al. (1999) use longitudinal data from students in 23 US colleges taking the CAAP test and find that peer composition modestly influences critical thinking in the first year of college but that its effect fades over an individual's college career. Saavedra and Saavedra (2011) use cross-sectional data from an administration of Australia's Graduate Skills Assessment (GSA) to estimate educational value added in a nationally representative sample of freshmen and seniors at 17 Colombian colleges.[4] After controlling for incoming student characteristics, Saavedra and Saavedra (2011) find that private ownership is related to value added but that measures of college quality—such as resources, selectivity, and reputation—are not.

Our work also relates to a long and growing literature measuring productivity in higher education (e.g., Cooke 1910; Sullivan et al. 2012). For instance, recent system-wide studies from Norway, the United States, and Chile that credibly address selection bias using administrative data find mixed evidence on the labor market payoffs to attending more-selective colleges (Hoxby and Bulman 2015; Hastings, Neilson, and Zimmerman 2013; Kirkeboen, Leuven, and Mogstad 2016). In chapter 2 of this volume, Hoxby uses administrative data to estimate the productivity of all postsecondary institutions in the United States. However, unlike prior studies that credibly address issues of selection bias, Hoxby is able to estimate both per-pupil lifetime earnings outcomes and per-pupil costs for each institution. She finds that more-selective colleges produce higher lifetime earnings but do so at a proportionally higher cost. As a result, among the 1,000 most-selective US colleges, there is little relationship between earnings value added per unit of input and institutional selectivity.

The remainder of the chapter is structured as follows. Section 4.2 presents background on the Colombian higher education sector, and section 4.3 describes our data and sample. Section 4.4 discusses the computation of our productivity measures, and section 4.5 presents results. Section 4.6 concludes with broader implications.

4.2   Background

This section provides background on Colombia's higher education system.

4.2.1   Access to College

In the past decades, Latin American countries have seen a marked expansion in access to secondary and tertiary education. Access to the latter has actually risen faster, although from a lower base. As figure 4.1 shows, the gap between secondary and tertiary enrollment in the region narrowed from 60 percentage points in 1996 to 50 percentage points by 2013. By 2013, about 43 percent of the population had enrolled in some type of tertiary education. The evolution in Colombia has generally mirrored that in the rest of the region, although the gap between both types of enrollment has remained stable at about 45 percentage points.[5]

4. The GSA, which is most similar to the CLA in the United States, measures four general skill domains: critical thinking, problem solving, writing, and interpersonal skills.
5. The salient difference between Colombia and the rest of the region is that secondary rose faster initially and then stagnated. Tertiary enrollment trends are essentially identical in Colombia and the region as a whole.

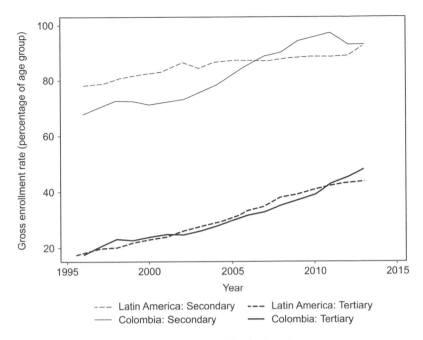

Fig. 4.1   Enrollment trends in Colombia and Latin America

Notes: The data come from the World Bank indicators (http://databank.worldbank.org, consulted on April 7, 2016). The figure plots gross secondary and tertiary enrollment rates for Colombia and the corresponding aggregate for Latin America as a whole. Gross secondary enrollment rate is the number of individuals enrolled in secondary school as a fraction of the total number of individuals 12 to 17 years of age. Gross tertiary enrollment rate is the number of individuals enrolled in tertiary education as a fraction of the total number of individuals 18 to 24 years of age.

Throughout the region, there are constraints for further tertiary expansion. In the case of Colombia, these partially reflect market structure. Private and public providers coexist, and while public colleges are significantly subsidized, their capacity is strained. Table 4.1 shows that public colleges account for 23 percent of institutions but 52 percent of total tertiary enrollments.[6]

There is little regulation on the entry of tuition-charging, unsubsidized private providers, and these generally offer few financial aid opportunities.[7] As a result, private colleges represent 77 percent of all institutions but only 48 percent of total enrollment.

6. Throughout this chapter, we use the term *colleges* to refer to both universities and technical institutions, as depicted in table 4.1.

7. Technically there are no for-profit colleges in Colombia. It is widely perceived, however, that many nonselective private colleges are de facto for-profit, as their owners are the residual claimants of excess revenue typically distributed through wages, rental charges, investments, and so on. In this sense, the situation resembles that which has existed during certain periods in other countries with large private college sectors, such as Chile.

Table 4.1   Colombian higher education market structure

	Institutions			Enrollment		
	Public	Private	Total	Public	Private	Total
Universities	47	142	189	495,855	799,673	1,295,528
	0.17	0.53	0.70	0.25	0.40	0.65
Technical schools	15	65	80	524,007	163,886	687,893
	0.06	0.24	0.30	0.27	0.08	0.35
Total	62	207	269	659,142	601,744	1,983,42
	0.23	0.77	1.00	0.52	0.48	1.00

Notes: Calculations based on the Colombian national higher education information system (SNIES) for 2013, the last year with data available. Enrollment data only include undergraduate students. The category "universities" combines universities and university institutes. "Technical schools" combines technical institutes, technological institutes, and the National Job Training Agency (SENA).

Colleges and universities are also geographically concentrated: 50 percent are in Colombia's three largest cities, which account for 26 percent of the population. Bogotá, the capital, is home to 31 percent of all colleges. About 75 percent of tertiary students attend a college in the city of their birth (Saavedra and Saavedra 2011). Furthermore, in our data, roughly 70 percent of graduates get their first formal sector job in the same municipality where they attended college. This suggests an important role for local labor markets in our analysis—part of the benefit of attending a college in an urban area, for example, is that it may increase access to high-wage jobs.[8]

4.2.2   College Entrance Exam

To apply to college, Colombian students must take a standardized entrance exam called the Icfes, which is administered by a government agency.[9] The Icfes is generally analogous to the SAT in the United States, but it is taken by the vast majority of high school seniors regardless of whether they intend to apply to college.[10] The Icfes also plays a larger role in admissions

8. We also find a positive relationship between college selectivity and the probability that an individual stays in the area upon graduation; a one-standard-deviation increase in a college's mean entrance exam score raises the likelihood that a graduate works in the municipality where she attended college by six percentage points.

9. Icfes stands for Institute for the Promotion of Higher Education, the former acronym for the agency that administers the exam. The Colombian Institute for Educational Evaluation, as it is now called, was created in 1968 and is a state agency under the authority of the national Ministry of Education. The Icfes exam is now known as Saber 11, reflecting the fact that students usually take it in the 11th grade. We use the name Icfes to match the designation during the period covered by our data.

10. Angrist, Bettinger, and Kremer (2006) and our personal communications with the Colombian Institute for Educational Evaluation suggest that more than 90 percent of high school seniors take the exam. The test-taking rate is high in part because the government uses Icfes exam results to evaluate high schools.

in Colombia than the SAT does in the United States. In addition to using it as an application requirement, many schools extend admission offers based solely on students' entrance exam performance. Others consider additional factors such as high school grades while heavily weighting the Icfes, and a handful administer their own exams. Applications and admissions are major specific; students apply to a college/major pair.

The Icfes tests multiple subject areas, including biology, chemistry, English, math, reading/language arts, social science, philosophy, and physics.

4.2.3   College Exit Exam

In 2004, the agency that administers the Icfes introduced, with considerable publicity, new field-specific college *graduation* exams. These exit exams are standardized and administered at every institution that offers a related program.[11] The exams are intended to assess senior students' competencies in fields ranging from relatively academic in orientation (e.g., economics and physics) to relatively professional (e.g., nursing and occupational therapy).

The creation of the exit exams was a major undertaking, as it required coordination among departments in multiple colleges. The stated intent of this effort was to improve quality, transparency, and accountability in the higher education sector. Consistent with this, school-level aggregate scores were made available and have been used by news outlets as part of college rankings.

Field-specific exams became available for most majors in 2004, with several majors receiving field exams in subsequent years. A few fields, such as political science, anthropology, history, and philosophy, never received a corresponding field-specific exam. In part because of this, for the first few years, taking the exit exam was optional, although the majority of students in tested fields took the exam. This changed in 2009, when the exit exam became a graduation requirement for all students. A generic test was introduced for majors that did not previously have a field-specific exam. In addition, from 2009 onward, the exam included several common components in subjects such as English and reading comprehension, which were taken by all students regardless of their field.

Increasingly, colleges and students use results on the college exit exam as a signal of ability. For example, students may report whether they obtained a top score nationally or their score in comparison to the university or the national average. Some universities use exit exam results in admissions to graduate programs, and the Colombian Student Loan Institute offers a postgraduate study credit line (of up to $16,000) exclusively to the best 10 nationwide scorers. In addition, every year the Colombian president and education minister publicly recognize the individuals with the top 10 scores

---

11. These tests were initially labeled Ecaes, which stands for *Exámenes de Calidad de Educación Superior*—that is, higher education quality exams. They are now called *Saber Pro*.

in each field. Anecdotally, the best scorers receive job offers based on public knowledge of their test scores, and MacLeod et al. (2015) provide evidence that the exit exams affect graduates' labor market earnings.

4.3   Data and Sample

This section describes our sources of data and the sample we use for our analysis.

4.3.1   Data

We use individual-level administrative data sets from three sources:

1. The Colombian Institute for Educational Evaluation, which administers the college entrance and exit exams, provided records for both tests. This includes scores for all high school seniors who took the entrance exam between 1998 and 2012 as well as college exit exam scores for all exam takers from 2004 to 2011.

2. The Ministry of Education provided enrollment and graduation records for students entering college between 1998 and 2012. These include each individual's college, program of study, and enrollment and graduation dates. These data cover roughly 90 percent of all college enrollees; the ministry omits a number of smaller colleges due to poor and inconsistent reporting.

3. The Ministry of Social Protection provided monthly earnings records for formal sector workers during 2008–12. These come from data on contributions to pension and health insurance funds.

We link these data sources using student names, birthdates, and national ID numbers. The resulting data set includes students from nearly all colleges in Colombia with information on their entrance exam scores and, if applicable, their exit exam performance and formal labor market earnings.

4.3.2   Sample

We select a sample that allows us to cleanly compare measures of college performance on earning and learning. Specifically, we restrict our sample to graduates who satisfy two important criteria. First, we include only students who took the college exit exam in 2009–11. As noted above, the exit exam was voluntary prior to 2009, so we exclude pre-2009 exam takers to limit selection into taking the exam. Second, we include only graduates for whom we observe initial labor market earnings. Since students typically take the exit exam one year before graduating, this means that we include only 2010–12 graduates with earnings observed in their graduation year.

This restriction sets aside other outcomes of interest to students and policy makers, such as graduation rates. In Colombia, as in the United States, the probability of graduating tends to increase with the selectivity of the

Table 4.2   **Sample and college types**

College type	No. of colleges	No. of grads	Admit rate	Annual tuition ($)	Mother went to college	Entrance exam percentile
Public (most selective)	12	15,642	0.20	369	0.42	0.82
Public (medium selective)	24	13,228	0.55	509	0.29	0.67
Public (least selective)	12	6,063	0.87	535	0.23	0.59
Top private	8	9,653	0.64	2,584	0.90	0.90
Other private (high cost)	51	19,229	0.82	1,696	0.59	0.72
Other private (low cost)	50	17,489	0.86	1,079	0.31	0.63
Total	157	81,304	0.65	1,134	0.46	0.72

Notes: Admission rate data are from Colombian national higher education information system (SNIES) and average over 2007–12. Tuition data are from the exit exam records, which report each exam taker's tuition in the previous year in six categories. We compute the average across all students using the midpoint of each category and convert to US dollars using 2012 exchange rates. Entrance exam percentiles are relative to all exam takers in each year, including those who did not attend college.

college a student attends. To the extent that graduation rates are highly correlated with college-level earnings, restricting the sample to graduates is unlikely to significantly change our findings.[12]

In addition to these restrictions, we drop individuals with missing values on any of the other variables we use, including entrance exam scores, high school of origin, mother's education, and previous year's tuition.[13] This ensures that all performance measures calculated below are based on the same set of individuals. Lastly, to obtain reasonable precision for each of our performance measures, we restrict our analysis to colleges that have at least 50 graduates satisfying the above criteria.

The resulting sample includes approximately 81,000 graduates from 157 colleges. This is much larger than samples available in previous studies that use longitudinal data to compute college performance measures (e.g., Klein, Steedle, and Kugelmas 2010). The last row in table 4.2 presents summary statistics on our sample.

4.3.3   College Categorization

Table 4.2 additionally categorizes colleges into six types with the aim of providing a useful portrayal of the college market in Colombia. The top

12. For example, we find that the correlation between mean college earnings in samples with and without college dropouts is 0.9.

13. The entrance exam underwent a major overhaul in 2000, so we also exclude the small number of students who graduated in 2010–12 but took the entrance exam prior to 2000. Since one of our learning outcomes below is a student's English exit exam score, we additionally drop the fewer than 1 percent of students who took the French or German entrance exams, which were offered until 2006, rather than the English exam.

three rows separate public colleges into three groups based on quartiles of their admission rates. We define the most-selective public colleges as those in the quartile with the lowest admission rates and the least-selective colleges as those in the highest admission rate quartile. Medium-selective colleges are those in the middle two quartiles.[14] Table 4.2 shows that the most-selective public colleges admit 20 percent of their applicants on average, while the least-selective are essentially open enrollment.[15]

Selectivity defined by admission rates has limited usefulness in categorizing private colleges in Colombia, as most private colleges admit nearly all of their applicants. Instead, sorting into private colleges is defined more strongly by the tuition rates they charge. We therefore define "top private" colleges as those few that are actually selective—that is, they reject some of their applicants—and in which average annual graduate tuition exceeds the equivalent of about $2,500.[16] This definition picks out eight colleges that represent the most elite private schools in the country. We divide the remaining private institutions—which we label "other private"—into two types based on the average tuition payments reported by their graduates. We define high-cost private colleges as those above the median tuition and low-cost colleges as those below.[17]

Average annual tuition varies significantly across private college types, with a mean of roughly $1,000 at low-cost private colleges. Average tuition is significantly lower at all public college types, as they offer substantial discounts to low-SES students.

The last two columns of table 4.2 summarize the socioeconomic and academic backgrounds of graduates from each college type. Graduates from private colleges are much more likely to have mothers with a college education; for instance, 90 percent of students at top private colleges do so. Academic preparation, as defined by each student's entrance exam percentile in the full distribution of test takers, also varies starkly across college types. Average entrance exam performance is at the 82nd percentile at the most-selective public colleges and the 90th percentile at top private schools. Graduates from the lowest college types, both public and private, have average entrance exam scores near the 60th percentile.

14. We use quartiles rather than terciles to define these three groups to provide more detail on colleges at the extremes of the distribution.
15. Note that nonselective colleges often have admission rates that are slightly less than one in table 4.2. This reflects that students may fail to follow all application procedures or may withdraw their applications before admission.
16. Specifically, we use a four million peso cutoff for top private colleges, and we define their selectivity using a 2002 report from the Colombian Institute for Educational Evaluation entitled *Estadísticas de la Educación Superior*. Selective private colleges are those for which the number of applicants exceeded the number of offered slots, according to this report.
17. We note that we do not use an institution's level of training (university or technical, as in table 4.1) to define these six college categories. We find that this distinction provides little additional information on average college characteristics conditional on the categories defined by financing, selectivity, and tuition.

We use the sample and college categorization in table 4.2 for our analysis of college performance measures below.

4.4   Measures

This section describes the outcome variables we use and the measures we employ to approximate college earning and learning productivity.

4.4.1   Earning and Learning Variables

Our earnings variable is log average daily formal labor market earnings, which we calculate by dividing base monthly earnings for pension contributions by the number of employment days in each month and averaging across the year. We use earnings in the year of each student's graduation (2010–12) and demean earnings in each year.

Our learning variables are based on students' scores on the college exit exam. During the exam years we analyze (2009–11), this test included a field-specific component related to a student's major (e.g., economics or mechanical engineering) as well as several components taken by all students. We focus on three of these: (1) the field-specific score, (2) a reading common component score, and (3) an English common component score.

These components have different strengths and weaknesses in measuring college productivity. The field exit score, because it typically reflects each student's college major, provides arguably the best measure of the material studied in college. However, in general, there is no direct analog on the entrance exam. The English component of the exit and entrance exams are very similar and thus well placed to measure progress, but English proficiency may be less directly related to college productivity. Since the exit and entrance exams include a similar but not identical reading / language arts component, the reading component lies arguably in the middle of the comparability and relevance spectrums.

Using these three exit exam scores, we calculate each student's percentile relative to all other students in our sample in the same exam field and cohort. We use exam score *percentiles* because the entrance and exit exams are not on a common scale and thus cannot measure growth in human capital. As a result, our learning measures will capture a college's relative rather than absolute performance. The same caveat applies to our earning measures, since we do not observe a precollege measure of earnings.

4.4.2   Calculation of Productivity Measures

We use four procedures to measure learning and earning performance. Some of these procedures are simple and require less-detailed information, and thus they correspond to measures that may be more commonly reported in the media or easier for policy makers to compute. Other procedures use comprehensive information on students' backgrounds and align more closely with "value-added" methods employed in other areas of economic research. These four procedures, which we describe in the following subsections, allow us to explore the sensitivity of our results to different data requirements and methodologies.

4.4.2.1 Raw Means

Our first performance measure is the average log earnings, or the average exit exam percentile, at each college:

$$(1) \qquad \bar{\theta}_c = E\{y_{ic} | i \in c\},$$

where y_{ic} is either outcome for individual i who graduated from college c. We label $\bar{\theta}_c$ the *raw means* measure, as it implements the simplest and least data intensive of our four procedures. Note that it does not adjust for differences across colleges in incoming student characteristics—that is, in the student "inputs" to college production.

4.4.2.2 Entrance Exam Residuals

Our second performance measure adjusts for differences in college inputs by controlling for students' entrance exam performance. We do this through an individual-level regression of the following form:

$$(2) \qquad y_{ic} = \beta' t_i + \tilde{\theta}_c + \tilde{\varepsilon}_{ic},$$

where t_i is a vector of student i's entrance exam percentiles on eight components, which include reading/language arts and English.[18] We decompose the residual from this regression into a school-specific term, $\tilde{\theta}_c$, and an idiosyncratic component, $\tilde{\varepsilon}_{ic}$. Our second college productivity measure, which we call *entrance exam residuals*, is the $\tilde{\theta}_c$ coefficient from equation (2).

4.4.2.3 Entrance Exam + SES Residuals

Our third performance measure is closely related to the second, but we include additional controls for students' socioeconomic background in regression (3):

$$(3) \qquad y_{ic} = \beta' t_i + \gamma' x_i + \hat{\theta}_c + \hat{\varepsilon}_{ic},$$

where x_i represents dummies for four categories of mother's education (primary, secondary, vocational, university), which are fully interacted with dummies for each of the approximately 6,000 high schools in our sample. The *entrance exam + SES residuals* measure for each college is the $\hat{\theta}_c$ coefficient from this regression. This coefficient is identified from variation in college attendance across students with the same high school and mother's educa-

---

18. The other components are biology, chemistry, math, social sciences, philosophy, and physics. As with the exit exam scores, we convert entrance exam scores into percentiles within each exit exam field and cohort.

tion combination. This measure is most analogous to benchmark "value-added" models in other work in economics, which control for a broad array of initial individual characteristics.

4.4.2.4 College-Level Residuals

Our fourth performance measure controls for college-level characteristics in addition to individual-level characteristics. This is motivated by research in Altonji and Mansfield (2014), which shows that in the estimation of group-level treatment effects, including group average characteristics can in some cases control for between-group sorting on unobservable individual traits.

We control for both individual and college characteristics using a two-step procedure. First, we estimate equation (3) and calculate residuals y_{ic}^* from the individual characteristics only. That is, we calculate $y_{ic}^* = y_{ic} - \hat{\beta}'t_i - \hat{\gamma}'x_i$, where $\hat{\beta}$ and $\hat{\gamma}$ are the estimated coefficients from regression (3).[19]

Second, we calculate the mean value of y_{ic}^* for each college, $y_c^* = E\{y_{ic}^* | i \in c\}$, and estimate the following college-level regression:

$$(4) \qquad\qquad y_c^* = \beta't_c + \gamma'x_c + \theta_c,$$

where t_c is the vector of college mean percentiles for each of the eight entrance exam components, and x_c is the fraction of students with a college-educated mother at college c.[20] The *college-level residuals* measure is the residual from regression (4), θ_c. As we discuss below, this measure has properties that differ from those of measures based on individual residuals because it is uncorrelated with college mean entrance scores by construction. Altonji and Mansfield (2014) note that under certain conditions, the variance in θ_c also serves as a lower bound to the true variance of college treatment effects, in part because these treatment effects are likely correlated with t_c and x_c.

4.4.3 Correlations of Productivity Measures with Inputs

For our earnings and each of our three learning variables, the above procedures yield four separate productivity measures—in short, 16 measures for each college in our sample. We normalize each of these to have mean zero and standard deviation one across the 157 colleges. This normalization is convenient because it makes the coefficient from a linear regression of one measure on another equal to their pairwise correlation coefficient.

To provide context on these measures, we show how they relate to a college characteristic that is, in principle, easily observable to many agents: colleges' mean entrance exam score. We begin with a graphical exposition using only

---

19. Note that this first-step regression also includes group-level (i.e., college) fixed effects, as is common in the teacher value added literature (Chetty, Friedman, and Rockoff 2014).

20. Observations in regression (4) are weighted by the number of graduates from each college. All college-level computations in this chapter use these same weights.

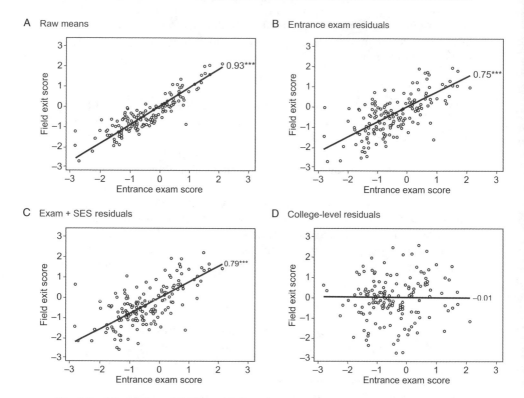

Fig. 4.2   Illustration of field-specific learning measures

Notes: Small circles represent the 157 colleges in our sample. The solid line depicts the linear relationship between the learning measures and college mean entrance scores, with colleges weighted by their number of graduates. Asterisks on the slope coefficients indicate statistical significance with robust standard errors.

$* p < 0.10$, $** p < 0.05$, $*** p < 0.01$.

one learning outcome: the field-specific exam score. The four panels of figure 4.2 depict our four measures for this outcome. The gray circles are the 157 colleges in our sample. The vertical axis in each panel represents the learning performance under each measure, while the horizontal axis depicts the raw mean entrance exam score at each college.[21] The solid line depicts the linear relationship between these two measures, with the slope indicated on the graph.

Panel A shows that the correlation between a college's raw mean field exit score ($\bar{\theta}_c$ from equation [1]) and its mean entrance exam score is 0.93. Panel B shows that controlling for individual entrance exam scores (using $\tilde{\theta}_c$ from equation [2]) reduces this correlation only slightly. Note that while $\tilde{\theta}_c$ ensures

---

21. Raw mean entrance score is the average percentile across the same eight components included in regressions (2)–(4), also normalized to mean zero and standard deviation one.

Table 4.3   **Correlations with college mean entrance scores**

	Raw means (A)	Entrance exam residuals (B)	Exam + SES residuals (C)	College-level residuals (D)
Field exit score	0.93***	0.75***	0.79***	−0.01
Reading exit score	0.90***	0.59***	0.65***	−0.03
English exit score	0.88***	0.73***	0.71***	−0.04
Log earnings	0.70***	0.63***	0.57***	0.06

Notes: This table displays coefficients from linear regressions of college mean entrance exam scores on each of our 16 learning and earning measures. All regressions have 157 observations with weights equal to each college's number of graduates. Asterisks indicate statistical significance with robust standard errors.
* $p < 0.10$, ** $p < 0.05$, *** $p < 0.01$.

that *individual* exit residuals are uncorrelated with *individual* entrance exam scores, it allows *college-level* exit scores to be correlated with *college-level* entrance exam performance. This can arise if other individual characteristics that affect exit exam performance, such as socioeconomic background, also affect the colleges students choose to attend.

Panel C partially addresses this issue by using the entrance exam + SES residual measure ($\hat{\theta}_c$ from equation [3]), which controls for students' observable background. Panel C shows that these controls have little effect on the correlation of the exit field score with college mean entrance exam performance; in fact, the correlation coefficient increases slightly. This illustrates that our individual learning productivity measures may still be correlated with unobservable student characteristics that affect both college choice and exit exam performance.

Panel D illustrates that our last productivity measure, the college-level residual (θ_c from equation [4]), is uncorrelated with college mean entrance exam performance by construction.[22] This addresses the issue that individual characteristics may be correlated with college mean entrance scores (as well as college mean mother's education). However, the college residual measure, θ_c, rules out the possibility that colleges with high mean entrance scores systematically produce better learning outcomes than colleges with low average scores. Rather, this measure is better suited for comparing the performance of colleges with similar inputs as defined by mean entrance scores.

As stated, we have 16 outcome measures in total (log earnings plus three learning measures, each calculated using the procedures in equations [1]–[4]). Table 4.3 displays the correlations of each of these measures with college mean entrance scores. The top row refers to the field exit score and replicates

22. The correlation between the two measures in panel D is not strictly zero because the horizontal axis is the average of the eight entrance exam components, not any individual component from regression (4).

Table 4.4   Correlations with earning measure

	Raw means (A)	Entrance exam residuals (B)	Exam + SES residuals (C)	College-level residuals (D)
Field exit score	0.62***	0.45***	0.45***	0.07
Reading exit score	0.58***	0.29***	0.41***	0.16**
English exit score	0.71***	0.62***	0.51***	–0.09

Notes: This table displays coefficients from linear regressions of our earning measures on each of our learning measures. All regressions have 157 observations with weights equal to each college's number of graduates. Asterisks indicate statistical significance with robust standard errors.

* $p < 0.10$, ** $p < 0.05$, *** $p < 0.01$.

the correlation coefficients depicted in figure 4.2. The remaining three rows cover the other measures. The manner in which the correlation measures change as one moves across columns is similar across all rows; in other words, the above discussion applies to all of our learning and earning measures. This provides an additional justification for using multiple methods to calculate productivity in examining our key findings below.

4.5   Results

This section presents empirical results related to three questions: (1) How are the earning and learning measures related to each other? (2) How are they related to other factors that influence students' choice of colleges? (3) How do these measures vary with the majors a college offers?

4.5.1   Comparing Learning and Earning Measures

Our first empirical task is to explore how the learning and earning measures relate to each other. Table 4.4 shows the correlation coefficients for each of our three learning measures with our earning measure, where each has been calculated according to the procedure listed in the column.

A simple but important result is that the learning measures are mostly positively related to our earning measure, but far from perfectly so, with correlations ranging from –0.09 to 0.71 across the learning outcomes and the four procedures. The raw mean learning and earning measures are more strongly correlated than those that control for individual characteristics. The college-level residual measures are mostly uncorrelated, with only one correlation coefficient that is statistically different from zero. It is also notable that the English learning measures are generally more correlated with earnings, which may reflect a stronger socioeconomic component to English education relative to the other subjects.

Figure 4.3 depicts the relation between the earning measures (vertical axis) and the field-specific learning measures (horizontal axis). The imperfect cor-

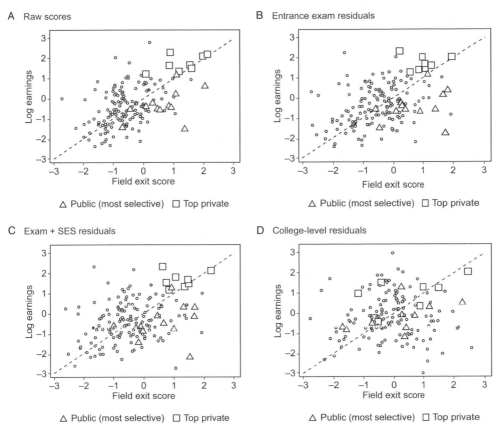

Fig. 4.3   Earning vs. field-specific learning

Notes: Triangles represent the most-selective public colleges as defined in table 4.2. Squares represent top private colleges, and small circles depict all other colleges.

relations from table 4.4 are evident here in the dispersion of the dots, which is most prevalent for the college-level residual method in panel D. Each panel also contains a 45-degree line that represents the boundary between whether colleges appear more productive on the learning or earning measures. In all four panels, the most-selective public colleges (indicated by the triangles) typically lie below the diagonal line—these colleges appear in a more favorable light when we define productivity by learning. Conversely, top private colleges (squares) mostly lie above the 45-degree line; this means that they appear in a more favorable light when performance is defined in terms of earnings. Note that these conclusions hold across all four procedures for calculating productivity despite the different properties discussed above. We also find that they hold when we measure earnings eight years after graduation rather than in the year of graduation. We note, however, that

Table 4.5   Average institution rank by college type

College type	Field exit score	Log earnings	Field exit score	Log earnings
	Panel A: Entrance exam residuals		*Panel B: College-level residuals*	
Public (most selective)	0.88	0.58	0.63	0.56
Public (medium selective)	0.54	0.44	0.47	0.57
Public (least selective)	0.26	0.20	0.45	0.48
Top private	0.89	0.95	0.44	0.68
Other private (high cost)	0.63	0.70	0.59	0.51
Other private (low cost)	0.36	0.49	0.42	0.58

Notes: This table displays percentile ranks of colleges using the measures listed in the column header. We sort all colleges according to each measure and then calculate average ranks within the college types depicted in table 4.2. Averages are weighted by each college's number of graduates.

this comparison requires that we calculate earning and learning measures using different samples, as we discuss in further detail below.

Table 4.5 elaborates on this point by presenting the average institution rank that arises from the use of learning or earning measures. Specifically, we sort colleges according to each measure and calculate their percentile rank among the 157 schools. We then compute the average rank in each of the six college types defined in table 4.2. We repeat this calculation for the field-specific learning measures and the earning measures from the entrance exam residual method (panel A) and the college-level residual procedure (panel B). For instance, using the field exit score and individual entrance exam residuals, the most-selective public colleges have an average rank at the 88th percentile, while the average rank of a top private college is in the 89th percentile.

The main conclusion from table 4.5 is that public colleges receive higher rankings from the learning measures than from the earning measures. Conversely, private colleges are relatively higher ranked using earnings. This finding holds for all college categories using the individual-level measures. It also holds for most categories under the college-level measures, though the result is flipped for middle-ranked public and private institutions.

The different measures can thus lead to starkly different conclusions about colleges' relative productivity. In panel A, for example, high-cost private colleges are ranked higher on average than the most-selective public colleges using earnings, but their average rank is 25 percentile points lower using the learning measure. As discussed above, comparisons of colleges with different mean entrance scores are more complicated under the college-level residual method of panel B. Nonetheless, a similar conclusion applies to the relative rankings of the most-selective public colleges and top private colleges, which have similar mean entrance scores (see table 4.2). Top private colleges receive higher ranks under the earning measure, while selective public colleges appear more favorably when one uses the learning measure.

The ranking differences between public and private institutions are consistent with the hypothesis that these colleges add value in different dimensions. For example, students at private colleges may benefit more from peer and alumni networks in the labor market. Conversely, public colleges typically offer a more diverse set of majors, which could allow for better sorting of students into their fields of comparative advantage. An alternative hypothesis is that these colleges vary in the types of students they attract and that these differences are correlated with students' earning and learning potential. We consider this possibility in the next section.

4.5.2 Correlations with Other College Characteristics

The fact that the learning and earning measures are not perfectly correlated suggests that they likely have different relationships with other student and college characteristics. In this section, we explore how learning and earning productivity are related to two other factors that influence students' college choice. We first consider socioeconomic status as defined by whether a student's mother attended college. We then consider a proxy for student demand: each graduate's annual tuition in the prior year.

For both the SES and tuition variables, we follow the same procedures described in section 4.4.2 to compute college averages. This yields measures of college mean SES and college mean tuition corresponding to the raw means, entrance exam residuals, entrance exam + SES residuals, and college-level residuals methods. Note that we do not present the SES measures from equation (3), as this method includes SES controls also defined by mother's education. Similarly, we exclude the SES variables (x_i and x_c) from equation (4) when we calculate the college-level residual measures for figure 4.4 and table 4.6 below; this allows us to compare their correlations with mother's education. As above, we normalize each measure to mean zero and standard deviation one across the sample of 157 colleges.

Figure 4.4 displays the correlations of SES with the field-specific learning measures and the earning measures. In all cases, the earning measures are more strongly correlated with SES than the learning measures, though the difference between the two is not statistically different from zero using raw means.[23]

Table 4.6 presents these correlations for all our learning and earning measures. The top panel displays the correlation of the measures with college mean SES, while the bottom panel displays the difference between each learning measure and the earning measure. In nearly all cases, the learning measures are less correlated with SES than the earning measures, and this difference is statistically significant using the two residual methods (columns B and C). The only exceptions arise with two of the English learning

---

23. The same patterns arise when we measure earnings eight years after graduation rather than in the year of graduation.

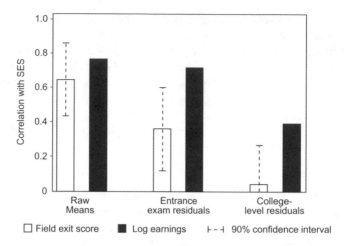

Fig. 4.4   Correlations with SES

Notes: White bars depict the correlations of our SES measures with our field-specific learning measures (the first row in table 4.6). Black bars show the correlation of our SES measures with our earning measures (the fourth row in table 4.6). Dashed lines are 90 percent confidence intervals using robust standard errors. We exclude the x_i and x_c variables in calculating the college-level residual measures for this figure (see equation [4]).

Table 4.6   Correlations with SES

		Raw means (A)	Entrance exam residuals (B)	College-level residuals (C)
Correlations	Field exit score	0.65***	0.36***	0.04
	Reading exit score	0.59***	0.16	0.08
	English exit score	0.83***	0.75***	0.20***
	Log earnings	0.77***	0.72***	0.39***
Differences from earnings	Field exit score	−0.12	−0.36**	−0.35**
	Reading exit score	0.18	0.56***	0.31**
	English exit score	0.07	0.03	−0.19*

Notes: The top panel displays coefficients from linear regressions of SES (defined by mother's education) measures on each of our learning and earning measures. All regressions have 157 observations with weights equal to each college's number of graduates. The bottom panel shows the difference between each of the learning coefficients and the earnings coefficient. We exclude the x_i and x_c variables in calculating the college-level residual measures for this table (see equation [4]). Asterisks indicate statistical significance with robust standard errors.
* $p < 0.10$, ** $p < 0.05$, *** $p < 0.01$.

measures, which, as noted above, may be more influenced by socioeconomic background than the field and reading scores.

Table 4.7 is analogous to table 4.6, but it presents the correlations of learning and earning measures with tuition rather than with SES. The same pattern holds; the learning measures are in all cases substantially less correlated with graduates' average tuition than the earning measures.

Table 4.7   Correlations with tuition

		Raw means (A)	Entrance exam residuals (B)	Exam + SES residuals (C)	College-level residuals (D)
Correlations	Field exit score	0.32*	0.16	0.24	0.02
	Reading exit score	0.24	−0.05	0.10	0.02
	English exit score	0.59***	0.63***	0.54***	−0.03
	Log earnings	0.67***	0.67***	0.60***	0.27***
Differences from earnings	Field exit score	−0.36*	−0.52***	−0.36*	−0.26*
	Reading exit score	−0.44**	−0.72***	−0.50***	−0.25**
	English exit score	−0.08	−0.04	−0.06	−0.31**

Notes: The top panel displays coefficients from linear regressions of tuition (defined as in table 4.2) measures on each of our learning and earning measures. All regressions have 157 observations with weights equal to each college's number of graduates. The bottom panel shows the difference between each of the learning coefficients and the earnings coefficient. Asterisks indicate statistical significance with robust standard errors.
* $p < 0.10$, ** $p < 0.05$, *** $p < 0.01$.

The results in tables 4.6 and 4.7 are consistent with a college's earning performance being a stronger driver of its demand than its learning performance. Though none of our measures may fully isolate college value added, these findings suggest that learning measures may be less related to other factors that affect student outcomes, which may not be observable in all contexts. This is particularly relevant if learning outcomes are ultimately under greater control on the part of colleges than earning results. In particular, earning measures, unlike those based on learning, have a natural dynamic component in the years after students enter the labor market. Throughout our analysis, we have used earnings measured in the year of each student's graduation, but there are both conceptual and data-related reasons why earnings might be measured later in a worker's career.

To explore the potential implications of the timing of earning measurement, we use a different sample than in the above analysis that allows us to measure earnings later in workers' careers. Specifically, we include 2003–12 graduates with earnings observed in 2008–12. With this sample, we can observe earnings between zero and eight years of potential experience, defined as earnings year minus graduation year.[24] Note that this analysis relies on cross-cohort earning comparisons, meaning that the sample differs across experience levels.

The earning measures analyzed above normalize measures to have a constant standard deviation. Before computing such measures, we display the raw data in figure 4.5. This figure shows average log earnings at the 128 col-

24. We can actually observe a ninth year of potential experience using 2012 earnings for 2003 graduates, but these ninth-year measures are noisy because they come from only a single cohort and year.

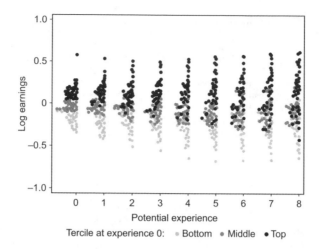

Fig. 4.5   Log earnings by potential experience

Notes: The sample includes 2003–12 graduates with earnings measured at 0–8 years of potential experience, defined as earnings year minus graduation year. Dots depict average log earnings at the 128 colleges in our sample with at least 10 earning observations for each experience level. Log earnings are demeaned by graduation year and experience. We group colleges into three terciles based on experience zero earnings and add horizontal spacing to improve visibility.

leges that we observe at all experience levels, where we demean earnings by graduation cohort and year. We group the 128 colleges into three terciles of different shadings based on their average earnings at experience zero and hold these terciles constant for all experience levels.

Figure 4.5 shows that the variance in average earnings across colleges increases with worker experience, a result first documented by MacLeod et al. (2015). At experience zero, nearly all colleges have average earnings within 30 percent of the mean, while many colleges lie outside this range after eight years. Further, there is substantial mixing of the terciles over time such that some colleges with low initial earnings ultimately have mean earnings above those of top tercile colleges. These two findings show that both the magnitude and the ordering of differences in earnings across colleges can change substantially depending on when one measures earnings.

Table 4.8 formalizes this point by showing how the correlation of earnings with initial measures of college productivity evolves with worker experience. For this table, we calculate earnings measures analogous to those above using the same students and colleges as in figure 4.5. Panel A displays the raw mean measures (from equation [1]), and panel B depicts residuals from a regression on college mean entrance exam scores (equation [4]).[25]

25. We do not present individual entrance exam residual measures in table 4.8 because we do not observe the full vector of individual exam scores for all 2003–12 graduates. For this reason, we also do not use a first-step regression to net out individual characteristics in calculating the college-level measures (see section 4.4.2.4).

Table 4.8   **Correlations by potential experience**

		Panel A: Raw means		Panel B: College-level residuals	
		Log earnings at exp. 0	Field exit score	Log earnings at exp. 0	Field exit score
Correlations	Log earnings at exp. 0	1.00***	0.44***	1.00***	0.04
	Log earnings at exp. 2	0.93***	0.63***	0.92***	0.16*
	Log earnings at exp. 4	0.88***	0.68***	0.85***	0.17*
	Log earnings at exp. 6	0.83***	0.70***	0.78***	0.15*
	Log earnings at exp. 8	0.76***	0.69***	0.67***	0.10
Differences from earnings at exp. 0	Log earnings at exp. 2	−0.07*	0.20	−0.08**	0.11
	Log earnings at exp. 4	−0.12***	0.25*	−0.15**	0.12
	Log earnings at exp. 6	−0.17***	0.26**	−0.22***	0.11
	Log earnings at exp. 8	−0.24***	0.26**	−0.33***	0.06

Notes: The top panel displays coefficients from linear regressions of earning measures at different experience levels on experience zero earning measures and the field-specific learning measures. The sample is the same as that for figure 4.5. All regressions have 128 observations with weights equal to each college's number of graduates. The bottom panel shows the difference between each of the experience 2–8 coefficients and the experience zero earnings coefficient. Asterisks indicate statistical significance with robust standard errors.
* $p < 0.10$, ** $p < 0.05$, *** $p < 0.01$.

The top panel of table 4.8 shows the correlation of earnings measured at different experience levels with earnings at experience zero and with our field-specific earnings measure from above. The bottom panel shows how the correlations at each experience level change relative to those at experience zero. The results show that the correlation of earning measures with initial earnings declines substantially over time and that this holds for both the raw and residual methods. By contrast, the earning measures become *more* correlated with the field-specific exit scores over time, though the differences are not significant for the residual measures.

The main takeaway from figure 4.5 and table 4.8 is that one can arrive at very different conclusions for a college's earning productivity depending on when one measures earnings. This highlights the fact that colleges do not have complete control over their graduates' earnings, which also depend on the postschooling actions of workers and employers. This leaves open the possibility that learning measures do a better job of isolating a college's contribution to students' human capital.

4.5.3   Learning and Earning across Majors

Our final set of results concern one way in which colleges might be able to influence these productivity measures: their choice of which majors to offer. To explore how our measures vary across majors, we repeat the four procedures described in section 4.4.2, but instead of calculating productiv-

Table 4.9   Average institution/major rank by major area

| | | Panel A: Entrance exam residuals | | Panel B: College/major-level residuals | |
Major area	Proportion of grads	Field exit score	Log earnings	Field exit score	Log earnings
Business/economics	0.35	0.50	0.53	0.53	0.59
Engineering	0.29	0.51	0.60	0.45	0.59
Law	0.14	0.48	0.81	0.43	0.75
Social sciences	0.14	0.55	0.41	0.51	0.33
Health	0.07	0.52	0.66	0.54	0.68
Education	0.06	0.55	0.27	0.57	0.36
Fine arts	0.05	0.50	0.46	0.41	0.27
Agronomy	0.02	0.52	0.35	0.47	0.37
Natural sciences	0.02	0.75	0.62	0.55	0.50

Notes: This table includes all college/major pairs with at least 20 graduates in our sample, where majors are defined by the program name at each college. The Ministry of Education records aggregate these majors into the nine listed "areas." The first column shows the proportion of graduates from each major area, and the remaining columns display percentile ranks of college/major pairs using the learning and earning measures in the column header. For these, we sort college/majors according to each measure and then calculate average ranks within the major areas. Averages are weighted by each college/major's number of graduates.

ity at the institution level, we do so at the institution/major level. In other words, we calculate separate learning and earning productivity measures for each major offered by each college.[26] We then sort the roughly 1,100 college/major pairs according to each measure and calculate each college/major's percentile rank. This is analogous to the procedure used to calculate institution ranks in table 4.5.

Table 4.9 summarizes the resulting ranks using nine broader major "areas" defined by the Ministry of Education.[27] The first column displays the proportion of all graduates in our sample in each major area. More than half of all graduates are in majors related to business and engineering, which are offered by almost all colleges in the country. Majors related to fine arts and natural sciences are less popular and are offered by only a small number of colleges.

The other columns in table 4.9 show the average ranks from the 1,100 college/major pairs using different learning and earning measures. Panel A presents ranks based on the entrance exam residuals method, and panel B displays ranks based on the college/major-level residual method. Using either method, the results show that some majors—such as those in engi-

26. We include only institution/major pairs that have at least 20 graduates in our sample.
27. The ministry's categorization actually combines social sciences and law, but we split these major groups because they have vastly different properties with respect to our productivity measures.

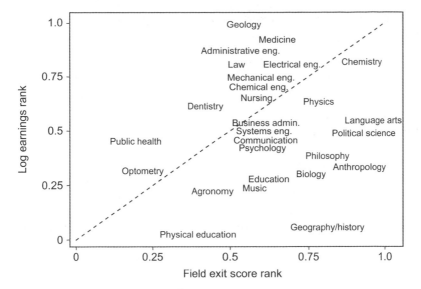

Fig. 4.6   Earning vs. field-specific learning ranks by major group

Notes: This figure plots percentile ranks for college/major pairs using the entrance exam, re-sidual earning, and field-specific learning measures. We calculate these ranks as in panel A of table 4.9, but we display average ranks within a more granular categorization of majors into 51 groups defined by the Ministry of Education. Averages are weighted by each college's/major's number of graduates.

neering, business, and law—receive much higher ranks under the earning measures than under the learning measures. Conversely, majors related to education, fine arts, and social or natural sciences are much lower ranked using the earning measures.

Figure 4.6 elaborates on this result using a slightly more granular grouping of majors. The horizontal axis displays the average rank in each major group using the field-specific learning measure from panel A of table 4.9. The vertical axis depicts the average rank using the earning measure from the same procedure. Major groups that lie below the 45-degree line are ranked more highly on learning than on earning; these include many majors in social and natural sciences. Major groups above the 45-degree line, including many related to engineering and health, appear more favorable when rankings are based on earnings.

The results in table 4.9 and figure 4.6 suggest that the use of different productivity measures may create incentives for colleges to favor some majors over others. In particular, if policy makers primarily use earnings to measure performance, this could encourage college administrators to shift resources away from more specialized majors. Furthermore, in a separate analysis, we find that—holding fixed the measure of productivity—a college's ranking in one major is only moderately correlated with its ranking in another major.[28] Thus there is substantial scope for colleges to respond to accountability schemes by favoring some majors over others.

4.6 Conclusion

Increasingly, policy makers are looking to provide information on the outcomes that different colleges produce for their graduates. In many ways, this reflects a desire to extend school accountability to higher education. Casual observation suggests this desire is particularly prevalent in countries that have seen some combination of significant growth in access to college, growth of a substantial (and often relatively unregulated) private sector, and increasing amounts of student debt.[29] As with school accountability in K–12 education—despite its much longer history—questions remain as to the informational content and the ultimate effects of initiatives in this area.

Our goal here has been to contribute by calculating, for the country of Colombia, system-wide measures of college productivity in terms of earning and learning. While we do not claim that our measures isolate causal college value added, they allow for analyses beyond those that have been previously feasible. Our findings suggest that measures of college productivity on earning and learning are far from perfectly correlated.

A key implication of this is that the design of accountability systems will affect how these portray different types of colleges and potentially also how these colleges respond. For instance, we find that in the case of Colombia, top private colleges generally perform better under our earning measure, while selective public colleges appear more favorably under our learning measure.

In addition, in the earnings dimension, one can arrive at starkly different conclusions regarding colleges' relative productivity depending on when one measures earnings. This is problematic because the more chronologically removed the observation is from graduation, the more that factors extraneous to colleges—such as postschooling human capital investment decisions made by employers and employees—will have a chance to affect wages. This leaves open the possibility that learning measures do a better job of isolating a college's contribution to students' human capital. Of course, trade-offs abound, as shifting weight toward learning measures may induce gaming similar to that which has been observed around "No Child Left Behind" and analogous K–12 accountability initiatives.

Finally, our results illustrate that the use of different productivity measures may create incentives for colleges to favor some majors over others.

28. For example, the correlation between a college's business/economics ranking and its engineering ranking is 0.53 using field exit score residuals from equation (2) and 0.54 using log earnings residuals.

29. For instance, the United States, Chile, and Colombia fit some of these criteria.

For example, our findings suggest that they might encourage institutions to shift resources away from more specialized majors and toward areas such as business and engineering.

References

Altonji, J. G., and R. K. Mansfield. 2014. "Group-Average Observables as Controls for Sorting on Unobservables When Estimating Group Treatment Effects: The Case of School and Neighborhood Effects." NBER Working Paper no. 20781, Cambridge, MA.

Angrist, J., E. Bettinger, and M. Kremer. 2006. "Long-Term Consequences of Secondary School Vouchers: Evidence from Administrative Records in Colombia." *American Economic Review* 96 (3): 847–62.

Arum, R., and J. Roksa. 2011. *Academically Adrift: Limited Learning on College Campuses.* Chicago: University of Chicago Press.

Chetty, R., J. N. Friedman, and J. Rockoff. 2014. "Measuring the Impacts of Teachers I: Evaluating Bias in Teacher Value-Added Estimates." *American Economic Review* 104 (9): 2593–2632.

Cooke, M. 1910. *Academic and Industrial Efficiency.* New York: Carnegie Foundation for the Advancement of Teaching.

Council for Aid to Education. 2013. *Does College Matter? Measuring Critical-Thinking Outcomes Using the CLA.* Technical report. Accessed August 2016. http://cae.org/images/uploads/pdf/Does_College_Matter.pdf.

Dale, S. B., and A. B. Krueger. 2014. "Estimating the Effects of College Characteristics over the Career Using Administrative Earnings Data." *Journal of Human Resources* 49 (2): 323–58.

Hagedorn, L. S., F. T. Pascarella, M. Edison, J. M. Braxton, A. Nora, and P. T. Terenzini. 1999. "Institutional Context and the Development of Critical Thinking: A Research Note." *Review of Higher Education* 22 (3): 265–85.

Hastings, J., C. Neilson, and S. Zimmerman. 2013. "Are Some Degrees Worth More Than Others? Evidence from College Admissions Cutoffs in Chile." NBER Working Paper no. 19241, Cambridge, MA.

Hoekstra, M. 2009. "The Effect of Attending the Flagship State University on Earnings: A Discontinuity-Based Approach." *Review of Economics and Statistics* 91 (4): 717–24.

Hoxby, C., and G. Bulman. 2015. "Computing the Value Added of American Postsecondary Institutions." Mimeo, Stanford University.

Kirkeboen, L., E. Leuven, and M. Mogstad. 2016. "Field of Study, Earnings, and Self-Selection." *Quarterly Journal of Economics* 131 (3): 1057–1111.

Klein, S., J. Steedle, and H. Kugelmass. 2010. "The Lumina Longitudinal Study: Summary of Procedures and Findings Comparing the Longitudinal and Cross-sectional Models." Unpublished manuscript.

MacLeod, W. B., E. Riehl, J. E. Saavedra, and M. Urquiola. 2015. "The Big Sort: College Reputation and Labor Market Outcomes." NBER Working Paper no. 21230, Cambridge, MA.

Pascarella, E. T., and P. Terenzini. 2005. *How College Affects Students: A Third Decade of Research.* San Francisco: Jossey-Bass.

Saavedra, A., and J. E. Saavedra. 2011. "Do Colleges Cultivate Critical Thinking,

Problem Solving, Writing and Interpersonal Skills?" *Economics of Education Review* 30 (6): 1516–26.

Saavedra, J. 2009. "The Learning and Early Labor Market Effects of College Quality: A Regression Discontinuity Analysis." Mimeo, Harvard University.

Stange, K. 2012. "Ability Sorting and the Importance of College Quality to Student Achievement: Evidence from Community Colleges." *Education Finance and Policy* 7 (1): 74–105.

Sullivan, T., C. Mackie, W. F. Massy, and E. Sinha. 2012. *Improving Measurement of Productivity in Higher Education*. Online book. Washington, DC: National Academies Press.

The Costs of and Net Returns to College Major

Joseph G. Altonji and Seth D. Zimmerman

5.1 Introduction

Both casual observation and detailed survey data indicate that postcollege earnings for graduates vary widely by field of study. Though this is in part driven by differences in the mix of students majoring in different subjects, both regression studies that control in detail for student background and studies relying on quasi-experimental variation in student assignment to different majors indicate that major choice plays a causal role in earnings determination (Altonji, Arcidiacono, and Maurel 2016; Altonji, Blom, and Meghir 2012; Hastings, Neilson, and Zimmerman 2013; Kirkeboen, Leuven, and Mogstad 2016). State and national policy makers observing cross-field wage differentials have proposed policies encouraging students to pursue degrees in perceived high-return areas such as the STEM (science, technology, engineering, and mathematics) fields while suggesting that students think carefully before pursuing degree programs in liberal arts with perceived low returns (Alvarez 2012; Jaschik 2014). The idea is that by

Joseph G. Altonji is the Thomas DeWitt Cuyler Professor of Economics at Yale University and a research associate of the National Bureau of Economic Research.

Seth D. Zimmerman is assistant professor of economics and the Richard N. Rosett Faculty Fellow at the University of Chicago Booth School of Business and a faculty research fellow of the National Bureau of Economic Research.

We thank Ling Zhong, Justin Young, Stephen Lamb, Melody Haxton, Jordan Rosenthal-Kay, and Elyse Adamic for outstanding research assistance. We thank Dale Bradley and the staff of the Florida Board of Governors for help accessing cost records and Caroline Hoxby, Kevin Stange, and participants at the NBER Productivity in Higher Education conference for valuable comments. We also thank Jamie Champion, Nancy Copa, and Tammy Duncan at the Florida Department of Education Data Warehouse for helping us access student data extracts. All errors are our own. For acknowledgments, sources of research support, and disclosure of the authors' material financial relationships, if any, please see http://www.nber.org/chapters/c13878.ack.

choosing higher-earning degree programs, students will help raise the return on public and private investments in higher education.

While policy discussions tend to focus on labor market outcomes, pecuniary returns on educational investments depend on costs as well as future earnings. At least until recently, tuition costs have not varied across fields or have not varied much (CHERI 2011; Ehrenberg 2012; Stange 2015). However, the available evidence suggests that the costs of producing graduates or credit hours vary substantially by field (Conger, Bell, and Stanley 2010; Johnson 2009). Some majors may lead to high earnings but also may be costly to produce, offering lower net returns per graduate or per invested dollar than lower-earning but less-costly majors. An understanding of *net* private returns (private returns net of instructional costs) may be valuable for policy makers seeking to maximize the efficacy of higher education spending.

This chapter brings together evidence on major-specific earnings outcomes and production costs to provide what is to the best of our knowledge the first assessment of the net returns to college major. We evaluate earnings outcomes using two data sources: administrative records of educational and early career labor market outcomes for a large sample of in-state, first-time-in-college students enrolling in the Florida State University System (SUS) and nationally representative data from the American Community Survey (ACS). Though we lack experimental or quasi-random variation in the assignment of students to college major, the Florida data do contain a detailed set of control variables, including high school grades and college admissions test scores. We evaluate the costs of producing graduates and credits in different fields using publicly available administrative expenditure reports from the SUS Board of Governors (FLBOG). These reports detail total and per-credit direct and indirect instructional expenditures within institution-major-course-level cells. Majors are defined by two-digit Classification of Instructional Programs (CIP) codes. We link the expenditure reports to microdata on student course-taking to compute total instructional expenditures over college careers for the same graduates and dropouts for whom we observe earnings outcomes.

We use these data to construct two measures of net returns. The first is the present discounted value (PDV) of net earnings returns per graduate by major. These values are potentially relevant for a university or policy maker trying to decide whether to open an additional spot in one major versus another. The second measure is the PDV of net returns per dollar of incurred cost. This is potentially relevant for universities or policy makers with a fixed budget trying to decide which major or majors to expand.

We find that costs per credit and per graduate vary by field and that measures of earnings returns net of cost are in many cases significantly different from returns measured using labor market outcomes only. Engineering majors are the most expensive, with total costs of $62,297. This compares to a graduate-weighted median degree cost of $36,369 across all majors and a cost of $31,482 for business, the second cheapest major. The graduate-weighted standard deviation of the distribution of the PDV of costs by major is $7,187 (in 2014 USD). This is roughly one quarter the size of the standard deviation of the PDV of the earnings effects through age 32, the oldest age at which we observe earnings in the Florida data, and 13.5 percent of a standard deviation of the PDV of earnings effects if we extrapolate those effects out to age 45.[1] Measuring returns on a per-graduate basis, we find that low-cost but relatively high-earning fields such as business and computer science offer higher net returns through age 32 than higher-earning but higher-cost majors such as engineering. On the whole, however, differences in per-graduate net returns across degree programs are driven primarily by differences in earnings. The correlation between per-graduate PDVs of earnings net of costs through age 32 and estimates of log earnings effects is 0.95. The role of earnings differences in driving PDVs is even larger when we consider earnings through age 45.

Differences between net returns and earnings returns are more striking when evaluated per dollar of instructional expenditure. High-earning but high-cost degree programs in engineering and health offer per-dollar returns that are similar to lower-earning but lower-cost programs in fields such as education and philosophy. High-earning but low-cost degree programs in fields such as business and computer science have the highest net returns by this measure. The graduate-weighted correlation between per-dollar estimates of net PDVs through age 32 and estimates of log earnings effects is 0.52.

The last component of our empirical work considers trends in field-specific per-credit expenditures over the 1999–2013 period. On average, per-credit expenditures dropped by 16 percent in the Florida SUS over this period. Rates of decline differ by field. The largest drops occurred in engineering and health, growing fields with high per-graduate returns. Per-credit funding in these fields fell by more than 40 percent over the period. Overall, costs per credit fell more in fields with large increases in credit hours. The changes have little relationship with average per-credit costs or with earnings effects. Our findings suggest that long-run declines in funding at the institution level affect fields differentially. This may alter the distribution of degree types in addition to reducing overall completion rates, as reported in Bound and Turner (2007) and Bound, Lovenheim, and Turner (2010). An analysis of staffing data for the University of Florida suggests that changes in faculty and staff inputs per credit can explain about half of the overall decline. Faculty full-time equivalents (FTEs) per credit declined 16 percent between 2000 and 2012.

---

1. The ratio does not account for sampling error in the earnings effects estimates, which is substantial in the case of the estimates based the Florida administrative data. We find similar results using ACS data.

The chapter proceeds as follows. In section 5.2, we discuss our contribution to existing work on the topic. In section 5.3, we present a model of the trade-offs facing policy makers deciding how to allocate program spots and funding across majors. In section 5.4, we describe our data. Sections 5.5 and 5.6 present our findings, and section 5.7 concludes.

5.2   Related Literature

Our work builds on two strands of literature. The first is the rapidly growing literature on the return to education by field of study, surveyed by Altonji, Blom, and Meghir (2012; henceforth ABM) and Altonji, Arcidiacono, and Maurel (2016; henceforth AAM). A core challenge in this literature is to understand how the process by which students choose different fields affects observed earnings outcomes. A small set of studies, including those by Arcidiacono (2004) and Beffy, Fougere, and Maurel (2012), use structural models of field choice and wages to address this issue. A few other studies use plausibly exogenous variation in access to fields of study to identify returns. Hastings, Neilson, and Zimmerman (2013; henceforth HNZ) and Kirkeboen, Leuven, and Mogstad (2016; henceforth KLM) use the fact that Chile and Norway (respectively) determine admission to particular school / field-of-study combinations using an index of test scores and grades. This admissions structure provides the basis for a fuzzy regression discontinuity design. Findings from these studies indicate that admission to different fields of study can have large effects on earnings outcomes.

In the absence of quasi-experimental variation, we follow the vast majority of studies that use multivariate regression with controls for student characteristics.[2] While omitted variables bias is a concern, we do have access to high school transcript information and test scores. Consequently, our control set is richer than that of most previous studies. We find large differences in the returns across majors that follow the general pattern in previous studies (see ABM and AAM). Using the earnings regressions, we compute the present discounted value of earnings by field, taking the education major as the omitted category. As we discuss in section 5.4, we have some concerns about earnings outcomes measured using our Florida data because (a) the data cover early career outcomes only and (b) we do not observe earnings outcomes for students who leave Florida. We therefore use the ACS to construct alternate measures of earnings effects. These are very similar to estimates described in ABM, with the key differences being that we create more aggregated major categories to correspond with what we observe in the Florida administrative records and that we use annual earnings rather than hourly wage rates as our earnings measure.

---

2. Examples include Berger (1988), Chevalier (2011), Grogger and Eide (1995), Webber (2014), and Hamermesh and Donald (2008).

We also contribute to a much smaller literature on education production costs. Bound and Turner (2007) and Bound, Lovenheim, and Turner (2010) show that reductions in per-student resources have played an important role in the decline in rates of college graduation since the 1970s. In research focusing on cost heterogeneity by major, Middaugh, Graham, and Shahid (2003); Johnson (2009); American Institutes for Research (2013); and Conger, Bell, and Stanley (2010) provide evidence that instructional costs vary across fields and tend to be higher for STEM courses as well as courses in instruction-intensive non-STEM fields such as education, art, and nursing (Middaugh, Graham, and Shahid 2003). Thomas (2015) uses data on course selection and instructor costs for particular courses at the University of Central Arkansas to estimate a model of how universities decide what courses to offer. Our cost-side analysis most closely parallels that of Johnson (2009), who also uses data on expenditures and course-taking from the Florida State University System. Our findings on the average and major-specific per-credit and per-graduate costs are similar to his. Though our research focuses exclusively on Florida, evidence on costs from Ohio, New York, and Illinois suggests that other states exhibit similar patterns of expenditure across field and trends over time (Conger, Bell, and Stanley 2010).

Our main contributions are to (a) highlight the importance of considering costs as well as earnings when evaluating the efficacy of field-specific educational investments and (b) bring earnings and cost estimates together to produce what to our knowledge are the first available measures of per-person and per-dollar net returns. We interpret our findings cautiously. Our estimates of earnings effects may be biased. Our measures of costs are based on average expenditures, which may diverge from the marginal cost concepts that should guide institutional decision making. Still, we believe our results represent a jumping-off point for future research into universities' production functions.

We also provide new evidence on heterogeneity in major-specific spending trends. Much previous work on major-specific spending has focused on snapshots of spending for particular cohorts of graduates. One exception, Conger, Bell, and Stanley (2010), documents trends in major-specific spending in the SUS system over the 2002–7 period, when both our data and theirs show little change in per-credit spending. Using a longer time window, we document a secular decrease in spending, with timing that coincides with economic downturns in 2001 and 2008.

5.3 Private Incentives, Externalities, and Choice of Major

In this section, we motivate our focus on instructional costs using a simple model of optimal major choice from the point of view of both the individual and the social planner. Our focus is on how labor market returns, instructional costs, and tuition influence choice in an environment where taxation and externalities cause the private and social values of majors to differ. We abstract from the extensive margin choice to attend college as well as from the college completion margin.

Students choose majors to maximize utility. The utility from a given major depends on earnings returns, tuition, and the nonpecuniary benefits associated with its coursework and the occupations it leads to. Assuming additive separability, the utility U_i^f that student i receives from enrolling in major f is

$$(1) \qquad U_i^f = u_i((1-t)Y^f - \tau^f) + V_i^f,$$

where Y^f is the present discounted value of earnings for individuals who enroll in f, t is the tax rate on earnings, τ^f is the tuition in major f, and V_i^f is i's nonpecuniary utility from major f. We assume for simplicity of exposition that earnings and tuition do not vary across individuals within a major and that tax rates are constant. We also abstract from general equilibrium effects on skill prices of large changes in the allocation of students across majors. The function u_i captures utility from the consumption of goods and services financed out of earnings net of tuition costs. V_i^f depends on preferences over subject matter and occupations, academic preparation, and ability.

Students rank fields based on their preferences and choose the highest-utility field available to them from some set of F majors, perhaps given some capacity constraints. We discuss these in more detail below. Note that students consider earnings Y^f and tuition τ^f but not the costs of providing major f.

The social planner's problem differs from the individual's problem in three respects. First, the planner values Y^f, not just the after-tax component. Second, the planner considers education production costs C^f, which may vary by major. Third, the planner considers the externalities associated with graduates in different fields. The value SU_i^f that the planner places on a degree in f for student i is

$$(2) \qquad SU_i^f = U_i^f + \lambda[tY^f + \tau^f - C^f] + EXT^f$$

$$(3) \qquad = u_i((1-t)tY^f - \tau^f) + V_i^f + \lambda[tY^f + \tau^f - C^f] + EXT^f.$$

In the above equation, λ is the marginal utility generated by an extra dollar of government transfers and expenditures made possible by tax and tuition revenue. EXT^f is the net social externality associated with an extra graduate in field f.[3]

---

3. Lange and Topel (2006), Moretti (2004), and McMahon (2009) discuss the social benefits of higher education in general. Studies such as Currie and Moretti (2003) focus on effects on political participation and citizenship, on crime, and on parenting. There is much less evidence regarding differences across fields in externalities. Much of the policy discussion of field-specific externalities centers on STEM education. For a recent example, see Olson and Riordan (2012). Note that large changes in the relative supply of majors would alter EXT^f in addition to Y^f.

An instructive special case is when utility is linear in consumption so that

$$u_i(Y^f(1-t) - \tau^f) = \theta_i[Y^f(1-t) - \tau^f].$$

Assume the marginal utility of income does not vary so that $\theta_i = \theta$. Since a benevolent planner would choose taxes and transfers and public expenditures so that the marginal utility generated by expenditures matched the marginal benefit of private consumption, we set $\theta = \lambda$. Then i's utility from enrolling in f is

$$U_i^f = \lambda[(1-t)Y^f - \tau^f] + V_i^f,$$

and the planner's valuation simplifies to

(4)
$$SU_i^f = \lambda[Y_i^f - C^f] + V_i^f + EXT^f$$

$$= U_i^f + \lambda[tY^f + (\tau^f - C^f)] + EXT^f.$$

We make two observations based on equation (4). First, the individual's preferences will be identical to the planner's when $C^f - \tau^f = tY^f + EXT^f/\lambda$. Left unconstrained, individuals will choose the same allocation as the planner when tuition subsidies $C^f - \tau^f$ are sufficient to (a) offset the wedge between individual and planner preferences created by the tax rate and (b) account for positive or negative externalities generated by enrollment. In the first part of our empirical work, we document differences in tuition subsidy levels by field of study. Second, the planner's valuation depends on $Y^f - C^f$—that is, earnings net of costs for enrolled students. Our empirical work presents estimates of these quantities, which would determine the planner's preferences in the absence of externalities and nonpecuniary differences across majors.

Our empirical work also considers differences in per-dollar returns to fields of study. To understand why this quantity is relevant for policy, consider a case in which student and planner preferences are as above but where students cannot sort freely across fields.

Specifically, assume that at least some fields are subsidized in the sense that $C^f > \tau^f$ and have budget limits B^f with corresponding enrollment caps of $N^f = B^f/(C^f - \tau^f)$. Students are allocated to fields in a way that may depend on student preferences over fields and admissions committee preferences over students.

The idea of a hard cap on major-specific enrollment corresponds closely with institutional details in many non-US countries, such as Norway and Chile (see HNZ and KLM for more details). It is a reasonable approximation of US institutions that, for example, establish minimum grade point average (GPA) standards for enrollment in some majors or where lack of available seats in required courses leads to de facto limits on enrollment.

The planner has an opportunity to expand the budget in major f to allow for increased enrollment. For simplicity, we assume that students who benefit from this expansion would otherwise have enrolled in a reference major g, where tuition is equal to costs and where the capacity constraint is slack. Let D_{if} be an indicator function equal to 1 if i enrolls in f, and let

$$SU = \sum_i \sum_f D_{if} SU_i^f$$

be the sum of social utility over all students. Then the gain in social utility from a marginal increase in B^f is given by

$$
\begin{aligned}
(5) \qquad \frac{dSU}{dB^f} &= \frac{dSU}{dN^f} \times \frac{dN^f}{dB^f} = \frac{dSU}{dN^f} \times \frac{1}{C^f - \tau^f} \\
&= \frac{\lambda((Y^f - C^f) - (Y^g - C^g)) + (E^f - E^g) + \bar{V}^{fg}}{C^f - \tau^f},
\end{aligned}
$$

where $\bar{V}^{fg} = E[V_i^f - V_i^g \,|\, i \in$ marginal group]. Differences in returns net of costs are scaled by the net cost of producing majors in the destination field. We consider measures of earnings scaled by costs in section 5.5.5.

In practice, the social returns from marginally relaxing major-specific budget constraints will depend on the mix of majors from which students affected by the policy are drawn and on students' relative skills in and preferences for those majors. HNZ and KLM explore these issues in detail.

5.4   Data

5.4.1   Cost Data

Our cost data come from administrative expenditure reports compiled by the Board of Governors of the Florida State University System (FLBOG 2000–2014). The data span the 12 universities in the State University System.[4] These are four-year public institutions that primarily offer degrees at the bachelor's level or higher. The Florida College System, which includes mostly two-year institutions, is excluded. The reports document course-taking and expenditures for the state university system as a whole and within groups defined by the intersection of college major and offering institution. Majors are identified at the two-digit CIP code level. This is a relatively high level of aggregation: in 2000, there were 33 distinct major codes, of which 30 reported a positive number of undergraduate student credit hours. Examples include engineering or English language and literature. A full list is provided in table 5.A1. We use data obtained from academic year (AY) 1999–2000 through AY 2013–14 versions of these reports.

---

4. Florida A&M, Florida Atlantic University, Florida Gulf Coast University, Florida International University, Florida Polytechnic University, Florida State University, the New College of Florida, the University of Florida, the University of North Florida, the University of South Florida, and the University of West Florida.

Table 5.1   **Spending by type, AY 2000–2001**

Type	Direct	Indirect	Total	Credit hours	Direct PC	Indirect PC	Total PC
A. Instruction							
Lower	232	273	505	2,147	108	127	235
Upper	502	467	969	2,781	181	168	349
Graduate	371	199	570	803	462	248	710
All	1,106	939	2,044	5,731	193	164	357
B. Noninstruction							
Research	282	155	437				
Public service	31	15	46				

Spending and credit hours by direct expenditure category in SUS system, AY 2000–2001. Units in left three columns are millions of USD. Units in credit hours column are thousands of credits. Per-credit (PC) expenditures in dollars. Panel A: instructional expenditures by level and type. "Upper" and "Lower" are undergraduate-level expenditures. Panel B: noninstructional expenditures. See Section 5.4.1 for a discussion of direct and indirect expenditures.

Each report breaks down spending by course level and expenditure type. There are four relevant course levels for graduate and undergraduate education: lower undergraduate, upper undergraduate, master's-level courses, and doctoral courses.[5] Reports describe direct expenditures for instruction, research, and public service within institution-major cells. Direct expenditures are primarily for personnel. They also compute indirect costs for activities including academic advising, academic administration, financial aid, plant maintenance, library costs, and student services. They allocate these indirect costs to institution-major cells based on either student credit hours (for academic advising and student services) or faculty/staff person-years (for the other listed cost types). See Johnson (2009) for a more detailed description of these data.

Table 5.1 describes SUS expenditures by level and type for the 2000–2001 academic year. Instructional spending totaled just over $2 billion in that year, with direct spending accounting for 54 percent and indirect accounting for the rest.[6] Spending on undergraduate instruction made up 72 percent of total instructional spending, and direct expenditures accounted for 49.7 percent of the undergraduate instructional total. Together, these expenditures purchased a total of more than 5.7 million student credit hours, equivalent to about 190,000 student FTEs at 30 credits per year; 37 percent of student credit hours were at the lower undergraduate level, 49 percent at the upper-undergraduate level, and the remainder at the graduate level. Average per credit spending was $357, with per-credit expenses increasing with course

5. There are also separate codes for medical school courses and clinical education for medical residents.
6. All dollar values reflect 2014 USD deflated using the CPI-U except where noted.

level. Noninstructional spending on research and public service added up to $483 million.

How reliable are these cost measures? Johnson (2009) compares aggregate cost measures in the FLBOG expenditure reports to expenditure measures reported in US Department of Education's Integrated Postsecondary Education Data System (IPEDS). The main difference between the two data sources is that the FLBOG reports include only expenditures in out-of-state appropriations and student fees. The reports do not include expenditures from other sources, such as grants, contracts, or endowment income. Comparisons with IPEDS data indicate that the omission of these revenue sources may lead the expenditure reports to understate costs by 15 to 25 percent. It is also worth noting that although expenditure records do include operations and maintenance, they do not include the (amortized) costs of capital investment.

Our analysis hinges on comparisons of costs across majors. Existing evidence suggests that direct expenditures consist largely of instructor salaries (Johnson 2009; Middaugh, Graham, and Shahid 2003). They will therefore allow for meaningful cross-major comparisons to the extent that either (a) faculty and other instructors allocate their time to teaching in a manner consistent with the time breakdowns they report to (or are assigned by) universities or (b) differences between reported and actual time allocations are similar across majors. Comparisons will be uninformative if, for example, both engineering and English professors report spending 40 percent of their time on teaching and 60 percent on research but in practice English professors spend 80 percent of their time on research and only 20 percent on teaching while engineering professors stay closer to the nominal allocation. The assumptions required to believe cross-major comparisons in indirect expenditures are harder to justify. How to divide costs of building maintenance, academic advising, and similar activities across majors is not obvious. Allocating expenses based on student credit shares and faculty/staff person-year shares is an a priori reasonable strategy, but it will yield faulty comparisons if usage intensity of different resources varies by discipline.

Our analysis of per-credit expenditures will focus primarily on total instructional spending at the lower- and upper-undergraduate levels. This parallels our focus on undergraduate majors in the earnings analysis. When we compute costs per graduate, we use data on all courses taken by graduating students. We focus on total as opposed to direct instructional spending because we want our cost measure to come as close as possible to capturing cost levels across majors. This choice follows that of Johnson (2009), who notes that this is the approach taken by the FLBOG in internal cost calculations. The trade-off is that indirect costs may be measured less accurately. We note that direct costs are strong predictors of both indirect and total costs. In credit-weighted univariate linear regressions, direct costs explain 95.4 percent of the variation in total costs and 77.9 percent of the variation in indirect costs. Similarly, changes in direct costs explain 91.3 percent of changes in total costs and 60 percent of changes in indirect costs. In sum, we view our cost measures as reasonable though imperfect first-order approximations of the production costs of different types of college credits.

We emphasize that our cost data measure average costs, not marginal costs. The marginal cost to a university of adding an additional student in any particular major may be small if the university does not have to hire new faculty or allocate additional funds to student programming. However, even one additional student changes expected costs by altering the probability that extra class sections will be required across the set of courses the student takes. Our estimates are likely most appropriate in the context of changes in major size or class size that are large enough to require at least some new investment in faculty and staff. Over the long run, we believe it is these types of changes that are most relevant from a policy perspective.

5.4.2   Instructor Data

We use FLBOG data on instructional personnel by field, institution, and year as part of our analysis of trends in costs and credits. The data are from the FLBOG reports discussed above. They are reported in person-years and are broken out into three categories—faculty, support staff, and a combined category that includes graduate assistants, house staff, adjunct faculty, and other (hereafter GA-AF). We have staffing data for the 2000–2001 through 2013–14 academic years.

5.4.3   Microdata Extracts

We compute earnings and total spending for graduates using aggregated extracts and regression output drawn from administrative student microdata collected by the Florida Department of Education. We have data on the population of high school graduates from 15 Florida counties over six cohorts between 1995 and 2001. There are a total of 351,198 students in this sample. These data track students from high school, through any public college or university they may attend, and into the labor market. We focus on the subset of 57,711 students who enroll in the state university system in the year following high school graduation. Labor market data come from Florida unemployment insurance (UI) records and include in-state labor market outcomes only. In addition to academic and labor market outcomes, these data include standard demographic variables like racial/ethnic background and free lunch status, as well as math and reading SAT scores for students who took those exams. See Zimmerman (2014) for a more detailed description.

For the purposes of this study, key academic outcomes are course-taking behavior while in college and data on degree type, graduation date, and major. The microdata on college course-taking contain administrative course identifiers and a set of narrow subject descriptors that divide courses into 483 subject categories. We combine these records with publicly available administrative data that map course identifiers to CIP codes (Florida Department of Education [FLDOE] 2011) and course levels (FLDOE 2015). We then merge on AY 2000–2001 SUS average per credit cost data at the course level by two-digit CIP level. We match 96 percent of course to CIP codes and 74 percent to both CIP and course level.[7] We replace cost data for courses with missing level information with CIP-specific averages. We replace cost data for students with missing CIP codes with average per-credit costs across all majors and levels. We then compute total incurred direct, indirect, and total costs at the individual level, based on all courses each student takes within the state university system.

Our earnings data track students through early 2010, so the oldest students in the earnings records are 14 years past high school graduation, or approximately age 32. For each individual, we compute mean quarterly earnings over the period eight or more years following high school completion, so the youngest individuals in our earnings outcome sample are approximately age 26. Our earnings specifications take either this variable or its log as the outcome of interest. Our earnings measure has a number of limitations in this application. First, as mentioned above, we do not observe earnings for individuals who leave Florida. Because missing values of earnings may reflect both true zeros and students who do have earnings but leave the state, we consider only quarters with positive earnings values when computing means. We observe no earnings records for about 25 percent of individuals in our data. We discuss the relationship between earnings censoring and major choice in section 5.5.4. Second, it does not capture differential growth in earnings across majors over time. Two majors with similar average earnings over the immediate postcollege period could have different long-run trajectories. Third, because we cannot differentiate between nonemployment and out-of-state migration, we cannot compute labor force participation rates, which may differ by major. When computing the present discounted value of cross-major earnings differences, we scale our estimated level effects by the number of elapsed quarters times 0.84, the labor force participation rate for college graduates aged 25–34 in 2005 (National Center for Education Statistics [NCES] 2015, table 501.50).

We consider two samples of students in our earnings and cost analysis. The first consists of students who enroll in a state university in their first year following high school graduation and go on to complete a bachelor's

7. Note that our administrative course records date to the 2010s, while our microdata on student course-taking span the early 1990s through late 2000s. Merge rates are less than one because some courses offered in, say, 2000 do not appear in 2015 administrative data. Merge rates for CIP code are high because we observe narrow subject classification in both the administrative records and the course microdata. This allows us to merge CIP classifications to microdata at the subject level even where we do not observe a direct course match. Merge rates for level are relatively low because there is no level classification in the microdata, so we only observe level where we can precisely match a course from the late 1990s through mid-2000s to a course offered in 2011.

degree program at a state university. We use data on these students for the cross-major earnings and cost comparisons. The second consists of students who satisfy the initial enrollment criterion but do not graduate. We consider earnings and cost outcomes for these students in section 5.5.6.[8]

Our microdata cover in-state students only. Out-of-state students who enroll in Florida public universities are not part of our sample. In-state students make up the vast majority of undergraduate enrollees at all Florida public universities. As reported in appendix figure 5.A1, the average in-state student share was 89 percent or higher throughout the late 1990s and early 2000s. All institutions drew at least 75 percent of their undergraduate students from in state in each year over the period. We interpret our main estimates as reflecting earnings and cost outcomes for the in-state population. Out-of-state students pay higher tuition than in-state students. However, differences in tuition levels do not affect our main analysis of net returns, which compares earnings to incurred instructional costs. If out-of-state students take similar classes and earn similar amounts to in-state students in the same major, then their net returns will be similar to those for in-state students.[9]

To address concerns related to censoring and the lack of late- and midcareer data in the Florida earnings data, we supplement our earnings analysis with estimates of midcareer earnings from the ACS. We use data from the 2009 to 2012 ACS surveys and estimate earnings value added specifications that control for gender, race, and labor market experience within the set of individuals aged 24 to 59 who had earnings of at least $2,000 per year. These estimates closely parallel those discussed in ABM (2012), except that we aggregate majors into coarser categories to correspond with two-digit CIP codes. We discuss results obtained using these data in parallel with our findings using the Florida data extracts.

5.5   Costs, Returns, and Net PDVs

5.5.1   Methods

Our analysis focuses on earnings and cost "value added" specifications of the form

$$(6) \qquad y_i = \theta^y_{f(i)} + X'_i\beta^y + e^y_i$$

and

$$(7) \qquad c_i = \theta^c_{f(i)} + X'_i\beta^c + e^c_i.$$

---

8. Due to changes in data access policies, we no longer have access to the microdata used to estimate the earnings models and construct the cost estimates. Consequently, for part of the analysis, we are limited to using data extracts based on the microdata. We were unable to compute summary statistics for our earnings and costs analysis samples.

9. Out-of-state students may be more likely to leave the state following college. This is a potential concern for state-level policy makers trying to maximize future state tax revenues. We abstract from this concern here.

Equation (6) estimates the effects of college major, indexed by f, on earnings outcome y_i. We consider specifications with both log earnings and earnings levels as the dependent variable. In the Florida data, X_i is a set of controls for individual and institutional characteristics. It includes race, gender, free lunch status while in high school, a dummy variable equal to one for students born in the United States, a third-degree polynomial in high school GPA, and third-degree polynomials in SAT math and reading scores. It also includes sets of dummy variables for high school graduation cohort and the university a student attends. We estimate this specification within the sample of students who graduated from college. The coefficients of interest here are the $\theta^y_{f(i)}$, which correspond to the effect of major on earnings conditional on other student observables. Although our control set is fairly rich, students may sort into majors in ways that are correlated with unobservable determinants of income levels. Students may also sort into majors on the basis of comparative advantage. We therefore interpret our estimates cautiously: they may not capture the earnings changes that would occur if students were arbitrarily selected to move from one degree to another. This concern is stronger in the case of the ACS earnings regressions, which do not control for test scores, high school grades, or free lunch status while in high school.

Equation (7) has a control set identical to the earnings regression but takes as the outcome the total costs a student incurs while in college. We regression-adjust costs to account for the fact that some students may take more- or less-expensive routes through college regardless of major. For example, students with lower high school grades may take more remedial courses. Consequently, our estimates of degree costs by major hold constant differences across majors in student characteristics.

We use estimates of θ^y_f and θ^c_f from versions of equations (6) and (7), where the dependent variables are earnings and cost levels, to compute present discounted values of earnings and cost streams. We compute the present discounted value of a stream of earnings by (a) multiplying the estimated quarterly earnings effects by four to get annual effects, (b) scaling annual effects by 0.84 (the average rate of labor force participation among college graduates age 25–34 in 2005) to approximate labor force participation rates, and (c) computing the discounted value of a stream of payments of this size beginning in the eighth year following high school graduation and continuing until some stop time T. We discount values back to the year before students begin college at an interest rate of 5 percent per year. We focus on two stop times: age 32 (14 years after high school completion), and age 45. The former corresponds to the limit of our support for earnings outcomes in the Florida data. We choose the latter to approximate earnings effects through midcareer. We also present estimates through age 55. To compute the PDVs of college costs, we assign estimated total cost effects evenly across the first four years following high school completion and discount back to the year of completion. This discounting will result in values that are too large for

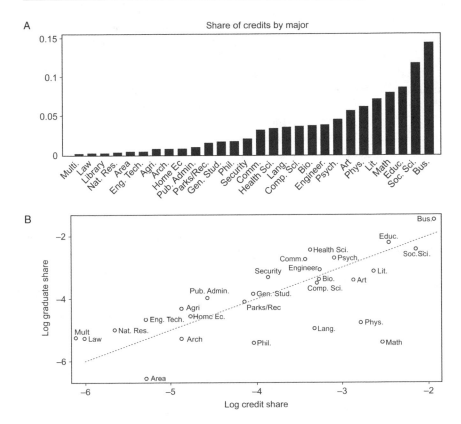

Fig. 5.1   Credits and graduates by major

A. Share of undergraduate-level credits by major in AY 2000–2001. Sample includes all Florida SUS institutions. Majors are divided by two-digit CIP code.

B. Log share of credits by major AY 2000–2001 on horizontal axis. Log share of graduates by major for AY 2000–2001 on vertical axis.

Source: Authors' calculations from FLBOG expenditure and enrollment reports and graduate reports.

students who stay in college longer than four years but too small for students who front-weight credits to their first few years of college.

5.5.2   Distribution of Credits and Graduates over Majors

The upper panel of figure 5.1 shows the shares of undergraduate credits by major for the 2000–2001 school year, sorted from smallest to largest share. In total, we observe cost data for 4.9 million student credit hours, or roughly 164,000 student FTEs. Business courses are the most common, accounting for 14.3 percent of all credit hours. The next most popular fields are social science and education, which make up 11.7 percent and 8.5 percent of credit hours, respectively. The most common type of STEM credit is math. Math courses make up 7.9 percent of all credit hours. Within the STEM category, math is followed by engineering, biology, and computer science, which each make up between 3.7 percent and 3.8 percent of all credit hours.

The distribution of degree programs for graduating majors is strongly but not perfectly correlated with the distribution of credits. The lower panel of figure 5.1 plots the log share of credits on the horizontal axis against the log share of graduates on the vertical axis. Most majors track the 45-degree line, which we plot for reference. A handful of majors—math, physical science, languages, and philosophy—fall far below the line. Many students take courses in these subjects but do not major in them. The most common major, business, accounts for nearly one-quarter of all graduates.

5.5.3   Cost Heterogeneity

As shown in panels A and B of figure 5.2, spending per credit varies widely by field. Table 5.2 presents descriptive statistics about the distribution of costs over field, while table 5.3 shows spending for each field individually. Per-credit spending on direct instruction in the highest-cost major, engineering, is $322—272 percent higher than per credit spending in the lowest-cost major, parks and recreation. It is 237 percent higher than the field with the second-lowest cost, mathematics. Levels of total instructional spending are roughly twice as high, but both the ordering of degree programs and relative magnitudes of differences (in percentage terms) are quite similar. For example, the total cost per credit of an engineering course is $569, which is 209 percent more than the $184 per-credit cost of a mathematics credit. Though STEM fields such as engineering, health sciences, and engineering technology are among the highest-cost fields, not all high-cost fields are STEM fields. For example, visual art, architecture, and library science all have above-average per-credit costs. The (credit-weighted) interquartile range (IQR) of the total cost per credit distribution is $120, or 43 percent of the median per-credit cost, and the standard deviation of per-credit cost distribution is $89.

The cost differences we observe suggest that some majors cross subsidize others. Under the assumption that levels of institutional aid are consistent across majors, we can read off the relative net costs of credit hours in different majors to the institution by subtracting per-credit tuition from major-specific per-credit costs. Because the students in our data are in-state students, we focus on in-state tuition.[10] Per-credit average in-state tuition in the State University System was $108 (2014 USD) in the 2000–2001 academic year, including mandatory fees (FLBOG 2001). The upper panel in figure 5.2 shows that tuition covers direct instructional costs in only a handful of

---

10. Assuming the same cost structure across majors, out-of-state students paying higher tuition will have lower subsidy levels overall but identical relative subsidies. Average cross subsidies in each major will depend on the share of in-state and out-of-state students. Unfortunately we do not have data on major choice for out-of-state students.

A

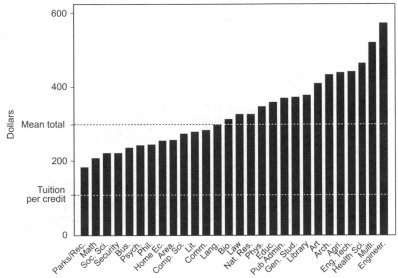

B

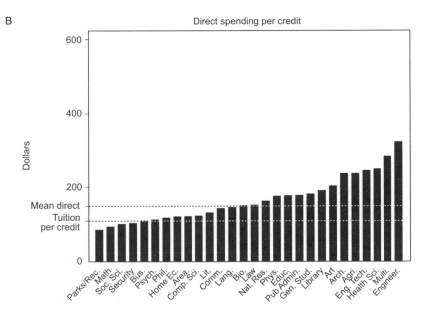

Fig. 5.2 Costs by major

A. and B. Total and direct spending per credit by major, AY 2000–2001. Panel uses administrative per-credit data for undergraduate-level credits averaged across SUS system. Tuition per-credit line represents (deflated) 2000–2001 in-state per-credit tuition and mandatory fees. "Mean total" and "Mean direct" lines are credit-weighted average of per-credit costs across majors.

C. and D. Total and direct spending per graduate. Average total and direct course costs over course of study for graduates in microdata extracts. "Mean total" and "Mean direct" lines are graduate-weighted cost averages.

C

Total spending per graduate

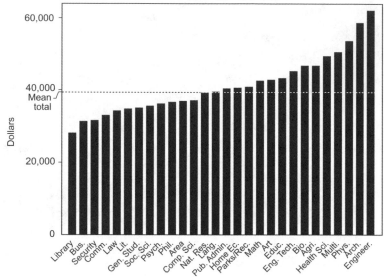

D

Direct spending per graduate

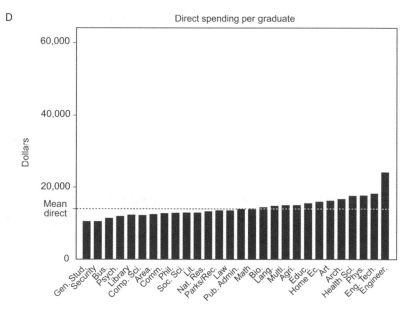

Fig. 5.2 (cont.)

Table 5.2   **Spending variation by major, AY 2000–2001**

	Direct PC	Total PC	Direct per graduate	Total per graduate
Mean	149	299	14,009	39,184
SD	54	89	3,013	8,025
p5	95	209	10,792	31,482
p10	102	222	11,501	31,482
p25	109	236	11,501	31,689
p50	123	280	12,958	36,369
p75	178	357	15,597	43,200
p90	205	407	17,600	49,335
p95	250	461	18,196	58,764

Distribution of per-credit and per-graduate expenditures by major for SUS system, AY 2000–2001. N = 28. Graduate data from extract with N = 38,336. The left two columns describe credit-weighted per-credit direct and total expenditures for undergraduate credits. The right two columns describe graduate-weighted direct and total per-graduate expenditures for graduates in microdata extracts. All values in dollars. p5 is the 5th percentile of cost distribution, p10 the 10th, and so forth.

Table 5.3   **Spending per credit and per graduate by major**

Major	Per credit Total	Per credit Direct	Per graduate Total	Per graduate Direct	Major	Per credit Total	Per credit Direct	Per graduate Total	Per graduate Direct
Fitness	184	87	40,775	13,587	Bio	311	154	46,735	14,319
Math	209	95	42,543	14,077	Nat Res	326	164	39,141	13,137
Soc Sci	222	102	35,744	12,958	Gen Stud	370	177	35,173	10,743
Security	223	103	31,689	10,792	Educ	357	178	43,200	15,597
Phil	245	109	36,899	12,873	Law	325	179	34,338	13,672
Home Ec	255	112	40,534	16,074	Phys	346	183	53,716	17,736
Bus	236	119	31,482	11,501	Pub Admin	368	193	40,417	13,823
Psych	241	121	36,369	12,189	Art	407	205	42,710	16,222
English	280	123	34,656	12,979	Agri Bus.	437	237	46,765	14,986
Area	256	123	36,951	12,701	Arch	432	238	58,764	16,599
Lang	296	132	39,448	14,676	Eng Tech	439	246	45,126	18,196
CompSci	274	144	37,236	12,572	Health Sci	461	250	49,335	17,600
Comm	282	147	33,070	12,841	Multi	519	283	50,569	14,950
Library	376	151	28,223	12,480	Engineer	569	322	62,297	23,937

Per-credit and per-graduate total and direct expenditures by major. Credit data for SUS system, AY 2000–2001. Graduate data for microdata extract. Graduate data from sample with N = 38,336. All values in dollars. For distribution summary statistics, see table 5.2.

majors and does not cover total costs in any of them. Relative to tuition, the per-credit subsidy in engineering degrees was $461, compared to a $76 subsidy for mathematics credits. The credit-weighted average subsidy level is $191 per credit. Relative to this average, classes in fields such as business, psychology, and computer science cross subsidize fields in engineering, health, education, and the visual arts.

We observe similar patterns across fields when assessing the costs on a per-graduate basis. Compared to an average total degree cost of $39,184, engineering graduates incur costs of $62,297 over their schooling career, while graduates in business (the third-lowest-cost major) incur costs of $31,482. The graduate-weighted interquartile range is $11,511, equal to 32 percent of the median value. The graduate-weighted correlation between total per-credit costs and total incurred costs for graduates is 0.89, while the credit-hour weighted correlation is 0.75. The values of total costs we compute are very similar to results reported for a subset of degrees in Johnson (2009) based on the 2003–4 graduating cohort from the Florida SUS. For example, Johnson reports average total costs for graduates of $40,339 (after converting to 2014 USD), similar to our estimate of $39,184, and he reports average costs for engineering graduates of $60,703, compared to our estimate of $62,297.

5.5.4   Earnings Heterogeneity

Earnings outcomes also differ across majors. Figure 5.3 and table 5.4 show mean log earnings and regression-adjusted log earnings differences based on the Florida data. Values are expressed relative to the omitted education major. Without adjusting for student covariates, education majors earn an average of $10,279 per quarter that they work, or roughly $41,000 if they work for the entire year. This is 42.6 log points less than students in the highest-earning major, engineering technology, and 39.8 log points more than the lowest-earning major, art. Value-added measures that control for student observable characteristics yield similar patterns. Engineering technology majors earn 43.5 percent more than education majors with similar observable characteristics, while art majors earn 37 percent less. Though STEM majors such as engineering technology, engineering, computer science, and health science are among the highest-paying majors, non-STEM majors such as business are also high paying, while other STEM majors such as biology, math, and the physical sciences offer lower returns. Overall, the graduate-weighted standard deviation of estimated earnings effects is 0.17 log points, and the difference between the lowest- and highest-earning degrees is 80 log points, or 123 percent.

Our findings are qualitatively similar to those reported in ABM (2012) in that the gap between the highest- and lowest-earning majors is comparable in size to the college wage premium. However, our finding of fairly low returns (relative to education) in math and the physical sciences is inconsistent with results displayed there and in many of the studies they survey. This discrepancy may reflect real differences in program quality, labor market conditions, or student sorting in our data versus in the nation as a whole.[11]

11. It is worth noting the Florida was particularly hard hit by the Great Recession. Oreopoulos, vonWachter, and Heisz (2012) and Altonji et al. (2016) show that labor market conditions have a substantial effect on the early career earnings of college graduates that vary across fields.

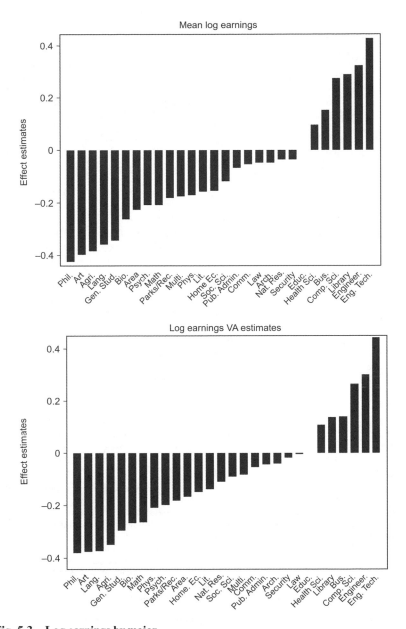

Fig. 5.3   Log earnings by major

Notes: Raw (top) and regression-adjusted (bottom) means of log earnings estimates for FL graduates in microdata extracts. Coefficient estimates expressed relative to omitted education category. N = 28,469 in top panel and 26,189 in bottom panel.

	Florida administrative records			ACS 2009–12 Age 24–59		ACS Age 26–32 Born and live in Florida	
Field	Mean	Coefficient	SE	Coefficient	SE	Coefficient	SE
Agri	−0.383	−0.342	0.094	0.050	0.007	0.202	0.087
Nat Res	−0.038	−0.108	0.072	0.072	0.008	−0.107	0.091
Arch	−0.049	−0.042	0.058	0.139	0.010	0.079	0.107
Area	−0.227	−0.164	0.078	0.163	0.016	0.045	0.132
Comm	−0.055	−0.053	0.023	0.171	0.004	0.099	0.047
CompSci	0.272	0.260	0.032	0.379	0.004	0.148	0.074
Educ	0.000	0.000	0.000	0.000	0.000	0.000	0.000
Engineer	0.324	0.295	0.026	0.428	0.003	0.238	0.048
Eng Tech	0.426	0.435	0.043	0.218	0.008	0.341	0.211
Lang	−0.357	−0.366	0.090	0.077	0.008	0.148	0.205
Home Ec	0.155	−0.145	0.038	0.032	0.009	0.130	0.097
Law	−0.050	−0.003	0.072	0.120	0.020	0.073	0.133
Lit	−0.159	−0.137	0.026	0.092	0.005	−0.051	0.067
Gen Stud	−0.345	−0.289	0.042	0.085	0.007	−0.046	0.067
Library	0.289	0.135	0.214	−0.044	0.030	0.055	0.026
Bio	−0.263	−0.261	0.034	0.239	0.004	0.184	0.059
Math	−0.210	−0.259	0.096	0.328	0.006	0.205	0.225
Multi	−0.175	−0.081	0.083	0.141	0.008	0.313	0.073
Parks/Rec	−0.182	−0.180	0.047	0.057	0.008	0.260	0.095
Phil	−0.424	−0.372	0.089	−0.018	0.011	0.006	0.168
Phys	−0.173	−0.205	0.065	0.258	0.005	−0.150	0.115
Psych	−0.210	−0.193	0.023	0.283	0.031	−0.063	0.056
Security	−0.037	−0.017	0.026	0.088	0.004	−0.050	0.079
Pub Admin	−0.069	−0.044	0.033	0.125	0.005	−0.047	0.058
Soc Sci	−0.120	−0.089	0.021	0.012	0.006	0.108	0.045
Art	−0.398	−0.369	0.036	0.244	0.004	−0.077	0.062
Health Sci	0.096	0.106	0.023	0.004	0.005	0.232	0.047
Bus	0.153	0.137	0.017	0.330	0.003	0.140	0.036

Notes: Column 1 reports the mean of log earnings by major based on the Florida administrative records. Columns 2 and 3 report regression-adjusted estimates and standard errors (SEs). Estimates are relative to the education major. Controls include indicators for ever having graduated from high school; gender; Spanish language; US born; black, Hispanic, and other race; ever having received free or reduced lunch; cohort indicators; district indicators; university indicators; a cubic in high school GPA; and cubics in reading and math tests scores. Standard deviation/IQR of log means: 0.189/0.312. Standard deviation/IQR of VA estimates: 0.174/0.274. Unadjusted means from regression sample with N = 28,469, adjusted from sample with N = 26,189. Columns 4 and 5 report regression-adjusted estimates and standard errors using the ACS data for 2009–12. The ACS sample is restricted to workers between the ages of 24–59 inclusive of those who earned at least $2,000/year. It includes controls for race/ethnicity interacted with gender, a cubic in age interacted with gender, and dummies for master's, professional, and PhD degrees. The final two columns report estimates after restricting the ACS sample to persons born in and living in Florida.

The availability of a richer set of controls in the Florida data probably plays a role, and one should be mindful of the fact that the standard errors are quite large for some of the Florida parameters. It is also possible that our findings are affected by differential censoring across majors or our focus on early career outcomes. Table 5.A2 describes the difference in rates of earnings censoring by major.

To supplement our coefficient estimates, we present parallel estimates of equation (6) using nationally representative ACS data for college graduates aged 24 to 59. These estimates control for gender, race, a third-degree polynomial in age, and interactions among these variables. Table 5.4 reports coefficient estimates and standard errors. The graduate-weighted correlation between the Florida and ACS estimates is 0.678. The most salient difference between the Florida estimates and the ACS estimates is that in the ACS data, education is a relatively low-earning degree program, while in the Florida data, it falls in the middle of the earnings effect distribution. Physical science, life science, and math majors also perform well in the ACS data relative to the Florida data. The ACS estimates of the effects of physical sciences, math, and life sciences and most other majors are lower relative to education even when we restrict the ACS sample to persons who were born in and living in Florida at the time of the survey and between the ages of 26 and 32 (roughly the age range of the Florida data), though we note that the Florida-only ACS estimates are noisy. We will continue the comparison of Florida and ACS earnings estimates when comparing earnings to costs. Estimates are based on the Florida administrative earnings data unless stated otherwise. Appendix figure 5.A2 plots the estimated coefficients from the Florida data on the horizontal axis against ACS coefficients on the vertical axis.

5.5.5 Net Returns

Table 5.5 and figure 5.4 compare regression-adjusted earnings and costs for graduates from different majors and compute present discounted values of net effects for graduates. We focus on levels specifications to facilitate simple comparisons between earnings and costs. We find that (a) differences across major in net PDVs are primarily driven by earnings outcomes but that (b) differences in costs have a sufficiently large effect on PDVs to make an economically significant difference in relative returns.

Figure 5.4 compares value-added measures of earnings effects (measured in levels) on the horizontal axis to returns net of costs through age 32 on the vertical axis. As with the earnings estimates above, we measure earnings-level effects and net PDVs relative to the values observed for education, which we normalize to zero. Because the PDVs of earnings and costs are weakly correlated (the graduate-weighted correlation between these variables is 0.21), PDVs net of costs on average rise one to one with PDVs of earnings, closely tracking the 45-degree line, which we plot for reference. The highest-earning degrees, such as engineering technology, engineering, and computer science,

Table 5.5   Per-graduate PDVs of costs, earnings, and earnings net of costs by major

Major	Costs	Florida admin earnings data				ACS	
		Earn 32	NetPDV 32	NetPDV 45	NetPDV 55	NetPDV 45	NetPDV 55
Parks/Rec	−3.4	−18.7	−15.3	−31.2	−38.2	23.8	27.9
Math	−2.8	−25.7	−23.0	−44.9	−54.5	120.5	144.0
Soc Sci	−8.2	−3.3	4.9	2.0	0.8	95.6	113.1
Security	−10.6	5.1	15.6	19.9	21.8	55.5	64.5
Bus	−11.6	35.9	47.6	78.2	91.6	114.5	135.2
Psych	−7.2	−20.9	−13.7	−31.5	−39.2	38.5	44.8
Phil	−6.9	−38.6	−31.7	−64.6	−78.9	0.3	−1.0
Home Ec	−3.9	−15.6	−11.7	−25.0	−30.8	15.2	17.5
Area	−6.6	−25.8	−19.2	−41.2	−50.8	64.9	76.6
CompSci	−6.8	52.5	59.3	104.0	123.5	142.8	170.1
Lit	−8.7	−13.9	−5.3	−17.2	−22.3	41.6	48.3
Comm	−10.4	−0.4	10.0	9.7	9.6	71.8	84.1
Lang	−5.8	−35.6	−29.8	−60.2	−73.4	33.3	38.9
Bio	1.8	−16.0	−17.8	−31.4	−37.3	83.8	101.0
Law	−7.1	11.9	19.1	29.2	33.6	50.0	58.6
Nat Res	−4.7	−25.0	−20.3	−41.6	−50.9	30.6	35.8
Phys	7.4	−17.3	−24.7	−39.5	−45.9	85.0	103.5
Educ	0.0	0.0	0.0	0.0	0.0	0.0	0.0
Pub Admin	−2.5	−6.9	−4.4	−10.3	−12.8	6.8	7.7
Gen Stud	−6.5	−29.7	−23.2	−48.4	−59.5	37.1	43.2
Library	−12.0	32.2	44.2	71.6	83.5	−3.8	−7.0
Art	−1.3	−42.1	−40.8	−76.7	−92.3	2.6	2.9
Arch	12.7	−5.7	−18.4	−23.2	−25.3	37.0	47.0
Agri	0.2	−18.6	−18.8	−34.7	−41.6	17.8	21.4
Eng Tech	1.1	88.2	87.1	162.2	195.0	77.2	92.9
Health Sci	4.8	35.2	30.4	60.4	73.4	113.6	137.3
Multi	4.5	4.8	0.3	4.3	6.1	46.0	56.2
Engineer	15.5	68.6	53.1	111.5	137.0	137.9	168.7

Notes: Columns 1 and 2 report PDVs of costs and earnings (to age 32) by major. The remaining columns report PDV of earning net of costs by major. Units are thousands of 2014 USD. Column headings indicate the age through which earnings are considered. Columns 2–5 are based on the Florida administrative earnings records. Columns 6 and 7 are based on the ACS. All estimates expressed relative to education major, which is normalized to have earnings and cost PDVs of zero. See section 5.5.1 for details on NPV calculation. For the Florida date, SD/IQR of cost PDV: 7.19/10.58. SD/IQR of earning 32 PDV: 28.85/49.88. SD/IQR of net PDV is 28.4/52.84 through age 32, 52.7/95.27 through age 45, and 63.40/113.88 through age 55. For the ACS data, the SD/IQR of net PDV is 45.9/71.6 through age 45 and 54.87/90.33 through age 55.

have the highest PDVs net of costs, while the lowest-earning degrees have the lowest net PDVs.

Deviations from the 45-degree line are driven by cost differences across degrees. One way to quantify the importance of these differences is to compare variation in costs to variation in the distribution of earnings. The graduate-weighted standard deviation of the cost PDV distribution is $7,187, roughly one quarter the size of the graduate-weighted standard

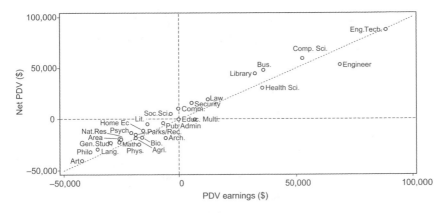

Fig. 5.4   Earnings vs. per-graduate net value by major

Notes: Horizontal axis: PDV of earnings effects through age 32 by major. Vertical axis: net PDV (earnings less costs) through age 32. Earnings and cost estimates come from equations (6) and (7) with quarterly earnings and total costs as dependent variables. Earnings and costs normalized to zero for education major. See section 5.5.1 for a discussion of the PDV calculation in more detail.

deviation of the earnings PDV distribution ($28,845). It is 13.5 percent of a standard deviation of the graduate-weighted PDV of earnings effects extrapolated out to age 45. It is 15.6 percent and 15.7 percent using the PDV through age 45 and age 55 (respectively) of earnings effects based on the ACS data. The graduate-weighted interquartile range of the cost PDV distribution is $10,582, and the difference between the highest- and lowest-cost degree is $27,184. The former value is somewhat larger than the difference between the 10th and the 25th percentile of the distribution of earnings PDVs through age 32 ($6,940) and somewhat smaller than the difference between the 25th and 50th percentile ($13,934).

It is also helpful to draw concrete comparisons between earnings and cost rankings of specific degree programs. For example, the PDV of early career earnings is more than $32,000 higher for engineering majors than for business majors. However, higher costs for engineers lead these two majors to have net PDVs that are close to equal. Similarly, business and health majors have earnings PDVs that are essentially the same, but lower costs for business degrees lead to a higher net present value (NPV). Shifting focus to the lower-earning degree programs, we can make similar comparisons. For example, English degrees have a higher NPV than physical science despite fairly similar earnings because costs are much lower. Broadly speaking, we observe a relatively small number of degree programs where earnings are substantially higher than in education. Using a difference of 10 log points as a cutoff, these degrees are in the fields of health, business, computer science, engineering, engineering technology, and (somewhat surprisingly) library science. Cost differences are sufficient to reorder these programs relative to one another based on early career earnings but not to shift them to lower values than the set of lower-return programs. When we consider PDVs of earnings to age 45 or beyond, rank reversals are rare, but the cost differentials are still substantial.

5.5.5.1   Returns per Instructional Dollar

If we believe that estimates of earnings and cost effects are causal, that earnings effects are not heterogeneous across individuals, and that our cost estimates are representative of differences in marginal costs, then the above discussion identifies the earnings return net of costs of adding an additional graduate in a given field. The effects of additional spending on a per-dollar basis are also of interest. While the net earnings returns on a per-degree basis are relevant for individuals who face the true costs of degree provision or for policy makers maximizing the sum of net earnings returns who must choose how to allocate an additional graduate, net earnings returns on a per-dollar basis are relevant for policy makers trying to figure out how to get the most net value given a fixed budget for additional students.

To consider per-dollar effects, we first fix earnings and cost intercepts by conditioning on a specific set of covariates. We consider the case of a Hispanic, female, US-born student from the Miami-Dade school district in the 2000 high school graduating cohort who attends Florida State, had an unweighted high school GPA of 3.5, and scored 500 on the math and verbal sections of her SATs. We compute predicted PDVs of earnings and costs for this individual based on estimated effects from table 5.5 and divide the earnings PDV by the cost PDV to get a per-dollar measure of the return to spending in each major. Figure 5.5 plots estimates of per-dollar returns by major through age 32 as a fraction of the per-dollar return to education on the vertical axis versus estimated log earnings effects on the horizontal axis. We normalize the return for the education major to zero. We report estimates for each major in table 5.6.

The graduate-weighted correlation between per-dollar spending effects and estimated earnings effects is 0.52. Health and engineering majors, where earnings returns are large on a per graduate basis, have per-dollar returns similar to those observed in education, math, philosophy, and language degrees, where earnings are much lower. The degrees that fare best on a per-dollar basis are business and computer science, which are both high earning and relatively cheap. These majors have per-dollar earnings returns that are 60 percent to 80 percent higher than in education degrees. The degrees that fare worst are architecture, art, and the physical sciences, which are fairly expensive and have relatively low earnings; these majors have per-dollar earnings returns that are 20 percent to 30 percent below that for education.

We also consider measures of per-dollar returns computed using ACS earnings data. Paralleling figure 5.5, appendix figure 5.A3 plots ACS estimates of log earnings effects on the horizontal axis and earnings PDV per

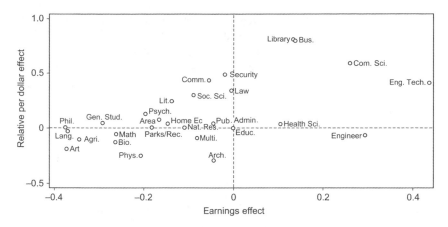

Fig. 5.5   Earnings vs. per-instructional-dollar net value by major

Notes: Horizontal axis: estimated log earnings effects from equation (6) relative to omitted major—education. Vertical axis: ratio of earnings to cost PDVs relative to ratio for education, conditional on $X_i = x$, i.e., $(EARNPDV_{j(x)}/COSTPDV_{j(x)})/(EARNPDV_{educ(x)}/COSTPDV_{educ(x)})$ – 1. See section 5.5.5 for more details on per-dollar effect calculations.

Table 5.6   PDVs by major per instructional dollar

Major	Earn PDV per dollar	Major	Earn PDV per dollar
Fitness	0.003	Law	0.342
Math	0.056	Nat Res.	0.009
Soc Sci	0.294	Phys Sci	−0.252
Security	0.486	Educ.	0
Bu	0.799	Pub Admin	0.04
Psych.	0.129	Gen Stud	0.047
Phil	0.004	Library	0.801
Home Ec	0.038	Art	−0.185
Area Stud	0.074	Arch	−0.292
CompSci	0.59	Agri	−0.101
English	0.243	Eng Tech	0.411
Comm	0.434	Health Sci	0.037
Lang	−0.018	Multi	−0.095
Bio	−0.129	Engine	−0.069

The table reports the ratio of the PDV of earnings (through age 32) to instructional costs relative to the ratio for the reference education category conditional on $X_i = x$, i.e., $(EARNPDV_{j(x)}/COSTPDV_{j(x)})/(EARNPDV_{educ(x)}/COSTPDV_{educ(x)})$ – 1. The value is zero for education. See section 5.5.5 for more details on the earnings per dollar of cost calculations.

spending dollar on the vertical axis. We obtain per-dollar earnings PDV estimates using the procedure described above but substituting ACS earnings estimates for Florida earnings estimates and use earnings through age 45. A similar pattern emerges in the sense that high-earning, low-cost degrees such business and computer science have the highest per-dollar PDVs. As in the Florida analysis, health and engineering degrees have fairly similar per-dollar PDVs to education despite much higher earnings. Most degrees, including math, life sciences, and social science, have higher per-dollar PDVs relative to education in the ACS data than in the Florida analysis. This pattern reflects the difference in estimates of earnings effects that we discussed earlier, particularly the lower return to the education major in ACS data.

5.5.6   Dropouts

The analysis above focuses on college graduates. Students who attend college but do not graduate incur costs as well but may have very different labor market outcomes. Unfortunately, we do not observe declared major prior to graduation. Nor do we observe specific patterns of course-taking for nongraduates that might allow us to divide students by major prior to graduation. However, we are able to observe the total costs incurred by students who obtain varying amounts of course credits. Specifically, we observe results from specifications of the form

$$(8) \qquad c_i = \theta_{t(i)}^c + X_i\beta^c + e_i^c$$

and

$$(9) \qquad y_i = \theta_{t(i)}^y + X_i\beta^y + e_i^y$$

in the sample of students who enroll in a state university but do not complete their degrees. Here y_i is earnings, again measured between 8 and 14 years following high school completion; c_i is total spending on courses taken by student i; $\theta_{t(i)}$ is a set of dummy variables corresponding to amounts of total completed credits; and X_i are the same set of individual covariates described in section 5.5.1. The categories indexed by t are divided into 24-credit bins. This is the minimum number of credits required to maintain full-time enrollment for two semesters, so we describe persistence in college for noncompleters in terms of years. We focus on earnings effects in levels to make the comparison with costs more straightforward. Recall that earnings are measured on a quarterly basis.

Table 5.7 shows estimates of earnings and cost effects of the θ_t for students who persist through their second, third, fourth, or more years relative to those who drop out within the first year. Costs increase rapidly with additional years of attendance, rising by $5,419 in the second year to $11,915 in the third year and to $28,276 for students who stay for three or more years but do not graduate. In contrast, earnings for noncompleters do not rise much with additional years of attendance. We cannot reject the null hypothesis that noncompleters who remain in college for two or three years have earnings equal to those who remain in college for only one year. Students who remain in college for three or more years earn $261 more per quarter than those who complete at most one year's worth of credits. However, the PDV of these earnings gains is $4,812 through age 32, which is 18.3 percent of the PDV of the additional costs these students incur.

One possible explanation for our finding of limited earnings gains per

Table 5.7   **Earnings and costs for noncompleters**

Spell length	Earnings	Costs	Censoring
1–2 years	–21	5,419	–0.016
	(127)	(54)	(0.010)
2–3 years	141	11,915	–0.033
	(143)	(72)	(0.011)
3+ years	261	28,276	–0.084
	(130)	(161)	(0.010)

Earnings and costs for noncompleters in extract data. Rows correspond to approximate lengths of enrollment before dropout. Earnings and cost columns present estimates of equations 8 and 9, respectively. Coefficients are expressed relative to omitted category of one or fewer enrollment years (within sample of students who enroll in university in year after high school completion).

Earnings are quarterly earnings. Costs are total incurred costs. "Censoring" outcome is a dummy equal to one if we do not observe mean earnings for a student. N = 12,301 in earnings regression and 16,651 in cost and censoring regression.

additional year of schooling in the dropout sample is that students who persist in an SUS institution but do not complete are likely to move out of state (e.g., to complete college at a different institution). We note that (a) this would not mechanically reduce estimated earnings effects, which are computed using earnings for stayers only, and (b) rates of earnings censoring decline with additional schooling in the dropout sample. We display estimates of equation (9) with an indicator variable for missing earnings outcomes as the dependent variable in the third column of table 5.7.

Dropouts account for a substantial share of overall costs in our data. Within our sample of students who enroll in college in the year following high school graduation, 38,336 students go on to graduate and are included in our analysis of college major returns, while 19,375, or one-third of the total sample, do not receive a bachelor of arts (BA) degree from any institution in the SUS. Based on average per-graduate expenditures of $39,184 and average per-dropout expenditures of $16,101, dropouts account for 17.2 percent of total expenditures in our sample. This estimate is similar to internal calculations conducted by the FLDOE and reported in Johnson (2009). The FLDOE calculations indicate that 19.6 percent of costs for entering first-time-in-college students in the 2001–2 school year accrued to students who had not graduated from any SUS institution by 2006–7. Due to data limitations, allocating dropouts in a way that would allow the costs of dropouts to be attributed to specific majors is a topic we leave for future work.

5.6   Trends in Costs per Credit

5.6.1   Overall Trends in Spending

Our analysis thus far captures a snapshot of instructional expenditures at a point in time. Results indicate that average earnings returns per graduate

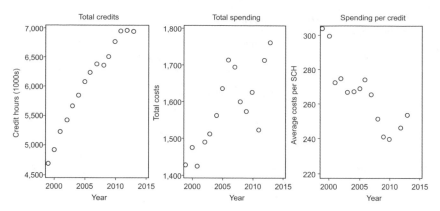

Fig. 5.6   Trends in credits and spending
Notes: Trends in total credits, total expenditures, and per-credit expenditures over time. Undergraduate-level credits only. Statistics computed over all SUS campuses. Credit hours reported in 1,000s; total costs in millions of 2014 USD.
Source: FLBOG expenditure reports.

and per dollar differ substantially across majors. This implies that a given increase (or decrease) in instructional expenditures may have very different implications for total income depending on how it is allocated across fields of study. In this section, we analyze changes in expenditures and course-taking over the 1999–2013 pattern through the lens of our findings on differential returns and subsidies across majors. Our goal is to understand how the allocation of resources and subsidies across majors changed over this period. Under the strong assumption that per-person and per-dollar returns to major did not change over the period and that our estimates of average returns and costs are predictive of marginal returns and costs, this exercise can provide insight into the overall return to instructional spending. We note, however, that changes in spending may also reflect changes in production technology. For example, expenditures may decline without any change in student earnings if professors become able to teach more students in the same time span without a reduction in quality. We return to this point in section 5.7.

We begin by documenting overall trends in course-taking and spending. Figure 5.6 shows how total credits, total instructional spending, and average spending per student credit hour changed over the 1999–2013 period. Total undergraduate credit hours rose by roughly 50 percent over the period, from approximately 4.6 million in 1999 to 7 million by 2013. This represents a rise from 150,000 FTEs to 233,000. Expenditures, shown in the middle panel, also rose, though less steadily and by a lower percentage. Total expenditures on undergraduate instruction rose roughly 25 percent from 1999 to 2013, from $1.4 billion to $1.7 billion. The result of these simultaneous trends was a 16 percent fall in per-credit spending over the period. It is worth noting that per-credit spending patterns correspond to the business cycle, with large drops in spending during downturns in 2001 and 2007–10.

5.6.2   Major Specific Trends in Credits and Spending

The allocation of student credit hours and expenditures also shifted between 1999 and 2013. Figure 5.7 breaks down enrollment and spending trends by major for the 12 largest majors. Together, these 12 majors account for 75 percent of credits over the period. The upper panel of figure 5.7 shows the ratio of each major's share of total credits in a given year to its credit share in 1999, which we normalize to one. The middle panel shows shares of total within-year spending over the same period, again normalizing the 1999 spending share to one. The lower panel shows total per-credit expenditures by major relative to the 1999 per-credit spending level. Within each panel, we split the majors into high-, middle-, and low-cost groups using terciles of average per-credit cost over the period.

Course enrollment trends vary by major within each cost category and are not strongly related to the earnings or net PDVs we observe in our analysis of microdata. The degrees with the greatest increase in credit share over the period were, in order, biology, health science, psychology, and engineering. Recall from table 5.5 that health science and engineering were among the majors with the highest NPVs, while biology and psychology were near the middle of the PDV distribution. The degrees with the largest losses over the period were, in order, education, computer science, and English. Computer science was among the highest-return degree programs in our data by any measure, while English and education were near the middle of the PDV distribution.

Changes in cost shares bear a limited relationship to changes in credit shares for many degree programs. Focusing on the middle panel of figure 5.7, we see that while the 52 percent increase in credit share for biology courses was nearly matched by a 41 percent increase in cost share, the 42 percent increase in health science credits did not correspond to any rise in cost share (in fact, there was a 3 percent decline in cost share over the period), while the 17 percent rise in engineering credit share corresponded with a 17 percent decrease in cost share. Overall, a 10 percent within-major increase in credit hour share between 1999 and 2013 corresponded to a 5.8 percent increase in relative cost share, meaning that spending per credit share tended to decline in degrees with growing credit shares. On average, a 10 percent shift in enrollment share between 1999 and 2013 was met by a 3.5 percent decline in average costs per credit. The lower panel of figure 5.7 explores this relationship in more detail. Some of the highest-growth fields saw the largest declines in spending per credit. Average spending per credit in engineering and health science fields fell by more than 40 percent between 1999 and 2013. Conversely, the only field of the 12 considered here that had higher average spending per credit in 2013 than in 1999 was English literature, which saw one of the biggest declines in credit share.

Within-year share of credits by year, with 1999 share normalized to one for each major.

Share of credits

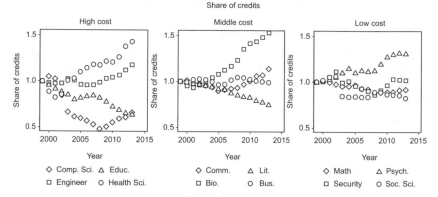

Within-year share of total costs by year, with 1999 share normalized to one for each major.

Share of costs

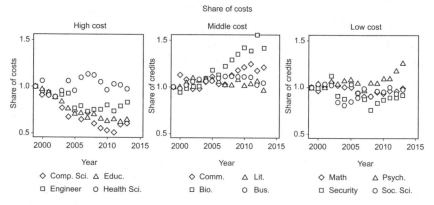

Average costs in each major relative to costs in 1999.

Average costs

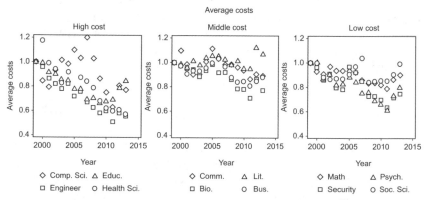

Fig. 5.7 Enrollment and spending trends by major

Notes: Enrollment and spending trends by major. Only 12 majors with the highest number of credits are included in graphs. Within each panel, graphs split majors by average per-credit costs over the period.

To explore the relationship between spending per credit and number of credits, we regressed log spending per credit by course level, field, institution, and year on log credits, including course level, field, institution, and year indicators as controls (not reported). The coefficient on log credits is –0.167 (0.030) for direct costs and –0.115 (0.027) for total costs. Appendix table 5.A3 allows for dynamics by adding the first and second lags to the regressions. The coefficients relating log total spending per credit to the current value, first lag, and second lag of log credits are –0.263 (0.044), –0.010 (0.019), and 0.171 (0.044), respectively.

The sign pattern suggests that resources respond with a lag to changes in course demand, and we obtain similar results using the log of direct costs and the log of faculty FTEs as the dependent variable. We also looked for evidence that, at least in the short run, cost per credit responds asymmetrically to increases and decreases in enrollment in a given subject area. One might expect this if some staff inputs (particularly tenure-track faculty) and classroom facilities are fixed in the short run. In appendix table 5.A4, we regress one-year changes in log total spending per credit (by field, level, and institution) on one-year changes in the log of total credits, allowing the coefficient to depend on the sign of the change in credits. The coefficient estimates do not vary much with the sign of the change. The change in faculty inputs is less responsive to increases in credits than decreases. The analysis of how schools adjust resource allocation in response to changes in the demand for credits is an interesting topic for future research.

5.6.3   Staff Inputs and Spending per Credit

In this subsection, we explore the degree to which trends in spending per credit reflect changes in faculty and staff inputs. The association reflects the extent to which educational inputs are adjusted as demand for credits varies and will also depend on policy choices about class size and instructor type. Some caution is called for in interpreting the relationship between credits and inputs because causality may also run in the other direction—from education inputs to supply of credits for the student to take. For concreteness, we focus our analysis on the University of Florida.

Figure 5.8 reports the trend in costs per credit for the same groups of high-, middle-, and low-cost majors at the University of Florida for the years 1999–2000 to 2012–13.[12] The figure shows a substantial decline in spending per credit and is broadly similar to that in figure 5.7 for all universities. Figure 5.9 reports the trends in faculty FTEs per credit hour for the University of Florida by cost grouping. Faculty inputs in the high- and middle-cost majors show a decline, with the exception of computer science and literature. All low-cost majors show a decline.

---

12. We report data through 2012–13 rather than 2013–14 as in the previous figures for comparability with staffing data, which is available through 2012–13.

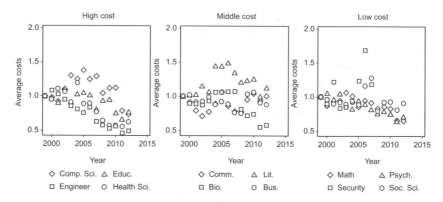

Fig. 5.8   Major specific per-credit costs at University of Florida

Note: This figure reports average costs in each major relative to costs in 1999 for the University of Florida only. Only the 12 majors with the highest number of credits are included in graphs. Panels split majors by average per-credit costs over the period.

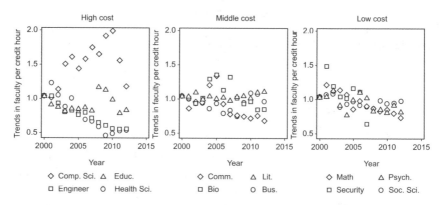

Fig. 5.9   University of Florida faculty and staff inputs per credit hour

Notes: This figure reports staff personnel years per credit hour relative to 2000–2001 by staff type. "Faculty" refers to regular faculty. "Graduate" (GA-AF) refers to graduate assistants, adjunct faculty, and house staff. The final category is support staff. Only the 12 majors with the highest number of credits are included in graphs. Panels split majors by average per-credit costs over the period.

Figure 5.10 aggregates across all undergraduate majors. The upper panel of the figure shows that faculty per credit drops by about 16 percent between 2000 and 2012. This decline parallels the drop in the number of faculty FTEs devoted to instruction, displayed in the lower panel. Graduate assistant-adjunct faculty (GA-AF) per credit rose by about 21 percent during the period, particularly between 2009 and 2012. GA-AF FTEs rose by a similar amount. Support staff per credit and in total rose by about 13 percent over the period. Use of GA-AF and support staff rose prior to the Great Recession, dropped during the Great Recession, and then recovered.

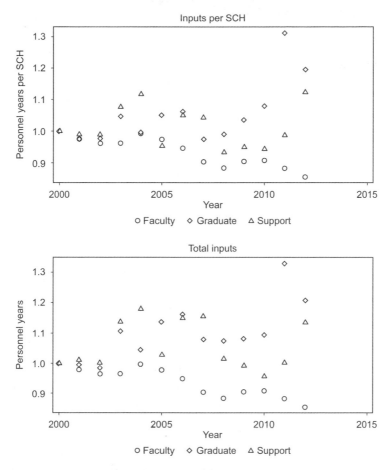

Fig. 5.10   Trends in faculty inputs for all undergraduate courses at University of Florida

Notes: Figures report trends in instructional personnel years per credit and in instructional personnel years. The values are for all undergraduate courses at the University of Florida for the 2000–2001 to 2012–13 academic years. The values are relative to 2000–2001, which is normalized to 1. "Graduate" refers to graduate assistants, adjunct faculty, house staff, and other (referred to as GA-AF in the text). "Support" refers to support staff.

We decompose the change in log total spending per credit over the 2000–2012 period into a component driven by changes in instructional inputs and a component unexplained by instructional inputs. The decomposition is based on coefficient estimates from a regression of spending per credit by course level, field, and year on the three instructional input measures and year indicators. The regression also controls for course level and field of study. We weight using the course shares of each field of study in a given year. Consequently, more-popular fields get more weight. The coefficient on

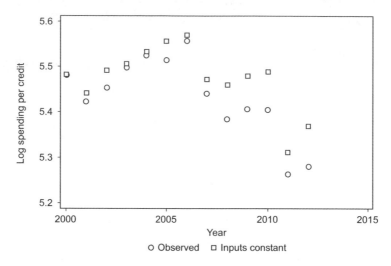

Fig. 5.11   University of Florida spending per credit on undergraduate instruction
Notes: The figure reports observed log spending per credit and log spending per credit, holding instructional inputs constant at their 2000–2001 values. See section 5.6.3 for a description of the adjustment procedure. The data are for all undergraduate courses at the University of Florida.

log faculty per credit is 0.317. The coefficients on log GA-AF per credit and log support staff per credit are 0.156 and 0.188, respectively.

We use the coefficients on the instructional inputs along with the weighted means of the input measures to compute an index for each year summarizing the effect of inputs on costs. Figure 5.11 displays the trend in the actual value of log spending per credit and the trend holding inputs per credit at the 2000 level. Spending per credit drops by 0.08 log points between 2000 and 2001 and then steadily rises between 2001 and 2006 to about 0.06 above the 2000 level. This increase is followed by a decline during the Great Recession. Overall, costs per credit fall by 0.21 log points between 2000 and 2012. About half of the decline is accounted for by instructor inputs and about half is a decline holding instructor inputs constant. Many factors, including changes in compensation, a shift toward lower-paid instructors within the three instructor categories, and more intense utilization of other inputs may have contributed to the share not determined by changes in counts of faculty, GA-AF, and support staff per credit. A full analysis of this issue is an interesting topic for future research.

5.7   Conclusion

This chapter studies the differences in the costs of producing course credits and graduates across majors and compares them to differences in earnings outcomes. We have two main findings. First, costs per credit and per graduate vary widely by major. The average cost per graduate across all fields is $39,184; the standard deviation of costs is $7,187. This is equal to one-quarter of the standard deviation of cross-major differences in earnings PDVs through age 32 and 13.5 percent of a standard deviation of the graduate-weighted PDV of earnings effects extrapolated out to age 45. While major-specific earnings estimates differ somewhat across data sets, they show that differences in costs are sufficiently large to have an economically significant effect on the relative net returns to various majors. The importance of costs as a determinant of relative returns is even more striking on a per-dollar basis. For example, the mean PDV of earnings for an engineering major is similar to that for a much lower-earning education major per dollar of instructional cost. Earnings returns are highest per dollar of instructional expenditure for inexpensive but high-earning majors such as computer science and business.

An important question for public policy is whether higher education institutions could become more productive by shifting the allocation of resources across majors given some fixed budget constraint. If one is willing to make the assumption that our estimates of earnings effects and average costs capture returns and costs for marginal students under such a policy, then one way to view our findings is as describing what would need to be true about major-specific externalities and nonpecuniary utilities for current tuition setting and enrollment policies to yield an optimal outcome. Specifically, at a utility-maximizing allocation, the marginal dollar spent should have equal value in any field of study. This means that observed per-dollar differences in earnings net of costs must be balanced out by per-dollar differences in nonpecuniary utility and utility from externalities. Our findings indicate that if schools are currently allocating funding optimally across majors, it must be the case that degrees in fields with low per-dollar returns such as art, architecture, and even engineering and the physical sciences must offer larger nonpecuniary and public benefits than programs in fields such as computer science, business, or law. It is not impossible that universities are finding this balance, but it does seem a priori unlikely. Given some set of beliefs about nonpecuniary and public returns by field, possible levers for equalizing marginal returns across degree programs are changes in tuition or shifts in supply large enough to change skill prices.

Our second main finding is that recent trends in per-credit spending differ by major. Per-credit spending fell 16 percent between 1999 and 2013, with especially rapid declines in majors with an increasing number of credit hours. These include high-return majors such as engineering and health science, where per-credit funding fell by more than 40 percent over the period. Though we cannot rule out that these declines reflect increased pedagogical efficiency on a per-dollar basis as opposed to any reduction in program quality, other research suggests that reduced expenditures at the level of the institution lead to declines in student outcomes. Bound and Turner (2007) and Bound, Lovenheim, and Turner (2010) highlight the extent to which reductions in per-student resources at two-year colleges and less-selective four-year public universities depress college completion rates in the aggregate. The declines in median per-student expenditures they observe are on the order of 5 percent to 15 percent depending on institution type. Our findings suggest that these average declines may mask larger declines in some majors than others and that these large declines may occur in high-return areas. Overall declines in graduation rate may understate the degree to which declining investment reduces human capital accumulation because the mix of graduates across fields may also be shifting. The effects of changes in major-specific educational expenditures on the majors students choose and earnings outcomes conditional on major choice are a topic for future study.

Finally, our results highlight how policies that fix tuition across majors create systems of cross-field cross subsidies. A natural question is how changes to this cross-subsidy system would affect the private and public returns to higher education. One approach would be to shift to major-specific tuition while keeping spending fixed (or not altering projected spending paths). As discussed in Stange (2015), Ehrenberg (2012), and CHERI (2011), an increasing number of universities allow tuition to vary for at least some majors. While some universities use these policies to more closely match tuition to instructional costs in majors such as nursing and engineering, others reduce tuition to encourage students to enroll in "high-need" majors regardless of costs. The majors labeled "high need" are often STEM majors with fairly high costs as well. Our results suggest that measures of need based on private labor market outcomes should take into account differences in production costs. We also emphasize that earnings returns may not reflect public returns. An alternate approach is to reallocate spending across majors while keeping tuition as it is. The effects of such a policy depend on the relative returns to a dollar of spending across majors. Further research on the marginal effects of additional subject-specific dollars would be valuable here.

Appendix

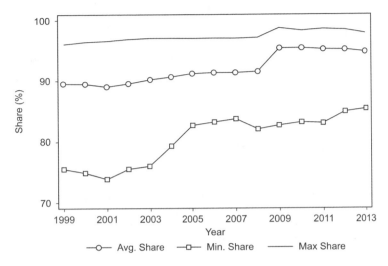

Fig. 5A.1 Share of in-state students at Florida public universities, 1999–2013

Note: Institution-level shares of in-state students by year. "Avg. share" is average across all institutions (student-weighted). "Min. share" is the lowest in-state share in a given year across institutions. "Max. share" is the highest in-state share in a given year. No statistics reported for 2004 and 2006.

Source: BOGfactbook, "Undergraduate Headcount Enrollment by Fee Classification."

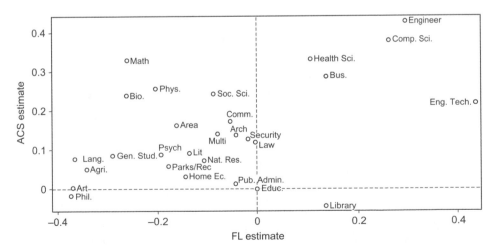

Fig. 5A.2 ACS vs. FL major effect estimates

Note: Estimated coefficients for ACS (vertical axis) versus FL (horizontal axis). Dependent variable is log earnings. ACS controls described in section 5.5.4. FL controls described in section 5.4.1. FL N = 38,336. ACS N = 1,272,597. Degree-weighted correlation between ACS and FL estimates is 0.678.

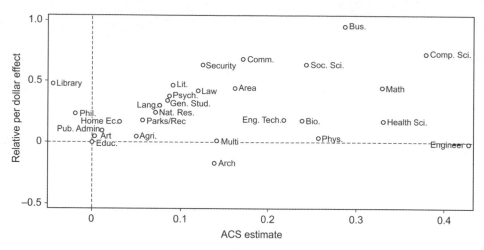

Fig. 5A.3   Earnings PDVs per instructional dollar using ACS earnings estimates

Note: Horizontal axis: estimated log earnings effects from equation (6) in ACS data relative to omitted education category. Vertical axis: ratio of earnings to cost PDVs relative to ratio for reference education category, conditional on $X_i = x$—i.e., $(EARNPDV_{j(x)}/COSTPDV_{j(x)})/$ $(EARNPDV_{educ(x)}/COSTPDV_{educ(x)}) - 1$. See section 5.5.5 for more details on per-dollar effect calculations.

Table 5.A1   Major classifications used in this chapter

CIP code	Full name	Abbreviation
1	Agribusiness and agricultural production	Agri
3	Natural resources and conservation	Nat Res
4	Architecture and environmental design	Arch
5	Area and ethnic studies	Area
9	Communications	Comm
11	Computer and information sciences	CompSci
13	Education	Educ
14	Engineering	Engineer
15	Engineering technologies	Eng Tech
16	Foreign languages	Lang
19	Home economics	Home Ec
22	Law	Law
23	English language/literature/letters	Lit
24	Liberal general studies	Gen Stud
25	Library and archival science	Library
26	Life sciences	Bio
27	Mathematics	Math
30	Multi-/interdisciplinary study	Multi
31	Parks/recreation/leisure/fitness studies	Parks/Rec
38	Philosophy and religion	Phil
40	Physical sciences	Phys
42	Psychology	Psych
43	Protective services	Security
44	Public administration and services	Pub Admin
45	Social sciences	Soc Sci
50	Visual arts	Art
51	Health sciences	Health Sci
52	Business and management	Bus

Table 5.A2 **Censoring by fields**

Major	Censoring rate	Major	Censoring rate
Fitness	0.076	Law	0.081
Math	0.1	Nat Res	0.113
Soc Sci	0.103	Phys	0.234
Security	0.076	Educ	0
Bus	0.054	Pub Admin	0.069
Psych	0.1	Gen Stud.	0.108
Phil	0.226	Library	0.228
Home Ec	0.103	Art	0.185
Area	0.185	Arch	0.115
CompSci	0.053	Agri	0.125
English	0.088	Eng Tech	−0.01
Comm	0.1	Health Sci	0.035
Lang	0.171	Multi	0.252
Bio	0.217	Engineer	0.127

Estimates of regressions of the form given in equation 6 with a dummy variable for presence in earnings data as the outcome. Estimates expressed relative to omitted education category. Censoring rate in education programs is 0.128. Estimates from regressions with $N = 38{,}336$.

Table 5.A3 **Regressions of costs and faculty on current and lagged credits**

	ln(Total Costs)	ln(Direct Costs)	ln(Faculty)
ln(Credit)	−0.263***	−0.346***	−0.348***
	(0.0444)	(0.0665)	(0.0368)
1 year lag ln(Credit)	−0.0108	−0.0202	−0.107**
	(0.0188)	(0.0339)	(0.0432)
2 year lag ln(Credit)	0.171***	0.208***	0.261***
	(0.0436)	(0.0599)	(0.0342)
Year fixed effect (FE)	Yes	Yes	Yes
Level FE	Yes	Yes	Yes
Institution FE	Yes	Yes	Yes
Major FE	Yes	Yes	Yes
Observations	5,056	5,054	5,027

* $p < 0.1$, ** $p < 0.05$, *** $p < 0.01$. Standard errors in parentheses. Regressions of log costs on the log of current student credit hours and its first two lags. Observations are defined by institution-major-course level-year. The sample is restricted to observations of greater than 100 credit hours. The regressions are weighted by the share of credits for a major at the lower or upper level over total credits in institution at the lower or upper level. These shares are constant over time for each institution/major/level by construction.

Table 5.A4   **Regressions of changes in costs and staff on changes in log credits**

	Δ Faculty	Δ Support staff	Δ Total staff	Δ Direct costs
Indicator for	−0.0399**	−0.0566*	−0.00955*	−0.0178
credit increase	(0.0157)	(0.0252)	(0.00518)	(0.00996)
Positive change	0.559***	0.904***	0.650***	0.576***
in ln(Credits)	(0.0681)	(0.123)	(0.0307)	(0.0626)
Negative change	0.778***	1.207***	0.673***	0.609***
in ln(Credits)	(0.0674)	(0.130)	(0.0575)	(0.0934)
Year FE	Yes	Yes	Yes	Yes
Level FE	Yes	Yes	Yes	Yes
Institution FE	Yes	Yes	Yes	Yes
Major FE	Yes	Yes	Yes	Yes
Observations	5,016	4,820	5,068	5,065

$* p < 0.1$, $** p < 0.05$, $*** p < 0.01$. Standard errors in parentheses. Regressions of changes in staffing and costs on changes in student credit hours. Observations are defined by institution-major-course level-year cells. Dependent variables (in columns) are log year-over-year changes in faculty, support staff, total staff, and direct costs, respectively, within institution-major-level cell. The sample is restricted to observations of greater than 100 credit hours. Observations are excluded if credit hours increase or decrease by more than a factor of 4. The regressions are weighted by the share of credits for a major at the lower or upper level over total credits in institution at the lower or upper level. These shares are constant over time for each institution/major/level by construction.

References

Altonji, J. G., P. Arcidiacono, and A. Maurel. 2016. "The Analysis of Field Choice in College and Graduate School: Determinants and Wage Effects." In *Handbook of the Economics of Education*, vol. 5, edited by E. Hanushek, S. Machin, and L. Woessmann, 305–96. Amsterdam: Elsevier.

Altonji, J. G., E. Blom, and C. Meghir. 2012. "Heterogeneity in Human Capital Investments: High School Curriculum, College Major, and Careers." *Annual Review of Economics* 4:185–223.

Altonji, Joseph G., Lisa B. Kahn, Jamin D. Speer et al. 2016. "Cashier or Consultant? Entry Labor Market Conditions, Field of Study, and Career Success." *Journal of Labor Economics* 34 (S1): S361–S401.

Alvarez, Lizette. 2012. "Florida May Reduce Tuition for Select Majors." *New York Times*, December 9.

American Institutes for Research (AIR). 2013. "How Much Does It Cost Institutions to Produce STEM Degrees?" The Price and Cost of Science Degrees Series, American Institutes for Research. Accessed March 26, 2019. https://www.air.org /project/price-and-cost-science-degrees-series.

Arcidiacono, P. 2004. "Ability Sorting and the Returns to College Major." *Journal of Econometrics* 121:343–75.

Beffy, M., D. Fougere, and A. Maurel. 2012. "Choosing the Field of Studies in Postsecondary Education: Do Expected Earnings Matter?" *Review of Economics and Statistics* 94:334–47.

Berger, M. C. 1988. "Predicted Future Earnings and Choice of College Major." *Industrial and Labor Relations Review* 41:418–29.

Bound, J., M. F. Lovenheim, and S. Turner. 2010. "Why Have College Completion Rates Declined? An Analysis of Changing Student Preparation and Collegiate Resources." *American Economic Journal: Applied Economics* 2 (3): 129–57.

Bound, J., and S. Turner. 2007. "Cohort Crowding: How Resources Affect Collegiate Attainment." *Journal of Public Economics* 91 (5): 877–99.

Chevalier, A. 2011. "Subject Choice and Earnings of UK Graduates." *Economics of Education Review* 30:1187–1201.

Conger, Sharmila Basu, Alli Bell, and Jeff Stanley. 2010. *Four-State Cost Study: Revised.* State Higher Education Executive Officers.

Cornell Higher Education Research Institute (CHERI). 2011. *2011 Survey of Differential Tuition at Public Higher Education Institutions.* Ithaca, NY: Cornell University.

Currie, Janet, and Enrico Moretti. 2003. "Mother's Education and the Intergenerational Transmission of Human Capital: Evidence from College Openings." *Quarterly Journal of Economics* 118 (4): 1495–1532.

Ehrenberg, Ronald G. 2012. "American Higher Education in Transition." *Journal of Economic Perspectives* 26 (1): 193–216.

Florida Department of Education (FLDOE). 2011. "Course Catalog Active Courses." October 27.

———. 2015. "Statewide Course Numbering System." Accessed July 12, 2015. https://flscns.fldoe.org/.

Grogger, J., and E. Eide. 1995. "Changes in College Skills and the Rise in the College Wage Premium." *Journal of Human Resources* 30:280–310.

Hamermesh, D. S., and S. G. Donald. 2008. "The Effect of College Curriculum on Earnings: An Affinity Identifier for Non-ignorable Non-response Bias." *Journal of Econometrics* 144 (2): 479–91.

Hastings, J. S., C. A. Neilson, and S. D. Zimmerman. 2013. "Are Some Degrees Worth More Than Others? Evidence from College Admissions Cutoffs in Chile." NBER Working Paper no. 19241, Cambridge, MA.

Jaschik, Scott. 2014. "Obama vs. Art History." *Inside Higher Ed*, January 31.

Johnson, N. 2009. "What Does a College Degree Cost? Comparing Approaches to Measuring 'Cost per Degree.'" Delta Cost Project white paper series.

Kirkebøen, Lars, Edwin Leuven, and Magne Mogstad. 2016. "Field of Study, Earnings, and Self-Selection." *Quarterly Journal of Economics* 132 (3): 1551–52.

Lange, Fabian, and Robert Topel. 2006. "The Social Value of Education and Human Capital." *Handbook of the Economics of Education* 1:459–509.

McMahon, Walter W. 2009. *Higher Learning, Greater Good: The Private and Social Benefits of Higher Education.* Baltimore: Johns Hopkins University Press.

Middaugh, M. F., R. Graham, and A. Shahid. 2003. "A Study of Higher Education Instructional Expenditures: The Delaware Study of Instructional Costs and Productivity." *Education Statistics Quarterly* 5 (2): 134–39.

Moretti, Enrico. 2004. "Estimating the Social Return to Higher Education: Evidence from Longitudinal and Repeated Cross-sectional Data." *Journal of Econometrics* 121 (1): 175–212.

National Center for Education Statistics (NCES). 2015. *Digest of Education Statistics: 2015.* Washington, DC: National Center for Education Statistics, Institute of Education Sciences, US Department of Education.

Olson, Steve, and Donna Gerardi Riordan. 2012. "Engage to Excel: Producing One Million Additional College Graduates with Degrees in Science, Technology, Engineering, and Mathematics. Report to the President." Executive Office of the President.

Oreopoulos, P., T. vonWachter, and A. Heisz. 2012. "The Short- and Long-Term Career Effects of Graduating in a Recession." *American Economic Journal: Applied Economics* 4:1–29.

Stange, K. 2015. "Differential Pricing in Undergraduate Education: Effects on Degree Production by Field." *Journal of Policy Analysis and Management* 34 (1): 107–35.

State University System of Florida Board of Governors (FLBOG). 2000. *State University System of Florida Expenditure Analysis 1999–2000.*

———. 2001. *State University System of Florida Expenditure Analysis 2000–2001.*

———. 2002. *State University System of Florida Expenditure Analysis 2001–2002.*

———. 2003. *State University System of Florida Expenditure Analysis 2002–2003.*

———. 2004. *State University System of Florida Expenditure Analysis 2003–2004.*

———. 2005. *State University System of Florida Expenditure Analysis 2004–2005.*

———. 2006. *State University System of Florida Expenditure Analysis 2005–2006.*

———. 2007. *State University System of Florida Expenditure Analysis 2006–2007.*

———. 2008. *State University System of Florida Expenditure Analysis 2007–2008.*

———. 2009. *State University System of Florida Expenditure Analysis 2008–2009.*

———. 2010. *State University System of Florida Expenditure Analysis 2009–2010.*

———. 2011. *State University System of Florida Expenditure Analysis 2010–2011.*

———. 2012. *State University System of Florida Expenditure Analysis 2011–2012.*

———. 2013. *State University System of Florida Expenditure Analysis 2012–2013.*

———. 2018. *State University System of Florida Expenditure Facts and Figures.*

Thomas, James. 2015. "What Do Classroom Spending Decisions Reveal about University Preferences?" Working paper, Duke University.

Webber, Douglas A. 2014. "The Lifetime Earnings Premia of Different Majors: Correcting for Selection Based on Cognitive, Noncognitive, and Unobserved Factors." *Labour Economics* 28:14–23.

Zimmerman, Seth D. 2014. "The Returns to College Admission for Academically Marginal Students." *Journal of Labor Economics* 32 (4): 711–54.

6

Faculty Deployment in Research Universities

Paul N. Courant and Sarah Turner

It is sometimes asserted that higher education institutions are inefficient and wasteful. Perhaps they are.[1] Whatever else is going on, however, faculty continue to be a major source of cost and account for more than two-thirds of instructional expenditures at public universities. Deploying faculty efficiently (or more efficiently) should surely be part of any optimizing strategy on the part of a college or university. The principal issue addressed in this chapter is the extent to which faculty in research universities are deployed efficiently in the context of an environment in which their institutions are called on to produce instruction and research.

Basic microeconomics about the theory of the firm provides some insight as to how a university would achieve productive efficiency in deploying faculty and other resources across and within departments given market wages

Paul N. Courant is the Harold T. Shapiro Collegiate Professor of Public Policy, Arthur F. Thurnau Professor of Economics and Information, and a Presidential Bicentennial Professor at the University of Michigan.

Sarah Turner is the University Professor of Economics and Education and the Souder Family Professor at the University of Virginia and a research associate of the National Bureau of Economic Research.

We would like to thank Austin Slaughter, Aaron Phipps, Fran Murphy, and Emily Cook for their patience and their exemplary research assistance. We are also grateful for the efforts of George Stovall of the University of Virginia and Ben Koester of the University of Michigan in helping us acquire and understand institutional data. We also received valuable comments from Kevin Stange and Ron Ehrenberg. For acknowledgments, sources of research support, and disclosure of the authors' material financial relationships, if any, please see http://www.nber.org/chapters/c13879.ack.

1. Critics of rising tuition levels in higher education commonly refer to growth in administrative and support services as evidence of "bureaucratic bloat" (see, e.g., Campos 2015), while increased amenities that would appear to be unrelated to student learning are cited as examples of wasteful expenditures (see, e.g., Jacob, McCall, and Stange 2018 and popular press articles that followed).

by discipline. Still, the case of the allocation of faculty time to teaching responsibilities in academe is distinct for at least three reasons. First, moving resources between academic departments is cumbersome. One cannot generally redeploy faculty across fields of expertise. Increasing the size of the philosophy department while reducing that of chemistry generally cannot be accomplished by moving a chemist's research from her lab to the library and her teaching from inorganic chemistry to epistemology. Rather, a decision to grow philosophy and shrink chemistry can only be fully implemented when a chemist (and not just any chemist; it depends on the configuration of expertise and the desirability of the same within the department) retires or leaves the department for other reasons. In effect, there is little (or *no*) short-run opportunity for substitution of faculty across disciplines, and the length of time required to make long-run adjustments can be long indeed. In contrast, within departments, faculty effort can be reallocated between teaching and research directly, and indeed there is a good deal of variation in faculty teaching loads and research expectations. Tenure-track faculty are often employed in the production of multiple outputs, including research and teaching students of different levels. Finally, the "technology of learning" as well as physical space limitations of universities may limit the extent to which universities can change class sizes in response to the differential cost of faculty.

The salaries of faculty exhibit substantial variation across disciplines, within disciplines, and over time. Yet particularly in undergraduate education and doctorate education in the arts and sciences, universities rarely engage in differential pricing (Stange 2015). Nevertheless, there are surely large differences in the cost of production for courses across departments and within departments at a university, and these differences derive in large part from differences in faculty salaries, class size, and teaching loads. These observations raise fundamental questions about whether and how differences in the cost of faculty affect resource allocation at research universities. In an effort to understand the production function of the research university, we examine how teaching allocations and costs vary both between and within departments.

The allocation of faculty to different activities is complicated because teaching and research are jointly produced by universities while they are also substitutes at some margin in faculty time allocation. It follows that the allocation of faculty time to teaching—determined by how many courses a faculty member teaches and how much effort is expended in the teaching— may bear little relationship to how many students a faculty member enrolls and, in turn, how much tuition revenue is generated. Recognizing different research productivity among faculty and different market prices for research across disciplines suggests a model in which university- and department- level decision-making incorporates input prices to approach efficiency in the deployment of faculty to teaching and research.

These issues are brought into sharp focus by the fairly dramatic changes in faculty salaries across fields in recent decades at research universities. Overall, a rise in faculty salaries should be relatively unsurprising in an overall labor market where returns to education are increasing. At the same time, there has also been considerable heterogeneity across fields. Disciplines such as economics have seen dramatic increases in faculty compensation, while salaries have increased only modestly in many fields in the humanities. Significantly, the salary increases seen at research universities are not shared across all sectors of higher education.

It is in research universities (in the United States, members of the Association of American Universities [AAU] and, to a substantial degree, members of the larger Association of Public and Land-grant Universities) where the same personnel (tenure-track faculty) do much of both the teaching and the research that are the focus of our analysis. These research-intensive public universities award a substantial share of graduate and undergraduate degrees, accounting for 36.5 percent of doctorate degrees and 16.7 percent of bachelor of arts (BA) degrees awarded by US institutions in 2015.[2] The university has two important margins as it allocates faculty resources. It can move resources between departments and schools—growing, say, computer science while shrinking, say, comparative literature[3]—and it can also move resources between teaching and research within departments. To set the stage for our analysis of instructional production in the research university, we begin with a brief overview of the trends in the faculty labor market, where supply generated by doctorate programs and demand from universities and the nonacademic market determine price. We focus our analysis on the public universities where data are generally available in the public domain. Section 6.3 sets forth the theoretical framework, where we outline a model of how universities allocate faculty to teaching across and within departments. Section 6.4 investigates the link between departmental compensation (payroll) and students and courses taught, leading to measures of the distribution of class sizes and "cost per seat." A simple and important takeaway is that faculty compensation per student varies less across departments than do salary levels. In turn, changes over time in relative salaries by discipline are much larger than changes in faculty compensation per student as universities adjust to these pricing pressures by increasing class size and increasing teaching inputs from other sources.

---

2. Authors' tabulations from the IPEDS survey, focusing on those classified as "Research I" under the Carnegie Classification.

3. In some places, these are in different colleges or schools within the university. We are ignoring the complications created by professional schools but supposing that there is some authority that can reallocate across broad lines of academic activity. For that matter, a university can grow the football team while shrinking the library, a margin that we will also ignore, sticking here to academic departments and, for reasons that will become clear, a subset of academic departments.

We find that within departments the highest-paid faculty teach fewer undergraduates and fewer undergraduate courses than their lower-paid colleagues. Following the logic of our theoretical discussion in Section 6.3, this finding confirms our view that salaries are determined principally by research output and associated reputation and that universities respond rationally to relative prices in deploying faculty.

Our finding that research universities respond rationally to differences in prices and opportunity costs of faculty deployment suggests, although it does not prove, that universities endeavor to be efficient in the classic economic sense of minimizing the cost of producing output. That university leadership recognizes and acts on opportunities to increase productivity in the important domain of allocating faculty to teaching and research suggests that we are likely to find similar efforts in other domains.

We end with a brief conclusion that summarizes our results and their implications and suggests further work.

6.1   Faculty Labor Markets: Trends and Compensation by Discipline

6.1.1   Faculty Salaries

Faculty salaries represent the price of the primary input in the higher education production function. The relative increase in the earnings of college-educated workers has been widely noted (see, e.g., Autor 2014), and one might think this premium is particularly concentrated among doctorate recipients, who are at the top of the distribution of years of educational attainment. Over the course of the last quarter century, faculty salaries have risen (figure 6.1), and these increases are somewhat larger than the earnings changes for college-educated workers more generally.[4] Since 1990, constant-dollar faculty salaries have increased by 14 percent at the level of full professors and by 10 to 11 percent for associate and assistant professors. For colleges and universities, an increase in the price of faculty, the most significant input in the university budget, affects costs of production. Yet as discussed in more detail below, the rising tide has not lifted all boats, and the increase in faculty salaries has been concentrated among universities in the research sector and faculty in a subset of academic disciplines.

Even as the faculty salary bill continues to dominate university expenditures on instruction, there has been little—if any—substitution of capital and technology for doctorate-level instructors in the university production for, quite literally, centuries. What some have labeled the "cost disease" would seem to be a significant force in explaining the long trend of rising

---

4. Data from the Current Population Survey P-20 series show an increase in the constant-dollar earnings of workers with at least a BA degree between 1991 and 2014 of 3.4 percent for men and 11 percent for women.

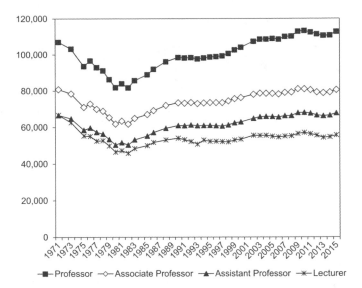

-■-Professor -◇-Associate Professor -▲-Assistant Professor -✳-Lecturer

Fig. 6.1   Overall trends in faculty salaries by rank, constant (2015) dollars
Source: US Department of Education, National Center for Education Statistics, Higher Education General Information Survey (HEGIS), "Faculty Salaries, Tenure, and Fringe Benefits" surveys, 1970–71 through 1985–86; Integrated Postsecondary Education Data System (IPEDS), "Salaries, Tenure, and Fringe Benefits of Full-Time Instructional Faculty Survey" 1987 2015. See Table 316.10 from 2015 Digest of Education Statistics.

costs in higher education.[5] Over the last two decades, there have been few changes in staffing ratios in aggregate, with the student-faculty ratio dropping only slightly at public degree-granting universities (16.6 to 16.1 from 1993 to 2013), while student-faculty ratios have dropped appreciably at private nonprofit colleges and universities (dropping from 12.4 to 10.6 over this interval), which would point broadly toward increasing labor costs absent changes in the composition of faculty.[6] These findings are generally inconsistent with substitution away from increasingly expensive faculty.

5. The original insight derives from the Baumol-Bowen analysis of the performing arts in the 1960s and has been broadly applied to higher education, including in an early study of the economics of private research universities Bowen. Essentially, because higher education is labor intensive and there are few opportunities for substituting capital for labor, unit labor costs in sectors such as higher education and the performing arts will increase more rapidly than in the economy overall (a contemporary discussion can be found in Bowen 2012). Recognizing that technology is not entirely absent from modern classrooms and characteristics of faculty (including research knowledge) may have adjusted, Bowen (2012) notes that any changes in the quality of teaching are not captured in unit output measures.
6. See *Digest of Education Statistics* 2014 (table 314.10). Note that for public universities, there is a substantial cyclical component in student-faculty ratios, with student-faculty ratios rising during recessionary periods (Turner 2015). What is more, as discussed below, there is substantial evidence of increased stratification or variance in student-faculty ratios over time. Bound, Lovenheim, and Turner (2010) show that the most selective institutions experienced declines in student-faculty ratios, while student-faculty ratios have risen at many less selective institutions.

Table 6.1   Faculty salaries by type of institution, selected years, constant dollar
                   (2015 USD)

	1971	1980	1990	2000	2015
Assistant professor					
Research 1 public	84,336	57,222	70,783	72,739	83,801
Research 1 private	73,741	54,417	73,088	84,895	101,244
Research 2 public	69,565	53,191	63,012	66,126	75,930
Other 4-year public	66,251	51,484	59,807	60,746	65,810
Other 4-year private	60,355	47,508	54,007	57,812	64,160
Private liberal arts 1	62,144	45,808	56,401	59,976	64,555
2-year public	67,875	52,778	59,766	58,990	57,912
Top 7 private universities	74,416	54,489	73,876	86,053	113,781
Top 5 public universities	70,742	56,459	74,575	80,973	95,053
Full professor					
Research 1 public	120,131	96,491	114,427	123,811	141,205
Research 1 private	127,120	101,796	129,787	149,459	186,582
Research 2 public	111,328	86,409	101,954	109,547	125,028
Other 4 year public	102,313	82,779	93,081	95,076	99,348
Other 4 year private	89,032	76,390	84,731	90,721	100,941
Private liberal arts 1	95,940	71,853	89,804	99,558	106,659
2-year public	90,788	87,329	91,645	80,683	75,507
Top 7 private universities	131,690	107,058	141,430	166,396	213,495
Top 5 public universities	125,591	102,229	128,886	144,801	168,710

Source: Authors' tabulations using US Department of Education, National Center for Education Statistics, Higher Education General Information Survey (HEGIS), "Faculty Salaries, Tenure, and Fringe Benefits" surveys, 1970–71 through 1985–86; Integrated Postsecondary Education Data System (IPEDS), "Salaries, Tenure, and Fringe Benefits of Full-Time Instructional Faculty Survey," 1987–2015. The top 7 private universities are coded as Princeton, Harvard, Yale, Columbia, Stanford, Chicago, and MIT. The top 5 public universities are coded as UC-Berkeley, UCLA, University of Virginia, University of Michigan, and UNC-Chapel Hill.

The national increase in faculty salaries misses two dimensions of increased stratification—discipline and research intensity. First, faculty salaries have not risen proportionately across all sectors of higher education, and in table 6.1, we distinguish colleges and universities by public control and research intensity, along with faculty rank. Indeed, constant-dollar salaries of faculty at community colleges and nondoctorate-granting public colleges have actually *lost* ground at all ranks since the early 1970s, with only modest gains at non-PhD institutions since 2000.[7] In contrast, faculty at research-intensive universities ("Research I" in the Carnegie Classifica-

7. Turner (2013) provides a detailed discussion of the divergence between the private and public sectors in student-faculty ratios and hiring during the recessionary period beginning in 2008, along with the widening of differences between research universities and open-access institutions in the public sector.

tions), most notably in the private sector, have made substantial real gains in compensation over the last quarter century. Between 1990 and 2015, salaries of full professors increased, on average, by 23 percent at public universities and nearly 44 percent at private universities in constant dollar terms. The increased stratification and competition in the market for research faculty is yet more evident when we compare faculty at top-ranked research institutions to the broader set of research universities (also shown in table 6.1), where the increase in full professor salaries was about 51 percent at the top privates and 31 percent at the top publics between 1990 and 2015. Salary increases have been concentrated at the universities where faculty are expected to produce both scholarly research and teaching, and it is the research contributions that are most broadly priced in the national marketplace. An implication is that the price of research has increased at a greater rate than the price of instruction.

The differential changes in faculty salaries across type of institution mirror the well-established pattern of increased input stratification across higher education, which is also a reflection of the increased "quality competition" in higher education (Hoxby 2009). Effectively, just as colleges and universities compete for students, they are also competing for top-tier faculty, and greater availability of resources increases an institution's capacity to attract these top-tier faculty.

Faculty salaries are also increasingly differentiated by discipline. Doctorate-level faculty are one of the most specialized educational classifications in the labor market. Because the field (and, indeed, subfield) of a PhD determines employment options, there are few opportunities for "substitution" across disciplines—a unique feature of the academic labor market that we return to shortly. What we see in the available aggregate data[8] is the increased divergence among fields in compensation: fields such as economics, engineering, and the physical sciences have higher salaries than those in the humanities and some social sciences, such as sociology and anthropology. The first columns of table 6.2 present data for public universities that are in the AAU (and participate in a central data exchange) for 2002–3 and 2014–15. While salaries have been fairly stagnant or have increased at single-digit rates in a number of fields, including English and sociology, the discipline of economics defines the other tail, with increases of about 30 percent across the ranks over this interval. To see faculty salaries over the longer time horizon of nearly four decades, we turn to data assembled on faculty salaries at the broader group of public land-grant universities in figure 6.2. Over time, the variance in real salaries across disciplines has increased markedly, moving from an era in which the better-compensated fields received only a

---

8. Note that faculty salaries by discipline are not collected as part of the standard IPEDS reporting process, and it is thus very difficult to assemble a long time series for a well-defined set of universities.

Table 6.2   Faculty salaries by discipline and rank, Association of American
                   Universities Data Exchange (AAUDE) public universities, the University
                   of Michigan, and the University of Virginia (2015 $)

Department	AAU public aggregate			University of Virginia	University of Michigan
	2002–3	2014–15	% Change		
Full professors					
Chemistry	139,450	148,698	6.6	149,832	154,673
Computer science	146,690	154,647	5.4	183,127	170,329
Economics	156,965	202,347	28.9	186,250	241,464
English	116,228	123,480	6.2	125,578	139,149
History	121,106	126,459	4.4	130,594	144,650
Mathematics	125,957	134,605	6.9	141,877	147,399
Philosophy	127,274	138,665	8.9	115,260	163,305
Physics	129,609	137,162	5.8	129,117	140,172
Political science	133,944	148,812	11.1	149,147	192,633
Psychology	132,491	138,617	4.6	151,530	167,564
Sociology	127,758	137,473	7.6	136,213	185,634
Assistant professors					
Chemistry	76,330	83,527	9.4	78,400	84,792
Computer science	103,438	98,563	–4.7	126,567	100,974
Economics	94,614	119,563	26.4	123,538	124,948
English	64,891	69,153	6.6	69,267	71,149
History	65,513	70,146	7.1	69,280	74,478
Mathematics	72,471	84,659	16.8	85,500	60,298
Philosophy	65,631	71,825	9.4	66,000	108,981
Physics	79,831	85,613	7.2	85,733	90,140
Political science	73,701	82,838	12.4	87,100	89,417
Psychology	72,190	78,906	9.3	96,700	87,124
Sociology	71,077	77,203	8.6	66,388	90,524

Source: Authors' tabulations from AAUDE institutional data from public universities and
institutional public-release files for the University of Virginia and the University of Michigan.

modest premium to the current period, in which salaries differ by orders of
magnitude across fields. As probably more than one exasperated dean has
noted, a rookie PhD economist commands a salary almost twice that of a
starting doctorate in English.

Our interest is in how the structure of these differences in salaries across
disciplines within research universities links to the organization of instructional activities. At the same time, salaries for faculty *within* discipline and
rank also vary markedly, which leads to the question of how faculty with
different skill and salary levels are allocated to different instructional and
research tasks within the university.

6.1.2   Market Forces and Faculty Salaries

As with any labor market, the determination of "price," or salary, in aca-
demics is a function of supply and demand. Thus for entry-level faculty,

A   Assistant Professors

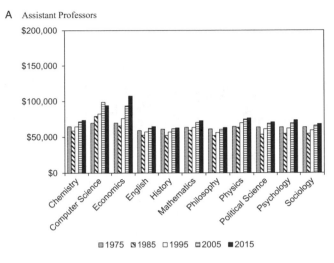

■1975 ◨1985 □1995 ▤2005 ■2015

B   Associate Professors

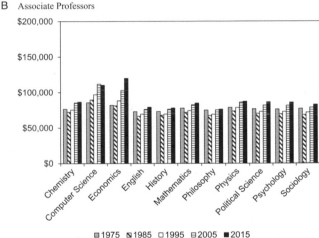

■1975 ◨1985 □1995 ▤2005 ■2015

Fig. 6.2   Faculty salaries by rank and discipline, public universities, constant (2015) dollars

Source: Faculty salary survey of institutions belonging to the National Association of State Universities and Land-Grant Colleges (NASULGC, now the Association of Public and Land-grant Universities; Oklahoma State University, various years).

the only avenue for supply is new doctorate production, while the supply of more-senior faculty is constrained by past production.[9] A noteworthy

9. A long research literature, with a particular focus on science and engineering fields, has assessed the particular challenges of projections in doctorate labor markets where the long period for degree attainment creates a substantial lag between program entry and degree receipt. Changes in market demand may then magnify any mismatch between supply and demand of new doctorates in the presence of myopic expectations (see Breneman and Freeman 1974;

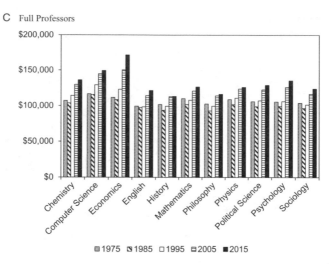

Fig. 6.2   (cont.)

point is that the flow of new doctorates varies in ways that only tangentially mirror the flow of new positions. Figure 6.3 shows the relative change in the number of new doctorates over the last quarter century by discipline. While computer science and mathematics, which may have considerable nonacademic labor markets,[10] are distinguished by the growth in the number of PhDs awarded, the relatively flat trajectories for the humanities and social sciences are also notable because they occur in the presence of a long-term excess of doctorates relative to academic positions. Considering the contrast between English and economics, the mismatch between new doctorates and new positions would explain much of the recent trend in salaries. Figure 6.4 shows the divergent trends in new job postings: whereas there is more than one position for each new PhDs in economics, the situation is reversed in English, where the number of jobs relative to PhDs is less than one and declining.

The decisions of colleges and universities to add faculty follow from demands for teaching and research, with the latter only a significant factor for a small set of doctorate-granting universities. Behind the job postings are basic demand determinants that can be expected to affect how universities choose to allocate hiring across fields. As the labor market and student preferences (both undergraduate and graduate) change, students will choose

---

Freeman 1976; National Academy of Sciences 2000). The result is that doctorates entering the labor market during weak job markets are likely to receive relatively low starting salaries.

10. Data from the 2013 Survey of Doctorate Recipients show that about 38 percent of computer science doctorates and 43 percent of chemistry doctorates are at colleges or universities, while about 73 percent of sociology doctorates and 67 percent of politics doctorates are employed at colleges and universities.

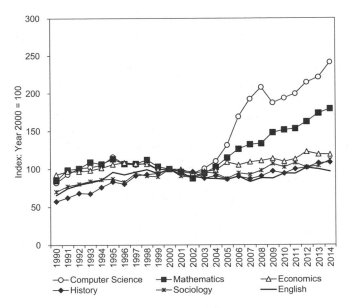

Fig. 6.3   Trends in doctorates conferred by discipline
Source: Survey of earned doctorates, various years.

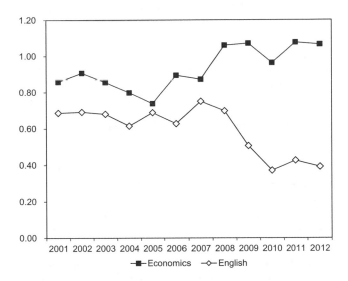

Fig. 6.4   New job postings by field relative to new doctorates awarded, 2001–12
Sources: Authors' tabulations from the American Economics Association and the MLA, with new PhDs by discipline from the Survey of Earned Doctorates.

to pursue different specializations to the extent afforded by the curriculum. Over time, fields like computer science that are known to have large changes in market demand demonstrate substantial cyclical patterns in undergraduate degree receipt. Still, universities may—wisely—be reluctant to address sharp changes in student demand generated by short-term factors with permanent tenure-track hiring.[11]

University goals to increase research output also place upward pressure on the demand for faculty. Fields in which external research funding is relatively plentiful will also experience relative booms in hiring and salaries as universities aim to compete for federal funds, which not only are inputs into rankings but also generate substantial opportunities for cost recovery. Research funding shocks in the last half-century have been large and differentiated across specific science disciplines. For the physical sciences, defense investments and federal funding spiked in the 1980s before reversing in the 1990s and then rebounding somewhat. For the life sciences, the doubling of the budget of the National Institutes of Health between 1998 and 2003 contributed to an increase in demand for faculty and salaries of research-active faculty.

Salary increases and reductions (at least in real terms) do not provide the only margin of adjustment to changes in demand in academic labor markets. For faculty at research universities, nonwage compensation often takes the form of benefits intended to increase research productivity. Additional benefits may include funded graduate students and access to money to purchase equipment, travel, and data, as well as lighter teaching loads and more frequent sabbatical leaves. When these latter forms of compensation are used to compete for faculty, they necessarily affect a university's resource allocation in the teaching domain.[12]

6.2   Faculty Deployment and Faculty Salaries: Sketching a Theoretical Framework

The market for academic labor just described determines the general pattern of salaries across fields and subfields. Individual universities, their departments, and their faculty have no influence on these general patterns. They are, for the most part, price takers in the conventional sense, although there may sometimes be cases where the fit between an individual university

11. Johnson and Turner (2009) explore some of the reasons beyond differences in faculty compensation that may limit adjustment to student demand, including the need to maintain a minimum scale in small departments, administrative constraints, and curricular requirements intended to temper demand in popular majors.
12. Writing more than two decades ago, Bowen and Sosa (1989) identify decreasing teaching loads as an avenue for adjustment and suggest that direct increases in salary would be a more efficient pathway to labor market clearing. Yet to the extent that universities may share the benefits of increased research productivity afforded by reduced teaching, incentives may be aligned in compensation arrangements providing the in-kind benefit of reduced teaching.

and faculty member is unusually good (in which case, there is some rent to be divided) or unusually bad (in which case, there is unlikely to be a long-lasting match).

We assume that the university maximizes an objective function[13] that depends positively on the quantity and quality of students taught and the quantity and quality of research. As noted above, we look only at arts and sciences departments, broadly defined to include computer science. In practice, the university has a complicated budget constraint because it has the possibility of engaging in a variety of activities that can generate revenue in excess of cost (or vice versa). Here we assume that in the background, the university has a well-defined budget constraint and understands the relationships among changes in research and teaching activity, revenue and cost, and the elements of the objective function.

Faculty members each have a utility function defined on salary, leisure, the quality of the work environment, time spent in various activities (e.g., teaching and research), quality of teaching, and research and reputation. Faculty tastes vary both within and across fields of expertise, as does faculty skill—that is, within departments, some faculty members are able to produce more or better research and teaching than others for the same measured input. At a given allocation of time to research and teaching, some faculty would prefer to increase teaching effort, and others would prefer to increase research, holding salaries constant.

The university's problem is to deploy its faculty (including both tenure- and nontenure-track) in a way that maximizes the value of the objective function. To keep the discussion simple, we adopt the conventional rubrics of teaching and research, subscripted by field, and we focus on the deployment of tenure-track faculty. Tenure-track faculty are especially interesting because, as a general matter, they can (and do) both teach and do research. A key margin regarding deployment of such faculty is the intradepartmental division between teaching and research, which will depend in part on the intradepartmental distribution of skills and tastes. This reasoning directly implies that within a department, we should observe that the best researchers should, on average, teach less than the best teachers (unless the best researchers have sufficiently—and surprisingly—strong preferences for teaching), where teaching less can be accomplished via course reduction (fewer courses) or less-onerous assignments (fewer students or students who are easier to teach per course).

The trick to evaluating this hypothesis is to measure research quality. In the absence of direct measures of research output, we can use our assump-

13. Universities are notorious for their complicated mechanisms of decision-making. Here we assume that the leadership nexus of president, provost, and dean has solved all the agency problems at those levels and has consistent preferences regarding what it would like chairs, faculty members, and everyone else to do, conditional on budget and so on, although that leadership nexus is not assumed to understand, say, the best way to teach physics or decode papyri.

tion that the university as a decision-maker is rational and cares about research reputation. The university values scholarly reputation and scholarly output. It doesn't know how to produce those things, but it is good at finding experts who do know how to produce those things in specific fields. Those experts are tenure-track faculty, organized into departments. The university tells the departments to hire great faculty, and by and large, it trusts the departments' judgments, in part because the university's goal of having an excellent scholarly reputation is aligned with departmental goals to advance departmental reputation.

Left to their own devices, the departments will hire the best research faculty that they can with the money that they are given, subject (probably) to meeting some minimum requirement for undergraduate teaching quality imposed by the preferences of members of the department and (almost certainly) by some set of constraints on quality and quantity of undergraduate education imposed by the university.[14] In particular, the university will often agree to supplement the department's salary and slot budgets in exchange for the department's teaching sufficiently more undergraduates in order to cover any increase in cost.

Scholarly reputation and output are produced, department by department, via technologies that are black boxes from the perspective of the university. In this setup, it is fairly straightforward to construct a model in which faculty salaries (and the net of other perks, such as graduate vs. undergraduate teaching) within a department should be a good indicator of quality-weighted research output. The marketplace in which field-specific faculty salaries are determined is driven almost entirely by research. Except for the fact that salaries are never reduced in nominal terms, the labor market should produce a set of salaries for tenure-track faculty in each department that give us a ranking (in the happy extreme, an exact measure of value marginal product) of faculty research production.

If salary levels (intradepartmentally only) are good measures of research quality/quantity and research skill isn't strongly positively correlated with a preference for allocating time to teaching, we should observe that highly paid faculty within a department do relatively little teaching on average and that the teaching they do has relatively high consumption value, either

---

14. Marc Nerlove (1972) constructs a model in which, at sufficiently low levels of teaching quantity and quality, teaching and research are complements. He draws a production possibility frontier for teaching and research (he includes graduate education as part of research) that has regions near the axes that slope up. In this formulation, even a department that cared only about research would do some teaching. Meanwhile, former Cornell University president Frank Rhodes (1998) asserts that the frontier slopes upward at low amounts of research. He quotes John Slaughter: "Research is to teaching as sin is to confession. If you don't participate in the former you have very little to say in the latter" (11). That these complementarities are evident to university leaders does not necessarily imply that they are evident to individuals or departments. In any case, departments in research universities generally act as if they live in the region where research and teaching are substitutes in production.

directly or as an input into research. This is exactly what we find in the empirical work below.[15]

A second margin of choice for faculty deployment is *inter*departmental. Noting that undergraduate tuition within the arts and sciences hardly varies by field (Stange 2015), the university has an interest in economizing on the cost of instruction, which in turn would suggest that it would want to have larger class sizes in fields where faculty are highly paid. But it's not that simple. The technology of teaching varies by field. Literature and other humanities are often taught in ways that require a high level of faculty-student interaction, including the provision of extended comments on multiple drafts of papers. Courses in science, math, and some social sciences, meanwhile, can often be organized without expressive writing and associated communication. Thus it's common to see introductory courses in quantitative fields that have hundreds of students, while courses at the same level in the humanities will have 30 students or fewer. The effect of such differences on the instructional cost per student seat can be much larger than the effect of differences (even by factors of two to one) in the average salaries of faculty in different fields.[16]

The technology of effective teaching and learning affects the nature of the game between the university and its departments. In all cases, the department would like to be generously supported in its research ambitions, while the university will generally undertake actions designed to lead the department to take into account the effects the volume and technology of its teaching have on the revenues available to the institution. Thus the total salary pool available to the department will generally depend positively on the number of students taught. To hire better research faculty (which is to say, more expensive faculty) the department must agree to teach more students. This is easier in some fields than in others. Indeed, where small classes are essential to effective teaching, there may be no feasible bargain to be struck that would increase the department's tuition-generated resources.

We note that in some universities, there are formal budget models that

15. Ron Ehrenberg has pointed out to us that there will be some cases where faculty stars with excellent research reputations can contribute to departmental and university reputations (and perhaps tuition levels) by teaching large undergraduate courses and allowing the institution to claim that undergraduates get to learn from, for example, Nobel Prize winners. This phenomenon is very much in the spirit of the optimizing framework we have sketched here. Where it occurs, it would weaken the negative relationship between research productivity and numbers of undergraduate students taught. Exploring the teaching deployment of "superstars" would be a useful exercise that we leave for future work.

16. It is also possible that faculty members in lower-paid fields, reflecting the relatively low opportunity cost of their time, are effective in influencing the administration and faculty governance to increase the number of slots in their departments. This hypothesis was suggested by Johnson and Turner (2009), who note the parallel with the finding from the corporate finance literature that weak divisions within firms are known to hold more than their optimal allocation of cash (from the perspective of shareholders), as the return to internal lobbying may be greater for executives in these units.

allocate tuition revenue to academic units, and in others, all or most such revenue is distributed centrally. For our purposes, what matters is that the university leadership can see and act upon the connection between teaching activities and tuition revenue, enabling it to negotiate (either directly or via manipulating budgeting formulas) with academic departments regarding faculty salaries, size, and workloads.[17]

6.3   Empirical Strategy and Data

Our model of faculty allocation and compensation in university production functions references the circumstances of research universities and, in particular, those disciplines in the arts and sciences, broadly defined. We do not look at professional schools in areas such as medicine and law. The assignments of faculty in professional schools to teaching and research are often separated from central university resource allocation because professional schools often have substantial autonomy with regard to pricing, admissions, and hiring decisions.[18]

6.3.1   Institutional Microdata

To examine how variation in compensation affects the allocation of faculty resources in the university context, we look at microdata from two public research universities—the University of Michigan and the University of Virginia. These institutions are broadly representative of AAU universities, which are intensive in research while also producing a significant number of undergraduate and graduate degree recipients. The University of Virginia and the University of Michigan share very competitive undergraduate degree programs that are generally ranked among the top 25 universities nationally and the top 2 or 3 public universities. The University of Michigan is somewhat larger than the University of Virginia,[19] generates considerably more research funding, and is generally regarded as having a greater number of highly ranked graduate programs. We believe it is reasonable to expect the

17. See Courant and Knepp (2002) for a discussion of activity-based budgeting. The kind of bargaining that we are talking about here would be facilitated by a system that allocated tuition revenue at the level of the school or college (or the department, although the latter configuration would be unusual and does not apply at either Michigan or Virginia). For the period we are analyzing in this chapter, Michigan allocated tuition revenue to deans such that the arts and sciences dean was empowered to engage in bargaining with departments, whereas at Virginia, the bargain was generally undertaken at a higher level of administration, with teaching activity only weakly aligned with school-level resources. Beginning in 2015, Virginia adopted a new budget model with a resource allocation broadly similar to the Michigan model.

18. It is also the case that the compensation of faculty in business schools and medical schools is determined differently in professional schools than in arts and sciences and, especially in medical schools, is much more complicated. So the exclusion of professional schools helps improve the tractability of the analysis.

19. In fall 2014, total enrollment was 43,625, with 28,395 undergraduates at the University of Michigan relative to 23,732 with 16,483 undergraduates at the University of Virginia.

findings from these universities to apply directly to peer public and private institutions in the AAU, even as there is surely some institution-specific variation. It is useful to underscore the observation that individual-level data on faculty salaries at private universities are nearly impossible to obtain, while public universities make such information available regularly.

In an effort to focus the analysis on a finite number of well-defined disciplines, we look at 11 disciplines that constitute separate administrative departments at nearly every research university and draw from the humanities (English, history, philosophy), the social sciences (economics, politics, sociology, psychology), and the natural and computational sciences (math, physics, chemistry, and computer science). These disciplines are intended to span broad differences in types of instruction, such as the emphasis on written expression, lab experiences, and quantitative analysis. In addition, there are notable differences among these disciplines in faculty compensation as well as student demand.

For both the University of Virginia and the University of Michigan, we have combined data on faculty compensation and course-level records of enrollment, which also identify the instructor of record.[20] For both universities, we are able to record salaries for all regular instructional faculty, which proves to cover the great majority of courses offered. The course-level data include the instructor, course title, course type, enrollment level, and course number, which allows for the distinction between graduate and undergraduate courses. For consistency, we focus on traditional "group instruction" courses and do not analyze independent study listings or speaker series (workshops). For the University of Michigan, courses and salary data extend from 2002 to 2015. For the University of Virginia, course offering data extend from the present to 1990, while the faculty salary data are available for only the three most recent years. There are 52,556 different records from our focal departments from the 1990–91 academic year to 2014–15 for the University of Virginia alone.

The empirical strategy proceeds in two related parts. The first set of questions focuses on department-level variation, where we assess differences by discipline and changes over time in teaching allocations in relation to salary levels. The second piece of the analysis examines within-department variation in compensation and teaching.

6.3.2   Descriptive Measures

For the purpose of this analysis, discipline-level variation in faculty salaries is assumed to be exogenous. In turn, we assume that individual faculty

20. Data from the University of Michigan were obtained from the Learning Analytics Task Force and from public records of salaries; data for the University of Virginia combine the publicly available faculty salary file with comprehensive "web scraping" of the course-offering directory, which was originally conducted by Lou Bloomfield.

salaries are determined on the national market by competitive forces.[21] To provide a baseline, columns in the right-hand panel of table 6.2 show faculty salaries by rank for the disciplines that are the focus of our analysis for the University of Virginia and the University of Michigan. One broad point is the notable correlation in salaries across fields—economics is the most highly paid field, while English is consistently at or near the bottom. Second, salary differences between the universities are much smaller at the assistant level than the full level, likely reflecting the greater reward for (highly variable) research productivity among the full professors. Overall, between-university differences in compensation reflect, in part, differences in the "ranking" or research productivity of departments. While faculty in English and history receive broadly similar compensation, faculty in sociology are far better compensated at the University of Michigan than at the University of Virginia, reflecting both the higher research ranking and greater quantitative focus of the Michigan department.[22] Table 6.3 illustrates some of the differences between the universities in rankings and research measures.

In terms of the program offerings, our focal departments all award both undergraduate and doctorate degrees. Again, there are some differences reflective of the overall institutional scale (the University of Michigan is larger than the University of Virginia), but there are similarities in terms of variations across disciplines in scale and the relative representation of graduate and undergraduate students.

6.4   Empirical Evidence

6.4.1   Between-Department Analysis

Teaching students is, perhaps, the most easily recognized "output" of an academic unit, with this coin of the realm often captured in measures of student enrollment or student credit hours.[23] Our interest is in the alignment between the faculty inputs and the courses taught between departments within universities. Table 6.4 shows the distribution of course seats in total and relative to the overall faculty counts. The provision of course seats relative to the faculty head count varies markedly across departments for both universities. Still, the "tails" of the distributions are quite similar between the two institutions: English has the lowest ratio of student course enroll-

21. Beyond faculty productivity, some differences in compensation between the University of Michigan and the University of Virginia may reflect differential program quality or compensating differences associated with the different geographic regions.

22. Indeed, the finding that between-institution variation in faculty compensation within disciplines is linked to variation in faculty research productivity between institutions follows the more general result from Ehrenberg, McGraw, and Mrdjenovic (2006).

23. While many universities have adopted budget models that tie revenue flows to enrollment (RCM), few such models allow for decentralization and incentives at the level of the individual department; instead, they limit incentives to the school level.

Table 6.3 Comparative characteristics by discipline, University of Virginia and University of Michigan

Program name	U.S. News ranking	Average citations per publication	Percentage of faculty with grants, 2006	Average number of PhDs graduated, 2002–6	Average GRE scores, 2004–6	Tenured faculty as a percentage of total faculty, 2006
University of Michigan–Ann Arbor						
Chemistry	15	2.49	84.0	31.20	732	86.0
Computer science	13	N/D	81.6	17.40	800	83.0
Economics	13	1.86	54.9	15.00	791	73.0
English language & literature	13	N/D	11.5	8.20	716	84.0
History	7	N/D	17.6	16.40	654	90.0
Mathematics	9	1.03	84.8	14.40	800	86.0
Philosophy		N/D	16.2	4.20	699	84.0
Physics	11	2.56	88.3	12.60	793	84.0
Political science	4	1.87	54.7	14.00	718	86.0
Psychology	4	3.52	66.4	25.60	728	83.0
Sociology	4	2.66	50.0	11.40	724	83.0
University of Virginia						
Chemistry	49	2.54	62.6	16.60	715	93.0
Computer science	29	N/D	75.0	4.40	789	64.0
Economics	30	1.23	34.8	8.20	783	52.0
English language & literature	10	N/D	15.9	12.40	697	90.0
History	20	N/D	17.9	14.20	657	90.0
Mathematics	52	0.71	65.1	4.80	792	79.0
Philosophy		N/D	15.4	1.40	676	92.0
Physics	44	2.46	87.9	7.40	779	66.0
Politics	36	0.47	25.0	9.20	699	86.0
Psychology	26	2.77	80.6	10.80	722	65.0
Sociology	35	0.95	46.2	4.40	674	59.0

Source: U.S. News and World Report and National Academies of Science "Assessment of Research and Doctoral Programs" (2010).

Table 6.4   Student course enrollment relative to faculty staffing, 2014–15

Field	Enrollment			Student-course/faculty ratio		
	Total	Undergraduate	Graduate	Total	Undergraduate	Graduate
University of Virginia						
Chemistry	4,990	4,580	410	161.0	147.7	13.2
Computer science	5,688	5,278	410	172.4	159.9	12.4
Economics	6,533	6,237	296	186.7	178.2	8.5
English	1,727	1,608	119	35.2	32.8	2.4
History	3,869	3,811	58	77.4	76.2	1.2
Math	2,656	2,088	568	83.0	65.3	17.8
Philosophy	1,852	1,572	15	108.9	92.5	0.9
Physics	2,749	2,509	240	91.6	83.6	8.0
Political science	4,529	4,425	104	122.4	119.6	2.8
Psychology	5,352	5,187	165	133.8	129.7	4.1
Sociology	2,131	2,082	49	106.6	104.1	2.5
University of Michigan						
Chemistry	10,067	9,672	395	193.6	186.0	7.6
Computer science	8,125	6,430	1,695	71.9	56.9	15.0
Economics	7,320	6,429	891	120.0	105.4	14.6
English	3,325	2,998	327	30.5	27.5	3.0
History	5,112	5,031	81	56.8	55.9	0.9
Math	10,123	8,967	1,156	82.3	72.9	9.4
Philosophy	1,786	1,722	64	63.8	61.5	2.3
Physics	4,290	4,026	264	71.5	67.1	4.4
Political science	3,691	3,416	275	67.1	62.1	5.0
Psychology	11,848	11,423	425	108.7	104.8	3.9
Sociology	2,758	2,522	237	86.2	78.8	7.4

Source: Authors' tabulations.

ment to faculty at 35.2 for Virginia and 30.5 for Michigan, while chemistry and economics are disciplines near the top, with ratios of student course enrollment to faculty 4 to 5 times higher at both institutions. Were faculty similarly priced across disciplines, such differences in the concentration of faculty relative to enrollments would create enormous variation in the cost of instruction across fields.

When we shift to thinking about expenditures on faculty relative to courses and students taught, the picture shifts dramatically. A rudimentary indicator of the average cost of a course offering in a department is the total faculty salary bill relative to course seats taught.[24] Table 6.5 shows two measures that portray similar evidence: the first column includes all faculty, including those

24. Of course, faculty are compensated for research as well as teaching. This metric is appropriate to the extent that the research share of faculty compensation is the same across departments. To the extent that research shares are larger in the most highly compensated departments, these measures will overstate the teaching costs in relatively research-intensive departments.

Table 6.5   **Estimated faculty cost per seat, University of Michigan and University of Virginia, 2014–15**

Field	Cost per enrolled student	
	All faculty ($)	Currently teaching ($)
University of Virginia		
Chemistry	760	741
Computer science	764	673
Economics	847	777
English	2,837	2,217
History	1,335	1,092
Mathematics	1,229	1,229
Philosophy	938	898
Physics	1,193	1,058
Political science	945	718
Psychology	921	736
Sociology	962	890
Total	985	854
University of Michigan		
Chemistry	554	528
Computer science	1,848	1,780
Economics	1,312	1,296
English	2,393	2,111
History	1,548	1,548
Mathematics	1,095	1,057
Philosophy	1,883	1,883
Physics	1,535	1,320
Political science	1,694	1,570
Psychology	1,121	800
Sociology	1,677	1,369

Source: Authors' tabulations.

on leave, while the second only includes those actively teaching in 2014–15. What we see is a very dramatic narrowing—and in some cases, a reversal—of the relative differences among departments in the cost per student, while departments with the highest salary levels are not those with the greatest cost of educational delivery. Two disciplines merit a particular focus. English is an outlier on the high end for both Virginia ($2,837) and Michigan ($2,393). In contrast, economics—which has the highest average salaries—is near the bottom of the distribution of the cost of course-seat provision.

Figure 6.5 illustrates the central finding that overall salary levels are negatively correlated with the cost of providing a course seat across disciplines. This finding is consistent with our theoretical prediction that universities adjust to variations in input costs by altering the organization of teaching. A corollary to this point is that we would expect faculty costs per seat to change by less than discipline-specific changes in faculty salaries over time.

It is worth noting that the consequences for educational quality of com-

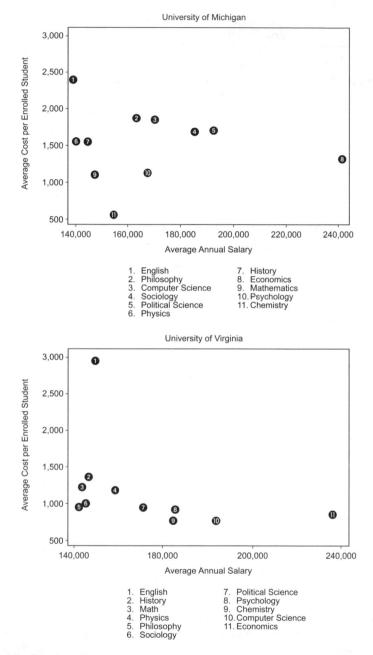

Fig. 6.5   Faculty salaries and cost per seat at University of Virginia and University of Michigan, 2014–15

Source: Authors' tabulations. This version of the table presents the average salary of full professors on the *x* axis; the next version will use the average salary of all faculty, which produces a qualitatively similar presentation.

pensating for higher salaries via larger class sizes will vary as a function of the way in which disciplines produce and share knowledge. In humanities fields, it is often the case that being able to express knowledge is inextricably bound up with the knowledge itself, in which case good pedagogy requires substantial writing (or filming, or podcast creating) with careful evaluating and editing on the part of the instructor. In contrast, many more quantitative fields can be taught and assessed without close interaction among the material, the student, and the instructor. We expect that in all cases it is possible to increase class sizes at the cost of reducing educational quality. However, the terms of the trade-off may differ greatly by field.

To test the hypothesis that the technology of teaching differs across disciplines in ways that may limit class size expansion and the organization of classroom activities, we coded syllabi from six fields (English, economics, history, philosophy, physics, and psychology) at the University of Virginia and the University of Michigan. Our sample is effectively one of convenience, as we chose randomly conditional on the availability of syllabi with the aim of coding one course each at the introductory, intermediate, and upper levels. We present some examples in table 6.6, and some basic intuitive points are clear: introductory courses are generally larger than upper-level courses, and some disciplines (particularly economics and psychology) have relatively large courses. Other points suggestive of differences in "technology" are apparent in the grading and writing requirements. In economics and physics, the majority of the evaluation is based on examination, while writing is minimal. In English, history, and philosophy, writing and participation components of evaluation are the norm. We summarize this information in the regressions results shown in table 6.7: both discipline and course scale have an appreciable effect on outcomes, such as the percent of the grade determined by examination and whether writing or participation is part of the evaluation. Our favored interpretation is that variation in the nature of the material and the nature of learning across disciplines drives these results.

6.4.2   Intradepartmental Analysis

In section 6.3, we hypothesized that within departments, research productivity should be negatively correlated with faculty teaching effort and that we could use salary as a measure of research productivity. That is, controlling for rank and recognizing that the market for faculty at this level is determined largely by research reputation, we would expect a negative relationship between salary and teaching activity within a department.

We controlled for rank by running the regression on full professors only. Variation in the salaries of assistant professors generally derives from accidents of history. The starting salary in the year of hire is determined in the relevant marketplace, and salaries then move according to budgetary circumstances. In our experience, it's unusual for differences in assistant professors' salaries to reflect much else. Associate professors come in two

Table 6.6   Field-specific examples of requirements in undergraduate courses

Name	Title	Instructor rank	Enrollment	Exam (0,1)	Writing (0,1)	Participate/ present (0,1)	Exam counts for > 50%	Paper/Writing counts for > 50%
University of Virginia								
ECON 2010	Principles of Microeconomics	Lecturer	298	1	0	0	1	0
ECON 3030	Money and Banking	Assistant prof.	83	1	0	0	1	0
ECON 4210	International Trade: Theory and Policy	Professor	17	1	1	1	1	0
ENMC 4530	J. M. Coetzee in His Times	Associate prof.	9	0	1	1	0	1
ENNC 3110	English Poetry and Prose of the Nineteenth Century	Professor	19	1	1	1	0	1
ENRN 3250	Milton: Origins, Transgressions, Revolutions	Associate prof.	29	1	1	0	0	1
HIEU 2101	Jewish History I: The Ancient and Medieval Experience	Associate prof.	40	1	1	1	0	0
HIEU 3390	Nazi Germany	Lecturer	61	1	1	1	1	0
HIST 4501	Scandals in History	Associate prof.	8	0	1	1	0	1
PHIL 2450	Philosophy of Science	Professor	7	1	1	0	0	1
PHIL 3710	Ethics	Professor	20	1	1	0	0	1
PHIL 3999	Philosophical Perspectives on Liberty	Professor	25	1	1	0	1	0
PHYS 2620	Modern Physics	Professor	84	1	0	0	1	0
PSYC 2150	Introduction to Cognition	Associate prof.	334	1	1	0	1	0
PSYC 3410	Abnormal Psychology	Professor	290	1	1	0	1	0
PSYC 4110	Psycholinguistics	Associate prof.	22	1	1	1	0	0

University of Michigan

Course	Title	Rank	N				
ECON 101-200	Principles of Economics I—Microeconomics	Lecturer	322	1	0	0	0
ECON 310-001	Money and Banking	Lecturer	184	1	1	0	0
ECON 340-001	International Economics	Professor	105	1	1	0	0
ENGLISH 298-007	Introduction to Literary Studies: Shakespeare, Race, and the 20th Century	Professor	22	0	0	1	1
ENGLISH 313-010	Topics in Literary Studies: The Road Trip in American Literature	Professor	68	0	1	0	1
ENGLISH 451-001	Literature 1600–1830	Professor	28	1	0	1	0
HISTORY 105-001	Introduction to Religion: From Rastafari to the Sun Dance	Professor	43	1	1	1	0
HISTORY 214-001	Modern Europe	Associate prof.	29	1	1	1	0
HISTORY 386-001	The Holocaust: The Fate of Jews, 1933–1949	Professor	89	1	1	1	0
HISTORY 451-001	Japan's Modern Transformations	Associate prof.	26	1	1	1	0
PHIL 180-001	Introductory Logic	Associate prof.	131	1	0	1	1
PHIL 355-001	Contemporary Moral Problems	Associate prof.	130	0	1	1	0
PHIL 361-001	Ethics	Professor	49	1	1	1	0
PHYSICS 240-100	General Physics II	Professor	147	1	0	0	1
PHYSICS 340-001	Waves, Heat, and Light	Assistant prof.	29	1	1	0	1
PHYSICS 401-001	Intermediate Mechanics	Assistant prof.	40	1	1	0	1
PSYCH 240-020	Introduction to Cognitive Psychology	Lecturer	293	1	0	0	1
PSYCH 250-020	Human Development	Lecturer	285	1	1	1	1
PSYCH 438-001	Hormones and Behavior	Associate prof.	131	1	0	1	0

Table 6.7   Association between course requirements and class size and department

Explanatory vars.	Exam pct (1)	Writing pct (2)	Writing (1/0) (3)	Participate/present (1/0) (4)
Enrollment	0.000668***	–0.000230	–0.000964*	–0.000858
	(0.000211)	(0.000152)	(0.000489)	(0.000596)
Economics	0.366***	–0.437***	–0.609***	–0.377
	(0.0937)	(0.0946)	(0.168)	(0.227)
English	–0.317***	0.144	0.130	0.0852
	(0.0742)	(0.0949)	(0.0826)	(0.178)
History	–0.0169	–0.164*	0.0114	0.260*
	(0.0884)	(0.0928)	(0.113)	(0.136)
Physics	0.181	–0.410***	–0.732***	–0.725***
	(0.111)	(0.109)	(0.124)	(0.136)
Psychology	0.213*	–0.311***	–0.233	–0.0614
	(0.111)	(0.116)	(0.205)	(0.215)
University of	0.0151	–0.00936	–0.217**	0.183*
Michigan	(0.0524)	(0.0524)	(0.0835)	(0.0970)
Constant	0.369***	0.517***	1.067***	0.634***
	(0.0703)	(0.0799)	(0.0680)	(0.173)
Observations	68	68	68	68
R-squared	0.722	0.630	0.648	0.531

Note: Philosophy is the omitted department. Convenience sample of 68 courses in 6 disciplines at the University of Virginia and the University of Michigan. *** $p < 0.01$, ** $p < 0.05$, * $p < 0.1$.

flavors. Some are progressing nicely toward a second promotion, and if we could identify these, it would be sensible to include them in the model with a control for their rank. Unfortunately, the other flavor of associate professor is progressing slowly if at all, and a model that describes their salary behavior well does not fit the first flavor of associate professor. Based on these considerations and our theoretical discussion of the expected power of salary as an indicator of research quality, we limit our empirical analysis to full professors, whose salaries are likely to reflect current or recent market circumstances.

Table 6.8 reports the effects of salary (in 2014 USD) and departmental fixed effects (the omitted department is history) on the numbers of courses and students taught using University of Michigan data from 2002 to 2014.[25] The regression also included fixed effects for each year (except 2002). The regression confirms quite powerfully our prediction regarding salary and teaching. The magnitudes are not trivial. The coefficients on salary reported in the table are in thousands of dollars, implying that an increase in salary of $10k leads to a reduction in the number of undergraduate courses of

25. Results for the University of Virginia are qualitatively similar though somewhat less precisely estimated given a shorter panel of salary data.

Table 6.8 Within-department determinants of courses and students taught, University of Michigan

Variables	All courses (1)	Undergraduate courses (2)	Graduate courses (3)	All students (4)	Undergraduate students (5)	Graduate students (6)
Salary (thousands)	-0.00461*** (0.000319)	-0.00568*** (0.000319)	0.00107*** (0.000229)	-0.343*** (0.0264)	-0.354*** (0.0270)	0.0114*** (0.00333)
Computer science	0.140** (0.0685)	-0.287*** (0.0655)	0.427*** (0.0391)	-0.628 (4.023)	-14.43*** (4.063)	13.80*** (0.819)
Chemistry	-0.131 (0.0941)	-0.452*** (0.0858)	0.321*** (0.0564)	35.86*** (10.41)	30.61*** (10.45)	5.250*** (0.692)
Economics	0.673*** (0.104)	-0.153** (0.0753)	0.826*** (0.0754)	43.93*** (8.001)	31.06*** (7.989)	12.87*** (1.325)
Math	0.202*** (0.0704)	-0.479*** (0.0665)	0.681*** (0.0445)	-13.54*** (4.107)	-25.43*** (4.155)	11.90*** (0.689)
Philosophy	0.390*** (0.0985)	0.210** (0.0926)	0.181*** (0.0536)	-0.426 (5.255)	-1.481 (5.254)	1.054*** (0.357)
Physics	-0.525*** (0.0768)	-0.540*** (0.0739)	0.0151 (0.0407)	-24.20*** (4.218)	-27.81*** (4.250)	3.604*** (0.632)
Politics	0.307*** (0.0910)	-0.204*** (0.0774)	0.511*** (0.0493)	48.52*** (8.055)	42.87*** (8.044)	5.653*** (0.511)
Psychology	-0.165** (0.0789)	-0.595*** (0.0685)	0.430*** (0.0473)	5.457 (5.486)	1.010 (5.493)	4.447*** (0.459)
Sociology	0.147 (0.117)	-0.423*** (0.0887)	0.569*** (0.0689)	-7.399 (5.283)	-14.94*** (5.040)	7.539*** (0.885)
English	-0.169** (0.0844)	-0.455*** (0.0776)	0.286*** (0.0402)	-21.47*** (5.803)	-25.09*** (5.819)	3.615*** (0.341)
Other	-1.053*** (0.0656)	-0.882*** (0.0604)	-0.171*** (0.0318)	-18.85*** (4.445)	-18.66*** (4.448)	-0.191 (0.381)
Constant	2.552*** (0.0916)	2.302*** (0.0860)	0.250*** (0.0562)	105.4*** (6.186)	104.8*** (6.238)	0.593 (0.793)
Observations	5,351	5,351	5,351	5,351	5,351	5,351
R-squared	0.158	0.138	0.140	0.075	0.076	0.124

Notes: Robust standard errors in parentheses. *** $p < 0.01$, ** $p < 0.05$, * $p < 0.1$.
Faculty-level data recording salary, courses taught, and number of students for academic years 2002–3 to 2014–15 for the University of Michigan. Regressions include year fixed effects.

about 5 percent of a course per year and a reduction in the number of undergraduate students by about 3.5 per year. The results suggest that superstars whose salary is $100k more than the mean teach half an undergrad course less and about 35 fewer undergraduate students. For some departments, 35 undergraduates per full professor per year is more than the average load. Additionally, the coefficients for graduate students and graduate courses are positive and significant, consistent with the idea that graduate teaching has amenity value for faculty, or is part of the production of research, or most likely, both in some combination.

The regression reported on in table 6.8 and the preceding paragraph looks at all faculty and controls for departmental differences via departmental fixed effects. In table 6.9, we organize the analysis somewhat differently, running separate regressions for each department at Michigan (with year fixed effects, as in table 6.9). As before, there is a consistent and generally significant negative relationship between full professors' salaries within departments and the number of undergraduate students and courses taught in that department. In this formulation, we also see clearly that there is substantial variation in the slope of the relationship. In psychology, economics, and chemistry, $10,000 in annual salary is associated with a reduction of about six students per year. In philosophy and history, our estimate is about a third the size, and in English and sociology, $10,000 in pay is associated with a reduction of fewer than 1.5 students per year. As in our earlier specification, the numbers of undergrads taught falls with full professors' salaries, while the number of graduate students taught rises. These patterns are also evident in figure 6.6, which multiplies the estimates by 50, showing the changes in students taught associated with a $50,000 difference in salary.

6.5   Conclusion and Thoughts Ahead

Tenure-track faculty in research universities teach and do research. Over the past several decades, the relative prices—in terms of wages paid to faculty—of those two activities have changed markedly. The price of research has gone up way more than the price of teaching. Salaries have risen much more in elite research universities than in universities generally. This is quite consistent with models in which compensation depends on tournaments and rankings, and the most successful workers can command a substantial premium relative to those who are merely successful (Lazear and Rosen 1981; Rosen 1981, 1986).

Departments in research universities (the more so the more elite) must pay high salaries in order to employ research-productive faculty. These faculty, in turn, contribute most to the universities' goals (which include teaching as well as research) by following their comparative advantage and teaching less often and also teaching in ways that are complementary with research—notably graduate courses. The university pays these faculty well because

Table 6.9   Field-specific within-field regressions of teaching assignment on salary, University of Michigan

	All courses (1)	Undergraduate courses (2)	Graduate courses (3)	All students (4)	Undergraduate students (5)	Graduate students (6)
Economics	-0.000147	-0.00774***	0.00759***	-0.482***	-0.609***	0.127***
	(0.00134)	(0.000846)	(0.00100)	(0.119)	(0.119)	(0.0205)
Chemistry	-0.00622***	-0.00532***	-0.000903*	-0.639***	-0.633***	-0.00598
	(0.00127)	(0.00136)	(0.000530)	(0.186)	(0.189)	(0.00855)
Computer science	-0.00474***	-0.00413***	-0.000602	-0.259***	-0.209***	-0.0496***
	(0.000781)	(0.000749)	(0.000623)	(0.0448)	(0.0480)	(0.0137)
English	-0.000609	-0.00420***	0.00259***	-0.120	-0.146*	0.0260***
	(0.00184)	(0.00162)	(0.000881)	(0.0846)	(0.0847)	(0.00882)
History	-0.00778***	-0.00772***	-5.59e-05	-0.241***	-0.244***	0.00292
	(0.00116)	(0.00108)	(0.000495)	(0.0464)	(0.0460)	(0.00323)
Math	-0.00680***	-0.00554***	-0.00127*	-0.181*	-0.172	-0.00883
	(0.00143)	(0.00171)	(0.000752)	(0.109)	(0.116)	(0.0162)
Philosophy	-0.00494*	-0.00526**	0.000322	-0.204*	-0.210*	0.00616
	(0.00251)	(0.00210)	(0.00151)	(0.112)	(0.112)	(0.0100)
Political science	-0.00111	-0.00417***	0.00306***	-0.172	-0.205	0.0331***
	(0.00131)	(0.000965)	(0.000726)	(0.123)	(0.126)	(0.00778)
Psychology	-0.00774***	-0.00967***	0.00194***	-0.583***	-0.599***	0.0163**
	(0.00106)	(0.000917)	(0.000747)	(0.0839)	(0.0808)	(0.00763)
Sociology	-0.00425***	-0.00354***	-0.000703	-0.105**	-0.104***	-0.00213
	(0.00111)	(0.000724)	(0.000748)	(0.0411)	(0.0366)	(0.00982)

Notes: Faculty-level data recording salary, courses taught, and number of students for academic years 2002–3 to 2014–15 for the University of Michigan. Each cell-standard error indicates the coefficient on salary (measured in thousands) for a regression with the indicated teaching measure (column headings); regressions include year fixed effects. *** $p < 0.01$, ** $p < 0.05$, * $p < 0.1$.

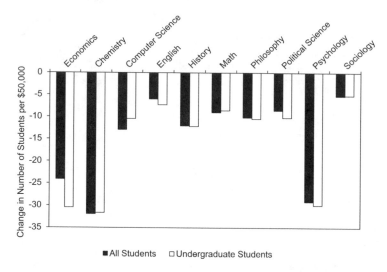

Fig. 6.6   Change in students taught within departments per $50,000 in salary
Source: See table 6.9. Estimates based on within-department regressions of the effect of individual faculty salary on teaching assignment.

they are especially good at research. It makes perfect sense that they would also have relatively low teaching loads (along with relatively high research expectations, which we don't observe directly).

In addition to deploying faculty productively within departments, the university has an interest in providing its curriculum efficiently—which is to say, at the lowest cost consistent with other desiderata, including quality and the ability to produce tuition revenue. The two most important features that relate to faculty deployment across departments are faculty salaries and class sizes. We observe large differences in both, with the faculty in the highest-paid departments tending to have the largest average class sizes, resulting in "cost per seat" being essentially uncorrelated with salaries for the departments we have studied at Michigan and Virginia.

A striking finding at both institutions is that the cost per seat is much higher in English than in any other department, notwithstanding the fact that salaries in English are at the low end of the distribution. As a matter of arithmetic, this is the result of relatively small class sizes in English. Why are class sizes there so small? We expect that it's because the technology of teaching and learning in English (and, plausibly, in other fields where detailed interpretation of text is an essential part of what is to be learned) is such that it is difficult or impossible to teach effectively in large classes. This is in contrast to, say, economics or chemistry, where learning what is in the textbook and working on relatively well-defined problems are much easier to scale up.

To be sure, economists would also like to teach small classes, both introductory and advanced, but they also like to have strong colleagues across the discipline. The loss in teaching quality and the amenity value of teaching associated with teaching large introductory sections (and large advanced courses) are easily worth the gain of paying (and being paid) what the market requires for good faculty.[26] Based on our analysis in table 6.9, that trade-off is on average less salutary in the humanities. Our analysis shows that departments in which close engagement with the text is likely to be an essential part of teaching and evaluation relies on interpretation (writing, presentation) face fewer trade-offs between increases in salary and reductions in students taught.

If we accept that the value placed on research in an elite research university is warranted, we conclude that the deployment of faculty is generally consistent with rational behavior on the part of those universities. Faculty salaries vary for a variety of reasons, and the universities respond to that variation by economizing on the most expensive faculty while attending to differences in teaching technologies across fields.

References

Autor, David. 2014. "Skills, Education, and the Rise of Earnings Inequality among the 'Other 99 Percent.'" *Science* 344 (6186): 843–51.

Bound, John, Michael Lovenheim, and Sarah Turner. 2010. "Why Have College Completion Rates Declined? An Analysis of Changing Student Preparation and Collegiate Resources." *American Economic Journal: Applied Economics* 2 (3): 129–57.

Bowen, William. 2012. "Cost Trends, the 'Cost Disease,' and Productivity in Higher Education." Tanner Lectures, Stanford University. http://www.ithaka.org/sites/default/files/files/ITHAKA-TheCostDiseaseinHigherEducation.pdf.

———. 2013. "Academia Online: Musings (Some Unconventional)." ITHAKA. http://ithaka.org/sites/default/files/files/ithaka-stafford-lecture-final.pdf.

Bowen, William, and Julie Ann Sosa. 1989. *Prospects for Faculty in the Arts and Sciences*. Princeton: Princeton University Press.

Breneman, David, and Richard Freeman. 1974. *Forecasting the Ph.D. Labor Market: Pitfalls for Policy*. Technical report no. 2. National Board on Graduate Education. Washington, DC: National Academy of Sciences Press.

Campos, Paul. 2015. "The Real Reason College Tuition Costs So Much." *New York Times*, April 4. http://www.nytimes.com/2015/04/05/opinion/sunday/the-real-reason-college-tuition-costs-so-much.html?_r=0.

Courant, Paul N., and Marilyn Knepp. 2002. "Activity Based Budgeting at the University of Michigan." In *Incentive-Based Budgeting Systems in Public Universities*, edited by Douglas Priest et al., 137–60. Cheltenham: Edward Elgar.

---

26. A related adjustment that may be adopted by departments with high salaries combined with teaching demands is further division of labor between faculty conducting research and those teaching to include the appointment of "master teachers" to teach core and introductory classes (Figlio, Schapiro, and Soter 2015).

Ehrenberg, Ronald, Marquise McGraw, and Jesenka Mrdjenovic. 2006. "Why Do Field Differentials in Average Faculty Salaries Vary across Universities?" *Economics of Education Review* 25 (3): 241–48.

Figlio, David, Morton Schapiro, and Kevin Soter. 2015. "Are Tenure Track Professors Better Teachers?" *Review of Economics and Statistics* 97 (4): 715–24.

Freeman, Richard. 1976. "A Cobweb Model of the Supply and Starting Salary of New Engineers." *Industrial and Labor Relations Review* 29:236–48.

Hoxby, Caroline. 2009. "The Changing Selectivity of American Colleges." *Journal of Economic Perspectives* 23 (4): 95–118. doi: 10.1257/jep.23.4.95.

Jacob, Brian, Brian McCall, and Kevin Stange. 2018. "College as Country Club: Do Colleges Cater to Students' Preferences for Consumption?" *Journal of Labor Economics* 36 (2): 309–48.

Johnson, William, and Sarah Turner. 2009. "Faculty without Students: Resource Allocation in Higher Education." *Journal of Economic Perspectives* 23 (2): 169–89.

Lazear, Edward, and Sherwin Rosen. 1981. "Rank-Order Tournaments as Optimum Labor Contracts." *Journal of Political Economy* 89 (5): 841–64.

National Academy of Science. 2000. *Forecasting Demand and Supply of Doctoral Scientists and Engineers: Report of a Workshop on Methodology.* Washington, DC: The National Academies Press. https://doi.org/10.17226/9865.

Nerlove, Marc. 1972. "On Tuition and the Costs of Higher Education: Prolegomena to a Conceptual Framework." *Journal of Political Economy* 80 (3, part 2: Investment in Education: The Equity-Efficiency Quandary): S178–S218.

Rhodes, Frank. 1998. "The University and Its Critics." In *Universities and Their Leadership,* edited by William G. Bowen and Harold T. Shapiro, 3–14. Princeton: Princeton University Press.

Rosen, Sherwin. 1981. "The Economics of Superstars." *American Economic Review* 71 (5): 845–58.

———. 1986. "Prizes and Incentives in Elimination Tournaments." *American Economic Review* 76 (4): 701–15.

Sallee, James M., Alexandra M. Resch, and Paul N. Courant. 2008. "On the Optimal Allocation of Students and Resources in a System of Higher Education." *B.E. Journal of Economic Analysis and Policy* 8 (1): 1–26.

Stange, Kevin. 2015. "Differential Pricing in Undergraduate Education: Effects on Degree Production by Field." *Journal of Policy Analysis and Management* 34 (1): 107–35.

Turner, Sarah. 2015. "The Impact of the Financial Crisis on Faculty Labor Markets." In *How the Financial Crisis and Great Recession Affected Higher Education,* edited by Jeffrey R. Brown and Caroline M. Hoxby, 175–207. Chicago: University of Chicago Press.

Measuring Instructor Effectiveness in Higher Education

Pieter De Vlieger, Brian Jacob, and Kevin Stange

7.1 Introduction

Professors and instructors are a chief input into the higher education production process, yet we know very little about their role in promoting student success. There is growing evidence that teacher quality is an important determinant of student achievement in K–12, with some school districts identifying and rewarding teachers with high value added. Yet relatively little is known about the importance of or correlates of instructor effectiveness in postsecondary education. Such information may be particularly important at the postsecondary level, in which administrators often have substantial discretion to reallocate teaching assignments not only within a specific class of instructors (e.g., tenured faculty) but across instructor types (e.g., adjuncts vs. tenured faculty).

There are a number of challenges to measuring effectiveness in the context of higher education. Unlike in K–12, there are rarely standardized test scores to use as an outcome. Furthermore, to the extent that college courses

Pieter De Vlieger is a graduate student in economics at the University of Michigan.

Brian Jacob is the Walter H. Annenberg Professor of Education Policy and professor of economics and education at the University of Michigan and a research associate of the National Bureau of Economic Research.

Kevin Stange is associate professor of public policy at the University of Michigan and a research associate of the National Bureau of Economic Research.

We are very grateful to Hinrich Eylers and Ashok Yadav at the University of Phoenix for many discussions and for providing access to the data. This chapter was prepared for the NBER Conference on Productivity in Higher Education, held on June 1, 2016. We also are grateful for useful feedback from Caroline Hoxby and other participants at the conference and at the University of Michigan Causal Inference in Education Research Seminar. For acknowledgments, sources of research support, and disclosure of the authors' material financial relationships, if any, please see http://www.nber.org/chapters/c13880.ack.

and majors intend to teach a very wide variety of knowledge and skills, it is harder to imagine an appropriate outcome as a conceptual matter. The issue of nonrandom student sorting across instructors is arguably more serious in the context of higher education because students have a great deal of flexibility in the choice of classes and the timing of these classes. Finally, one might have serious concerns about the attribution of a particular skill to a specific instructor given the degree to which knowledge spills over across courses in college (the importance of calculus in intermediate microeconomics or introductory physics, the value of English composition in a history class where the grade is based almost entirely on a term paper, etc.). For many reasons, the challenge of evaluating college instructors is more akin to the problem of rating physicians (see chapter 1 in this volume).

This chapter tackles these challenges to answer two main questions. First, is there variation in instructor effectiveness in higher education? We examine this in a highly standardized setting where one would expect minimal variation in what instructors actually do. Second, how does effectiveness correlate with teaching experience and salary? This informs whether teaching assignment and personnel policies could be used to increase effectiveness and institutional productivity. We examine these questions using detailed administrative data from the University of Phoenix (UPX), the largest university in the world, which offers both online and in-person courses in a wide array of fields and degree programs. We focus on instructors in the college algebra course that is required for all students in bachelor of arts (BA) degree programs and that often is a roadblock to student attainment.

This context provides several advantages. Our sample includes more than two thousand instructors over more than a decade in campuses all across the United States. This allows us to generate extremely precise estimates and to generalize to a much larger population than has been the case in previous studies. Most students in these courses take a common, standardized assessment that provides an objective outcome by which to measure instructor effectiveness. And as we describe below, student enrollment and course assignment are such that we believe the issue of sorting is either nonexistent (in the case of the online course) or extremely small (in the case of face-to-face [FTF] courses).

These institutional advantages possibly come at some cost, however, to generalizability. The UPX does not match the "traditional" model of higher education, in which tenured professors at selective institutions teach courses they develop themselves and have noninstructional responsibilities (such as research). The UPX is a for-profit institution with a contingent (i.e., nontenured, mostly part-time) faculty focused solely on instruction, and the courses are highly standardized, with centrally prepared curriculum materials and assessments (both online and FTF sections). While our findings may not generalize to all sectors of higher education, we believe they are relevant for the growing for-profit sector and possibly less-selective four-year and community colleges that also have many contingent instructors. A limitation of prior research is that it focuses on selective nonprofit or public institutions, which are quite different from the nonselective or for-profit sectors. It is in these settings with many contingent faculty and institutions whose primary purpose is instruction (rather than, say, research) where productivity-driven personnel policies could theoretically be adapted.

We find substantial variation in student performance across instructors. A 1.00 SD increase in instructor quality is associated with 0.30 SD increase in grades in the current course and a 0.20 SD increase in grades in the subsequent course in the math sequence. Unlike some prior work (Carrell and West 2010), we find a positive correlation between instructor effectiveness measured by current and subsequent course performance overall and in face-to-face courses. The variation in instructor effectiveness is larger for in-person courses but still substantial for online courses. These broad patterns and magnitudes are robust to extensive controls to address any possible nonrandom student sorting, using test scores that are less likely to be under the control of instructors, and other specification checks. These magnitudes are substantially larger than those found in the K–12 literature and in the Carrell and West's (2010) study of the Air Force Academy but comparable to recent estimates from DeVry University (Bettinger et al. 2014). Furthermore, instructor effects on future course performance have little correlation with student end-of-course evaluations, the primary metric through which instructor effectiveness is currently judged.

Salary is primarily determined by tenure (time since hire) but is mostly uncorrelated with measured effectiveness or course-specific teaching experience, both in the cross section and for individual teachers over time. However, effectiveness grows modestly with course-specific teaching experience but is otherwise unrelated to time since hire. Given the disconnect between pay and effectiveness, the performance differences we uncover translate directly to differences in productivity from the university's perspective. These large productivity differences imply that personnel decisions and policies that attract, develop, allocate, motivate, and retain faculty are a potentially important tool for improving student success and productivity at the UPX. Our study institution—like almost all others—measures faculty effectiveness through student end-of-course evaluations, despite only minimal correlation between evaluation scores and our measures of effectiveness. Thus current practices do not appear to identify or support effective instructors. Though policy makers and practitioners have recently paid a lot of attention to the importance of teachers in elementary and secondary school, there is surprisingly little attention paid to the importance of instructors or instructor-related policies and practices at the postsecondary level.

The remainder of this chapter proceeds as follows. We discuss prior evidence on college instructor effectiveness and our institutional context in section 7.2. Section 7.3 introduces our administrative data sources and our analysis sample. Section 7.4 presents our empirical approach and examines the validity of our proposed method. Our main results quantifying instructor effectiveness are presented in section 7.5. Section 7.6 examines how instructor effectiveness correlates with experience. Section 7.7 concludes by discussing the implications of our work for institutional performance and productivity.

7.2   Prior Evidence and Institutional Context

7.2.1   Prior Evidence

There is substantial evidence that teacher quality is an important determinant of student achievement in elementary and secondary education (Chetty, Friedman, Rockoff 2014; Rivkin, Hanushek, and Kain 2005; Rockoff 2004; Rothstein 2010). Many states and school districts now incorporate measures of teacher effectiveness into personnel policies in order to select and retain better teachers (Jackson, Rockoff, Staiger 2014). Yet little is known about instructor effectiveness in postsecondary education, in part due to difficulties with outcome measurement and self-selection. Standardized assessments are rare, and grading subjectivity across professors makes outcome measurement difficult. In addition, students often choose professors and courses, so it is difficult to separate instructors' contribution to student outcomes from student sorting. As a consequence of these two challenges, only a handful of existing studies examine differences in professor effectiveness.

Several prior studies have found that the variance of college instructor effectiveness is small compared to what has been estimated for elementary school teachers. Focusing on large, introductory courses at a Canadian research university, Hoffmann and Oreopoulos (2009a) find the standard deviation of professor effectiveness in terms of course grades is no larger than 0.08. Carrell and West (2010) examine students at the US Air Force Academy, where grading is standardized and students have no choice over coursework or instructors. They find sizeable differences in student achievement across professors teaching the same courses—roughly 0.05 SD, which is about half as large as in the K–12 sector. Interestingly, instructors who were better at improving contemporary performance received higher teacher evaluations but were less successful at promoting "deep learning," as indicated by student performance in subsequent courses. Braga, Paccagnella, and Pellizzari (2014) estimate teacher effects on both student academic achievement and labor market outcomes at Bocconi University. They also find significant variation in teacher effectiveness—roughly 0.05 SD for both academic and labor market outcomes. They find only a modest correlation of instructor effectiveness in academic and labor market outcomes.

Two recent studies have concluded that instructors play a larger role in student success. Bettinger et al. (2015) examine instructor effectiveness using data from DeVry University, a large, for-profit institution in which the average student takes two-thirds of her courses online. They find a variance of instructor effectiveness that is substantially larger than that seen in prior studies in higher education. Specifically, they find that being taught by an instructor who is 1.00 SD more effective improves student course grades by about 0.18 to 0.24 SD. The estimated variation is 15 percent lower when courses are online, even among instructors who teach in both formats. Among instructors of economics, statistics, and computer science at an elite French public university, Brodaty and Gurgand (2016) find that a 1.00 SD increase in teacher quality is associated with a 0.14 or 0.25 SD increase in student test scores, depending on the subject.

A few studies have also examined whether specific professor characteristics correlate with student success, though the results are quite mixed.[1] Using institutional-level data from a sample of US universities, Ehrenberg and Zhang (2005) find a negative relationship between the use of adjuncts and student persistence, though they acknowledge that this could be due to nonrandom sorting of students across schools. Hoffmann and Oreopoulos (2009a) find no relationship between faculty rank (including adjuncts and tenure-track faculty) and subsequent course enrollment. Two other studies find positive effects of adjuncts. Studying course-taking among students in public four-year institutions in Ohio, Bettinger and Long (2010) find adjuncts are more likely to induce students to take further courses in the same subject. Using a sample of large introductory courses taken by first-term students at Northwestern University, Figlio, Schapiro, and Soter (2015) find that adjuncts are positively associated with subsequent course-taking in the subject as well as performance in these subsequent courses. In their study of the US Air Force Academy, Carrell and West (2010) find that academic rank, teaching experience, and terminal degree are positively correlated with follow-on course performance, though negatively related to contemporary student performance.

There is also evidence that gender and racial match between students and instructors influence students' interest and performance (Bettinger and Long 2005; Fairlie, Hoffmann, Oreopoulos 2014; Hoffmann and Oreopoulos 2009b). Finally, Hoffmann and Oreopoulos (2009a) find that students' subjective evaluations of professors are a much better predictor of student academic performance than objective professor characteristics such as rank. This echoes the finding of Jacob and Lefgren (2008) that elementary school principals can identify effective teachers but that observed teacher characteristics tend to explain little about teacher effectiveness.

A limitation of this prior research is that it focuses largely on selective nonprofit or public institutions, which are quite different from the nonselective or for-profit sectors that constitute a large and growing share of the

---

1. Much of this evidence is reviewed in Ehrenberg (2012).

postsecondary sector. It is in these settings with many contingent faculty and institutions whose primary purpose is instruction (rather than, say, research) where productivity-driven personnel policies could theoretically be adapted. Students at these types of institutions also have lower rates of degree completion, so facilitating these students' success is thus a particularly important policy goal. The one prior study examining a setting similar to ours (Bettinger et al.'s 2014 study of DeVry University) focuses on differences in student performance between online and in-person formats, with very little attention paid to instructors. The simultaneous consideration of multiple outcomes and the exploration of how effectiveness varies with salary and teaching experience is also novel in the postsecondary literature.

7.2.2   Context: College Algebra at the University of Phoenix

We study teacher effectiveness in the context of the University of Phoenix, a large for-profit university that offers both online and face-to-face (FTF) courses. The UPX offers a range of programs, including associate in arts (AA), BA, and graduate degrees, while also offering à la carte courses. We focus on core mathematics courses, MTH208 and MTH209 (College Mathematics I and II), which are a requirement for most BA programs.

Below we describe these courses, the process through which instructors are hired and evaluated, and the mechanism through which students are allocated to instructors.[2] As highlighted above, the context of both the institution and the coursework does not translate to all sectors of higher education: the faculty body is largely contingent and employed part time, and admissions are nonselective.

7.2.2.1   MTH208 and MTH209

BA-level courses at UPX are typically five weeks in duration, and students take one course at a time (sequentially), in contrast to the typical structure at most universities. The MTH208 curriculum focuses on setting up algebraic equations and solving single and two-variable linear equations and inequalities. Additionally, the coursework focuses on relating equations to real-world applications, generating graphs, and using exponents. MTH209 is considered a logical follow-up course, focusing on more complicated non-linear equations and functions. Students in our sample take MTH208 after completing about eight other courses, so enrollment in the math course sequence does signify a higher level of commitment to the degree program than students in the most entry-level courses. However, many students struggle in these introductory math courses, and the courses are regarded by UPX staff as an important obstacle to obtaining a BA for many students.

Students can take these courses online or in person. In the FTF sections,

---

2. This description draws on numerous conversations between the research team and individuals at the University of Phoenix.

students attend 4 hours of standard in-class lectures per week, typically held on a single day in the evening. In addition, students are required to work with peers roughly 4 hours per week on what is known as "learning team" modules. Students are then expected to spend 16 additional hours per week outside of class reading material, working on assignments, and studying for exams.[3]

Online courses are asynchronous, which means that a set of course materials is provided through the online learning platform, and instructors provide guidance and feedback through online discussion forums and redirect students to relevant materials when necessary. There is no synchronous or face-to-face interaction with faculty in the traditional sense, but students are required to actively participate in online discussions by substantively posting six to eight times per week over three to four days. One instructor defined a substantive post as having substantial math content: "Substantial math content means you are discussing math concepts and problems. A substantive math post will have at least one math problem in it. Simply talking 'around' the topic (such as, 'I have trouble with the negative signs' or 'I need to remember to switch the signs when I divide by a negative coefficient') will not be considered substantive" (Morris 2016). Online participation is the equivalent of 4 hours of classes for the FTF sections.[4]

There are differences between the two course modes in terms of curriculum and grading flexibility. Both courses have standardized course curricula, assignments, and tests that are made available to the instructors. Grading for these components is performed automatically through the course software. However, FTF instructors sometimes provide students with their own learning tools, administer extra exams and homework, or add other components that are not part of the standard curriculum. In contrast, online instructors mainly take the course materials and software as given, and interaction with students for these teachers is mainly limited to the online discussion forum. In both online and FTF courses, teachers are able to choose the weights they assign to specific course components for the final grade. As discussed below, for this reason, we also use student performance on the final exam as an outcome measure.

7.2.2.2 Hiring and Allocation of Instructors

The hiring and onboarding process of teachers is managed and controlled by a central hiring committee hosted at the Phoenix, Arizona, campus, though much input comes from local staff at ground campuses. First,

3. There have been recent reductions in the use of learning team interactions in the past two years, but these changes occurred after our analysis sample.
4. The posting requirements actually changed over time. For the majority of the time of the study, the requirement was four days a week with two substantive posts per day (i.e., eight posts). In the past several years, it went to six times per week on at least three days (effectively allowing for two single post days).

this committee checks whether a new candidate has an appropriate degree.[5] Second, qualified candidates must pass a five-week standardized training course. This includes a mock lecture for FTF instructors and a mock online session for online instructors. Finally, an evaluator sits in on the first class or follows the online course to ensure the instructor performs according to university standards. Salaries are relatively fixed but do vary somewhat with respect to degree and tenure.[6] We should note that the actual hiring process for instructors may deviate from this description for certain campuses or in time periods when positions are particularly difficult to fill.

The allocation of instructors to classes is essentially random for online classes. About 60 MTH208 sections are started weekly, and the roster is only made available to students two or three days before the course starts, at which point students are typically enrolled. The only way to sidestep these teacher assignments is by dropping the course altogether and enrolling in a subsequent week. This differs from most settings in other higher education institutions, where students have more discretion over what section to attend. For FTF sections, the assignment works differently, since most campuses are too small to have different sections concurrently, and students may need to wait for a few months if they decide to take the next MTH208 section at that campus. While this limits the ability of students to shop around for a better teacher, the assignment of students to these sections is likely to be less random than for online sections. For this reason, we rely on value-added models that control for a host of student-specific characteristics that may correlate with both instructor and student course performance.

7.2.2.3 Evaluation and Retention of Instructors

The UPX has in place three main evaluation tools to keep track of the performance of instructors. First, instructors need to take a yearly refresher course on teaching methods, and an evaluator will typically sit in or follow an online section every year to ensure the quality of the instructor still meets the university's requirements. Second, there is an in-house data analytics team that tracks key performance parameters. These include average response time to questions asked through the online platform or indicators that students in sections are systematically getting too high (or too low) overall grades. For instance, if instructors consistently give every student in a section high grades, this will raise a flag, and the validity of these grades will

---

5. For MTH208 sections, for instance, a minimum requirement might be having a master's degree in mathematics or a master's degree in biology, engineering, or similar coursework along with a minimum number of credits in advanced mathematics courses and teaching experience in mathematics.

6. For instance, all else being equal, an instructor with a PhD can expect a higher salary than an instructor with a master's degree. Additionally, tenure in this context refers to the date of first hire at the University of Phoenix. Salary differences are larger among new instructors and tend to diminish at higher levels of experience.

be verified. Finally, additional evaluations can be triggered if students file complaints about instructor performance. If these evaluation channels show the instructor has not met the standards of the university, the instructor receives a warning. Instructors who have received a warning are followed up more closely in subsequent courses. If the instructor's performance does not improve, the university will not hire the person back for subsequent courses.

7.3 Data

We investigate variation in instructor effectiveness using data drawn from administrative UPX records. This section describes these records, the sample selection, and descriptive statistics. While the data we analyze has very rich information about the experiences of students and instructors while at the UPX, information on outside activities is limited.

7.3.1 Data Sources

We analyze university administrative records covering all students and teachers who have taken or taught MTH208 at least once between July 2000 and July 2014. The raw data contain information on 2,343 instructors who taught 34,725 sections of MTH208 with a total of 396,038 student-section observations. For all of these instructors and students, we obtain the full teaching and course-taking history back to 2000.[7] Our analysis spans 84 campuses (plus the online campus). There is typically one campus per city, but some larger metropolitan areas have multiple physical locations (branches) at which courses are offered.[8]

7.3.1.1 Instructors

We draw on three information sources for instructor-level characteristics. A first data set provides the full teaching history of instructors who have ever taught MTH208, covering 190,066 class sections. Information includes the campus and location of instruction, subject, number of credits, and start date and end date of the section.

For each instructor-section observation, we calculate the instructor's teaching load for the current year as well as the number of sections he or she had taught in the past separately for MTH208 and other courses. This allows us to construct a variety of different experience measures, which we use in the analysis below. As the teaching history is censored before the year 2000, we only calculate the cumulative experience profile for instructors hired in the year 2000 or later.

7. The administrative records are not available before 2000 because of information infra-structure differences, leading to incomplete teaching and course-taking spells for professors and students, respectively.
8. There are more than 200 physical locations (branches) corresponding to these 84 campuses.

The second data set contains self-reported information on ethnicity and gender of the instructor, along with complete information on the date of first hire, the type of employment (full time or part time), and the zip code of residence.[9] A unique instructor identifier allows us to merge this information onto the MTH208 sections.[10] A third data set contains the salary information for the instructor of each section, which can be merged onto the MTH208 sections using the unique section identifier.

7.3.1.2   Students

Student-level information combines four data sources: demographics, transcript, assessment, and student end-of-course evaluations. The demographics data set provides information on the zip code of residence, gender, age of the student, program the student is enrolled in, and program start and end dates.[11] A unique student identifier number allows us to merge this information onto the course-taking history of the student.

Transcript data contains complete course-taking history, including the start and end dates of the section, campus of instruction, grade, and number of credits. Every section has a unique section identifier that allows for matching students to instructors. Additionally, student-level information includes course completion, course grade, earned credits, and a unique student identifier that allows for merging onto the student demographics.

For sections from July 2010 to March 2014, or roughly 30 percent of the full sample, we have detailed information on student performance separately by course assignment or assessment, which includes everything from individual homework assignments to group exercises to exams. We use these data to obtain a final exam score for each student when available. Because the data do not have a single, clear code for final exam component across all sections and instructors have the discretion to add additional final exam components, we use a decision rule to identify the "best" exam score for each student based on the text description of the assessment object. Approximately 11 percent of observations have a single score clearly tied to the common computer-administered final assessment, 77 percent have a single assessment for a final exam (but we cannot be certain it is from the standardized online system), and the remainder have final exam assessments that are a little more ambiguous. Discussions with UPX personnel indicated that the vast majority of instructors use the online standardized assessment tool with

---

9. This instructor data set also contains information on birth year and military affiliation, though these variables have high nonresponse rates and are therefore not used for the analysis.

10. The instructor identifier is, in principle, unique. It is possible, however, that an instructor shows up under two different identifiers if the instructor leaves the university and then returns after a long time. While this is a possibility, UPX administrators considered this unlikely to be a pervasive issue in their records.

11. Similar to the instructor data set, demographic data are self-reported. While information on gender and age is missing for less than 1 percent of the sample, information on ethnicity, veteran status, and transfer credits exhibit much larger nonresponse rates and are therefore not used for the analysis.

no customization, but unfortunately this is not recorded in the administrative data. Nonetheless, results excluding this latter group are quite similar to analysis with the full sample. Our approach is outlined in Appendix B.

While the analysis focuses on course grades and final test scores, it also considers future performance measures, such as grades and cumulative grade point average earned in the 180 or 365 days following the MTH208 section of interest. Given the linear, one-by-one nature of the coursework, these measures capture the effect instructors have on moving students toward obtaining a final degree.

Finally, for sections taught between March 2010 and July 2014, we obtained student end-of-course evaluations. Students are asked whether they would recommend the instructor on a 10-point scale. Recommendation scores of 8 or above are considered "good" and are the primary way the evaluations are used by the University of Phoenix administration. We follow this practice and use a binary indicator for whether the recommendation score is at least 8 as our primary evaluation measure. End-of-course evaluations are optional for students, so they have a relatively low response rate. Only 37 percent of students provide a course evaluation score for MTH208, which is less than half of the students who have a final exam test score for MTH208. While nonrandom missing evaluations could create bias in our estimates of teacher effectiveness, this bias is also present in the evaluations as used by the institution. Our goal is to see how evaluations *as currently used in practice* correlate with more objective measures of teacher effectiveness.

7.3.1.3   Census Data

In addition to the UPX administrative school records, we use several census data resources to get additional variables capturing the characteristics of students' residential neighborhoods. In particular, we obtain the unemployment rate, the median family income, the percentage of family below the poverty line, and the percentage with a bachelor degree or higher of students' home zip code from the 2004–7 five-year American Community Survey (ACS) files.

7.3.2   Sample Selection

Starting from the raw data, we apply several restrictions to obtain the primary analysis sample. We restrict our analysis to the 33,200 MTH208 sections that started between January 2001 and July 2014. We then drop all students with missing data for the final grade or unusual grades (0.1 percent of students) as well as students who do not show up in the student demographics file (0.3 percent of remaining students).[12] We then drop all canceled sections (0.02 percent of the sections), sections with fewer than five enrolled

---

12. We keep students with grades A–F, I/A–I/F (incomplete A–F), or W (withdraw). Roughly 0.1 percent of scores are missing or not A–F or I/A–I/F (incomplete), and we drop these. These grades include AU (audit), I (incomplete), IP, IX, OC, ON, P, QC, and missing values.

students who had nonmissing final grades and did not withdraw from the course (11.4 percent of the remaining sections), and sections for which the instructor is paid less than $300 (5.2 percent of remaining sections). We believe the final two restrictions exclude sections that were not actual courses but rather independent studies of some sort. We also drop sections for which the instructor does not show up in the teacher demographics file, which is 3.5 percent of the remaining sections.

To calculate instructor experience, we use an instructor-section panel that drops observations where there is no salary information (about 3 percent of sections), where the section was canceled (0.04 percent), with fewer than five students (21.7 percent of the remaining sections), or for which the instructor is paid less than $300 (8.6 percent of the remaining sections). As above, these final two restrictions are meant to exclude independent-study-type courses or other unusual courses that may enter differently into the teacher-human capital function.[13] We then calculate several experience measures based on this sample. We calculate measures of experience, such as the number of courses taught in the previous calendar year and total cumulative experience in MTH208 specifically and in other categories of classes. The complete cumulative experience measures are only fully available for instructors who were hired after 2000, since the teaching history is not available in prior years.

Finally, we drop data from nine campuses because none of the instructors we observe in these campuses ever taught in another physical campus or online. As discussed below, in order to separately identify campus and instructor fixed effects, each campus must have at least one instructor who has taught in a different location. Fortunately, these nine campuses represent only 2 percent of the remaining sections and 4 percent of remaining instructors.

The final analysis sample consists of 339,844 students in 26,384 sections taught by 2,243 unique instructors. The subsample for which final exam data are available includes 94,745 students in 7,232 MTH208 sections taught by 1,198 unique instructors. We calculate various student characteristics from the transcript data, including cumulative grade point average and cumulative credits earned prior to enrolling in MTH208, as well as future performance measures. In the rare case of missing single-student demographic variables, we set missing to zero and include an indicator variable for missing.

7.3.3 Descriptive Statistics

We report key descriptive statistics for the final analysis sample, spanning January 2001 to July 2014, in table 7.1. We report these statistics for

---

13. There are three instructors who are first employed part-time and then employed full-time. As the part-time spells are longer than the full-time spells, we use the part-time demographics only. This restriction only impacts the employment type and date of first hire, as the other demographics are the same for the two employment spells for all three instructors.

Table 7.1a   **Descriptive statistics for sections and instructors (full sample)**

	All sections (n = 26,384)		Face-to-face sections (n = 13,791)		Online sections (n = 12,593)	
	Mean	SD	Mean	SD	Mean	SD
Online section	0.477	0.499	0.000	0.000	1.000	0.000
Male	0.735	0.441	0.755	0.430	0.714	0.452
White	0.649	0.477	0.633	0.482	0.664	0.472
Instructor compensation per section ($)	955.14	181.61	949.39	211.45	961.45	141.86
Section-average student age	34.89	3.25	34.33	3.38	35.50	3.00
Section-average share male	0.36	0.17	0.37	0.17	0.35	0.17
Section-average incoming GPA	3.35	0.23	3.34	0.24	3.36	0.21
Section-average incoming credits	22.87	8.39	25.56	8.82	19.93	6.77
Section-average repeat 208	0.11	0.11	0.08	0.10	0.14	0.11
Section-average number times taken 208	1.11	0.13	1.09	0.11	1.14	0.14
Section-average time since program start (years)	1.15	0.50	1.20	0.52	1.09	0.47
Section enrollment	12.88	4.40	13.98	5.38	11.68	2.48
Years since first hire	4.783	4.281	5.005	4.811	4.539	3.597
Years since first hire > 1	0.830	0.376	0.804	0.397	0.858	0.349
Total MTH208 sections taught prior to this section	15.310	16.792	11.038	13.132	19.988	18.975
Ever taught MTH208 prior to this section	0.920	0.272	0.888	0.316	0.955	0.208
Total sections instructor taught prior to this section	43.213	51.854	46.501	61.163	39.611	38.886
Total MTH209 sections taught prior to this section	9.871	12.915	10.690	13.170	8.975	12.569
Ever taught MTH209 prior to this section	0.776	0.417	0.873	0.333	0.670	0.470

all sections and for FTF and online sections separately. Table 7.1a reports section and instructor characteristics for the 26,384 MTH208 sections, while table 7.1b reports student background characteristics and student performance measures. About half of all sections are taught online, and instructors are paid about $950 for teaching a course, regardless of the instruction mode.[14] Instructors are majority white and male and have been at the university just under five years.[15] They typically have taught more than 40 total course sections since joining the faculty, of which 15 were MTH208 and 10 were MTH209. Instructors teaching online sections tend to specialize more in teaching MTH208 compared to their counterparts teaching FTF sections. Class size is about 13 students and is slightly larger for FTF than online sections. Tables 7.A1a and 7.A1b in Appendix A report descriptive statistics for the sample for which test scores are available (July 2010–March 2014). The

14. The earnings measures are deflated using the national CPI. For each year, the CPI in April was used, with April 2001 as the base.
15. Though omitted from the table, nearly 100 percent of instructors are part time.

Table 7.1b   **Descriptive statistics for students (full sample)**

	All sections (n = 339,844)		Face-to-face sections (n = 192,747)		Online sections (n = 147,097)	
	Mean	SD	Mean	SD	Mean	SD
Male	0.359	0.480	0.373	0.484	0.341	0.474
Age	34.816	9.097	34.264	9.127	35.538	9.008
Baseline GPA (0–4)	3.348	0.538	3.348	0.518	3.347	0.563
Credits earned prior to start of MTH208	23.386	18.363	25.714	18.451	20.337	17.791
Took MTH208 before	0.104	0.306	0.077	0.267	0.140	0.347
Number of times MTH208 taken	1.109	0.385	1.084	0.325	1.142	0.448
BS (general studies)	0.211	0.408	0.208	0.406	0.214	0.410
BS in nursing	0.050	0.217	0.026	0.159	0.081	0.272
BS in accounting	0.003	0.057	0.002	0.045	0.005	0.069
BS in business	0.503	0.500	0.587	0.492	0.393	0.488
BS in criminal justice administration	0.035	0.183	0.047	0.213	0.018	0.133
BS in education	0.022	0.145	0.013	0.112	0.033	0.179
BS in health administration	0.034	0.182	0.034	0.181	0.034	0.182
BS in human services	0.033	0.179	0.023	0.150	0.046	0.210
BS in information technology	0.028	0.166	0.027	0.162	0.030	0.172
BS in management	0.041	0.199	0.022	0.148	0.066	0.248
Nondegree program	0.014	0.117	0.002	0.042	0.030	0.169
BS in other program	0.015	0.122	0.009	0.092	0.024	0.152
Time since program start date (years)	1.160	1.399	1.203	1.334	1.105	1.478
Grade in Math 208	2.457	1.395	2.534	1.333	2.355	1.467
A / A–	0.319	0.466	0.323	0.468	0.314	0.464
B+ / B / B–	0.268	0.443	0.275	0.446	0.258	0.438
C+ / C / C–	0.174	0.379	0.192	0.394	0.151	0.358
D+ / D / D–	0.073	0.260	0.077	0.267	0.066	0.249
F	0.045	0.207	0.038	0.191	0.054	0.226
Withdrawn	0.122	0.327	0.095	0.293	0.156	0.363
Passed MTH208	0.834	0.372	0.867	0.340	0.790	0.407
MTH208 final exam score available	0.243	0.429	0.282	0.450	0.191	0.393
MTH208 final exam % correct (if available)	0.708	0.241	0.697	0.246	0.729	0.230
Took MTH209	0.755	0.430	0.824	0.380	0.664	0.472
Grade in MTH209 (if took it)	2.620	1.246	2.714	1.160	2.464	1.363
A / A–	0.318	0.466	0.328	0.470	0.300	0.458
B+ / B / B–	0.294	0.456	0.304	0.460	0.279	0.449
C+ / C / C–	0.201	0.401	0.217	0.412	0.174	0.379
D+ / D / D–	0.074	0.261	0.074	0.262	0.073	0.260
F	0.032	0.176	0.021	0.145	0.049	0.215
Withdrawn	0.068	0.251	0.046	0.209	0.104	0.305
MTH209 final exam score available	0.200	0.400	0.249	0.433	0.136	0.342
MTH209 final exam % correct (if available)	0.691	0.246	0.690	0.245	0.693	0.250
Credits earned in following 6 months	10.461	5.315	11.401	5.053	9.230	5.397
Have course evaluation	0.117	0.321	0.118	0.323	0.115	0.320
Course evaluation: Recommend instructor (if available)	0.658	0.474	0.693	0.461	0.610	0.488

test score sample is quite similar to the full sample, though the instructors are typically more experienced.

Table 7.1b provides an overview of student characteristics and performance. The students enrolled in these sections tend to be female and are around 35 years old, and they typically have taken 23 credits with a grade point average (GPA) of 3.35 prior to beginning MTH208. Students in online sections tend to have earned somewhat fewer credits than their counterparts in FTF sections and are more likely to have taken MTH208 before. Most students, in both FTF and online sections, are enrolled in a business or general studies program.

Students across both modes of instruction are equally likely to earn a grade of A (about 32 percent) or B (about 27 percent) and have similar final exam scores (70 percent) when available. Consistent with prior work, online students are more likely to withdraw from and less likely to pass MTH208 than students in FTF sections. In terms of student performance after taking MTH208, we find that FTF students are more likely to go on and take MTH209.[16] Students earn about 10.5 credits in the six months following the MTH208 section, with a 2-credit gap between FTF and online students. Participation in end-of-course evaluations is similar across formats, though FTF students generally report a greater level of instructor satisfaction.

7.4   Empirical Approach

Our main aim is to characterize the variation in student performance across instructors teaching the same courses. Consider the standard "value-added" model of student achievement given in equation (1):

$$(1) \qquad Y_{ijkt} = \beta_1 X_i + \beta_2 Z_{jkt} + \varnothing_t + \delta_c + \theta_k + e_{ijkt},$$

where Y_{ijkt} is the outcome of student i in section j taught by instructor k during term t. The set of parameters θ_k quantify the contribution of instructor k to the performance of their students above and beyond what could be predicted by observed characteristics of the student (X_i), course section (Z_{jkt}), campus (δ_c), or time period ($\varnothing_t$). The variance of θ_k across instructors measures the dispersion of instructor quality and is our primary parameter of interest. We are particularly interested in how the distribution of θ_k varies across outcomes and formats and how effectiveness covaries across outcomes.

Estimation of the standard value-added model in equation (1) must confront three key issues. First, nonrandom assignment of students to instructors or instructors to course sections could bias value-added models. In the presence of nonrandom sorting, differences in performance across sections

---

16. Conditional on taking MTH209, both online and FTF students typically take this class about a week after the MTH208 section.

could be driven by differences in student characteristics rather than differences in instructor effectiveness per se. Second, outcomes should reflect student learning rather than grading leniency or "teaching to the test" of instructors. Furthermore, missing outcomes may bias instructor effects if follow-up information availability is not random. Third, our ability to make performance comparisons among instructors across campuses while also controlling for cross-campus differences in unobserved factors relies on the presence of instructors who teach at multiple campuses. We address each of these in turn below.

7.4.1   Course and Instructor Assignment

In many education settings, we worry about the nonrandom assignment of instructors to sections (and students) creating bias in value-added measures (Chetty, Friedman, and Rockoff 2014; Rothstein 2009). In general, we believe that there is relatively little scope for sorting in our setting. Students do not know much about the instructor when they enroll, and instructors are only assigned to specific sections about two days before the start of the course for online sections. Students who have a strong preference with regard to the instructor can choose to drop the course once they learn the instructor's identity, but this would mean that they would likely have to wait until the start of the next session to take the course, at which point they would be randomly assigned to a section again. According to UPX administrators, there is no sorting at all in online courses, which is plausible given the very limited interaction students will have with instructors in the initial meetings of the course. UPX administrators admit the possibility of some sorting in FTF courses but believe this is likely minimal.

To explore the extent of sorting, we conduct two types of tests. First, we test whether observable instructor characteristics correlate with the observable characteristics of students in a section. To do so, we regress mean student characteristics on instructor characteristics, where each observation is a course section.[17] Table 7.2 reports the estimates from three regression models that differ in terms of the type of fixed effects that are included. Once we include campus fixed effects, there are very few systematic correlations between student and instructor characteristics, and any significant relationships are economically insignificant. To take one example, consider incoming student GPA, which is the single biggest predictor of student success in MTH208. Whether the instructor was hired in the last year is statistically significantly related to incoming student GPA once campus fixed effects are included, yet this difference is only 0.012 grade points, or 0.3 percent of the

---

17. An alternate approach would be to regress each student characteristic on a full set of course section dummies along with campus (or campus-year) fixed effects and test whether the dummies are jointly equal to zero. This is equivalent to jointly testing the equality of the means of the characteristics across class sections.

Table 7.2   **Randomization check**

	(1)	(2)	(3)	(4)	(5)	(6)	(7)	(8)	(9)
	Panel A: Outcome = average age (mean = 34.89)			Panel B: Outcome = fraction male (mean = 0.36)			Panel C: Outcome = fraction repeating (mean = 0.11)		
Years since first hire	-0.0147	0.00863	0.00207	0.0012	-0.00122**	-0.000613	-0.000429	0.000159	0.000305
	(0.012)	(0.010)	(0.009)	(0.001)	(0.001)	(0.000)	(0.000)	(0.000)	(0.000)
Years since first hire > 1	0.253***	0.0808	0.091	-0.00205	0.00750*	0.00713*	0.0108***	0.00337	-0.00137
	(0.080)	(0.073)	(0.074)	(0.005)	(0.004)	(0.004)	(0.003)	(0.002)	(0.002)
Total MTH208 sections taught prior to this section	0.0166***	0.00430**	-0.00161	-0.000769***	-0.000395***	-5.06E-05	0.000793***	0.0000	-0.0001
	(0.002)	(0.002)	(0.002)	(0.000)	(0.000)	(0.000)	(0.000)	(0.000)	(0.000)
Ever taught MTH208 prior to this section	0.155*	-0.0759	-0.0333	0.00276	0.00587	0.00269	0.0254***	0.00483*	0.00752***
	(0.084)	(0.080)	(0.078)	(0.005)	(0.005)	(0.005)	(0.003)	(0.003)	(0.003)
Total sections instructor taught prior to this section	-0.00139	-0.000813	-0.000186	9.60e-05*	7.69e-05**	3.34E-05	-7.39e-05***	-0.00002	-0.00002
	(0.001)	(0.001)	(0.001)	(0.000)	(0.000)	(0.000)	(0.000)	(0.000)	(0.000)
Total MTH209 sections taught prior to this section	-0.00546	-0.0012	0.000613	0.000152	0.000189	0.000209*	-0.0001	0.0000	0.000109
	(0.004)	(0.002)	(0.002)	(0.000)	(0.000)	(0.000)	(0.000)	(0.000)	(0.000)
Ever taught MTH209 prior to this section	-0.361***	0.0281	0.0141	-0.00352	-0.0127***	-0.0135***	-0.0206***	0.00304	-0.000631
	(0.073)	(0.064)	(0.061)	(0.004)	(0.004)	(0.004)	(0.002)	(0.002)	(0.002)
R-squared	0.047	0.121	0.176	0.034	0.105	0.167	0.054	0.13	0.167
	Panel D: Outcome = incoming GPA (mean = 3.35)			Panel E: Outcome = incoming credits (mean = 22.87)			Panel F: Outcome = section enrollment (mean = 12.88)		
Years since first hire	0.00167**	-0.000143	-0.000227	0.0871**	0.029	-0.00684	0.0651**	0.0215	0.00634
	(0.001)	(0.001)	(0.000)	(0.042)	(0.026)	(0.015)	(0.025)	(0.015)	(0.012)
Years since first hire > 1	-0.0168***	-0.0124***	-0.00124	0.174	0.593***	0.192	-0.278**	0.0592	0.0321
	(0.005)	(0.004)	(0.004)	(0.234)	(0.192)	(0.143)	(0.135)	(0.105)	(0.087)
Total MTH208 sections taught prior to this section	0.0000	0.0001	0.0000	-0.0455***	0.0235***	0.00052	-0.0119***	0.0186***	0.00512***
	(0.000)	(0.000)	(0.000)	(0.007)	(0.004)	(0.003)	(0.004)	(0.003)	(0.002)
Ever taught MTH208 prior to this section	0.00183	0.000257	-0.00197	-1.551***	0.174	0.326**	-0.535***	0.00424	0.269***
	(0.005)	(0.005)	(0.005)	(0.200)	(0.193)	(0.165)	(0.119)	(0.112)	(0.096)
Total sections instructor taught prior to this section	0.00004	0.00003	0.00001	0.00625*	-0.00370*	-0.000968	0.00562**	-0.00113	-0.000246
	(0.000)	(0.000)	(0.000)	(0.003)	(0.002)	(0.001)	(0.002)	(0.001)	(0.001)
Total MTH209 sections taught prior to this section	0.00024	0.00009	0.00002	0.0132	0.0025	0.00531	0.0234***	0.0158***	0.0114***
	(0.000)	(0.000)	(0.000)	(0.011)	(0.007)	(0.004)	(0.007)	(0.004)	(0.003)
Ever taught MTH209 prior to this section	0.000383	-0.00203	0.00303	1.890***	-0.0926	-0.0449	0.709***	-0.143	-0.0672
	(0.004)	(0.004)	(0.004)	(0.191)	(0.165)	(0.112)	(0.117)	(0.104)	(0.063)
R-squared	0.338	0.397	0.44	0.13	0.283	0.429	0.07	0.236	0.359
Observations	23,298	23,298	23,298	23,298	23,298	23,298	23,298	23,298	23,298
FE	None	campus	campus-year	None	campus	campus-year	None	campus	campus-year

Notes: Each panel-column is a separate regression of section-level student average characteristics (or total section enrollment) on instructor characteristics. All specifications also include year and month fixed effects. Robust standard errors clustered by instructor in parenthesis.

sample mean. Similar patterns are seen for all other observable student and instructor characteristics we examine. Furthermore, this pattern attenuates further when campus-year fixed effects are included. In results not reported here but available upon request, we continue to find no significant relationship between instructor and student characteristics for subsamples limited to only online sections and to sections with final exam scores.

In addition, we follow the procedure utilized by Carrell and West (2010) to test whether the distribution of student characteristics across sections is similar to what you would get from random assignment within campus and time. In a first step, we take the pool of students in a campus-year cell, randomly draw sections of different sizes (based on the actual distribution), and compute the statistic of interest for these random sections. Similar to test 1, the statistics of interest are average age, fraction male, average prior credits, and average prior GPA. By construction, the resulting distribution of these section-level characteristics is obtained under random assignment of students to sections. In a second step, we take each actual section and compare the actual student average of each baseline characteristic to the counterfactual distribution for the relevant campus-year combination by calculating the p-value. For instance, we take a section, compute the average age, and compute the fraction of counterfactual sections with values smaller than the actual value. For each campus-year combination, we therefore obtain a number of p-values equal to the number of sections held at that campus-year combination. In a final step, we test for random assignment by testing the null hypothesis that these p-values are uniformly distributed. Intuitively, we are equally likely to draw any percentile under random assignment, which should result in these p-values having a uniform distribution. If, for instance, we have systematic sorting of students according to age, we would find we are more likely to find low and high percentiles, and the p-values would not exhibit a uniform distribution.

Similar to Carrell and West (2010), we test the uniformity of these p-values using the chi-square goodness-of-fit test and a Kolmogorov-Smirnov test with a 5 percent significance level. We draw counterfactual distributions at the campus-year level, leading to 763 tests of the null hypothesis of uniformity of the p-values. We find that the null hypothesis is rejected in 56 cases using the chi-square goodness-of-fit test and in 51 cases using the Kolmogorov-Smirnov test, which is about 6 to 7 percent. Given that the significance level of these tests was 5 percent, we conclude that these tests do not reject the null hypothesis of random assignment of students to sections for these specific observables.

7.4.2 Outcomes

Unlike the elementary and secondary setting, in which teacher effectiveness has been studied extensively using standardized test scores, appropriate outcomes are more difficult to identify in the higher education context. Our unique setting, however, allows us to use a standardized testing framework in a higher education institution. Following prior studies in the literature, we examine not only contemporaneous course performance as measured by students' course grades but also enrollment and performance (measured by grades) in subsequent courses in the same subject.

An important limitation of grades as a measure of course performance is that they reflect, at least in part, different grading practices. This may be particularly worrisome in the context of FTF courses at the UPX because many students have the same instructor for MTH208 and MTH209. Thus lenient or subjective grading practices in MTH208 may be correlated with the same practices in MTH209, meaning that the MTH209 grade is not an objective measure of long-run learning from MTH208. For a subset of our sample, we are able to examine student performance on the final examination for MTH208 and/or MTH209. It also is informative to compare test-based measures to grade-based measures simply because the grade-based measures are easier for the universities to implement. It is informative to know how far using course grades deviates from the more "objective" measures. In order to maximize sample coverage, we first look at course grades and credits earned but then also look at final exam scores (for a smaller sample).

A practical challenge with both grade and test-score outcomes is that they may not be observed for students who do not persist to the final exam in MTH208 or who do not enroll in MTH209. Our main analysis imputes values for these outcomes where missing, though we also assess the consequences of this imputation. Our preferred method assumes that students who chose not to enroll in MTH209 would have received a failing grade, and those without test scores would have received a score at the 10th percentile of the test score distribution from their MTH208 class. Generally, results are not sensitive to the imputation method used. We also look directly at the likelihood of enrolling in MTH209 or of having nonmissing final exam scores as outcomes.

Persistence is less susceptible to these concerns. Given that roughly one-quarter of the sample either withdraw or fail MTH208 and an equal fraction fails to take MTH209 at any point, it is interesting to look at whether students eventually take MTH209 as an outcome. The number of credits accumulated in the six months following MTH208 is another outcome we examine that is also less susceptible to instructor leniency and missing value concerns.

7.4.3   Cross-campus Comparisons

A third challenge in estimating instructor effectiveness is that unobservable differences among students across campuses may confound instructor differences. This is the rationale for controlling for campus fixed effects in equation (1). But separately identifying campus and instructor effects requires that a set of instructors teach at multiple campuses.[18] For example,

---

18. Including fixed effects for each of the 200 physical locations requires instructors who teach at multiple locations within each campus. Within-campus switching is more common than cross-campus switching, and thus location fixed effects are only slightly more challenging to implement than campus fixed effects.

if an instructor's students do particularly well, it is impossible to say whether this reflects the contribution of the instructor herself or unobserved campus phenomena, such as the campus-specific facilities or student peers. Observing instructors across multiple campuses permits the separation of these two phenomena and permits instructors across campuses to be ranked on a common scale. This is analogous to the concern in studies that attempt to simultaneously estimate firm and worker effects as well as the literature that measures teacher value added at the K–12 level. Most prior work on postsecondary instructors has focused on single campus locations and thus has not confronted the cross-campus comparison problem.

The existence of the online courses and the fact that a sizeable fraction of instructors teach both online and at a physical campus, provides the "connectedness" that allows us to separately identify campus and instructor effects. Appendix table 7.A2 reports the degree of "switching" that exists across campuses in our data. About 8 percent of the exclusively FTF instructors teach at more than one campus, and about 21 percent of the online instructors also teach at an FTF campus.

7.4.4   Implementation

We implement our analysis with a two-step procedure. In the first step, we estimate the standard value-added model in (1) with ordinary least squares including a host of student characteristics, campus fixed effects, and instructor fixed effects (θ_k). Including θ_k's as fixed effects permits correlation between θ_k's and X characteristics (including campus fixed effects [FEs]), generating estimates of $\beta_1, \beta_2, \varnothing_t$, and δ_c that are purged of any nonrandom sorting by instructors (Chetty, Friedman, and Rockoff 2014). However, the estimated θ_k's are noisy, so their variance would be an inaccurate estimate of the true variance of the instructor effects. We then construct mean section-level residuals for each outcome:

$$(2) \qquad \tilde{Y}_{jkt} = \sum_{i \in j}(Y_{ijkt} - \hat{\beta}_1 X_i - \hat{\beta}_2 Z_{jkt} - \hat{\varnothing}_t - \hat{\delta}_c)$$

The section-level residuals $\tilde{Y}_{jkt}$ combine the instructor effects (θ_k) with any non-mean-zero unobserved determinants of student performance at the student or section levels. Our fully controlled first-stage model includes student characteristics (gender, age, incoming GPA, incoming credits, indicator for repeat of MTH208, number of times taking MTH208, 12 program dummies, years since started program), section averages of these individual characteristics, student zip code characteristics (unemployment rate, median family income, percent of families below poverty line, percent of adults with BA degree in zip code, missing zip), and total section enrollment. We control for aggregate temporal changes in unobserved student characteristics or grading standards by including calendar year and month fixed effects. Campus fixed effects control for any unobserved differences in student characteristics across campuses. Since the campus includes several physical locations for very large metro areas, as a robustness we replace campus fixed effects with effects for the specific physical location at which the class is taught. Finally, we also examine models with various subsets of these control variables and large sets of interactions between them.

In the second step, we use the mean residuals to estimate the variance of the instructor effects θ_k as random effects with maximum likelihood.[19] For a single outcome, not distinguishing by mode, the model is simply $\tilde{Y}_{jkt} = \theta_k + \tilde{e}_{jkt}$. The error term $\tilde{e}_{jkt}$ includes any section-specific shocks and also any non-mean-zero student-level unobserved characteristics, both of which are assumed to be independent across instructors and time. Our preferred approach stacks outcomes and lets effectiveness vary by outcome with an unrestricted covariance matrix. For instance, for two outcomes (o = grade in MTH208, grade in MTH209), we estimate

$$(3) \qquad \tilde{Y}_{jkt}^o = \theta_k^{M208}(M208_{ojkt}) + \theta_k^{M209}(M209_{ojkt}) + \tilde{e}_{ojkt},$$

where $M208_{ojkt}$ and $M209_{ojkt}$ are indicators for MTH208 and MTH209 outcomes, respectively.[20] The key parameters of interest are SD(θ_k^{M208}), SD(θ_k^{M209}), and Corr(θ_k^{M208}, θ_k^{M209}). The benefit of stacking outcomes and estimating multiple outcomes simultaneously is that the correlation across outcomes is estimated directly. As noted by Carrell and West (2010), the estimate of Corr(θ_k^{M208}, θ_k^{M209}) from equation (3) will be biased in the presence of shocks common to all students in a given MTH208 section if those shocks have a positive correlation across outcomes. For instance, groups of students who are high performing in MTH208 (relative to that predicted by covariates) are also likely to do well in MTH209, independent of the MTH208 instructors' ability to influence MTH209 performance. For this reason, our preferred specification also includes section-specific shocks (random effects μ_{jkt}^{M208} and μ_{jkt}^{M209}) with an unrestricted covariance matrix:

$$(4) \qquad \tilde{Y}_{jkt} = \theta_k^{M208}(M208_{ojkt}) + \theta_k^{M209}(M209_{ojkt}) + \mu_{jkt}^{M208}(M208_{ojkt}).$$

$$+ \mu_{jkt}^{M209}(M209_{ojkt}) + \tilde{e}_{jkt}$$

The Corr(μ_{jkt}^{M208}, μ_{jkt}^{M209}) captures any common shocks in MTH208 that carry over into MTH209 performance (regardless of instructor), such as unobserved student characteristics or similarities of environment between the classes (such as the same peers). The distribution of θ_k^{M208} and θ_k^{M209} is still estimated by systematic differences in student performance across sections taught by the same instructor, but now the correlation between these two effects nets out what would be expected simply due to the fact that individual

---

19. Second-stage models are estimated with maximum likelihood using Stata's "mixed" command. To ensure that estimated variances are positive, this routine estimates the log of the standard deviation of random effects as the unknown parameter during maximization. Standard errors of this transformed parameter are computed using the inverse of the numerical Hessian and then converted back to standard deviation units.

20. All models also include a constant and an indicator for one of the outcomes to adjust for mean differences in residuals across outcomes, which is most relevant when we estimate the model separately by mode of instruction.

students' performance in the two courses is likely to be correlated. Note that since the instructor and section effects are random effects (rather than fixed), their distributions are separately identified. Including section-specific random effects has no bearing on the instructor effects but does impact the estimated correlation between contemporary and follow-up course effectiveness. Analogous models are estimated separately by mode of instruction.

7.5   Results on Instructor Effectiveness

7.5.1   Main Results for Course Grades and Final Exam Scores

Table 7.3 reports our main estimates of the variances and correlations of MTH208 instructor effects for both grade and test score outcomes overall and separately by mode of instruction. This base model includes our full set of student and section controls in the first stage in addition to campus fixed effects. The odd columns report results without correlated section effects.

For the full sample, a one-standard-deviation increase in MTH208 instructor quality is associated with a 0.30 and 0.20 standard deviation increase in student course grades in MTH208 and MTH209, respectively. In course grade points, this is a little larger than one grade step (going from a B to a B+). Thus MTH208 instructors substantially affect student achievement in both the introductory and follow-on math courses. These estimates are statistically significant and quite a bit larger than effects found in prior research in postsecondary (e.g., Carrell and West 2010) and elementary schools (Kane, Rockoff, and Staiger 2008). In section 7.7, we return to the institutional and contextual differences between our study and these that may explain these differences.

We also find that instructor effects in MTH208 and MTH209 are highly positively correlated (correlation coefficient = 0.70). Including section-specific shocks that correlate across outcomes reduces (to 0.60) but does not eliminate this positive correlation. This tells us that MTH208 instructors who successfully raise student performance in MTH208 also raise performance in follow-on courses. Thus we do not observe the same negative tradeoff between contemporaneous student performance and "deep learning" highlighted by Carrell and West (2010).

Columns (4) and (6) split the full sample by whether the MTH208 section was held at a ground campus (face-to-face) or the online campus. Though slightly more than half of the sections are held at ground campuses, they make up three-quarters of the instructors in the full sample. The assignment of students to online sections is de facto randomized, while results from ground sections are more generalizable to nonselective two- and four-year institutions and community colleges. Instructor quality is slightly more variable at ground campuses than online (0.31 SD vs. 0.24 SD for MTH208) but with a much larger difference by format when measuring follow-on course performance (0.24 SD vs. 0.04 SD). There are a number of reasons

Table 7.3   **Main course grade and test score outcomes**

All models include full controls in first stage, impute zero MTH209 grade if missing, and impute 10th percentile of test scores if missing.

	FTF and online combined		FTF only		Online only	
	Full sample (no section shocks) (1)	Full sample (section shocks) (2)	Full sample (no section shocks) (3)	Full sample (section shocks) (4)	Full sample (no section shocks) (5)	Full sample (section shocks) (6)
	Panel A: Outcome = standardized course grade					
Instructor effect						
SD(MTH208 effect)	0.305	0.300	0.316	0.315	0.246	0.245
	(.006)	(.006)	(.007)	(.007)	(.008)	(.008)
SD(MTH209 effect)	0.201	0.195	0.250	0.243	0.041	0.039
	(.005)	(.005)	(.006)	(.006)	(.005)	(.005)
Corr (MTH208, MTH209)	0.695	0.596	0.763	0.657	0.374	0.168
	(.017)	(.02)	(.017)	(.02)	(.087)	(.095)
Section effect						
SD(MTH208 effect)		0.287		0.280		0.296
		(1.102)		(.206)		(.15)
SD(MTH209 effect)		0.299		0.300		0.298
		(1.058)		(.192)		(.149)
Corr (MTH208, MTH209)		0.425		0.478		0.364
		(3.132)		(.659)		(.367)
Observations (sections)	26,384	26,384	13,791	13,791	12,593	12,593
Number of instructors	2,243	2,243	1,710	1,710	676	676

(continued)

Table 7.3   (continued)

	FTF and online combined		FTF only		Online only	
	Test sample (no section shocks)	Test sample (section shocks)	Test sample (no section shocks)	Test sample (section shocks)	Test sample (no section shocks)	Test sample (section shocks)
Panel B: Outcome = standardized test score						
Instructor effect						
SD(MTH208 effect)	0.436	0.444	0.482	0.486	0.110	0.135
	(.012)	(.012)	(.014)	(.014)	(.012)	(.012)
SD(MTH209 effect)	0.425	0.408	0.490	0.481	0.100	0.047
	(.012)	(.012)	(.015)	(.015)	(.017)	(.032)
Corr (MTH208, MTH209)	0.680	0.609	0.680	0.597	0.248	−0.066
	(.025)	(.027)	(.026)	(.029)	(.204)	(.358)
Section effect						
SD(MTH208 effect)		0.380		0.384		0.384
		(.605)		(.828)		(.007)
SD(MTH209 effect)		0.478		0.439		0.547
		(.481)		(.724)		(.009)
Corr (MTH208, MTH209)		0.294		0.391		0.158
		(.763)		(1.489)		(.023)
Observations (sections)	7,232	7,232	4,707	4,707	2,560	2,560
Number of instructors	1,198	1,198	938	938	292	292

Notes: Random effects models are estimated on section-level residuals. First-stage models include instructor, campus, year, and month fixed effects in addition to individual controls, section average controls, and zip code controls. Residuals are taken with respect to all of these variables other than instructor fixed effects. Individual controls include male, age, incoming GPA, incoming credits, indicator for repeat MTH208, number of times taking MTH208, 12 program dummies, and years since started program. Section average controls include section averages of these same characteristics plus total enrollment in section. Zip controls include the unemployment rate, median family income, percent of families below poverty line, and percent of adults with BA degree in zip code from 2004–7 ACS (plus missing zip). Students who did not enroll in MTH209 were assigned a zero (failing), and students who did not possess a test score for 208 or 209 were assigned the 10th percentile of the test score from their 208 section. Robust standard errors clustered by instructor in parentheses.

that online instructors may have less variation in quality than face-to-face instructors. First, ground instructors have more discretion over course delivery and are more likely to modify the curriculum. Ground instructors also have more direct interaction with students. Both of these factors may magnify differences in their effectiveness in a ground setting. Second, personnel management is centralized for online sections, while many aspects of hiring, evaluation, and instructor training are done by individual campuses for ground sections. Finally, since faculty are not randomly assigned to section formats (FTF vs. online), variance differences across formats could reflect differences in instructor characteristics. For instance, if teaching experience relates to effectiveness and ground campuses have a greater variance of instructor experience, then this will be reflected in the variance of instructor quality. Furthermore, if there is less nonrandom sorting of students to instructors (conditional on our extensive control variables) in online sections than in ground sections, this will inflate the estimated variance of instructors at ground campuses. Interestingly, instructor quality in contemporaneous and follow-on course performance is more positively correlated for face-to-face sections than for online sections, though estimates for the latter are quite imprecise and not terribly robust across specifications.

Course grades are problematic as a measure of student achievement to the extent that systematic differences across instructors reflect different grading policies or standards rather than student learning. We address this by examining student performance on normalized final course exams.[21] Panel B of table 7.3 restricts analysis to sections that start between June 2010 and March 2014, for which we have such exam scores.[22] For FTF sections, the variance of instructor effects is actually larger when using final exam scores rather than course grades: 0.49 compared with 0.31. This is consistent with less-effective teachers grading more easily than more-effective teachers. In contrast, in online sections, the variance of instructor effects is smaller when using final exam scores, consistent with less-effective teachers grading more harshly. Effectiveness is also highly positively correlated (correlation = 0.61) between contemporaneous and follow-on course exam performance. The weak correlation between contemporaneous and follow-on course performance for online MTH208 sections is also observed with final exam scores (in fact, the point estimate of the correlation is negative), though it is imprecisely estimated and generally not robust (in magnitude or sign) across alternative specifications.

One way to interpret the magnitudes is to compare them to outcome dif-

---

21. Since exams differ in maximum point values across sections and for MTH208 and MTH209, the outcome is the fraction of points earned (out of the maximum). This fraction is then standardized to mean zero and standard deviation one for the individuals with scores across the entire sample.

22. Though not shown in the table, estimates for grade outcomes on the restricted sample of sections with exam scores are nearly identical to those for the full sample in panel A. Thus any differences between panels A and B are due to the outcome differences, not the difference in sample.

ferences by student characteristics. On the standardized final exam score, for instance, students who are 10 years older score 0.15 SD lower, and a one-grade-point difference in GPA coming into the class is associated with a 0.46 SD difference in exam scores. So having an instructor who is 1 SD more effective produces a test score change that is larger than the gap between 25- and 35-year-olds and comparable to the performance gap between students entering the class with a 3.0 versus a 2.0 GPA. So at least compared to these other factors that we know are important—age and prior academic success—instructors seem to be a quite important factor in student success.

One candidate explanation for the high positive correlation between instructor effects in contemporaneous and follow-on courses in the FTF setting is that many students have the same instructors for MTH208 and MTH209 at ground campuses. Fully 81 percent of students in ground sections have the same instructor for MTH208 and MTH209, while fewer than 1 percent of students taking MTH208 online do. This difference in the likelihood of having repeat instructors could also possibly explain differences between online and face-to-face formats. Having the same instructor for both courses could generate a positive correlation through several different channels. First, instructor-specific grading practices or tendencies to "teach to the test" that are similar in MTH208 and 209 will generate correlated performances across classes that do not reflect true learning gains. Alternatively, instructors teaching both courses may do a better job of preparing students for the follow-on course.

To examine this issue, table 7.4 repeats our analysis on the subset of MTH208 face-to-face sections where students have little chance of having the same instructor for MTH209. We focus on situations where the instructor was not teaching any classes or MTH208 again in the next three months and where few (< 25 percent) or no students take MTH209 from the same instructor. While instructor quality may influence some students' choice of MTH209 instructor, it is unlikely to trump other considerations (such as schedule and timing) for all students. Thus we view these subsamples as identifying situations where students had little ability to have a repeat instructor for other reasons. Though the number of sections is reduced considerably and the included instructors are disproportionately low tenure, the estimated instructor effects exhibit a similar variation as the full sample, for both course grades and exam scores. The correlation between MTH208 and MTH209 instructor effects is reduced substantially for grades and modestly for test scores but remains positive and significant for both, even with the most restricted sample.[23]

7.5.2 Robustness of Grade and Test Score Outcomes

Table 7.5 examines the robustness of our test score results compared to different first-stage models. Our preferred first-stage model includes numer-

---

23. These specifications all include correlated section shocks across outcomes, though they are not reported in the table. Excluding section shocks makes the instructor effects more positively correlated across outcomes.

Table 7.4 Robustness to having same instructor for MTH208 and MTH209, FTF sections

All models include full controls in first stage, correlated section effects, impute zero MTH209 grade if missing, and impute 10th percentile of test score if missing MTH209 test score.

	All FTF sections (1)	Not teaching next 3 months (2)	Not teaching 208 next 3 months (3)	FTF sections with < 25% same instructor (4)	FTF sections with 0% same instructor (5)
	Panel A: Outcome = standardized course grade (full sample)				
Instructor effect					
SD(MTH208 effect)	0.315	0.333	0.318	0.326	0.313
	(.007)	(.021)	(.007)	(.015)	(.016)
SD(MTH209 effect)	0.243	0.219	0.239	0.159	0.161
	(.006)	(.039)	(.007)	(.022)	(.024)
Corr (MTH208, MTH209)	0.657	0.333	0.669	0.205	0.140
	(.02)	(.137)	(.023)	(.107)	(.118)
Observations (sections)	13,791	856	7,224	1,587	1,402
Number of instructors	1,710	618	1,695	805	763
	Panel B: Outcome = standardized test score (test score sample)				
Instructor effect					
SD(MTH208 effect)	0.486	0.466	0.474	0.464	0.436
	(.014)	(.069)	(.015)	(.035)	(.039)
SD(MTH209 effect)	0.481	0.296	0.467	0.526	0.486
	(.015)	(.093)	(.016)	(.036)	(.042)
Corr (MTH208, MTH209)	0.597	(a)	0.597	0.523	0.546
	(.029)	(a)	(.033)	(.085)	(.11)
Observations (sections)	4,707	314	2,645	573	513
Number of instructors	938	255	933	371	351

Notes: Random effects models are estimated on section-level residuals. First-stage models include instructor, campus, year, and month fixed effects in addition to individual controls, section average controls, and zip code controls. Residuals are taken with respect to all of these variables other than instructor fixed effects. Individual controls include male, age, incoming GPA, incoming credits, indicator for repeat MTH208, number of times taking MTH208, 12 program dummies, and years since started program. Section average controls include section averages of these same characteristics plus total enrollment in section. Zip controls include the unemployment rate, median family income, percent of families below poverty line, and percent of adults with BA degree in zip code from 2004–7 ACS (plus missing zip). Students who did not enroll in MTH209 were assigned a zero (failing), and students who did not possess a test score for 208 or 209 were assigned the 10th percentile of the test score from their 208 section. Robust standard errors clustered by instructor in parentheses. (a) indicates that convergence was not achieved.

Table 7.5   Robustness of test score results to first-stage model (with section shocks)

All models include section-specific shocks and impute zero MTH209 grade if missing and impute 10th percentile of test score if missing.

| | No instructor FE in first stage | | | | | | Instructor FE included in first stage | | | | | |
| | | | | | | | | | | Base model | | |
	(1)	(2)	(3)	(4)	(5)	(6)	(1)	(2)	(3)	(4)	(5)	(6)
Panel A: All sections (just test score sample), n = 7,232 sections, 1,198 instructors												
SD(MTH208 test effect)	0.293	0.263	0.285	0.266	0.266	0.248	0.294	0.442	0.287	0.444	0.440	0.425
	(.01)	(.009)	(.009)	(.009)	(.009)	(.009)	(.01)	(.012)	(.009)	(.012)	(.012)	(.011)
SD(MTH209 test effect)	0.286	0.210	0.264	0.216	0.217	0.194	0.289	0.432	0.291	0.408	0.413	0.468
	(.01)	(.01)	(.01)	(.01)	(.01)	(.009)	(.01)	(.013)	(.01)	(.012)	(.012)	(.013)
Corr (MTH208, MTH209)	0.725	0.854	0.799	0.865	0.864	0.862	0.722	0.616	0.754	0.609	0.619	0.617
	(.028)	(.027)	(.025)	(.025)	(.025)	(.028)	(.028)	(.026)	(.026)	(.027)	(.027)	(.026)
Panel B: FTF sections (just test score sample) —4,673 sections, 935 instructors												
SD(MTH208 test effect)	0.341	0.304	0.328	0.305	0.305	0.283	0.342	0.480	0.331	0.486	0.482	0.466
	(.012)	(.011)	(.011)	(.011)	(.011)	(.011)	(.012)	(.014)	(.011)	(.014)	(.014)	(.014)
SD(MTH209 test effect)	0.293	0.259	0.293	0.263	0.264	0.236	0.294	0.507	0.296	0.481	0.487	0.546
	(.012)	(.011)	(.012)	(.011)	(.011)	(.011)	(.012)	(.015)	(.012)	(.015)	(.015)	(.016)
Corr (MTH208, MTH209)	0.857	0.896	0.866	0.906	0.906	0.919	0.855	0.601	0.867	0.597	0.606	0.590
	(.023)	(.023)	(.022)	(.022)	(.022)	(.023)	(.023)	(.029)	(.022)	(.029)	(.028)	(.028)

Panel C: Online sections (just test score sample)—2,559 sections, 292 instructors

SD(MTH208 test effect)	0.135	0.135	0.135	0.135	0.135	0.135	0.135	0.135	0.135	0.135	0.135	0.135
	(.013)	(.013)	(.012)	(.013)	(.012)	(.012)	(.013)	(.013)	(.012)	(.012)	(.012)	(.012)
SD(MTH209 test effect)	0.036	0.039	0.044	0.044	0.041	0.041	0.042	0.042	0.047	0.047	0.045	0.046
	(.042)	(.039)	(.034)	(.034)	(.036)	(.036)	(.037)	(.036)	(.032)	(.032)	(.033)	(.033)
Corr (MTH208, MTH209)	−0.200	−0.172	−0.008	−0.082	−0.148	−0.142	−0.156	−0.157	−0.062	−0.066	−0.122	−0.121
	(.557)	(.489)	(.378)	(.387)	(.431)	(.43)	(.449)	(.445)	(.36)	(.358)	(.381)	(.378)
Controls in first-stage model												
Individual controls	no	no	yes	yes	yes	yes	no	no	yes	yes	yes	yes
Zip controls	no	no	yes	yes	yes	yes	no	no	yes	yes	yes	yes
Section avg. controls	no	no	yes	yes	yes	yes	no	no	yes	yes	yes	yes
Flexible controls	no	no	no	no	yes	yes	no	no	no	no	yes	yes
Year FE, month FE	yes	yes	yes	yes	yes	yes	yes	yes	yes	yes	yes	yes
Campus FE	no	yes	yes	yes	no	no	yes	yes	yes	yes	yes	yes
Location FE	no	no	no	no	no	no	no	no	no	yes	yes	yes

Notes: Random effects models are estimated on section-level residuals. Individual controls include male, age, incoming GPA, incoming credits, indicator for repeat MTH208, number of times taking MTH208, 12 program dummies, and years since started program. Section average controls include section averages of these same characteristics plus total enrollment in section. Zip controls include the unemployment rate, median family income, percent of families below poverty line, and percent of adults with BA degree in zip code from 2004–7 ACS (plus missing zip). Flexible controls include program-specific cubics in incoming GPA and credits, cubic interactions between GPA and credits, gender-specific age cubic, and interactions between gender and GPA and credits. Students who did not enroll in MTH209 were assigned a zero (failing), and students who did not possess a test score for 208 or 209 were assigned the 10th percentile of the test score from their 208 section. Robust standard errors clustered by instructor in parentheses. ** Indicates that model failed to converge.

ous student characteristics, section averages of these individual characteristics, total section enrollment, campus fixed effects, instructor fixed effects,
calendar year fixed effects, and month fixed effects. Even models with only
time controls (column 1) exhibit patterns that are qualitatively similar to
our base model, with substantial instructor quality variation, particularly
for face-to-face sections. In fact, the extensive controls have little impact on
estimates of instructor quality, suggesting minimal systematic nonrandom
sorting of students to instructors based on observed characteristics (and
possibly unobserved characteristics too). Even including incredibly flexible
student-level controls (5) or fixed effects for each physical location of the
class (6) has minimal impact on our estimates.[24] The only consequential
controls we include are campus fixed effects when combined with instructor
fixed effects, which increase the estimated variance of instructor effects on
MTH208 and MTH209 exam scores and reduce their correlation. For online
sections, estimates of instructor effects do not change at all across first stage
specifications, but the estimated correlation across current and future course
outcomes is not robust and is very imprecisely estimated.

Table 7.6 addresses sample selection by assessing the robustness of our
estimates compared to different ways of imputing missing outcomes, overall and separately by instructional mode. For grade outcomes, estimated
instructor effects are quite similar regardless of whether MTH209 grades
are imputed if a student does not take MTH209. Our preferred method for
test scores assumes that students without test scores would have received a
score at the 10th percentile of the test score distribution from their MTH208
class. The results are generally quite similar, qualitatively and quantitatively, across imputation methods (including no imputation by only using
test scores for the select sample of students with test scores). These results
suggest that the substantial differences across instructors and the positive
(overall and for FTF sections) correlation across contemporary and follow-
up course outcomes is not driven by nonrandom selection of students into
test score and follow-up course outcomes.

7.5.3   Student Evaluations and Other Outcomes

Though course grades and final exam performance are two objective
measures of student learning that can be used to assess instructor quality,
end-of-course student evaluations are the primary mechanism for assessing
instructor quality at the UPX and most other institutions. At the UPX,
end-of-course evaluations are optional; fewer than 50 percent of students
who have an MTH208 final exam score (our proxy for being engaged in the
course at the end of the class) also have a completed evaluation. Students
are asked how much they would recommend the instructor to another stu-

---

24. There are approximately 200 physical locations included in the sample, in contrast to
the 75 campuses.

Table 7.6   Robustness to imputation method

All models include full controls in first stage and include section-specific shocks.

	Grade outcomes: Missing grades for MTH209 replaced with . . .		Test score outcomes: Missing test scores for MTH208 and MTH209 replaced with . . .					
	No imputation (1)	Base model: Set equal to 0 (failing) (2)	No imputation (3)	p10 for campus-year of MTH208 section (4)	Base model: p10 of students from MTH208 section (5)	Mean of students from MTH208 section (6)	Minimum of students from MTH208 section (7)	Mean for students who received same grade in MTH208 section (8)
Panel A: All sections								
Instructor effect								
SD(MTH208 effect)	0.286	0.286	0.416	0.395	0.444	0.469	0.406	0.402
	(.008)	(.008)	(.011)	(.01)	(.012)	(.012)	(.011)	(.01)
SD(MTH209 effect)	0.244	0.205	0.394	0.343	0.408	0.495	0.379	0.374
	(.008)	(.007)	(.011)	(.01)	(.012)	(.014)	(.012)	(.011)
Corr (MTH208, MTH209)	0.477	0.550	0.544	0.614	0.609	0.531	0.623	0.556
	(.034)	(.03)	(.028)	(.025)	(.027)	(.028)	(.027)	(.027)
Panel B: FTF only								
Instructor effect								
SD(MTH208 effect)	0.298	0.298	0.445	0.430	0.486	0.503	0.445	0.436
	(.009)	(.009)	(.013)	(.013)	(.014)	(.015)	(.013)	(.013)
SD(MTH209 effect)	0.288	0.239	0.457	0.392	0.481	0.572	0.447	0.430
	(.01)	(.008)	(.014)	(.012)	(.015)	(.017)	(.014)	(.013)
Corr (MTH208, MTH209)	0.593	0.597	0.549	0.629	0.597	0.550	0.614	0.595
	(.033)	(.032)	(.031)	(.028)	(.029)	(.031)	(.029)	(.029)
Panel C: Online only								
Instructor effect								
SD(MTH208 effect)	0.227	0.225	0.115	0.107	0.135	0.141	0.123	0.118
	(a)	(.012)	(.009)	(.009)	(.012)	(.01)	(.012)	(.009)
SD(MTH209 effect)	0.047	0.028	0.034	0.010	0.047	0.054	0.048	0.023
	(a)	(.013)	(.024)	(.007)	(.032)	(.022)	(.029)	(.029)
Corr (MTH208, MTH209)	(a)	0.365	−0.296	(a)	−0.066	0.172	−0.276	0.359
	(a)	(.234)	(.403)	(a)	(.358)	(.235)	(.382)	(.526)

Notes: Random effects models are estimated on section-level residuals. First-stage models include instructor, campus, year, and month fixed effects in addition to individual controls, section average controls, and zip code controls. Residuals are taken with respect to all of these variables other than instructor fixed effects. Individual controls include male, age, incoming GPA, incoming credits, indicator for repeat MTH208, number of times taking MTH208, 12 program dummies, and years since started program. Section average controls include section averages of these same characteristics plus total enrollment in section. Zip controls include the unemployment rate, median family income, percent of families below poverty line, and percent of adults with BA degree in zip code from 2004–7 ACS (plus missing zip). Robust standard errors clustered by instructor in parentheses. (a) indicates that convergence was not achieved.

dent on a 1 to 10 scale. Scores equal to 8 or above are considered "good" by the university, and we adopt this convention as well, constructing an indicator for whether the student rated the instructor at least an 8 on the 10-point scale. Table 7.7 presents estimates of model 4 with this evaluation score included pair-wise along with four different learning outcomes. We also include section-specific shocks that are permitted to correlate between learning and evaluation outcomes. The variance of these section shocks captures section-to-section variability that is not explained by instructors. We do not impute evaluation scores when missing, as our goal is to assess how well the course evaluation system—as it is currently used—captures our more objective measures of instructor effectiveness.[25]

As with learning outcomes, there is substantial variability across instructors: a one-standard-deviation increase in instructor quality is associated with a 0.219 percentage point increase in the fraction of positive student evaluations. This variability is smaller, though still large, among online instructors and is also comparable to the section-to-section variability (0.233). Interestingly, evaluation scores are most positively correlated with grades in the current course, suggesting that instructors are rewarded (through higher evaluations) for high course grades or that students experiencing temporary positive grade shocks attribute this to their instructor. Correlations with subsequent course performance and test scores are much weaker (and even negative for MTH209 test scores). Collectively, this suggests that end-of-course evaluations by students are unlikely to capture much of the variation in instructor quality, especially for more distant or objective outcomes.

Table 7.8 presents estimates of instructor effects for several different outcomes, for both the full sample and the restricted sample for which test scores are available. There is substantial instructor variability in students' likelihood of taking MTH209 and in the number of credits earned in the six months following MTH208. Both of these are important indicators of students' longer-term success at the UPX. A one-standard-deviation increase in MTH208 instructor quality is associated with a 5 percentage point increase in the likelihood a student enrolls in MTH209 (on a base of 76 percent), with the variability twice as large for face-to-face MTH208 sections as it is for online ones. A similar increase in instructor quality is associated with a 0.13 SD increase in the number of credits earned in the six months following MTH208, again with face-to-face instructors demonstrating more than twice as much variability as those teaching online sections. Total credits earned after MTH208 is an important outcome for students and the univer-

---

25. There is the additional complication that it is not entirely clear how missing evaluations should be imputed. In contrast, we are comfortable assuming that students with missing final exam scores (because they dropped out) are likely to have received low exam scores had they taken the exam.

Table 7.7   Relationship between course grade or test effect and teaching evaluation

All models include full controls in first stage, impute zero MTH209 grade if missing, and impute 10th percentile of test score if missing.

| | FTF and online combined | | | | FTF only | | | | Online only | | | |
| | Measure of student learning | | | | Measure of student learning | | | | Measure of student learning | | | |
	MTH208 grade (1)	MTH209 grade (2)	MTH208 test (3)	MTH209 test (4)	MTH208 grade (5)	MTH209 grade (6)	MTH208 test (7)	MTH209 test (8)	MTH208 grade (9)	MTH209 grade (10)	MTH208 test (11)	MTH209 test (12)
Instructor effect												
SD(learning effect)	0.286	0.205	0.444	0.410	0.299	0.240	0.487	0.484	0.227	0.028	0.137	0.048
	(.008)	(.007)	(.012)	(.012)	(.009)	(.008)	(.014)	(.015)	(.012)	(.013)	(.012)	(.032)
SD(eval effect)	0.219	0.219	0.219	0.219	0.240	0.239	0.240	0.240	0.140	0.141	0.141	0.141
	(.006)	(.006)	(.006)	(.006)	(.008)	(.008)	(.008)	(.008)	(.008)	(.009)	(.008)	(.009)
Corr (learning, eval)	0.439	0.237	0.084	-0.084	0.390	0.223	0.059	-0.074	0.751	0.597	0.520	-0.605
	(.033)	(.042)	(.039)	(.041)	(.039)	(.047)	(.044)	(.045)	(.041)	(.293)	(.084)	(.435)
Section effect												
SD(learning effect)	0.271	0.279	0.399	0.490	0.278	0.291	0.400	0.450	0.257	0.262	0.399	0.555
	(.003)	(.148)	(.352)	(.396)	(.624)	(.004)	(.266)	(.224)	(.255)	(.004)	(.006)	(.275)
SD(eval effect)	0.233	0.233	0.219	0.213	0.246	0.246	0.232	0.228	0.210	0.217	0.200	0.191
	(.003)	(.178)	(.641)	(.913)	(.706)	(.003)	(.457)	(.442)	(.313)	(.004)	(.004)	(.797)
Corr (learning, eval)	0.174	0.040	0.119	0.001	0.156	0.041	0.102	0.001	0.214	0.041	0.153	0.001
	(.015)	(.054)	(.452)	(.017)	(.799)	(.019)	(.27)	(.021)	(.534)	(.023)	(.024)	(.026)
Observations (sections)	7,267	7,267	7,267	7,267	4,707	4,707	4,707	4,707	2,560	2,560	2,560	2,560
Number of instructors	1,201	1,201	1,201	1,201	938	938	938	938	292	292	292	292

Notes: Random effects models are estimated on section-level residuals. First-stage models include instructor, campus, year, and month fixed effects in addition to individual controls, section average controls, and zip code controls. Residuals are taken with respect to all of these variables other than instructor fixed effects. Individual controls include male, age, incoming GPA, incoming credits, indicator for repeat MTH208, number of times taking MTH208, 12 program dummies, and years since started program. Section average controls include section averages of these same characteristics plus total enrollment in section. Zip controls include the unemployment rate, median family income, percent of families below poverty line, and percent of adults with BA degree in zip code from 2004–7 ACS (plus missing zip). Students who did not enroll in MTH209 were assigned a zero (failing), and students who did not possess a test score for 208 or 209 were assigned the 10th percentile of the test score from their 208 section. Robust standard errors clustered by instructor in parentheses.

Table 7.8   Instructor effects for alternative outcomes

First-stage model with full controls

	Outcome		
	Pass MTH208	Take MTH209	Credits earned 6 mos.
Panel A: Full sample			
SD (instructor effect) overall	0.073	0.051	0.126
(n = 26,384)	(.002)	(.002)	(.004)
SD instructor effect FTF	0.080	0.062	0.154
(n = 13,791)	(.002)	(.002)	(.005)
SD instructor effect online	0.059	0.031	0.059
(n = 12,593)	(.002)	(.002)	(.004)
Panel B: Test score sample			
SD (instructor effect) overall	0.072	0.059	0.130
(n = 7,267)	(.002)	(.003)	(.006)
SD instructor effect FTF	0.077	0.069	0.150
(n = 4,707)	(.003)	(.003)	(.007)
SD instructor effect online	0.056	0.032	0.040
(n = 2,560)	(.004)	(.004)	(.011)

Notes: Random effects models are estimated on section-level residuals. First-stage models include instructor, campus, year, and month fixed effects in addition to individual controls, section average controls, and zip code controls. Residuals are taken with respect to all these variables other than instructor fixed effects. Individual controls include male, age, incoming GPA, incoming credits, indicator for repeat MTH208, number of times taking MTH208, 12 program dummies, and years since started program. Section average controls include section averages of these same characteristics plus total enrollment in section. Zip controls include the unemployment rate, median family income, percent of families below poverty line, and percent of adults with BA degree in zip code from 2004–7 ACS (plus missing zip). Robust standard errors clustered by instructor in parentheses.

sity that is unlikely to be manipulated by individual instructors. In appendix table 7.A3, we report correlations between predicted instructor effects measured with these different outcomes for the test score sample, overall and separately by format.[26] Most of the outcomes are positively correlated overall and for face-to-face sections. Interestingly, value added measured by the likelihood of taking MTH209 after MTH208 is only weakly correlated with value added measured by final exam scores. Thus instructors who excel in improving student test scores are unlikely to excel at getting their students to enroll in the follow-up course.

26. These correlation matrices are formed by predicting the BLUP instructor effects for different outcomes one at a time and correlating these using section-level data. It would be more efficient to estimate all the effects and the correlations simultaneously as we did for pairs of outcomes (e.g., grades in MTH208 and MTH209 in table 7.3), but these models did not converge. Consequently, these models do not include section-specific shocks that correlate across outcomes. Thus the correlations reported in table 7.A3 differ from those in table 7.3. Correlations are quite similar for the full sample.

7.6   Does Effectiveness Correlate with Experience and Pay?

Having demonstrated substantial variation in instructor effectiveness along several dimensions of student success, particularly for face-to-face sections, we now consider how teaching experience and pay correlate with effectiveness. Are more experienced instructors more effective? Are more effective instructors paid more highly? While we do not attempt an exhaustive analysis of these questions, the answers have implications for whether instructional resources are used productively and how overall effectiveness could be improved. Teaching experience—both course specific and general—may be an important factor in instructor performance given results found in other contexts (e.g., Cook and Mansfield 2014; Ost 2014; Papay and Kraft 2015).

For this analysis, we focus on instructors hired since 2002 so that we can construct a full history of courses taught across all courses and in MTH208 specifically, not censored by data availability. This results in 18,409 sections (5,970 in the test score sample). Our main approach is to regress section-level residuals $\tilde{Y}_{jkt}$ on observed instructor experience at the time the section was taught:

$$(5) \qquad \tilde{Y}_{jkt} = f(Exp_{MTH208,t}) + \theta_k + e_{jkt},$$

where $f(.)$ is a flexible function of experience teaching MTH208. Our preferred model includes instructor fixed effects, θ_k, isolating changes in effectiveness as individual instructors gain experience. This model controls for selection into experience levels based on fixed instructor characteristics but does not control for time-varying factors related to experience and effectiveness. For instance, if instructors tend to accumulate teaching experience when other work commitments are slack, the experience effect may be confounded with any effects of these other work commitments. We also include other dimensions of experience, such as the number of sections of MTH209 and other courses taught. Papay and Kraft (2015) discuss the challenges in estimating equation (5) in the traditional K–12 setting given the near collinearity between experience and calendar year for almost all teachers. Many of these issues are not present in our setting, since the timing of when courses are taught and experience is accumulated differs dramatically across instructors. The nonstandard calendar of the UPX thus facilitates the separation of experience from time effects.

Figures 7.1 and 7.2 present estimates of equation (5) for a nonparametric version of $f(.)$, regressing section mean residuals on a full set of MTH208 experience dummies (capped at 20) along with year, month, and (when noted) instructor fixed effects.[27] Figure 7.1 depicts the results for

---

27. Approximately one quarter of the sections are taught by instructors who have taught MTH208 more than 20 times previously. Nine percent have not previously taught MTH208.

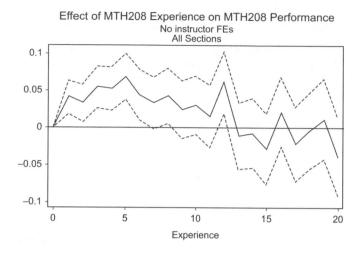

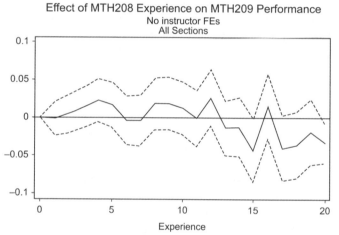

Fig. 7.1   Relationship between instructor effectiveness (grades) and teaching experience

Notes: Dashed lines denote 95 percent confidence interval (CI) with standard errors clustered by instructor. Section mean residuals are regressed on MTH208 teaching experience (capped at 20), instructor fixed effects (bottom row), and year and month fixed effects. Sample restricted to 18,418 sections taught by instructors hired since 2002. First-stage model includes full controls (see text).

course grade outcomes. Effectiveness increases very modestly the first few times instructors teach MTH208, as measured by MTH208 and MTH209 course grades. Interestingly, including instructor fixed effects stabilizes the effectiveness-experience profile, suggesting that less-effective instructors are more likely to select into having more MTH208 teaching experience. Figure 7.2 repeats this analysis, but for final exam test scores on the restricted test score sample. Estimates are quite imprecise but do suggest modest growth in

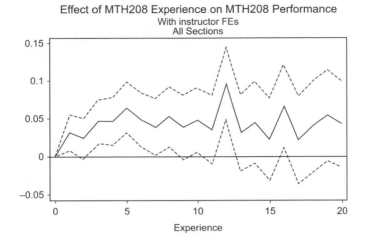

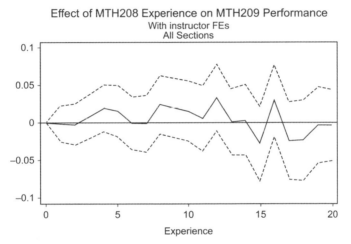

Fig. 7.1   (cont.)

MTH208 exam scores as instructors gain experience. Improvement with experience is not as clear-cut for MTH209 test score performance.

To gain precision, table 7.9 presents estimates from parametric specifications for f(.) while also including teaching experience in other courses and time since hire (in panel C). We find that teaching MTH208 at least one time previously is associated with a 0.03 to 0.04 SD increase in effectiveness (measured by MTH208 grade), but that additional experience improves this outcome very little. This holds even after controlling for additional experience in other subjects. The impact of instructors' experience on follow-on course grades is more modest and gradual. Test score results are much less precise but do suggest that instructor effectiveness increases with experi-

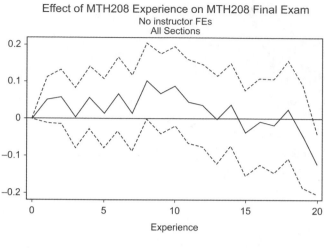

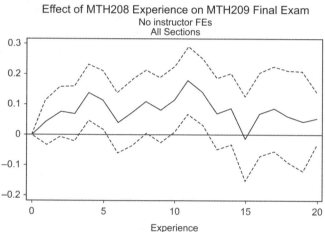

Fig. 7.2   Relationship between instructor effectiveness (test scores) and teaching experience

Notes: Dashed lines denote 95 percent CI with standard errors clustered by instructor. Section mean residuals are regressed on MTH208 teaching experience (capped at 20), instructor fixed effects (bottom row), and year and month fixed effects. Sample restricted to 5,860 sections taught by instructors hired since 2002. First-stage model includes full controls (see text).

ence for final exams in contemporaneous courses and (very modestly) in follow-on courses. We find that general experience in other subjects has little association with effectiveness in MTH208 (not shown). Finally, we find no systematic relationship between teaching experience and instructors' impact on the number of credits their students earn subsequent to MTH208. Whether the instructor was hired in the past year and the number of years since first hire date have no association with most measures of instructor

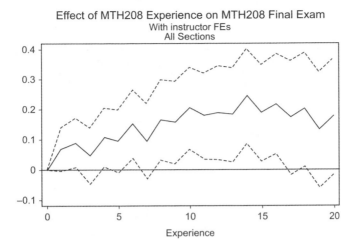

Effect of MTH208 Experience on MTH208 Final Exam
With instructor FEs
All Sections

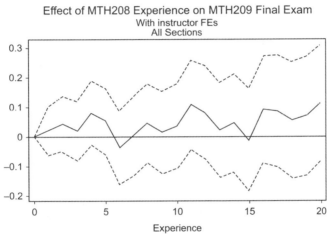

Effect of MTH208 Experience on MTH209 Final Exam
With instructor FEs
All Sections

Fig. 7.2   (cont.)

effectiveness (after controlling for MTH208 experience) but are associated with MTH208 test scores.

If pay was commensurate with effectiveness, then the substantial variation in measured effectiveness across instructors would not necessarily translate to productivity or efficiency differences (at least from the institution's perspective). Our discussions with leaders at the UPX suggest that pay is not linked to classroom performance in any direct way but rather is tied primarily to tenure and experience. We directly examine correlates of instructor salary quantitatively in table 7.10. Consistent with this practice, effectiveness (as measured by section-level mean residuals in MTH209 grades) is uncorrelated with pay, both in the cross section and within instructors over

Table 7.9 **Correlates of instructor effectiveness**

First-stage model with full controls. All sections, faculty hired since 2002.

	Outcome: Section-level mean residual for				
	MTH208 grade (1)	MTH209 grade (2)	MTH208 test (3)	MTH209 test (4)	Credits earned 6 months (5)
A. Linear, only MTH208 experience, instructor FEs					
Taught MTH208 previously	0.0384*** (0.0108)	0.00635 (0.0107)	0.0690** (0.0340)	0.0192 (0.0382)	−0.0162 (0.0104)
Times taught MTH208	0.00004 (0.0008)	0.000127 (0.0006)	−0.00333 (0.0045)	−0.0034 (0.0044)	0.00054 (0.0006)
B. Piecewise, only MTH208 experience, instructor FEs					
Times taught MTH208 = 1	0.0313*** (0.0121)	−0.00153 (0.0123)	0.0669* (0.0363)	0.0198 (0.0424)	0.00050 (0.0121)
Times taught MTH208 = 2 to 5	0.0409*** (0.0121)	0.00804 (0.0121)	0.0777* (0.0398)	0.045 (0.0440)	−0.0195* (0.0114)
Times taught MTH208 = 6 to 10	0.0403*** (0.0156)	0.00798 (0.0145)	0.137** (0.0541)	−0.000604 (0.0563)	−0.005 (0.0140)
Times taught MTH208 = 11 to 15	0.0412** (0.0200)	0.00129 (0.0176)	0.169** (0.0656)	0.0432 (0.0682)	−0.00106 (0.0170)
Times taught MTH208 = 16 to 20	0.0397* (0.0235)	−0.0087 (0.0195)	0.159** (0.0792)	0.0765 (0.0810)	0.0171 (0.0191)
Times taught MTH208 > 20	0.0348 (0.0278)	−0.00467 (0.0231)	0.131 (0.0893)	0.113 (0.0964)	0.0428* (0.0225)
C. Linear, control for MTH209 experience, other math, nonmath experience linearly, time since hire, instructor FEs					
Taught MTH208 previously	0.0277** (0.0135)	−0.00529 (0.0127)	0.0588 (0.0484)	−0.0449 (0.0547)	−0.0248** (0.0118)
Times taught MTH208	0.000248 (0.0009)	0.00004 (0.0006)	−0.00819 (0.0051)	−0.00256 (0.0048)	0.00084 (0.0006)
Taught MTH209 previously	0.0146 (0.0154)	0.0144 (0.0130)	−0.0135 (0.0536)	0.0809* (0.0487)	0.0154 (0.0117)
Times taught MTH209	0.0015 (0.0010)	0.000885 (0.0008)	0.00104 (0.0047)	0.00904** (0.0044)	−0.00003 (0.0008)
Years since first hire date	0.0023 (0.0158)	−0.00468 (0.0160)	0.0192 (0.0475)	0.0382 (0.0564)	0.0227 (0.0161)
First hire more than one year ago	0.0167 (0.0121)	0.0167 (0.0115)	0.0844*** (0.0320)	−0.0012 (0.0329)	0.0014 (0.0107)

Notes: Section mean residuals are regressed on teaching experience, instructor fixed effects, and year and month fixed effects. Sample restricted to 18,409 sections (5,970 for test scores) taught by instructors hired since 2002. First-stage model includes instructor, campus, year, and month fixed effects in addition to individual controls, section average controls, and zip code controls. Residuals are taken with respect to all of these variables other than instructor fixed effects. Individual controls include male, age, incoming GPA, incoming credits, indicator for repeat MTH208, number of times taking MTH208, 12 program dummies, and years since started program. Section average controls include section averages of these same characteristics plus total enrollment in section. Zip controls include the unemployment rate, median family income, percent of families below poverty line, and percent of adults with BA degree in zip code from 2004–7 ACS (plus missing zip). Students who did not enroll in MTH209 were assigned a zero (failing), and students who did not possess a test score for 208 or 209 were assigned the 10th percentile of the test score from their 208 section. Robust standard errors clustered by instructor in parentheses.

Table 7.10   **Correlates of instructor salary, all sections, faculty hired since 2002**

	Total salary paid for MTH208 section ($1,000) (mean = 1.077)				
	(1)	(2)	(3)	(4)	(5)
Section-level mean residual	−0.00521	0.00331	0.00642	0.00654	0.00648
for MTH209 grade	(0.00567)	(0.00475)	(0.00460)	(0.00437)	(0.00437)
Years since first hire date		0.02950***	0.02737***	0.04439***	0.04592***
		(0.00139)	(0.00137)	(0.00432)	(0.00442)
First hire more than one		0.01049***	0.00768**	0.00599	0.00537
year ago		(0.00368)	(0.00352)	(0.00368)	(0.00379)
Total sections taught		0.00051***	0.00047***	0.00006	
previously		(0.00012)	(0.00011)	(0.00015)	
Taught MTH208					0.00221
previously					(0.00353)
Times taught MTH208					−0.00056**
					(0.00026)
Times taught MTH209					0.00014
					(0.00028)
Times taught other math					−0.00014
courses					(0.00030)
Times taught nonmath					0.00015
courses					(0.00020)
Constant	1.03775	0.91904	0.90719	0.95343	0.95072
	(0.00351)	(0.00734)	(0.00719)	(0.01255)	(0.01273)
R-squared	0.26521	0.53594	0.56478	0.71340	0.71372
Fixed effects	None	None	Campus	Instructor	Instructor

Notes: Sample restricted to 18,080 sections taught by instructors hired since 2002. All specifications also include year and month fixed effects. Section-level residuals include the full set of individual and section controls and campus fixed effects, imputing zero MTH209 grades for students who did not enroll. Robust standard errors clustered by instructor in parentheses.

time.[28] However, the number of years since first hire is the one consistent predictor of the salary instructors are paid for MTH208 courses. Instructors receive approximately $44 more per course for each year of tenure (approximately 4 percent higher pay) after fixed instructor differences are accounted for. Overall and course-specific teaching experience have no association with instructor salary.

7.7   Conclusion and Discussion

In this study, we document substantial differences in effectiveness across instructors of required college algebra courses at the UPX. A 1 SD increase

---

28. It is possible that noise in our estimates of section-specific effectiveness attenuates our estimate of the relationship between effectiveness and pay. We are currently examining this issue, though we note that a finding of no relationship is consistent with the institution's stated pay policy.

in instructor quality is associated with a 0.20 SD increase in course grades and a 0.41 SD increase in final exam scores in the follow-on course, as well as a 0.13 SD increase in the number of credits earned within six months. Variation is much smaller for online sections yet still measurable and larger than that found in other contexts. Putting these magnitudes in context, having an instructor who is 1 SD more effective produces a test score change that is larger than the performance gap between 25- and 35-year-olds and comparable to the performance gap between students entering the class with a 3.0 versus a 2.0 GPA. Instructors are clearly quite an important factor in student success.

It is worth considering what institutional factors may contribute to such large differences across instructors, particularly in contrast to other settings. Prior work in postsecondary education has focused on selective and research-oriented public and nonprofit universities, courses taught by permanent or tenure-track faculty, institutions operating in a single geographic location, and institutions serving "traditional" students. Our setting focuses on a nonselective for-profit institution where the teaching force is contingent and employed part-time, the student body is diverse, the performance of the teaching force is solely based on teaching and instruction, and courses and testing procedures are highly standardized. It is possible that instructors are a more important factor in the success of "nontraditional" students or that there is more variation in instructor quality among contingent and adjunct faculty than among permanent or tenure-track faculty. The one prior study that finds instructor variation comparable to ours (Bettinger et al. 2015) shares all of these traits with our study institution. Having a better understanding of the importance of faculty at less-selective institutions and in settings where most faculty are contingent is important, as these institutions serve a very large (and growing) share of postsecondary students in the United States. Finally, it is possible that the fast course pace—five weeks—could magnify the consequences of behavioral differences across instructors. A delay in providing student feedback—even just a few days—could be devastating to students in a five-week course.

This substantial variation across instructors suggests the potential to improve student and institutional performance via changes in how faculty are hired, developed, motivated, and retained. Institutions like the UPX reflect the sector-wide trend toward contingent faculty (e.g., adjuncts and lecturers), which aims to save costs and create flexibility (Ehrenberg 2012). The debate about whether adjuncts are better or worse for instruction than permanent faculty obfuscates the feature that contingent arrangements create opportunities for improving student performance via personnel policies that are not available when faculty are permanent. However, instructor evaluation and compensation systems have not kept up with these changes; our study institution has an evaluation system (student course evaluations) that is similar to that at elite research universities and a salary schedule that varies only with tenure and credentials. Of course, the potential for improvement through changes in personnel policies—and how these policies should be designed—depends critically on the supply of instructors available (e.g., Rothstein 2015). Online and ground campuses likely face quite different labor markets for instructors, the former drawing on instructors across the country, suggesting that personnel policies should differ between them. A better understanding of the labor market for postsecondary faculty—particularly at less-selective institutions—is an important area for future attention.

Finally, we have focused on the role of individual faculty in promoting the success of students. In fact, differences in instructor effectiveness are one potential explanation for cross-institution differences in institutional performance and productivity that has yet to be explored. Our study suggests it should be.

Appendix A: Additional Data

Table 7.A1a   Descriptive statistics for sections and instructors (test score sample)

	All sections (n = 7,267)		Face-to-face sections (n = 4,707)		Online sections (n = 2,560)	
	Mean	SD	Mean	SD	Mean	SD
Online section	0.352	0.478	0.000	0.000	1.000	0.000
Male	0.683	0.465	0.699	0.459	0.656	0.475
White	0.641	0.480	0.633	0.482	0.652	0.476
Section-average student age	34.37	3.35	33.70	3.48	35.60	2.72
Section-average share male	0.38	0.18	0.41	0.19	0.32	0.14
Section-average incoming GPA	3.20	0.21	3.18	0.22	3.23	0.17
Section-average incoming credits	24.53	7.15	25.20	7.77	23.30	5.65
Section-average repeat 208	0.11	0.11	0.09	0.10	0.15	0.10
Section-average number times taken	1.12	0.13	1.10	0.12	1.16	0.13
Section-average time since program start (years)	1.23	0.52	1.20	0.51	1.30	0.53
Section enrollment	13.04	4.28	12.70	5.16	13.66	1.60
Years since first hire	6.271	5.008	5.908	5.450	6.939	3.987
Years since first hire > 1	0.832	0.374	0.802	0.399	0.887	0.317
Total MTH208 sections taught prior to this section	19.661	20.900	13.704	15.689	30.615	24.542
Ever taught MTH208 prior to this section	0.937	0.244	0.911	0.285	0.984	0.126
Total sections instructor taught prior to this section	59.854	66.590	58.833	75.495	61.733	45.869
Total MTH209 sections taught prior to this section	14.014	16.765	13.139	15.680	15.621	18.490
Ever taught MTH209 prior to this section	0.805	0.396	0.896	0.306	0.639	0.480

Table 7.A1b   Descriptive statistics for students (test score sample)

	All sections (n = 94,745)		Face-to-face sections (n = 59,787)		Online sections (n = 34,958)	
	Mean	SD	Mean	SD	Mean	SD
Male	0.384	0.486	0.419	0.493	0.323	0.468
Age	34.319	9.411	33.570	9.300	35.601	9.460
Baseline GPA (0–4)	3.206	0.576	3.195	0.565	3.227	0.594
Credits earned prior to start of MTH208	24.533	17.534	25.256	16.690	23.296	18.827
Took MTH208 before	0.112	0.316	0.089	0.285	0.152	0.359
Number of times MTH208 taken	1.124	0.407	1.103	0.360	1.160	0.475
BS (general studies)	0.164	0.371	0.159	0.366	0.173	0.378
BS in nursing	0.044	0.206	0.017	0.131	0.090	0.287
BS in accounting	0.009	0.094	0.005	0.071	0.015	0.123
BS in business	0.382	0.486	0.467	0.499	0.236	0.425
BS in criminal justice administration	0.100	0.300	0.124	0.330	0.058	0.234
BS in education	0.028	0.166	0.013	0.115	0.054	0.226
BS in health administration	0.091	0.288	0.092	0.288	0.090	0.287
BS in human services	0.044	0.204	0.036	0.186	0.057	0.232
BS in information technology	0.043	0.203	0.046	0.210	0.038	0.191
BS in management	0.055	0.228	0.027	0.162	0.103	0.304
Nondegree program	0.013	0.114	0.003	0.056	0.031	0.172
BS in other program	0.025	0.155	0.009	0.095	0.051	0.221
Time since program start date (years)	1.234	1.596	1.197	1.425	1.297	1.850
Grade in MTH208	2.385	1.361	2.405	1.324	2.352	1.422
A / A–	0.283	0.451	0.275	0.447	0.296	0.457
B+ / B / B–	0.277	0.448	0.283	0.451	0.267	0.442
C+ / C / C–	0.189	0.392	0.203	0.402	0.167	0.373
D+ / D / D–	0.092	0.289	0.099	0.299	0.080	0.272
F	0.052	0.221	0.050	0.217	0.055	0.227
Withdrawn	0.106	0.308	0.090	0.286	0.135	0.342
Passed MTH208	0.842	0.365	0.861	0.346	0.810	0.392
MTH208 final exam score available	0.854	0.354	0.894	0.308	0.785	0.411
MTH208 final exam % correct (if available)	0.707	0.241	0.696	0.246	0.728	0.230
Took MTH209	0.779	0.415	0.833	0.373	0.686	0.464
Grade in MTH209 (if took it)	2.467	1.249	2.524	1.187	2.347	1.361
A / A–	0.265	0.442	0.265	0.442	0.265	0.441
B+ / B / B–	0.296	0.457	0.307	0.461	0.273	0.445
C+ / C / C–	0.220	0.414	0.233	0.423	0.192	0.394
D+ / D / D–	0.102	0.302	0.107	0.309	0.091	0.288
F	0.040	0.195	0.031	0.174	0.057	0.232
Withdrawn	0.067	0.250	0.049	0.215	0.105	0.306
MTH209 final exam score available	0.670	0.470	0.758	0.428	0.518	0.500
MTH209 final exam % correct (if available)	0.690	0.245	0.691	0.243	0.688	0.251
Credits earned in following year	10.947	5.348	11.561	5.078	9.897	5.628
Have course evaluation	0.369	0.483	0.342	0.474	0.416	0.493
Course evaluation: Recommend instructor	0.661	0.473	0.694	0.461	0.614	0.487

Table 7.A2   **How much switching is there between online and FTF campuses?**

Number of MTH208 faculty by online and FTF participation

	Total FTF campuses taught at					
	0	1	2	3	4	Total
Never online	0	1,498	110	10	1	1,619
Taught online	534	126	14	3	0	677
Total	534	1,624	124	13	1	2,296

Table 7.A3   Correlation across outcomes (restricted to test sample)

All models include full controls in first stage, impute zero MTH209 grade if missing, and impute 10th percentile of test score if missing.

	Test MTH208	Test MTH209	Grade MTH208	Grade MTH209	Credits earned 6 mos.	Pass MTH208	Take MTH209	Good evaluation in MTH208
All sections restricted to test and evaluations sample (N = 7,135 sections)								
Test MTH208	1.00							
Test MTH209	0.57	1.00						
Grade MTH208	0.53	0.27	1.00					
Grade MTH209	0.30	0.30	0.51	1.00				
Credits earned 6 mos.	0.23	0.08	0.40	0.47	1.00			
Pass MTH208	0.39	0.13	0.83	0.43	0.54	1.00		
Take MTH209	0.13	0.01	0.38	0.63	0.52	0.51	1.00	
Good evaluation in MTH208	0.11	-0.04	0.38	0.21	0.17	0.35	0.14	1.00
FTF sections restricted to test and evaluations sample (N = 4,581 sections)								
Test MTH208	1.00							
Test MTH209	0.61	1.00						
Grade MTH208	0.54	0.35	1.00					
Grade MTH209	0.34	0.31	0.60	1.00				
Credits earned 6 mos.	0.35	0.12	0.46	0.47	1.00			
Pass MTH208	0.39	0.19	0.79	0.50	0.60	1.00		
Take MTH209	0.10	0.03	0.34	0.64	0.51	0.49	1.00	
Good evaluation in MTH208	0.07	-0.03	0.31	0.21	0.14	0.27	0.06	1.00

Online sections restricted to test and evaluations sample (N = 2,554 sections)

	Test MTH208	Test MTH209	Grade MTH208	Grade MTH209	Credits earned 6 mos.	Pass MTH208	Take MTH209	Good evaluation in MTH208
Test MTH208	1.00							
Test MTH209	0.06	1.00						
Grade MTH208	0.43	−0.30	1.00					
Grade MTH209	0.23	0.30	0.13	1.00				
Credits earned 6 mos.	0.23	−0.06	0.54	0.56	1.00			
Pass MTH208	0.39	−0.32	0.91	0.20	0.62	1.00		
Take MTH209	0.28	−0.12	0.53	0.71	0.66	0.59	1.00	
Good evaluation in MTH208	0.37	−0.15	0.65	0.19	0.35	0.63	0.42	1.00

Notes: Random effects models are estimated on section-level residuals on a outcome at a time. Tables show pair-wise correlations between predicted best linear unbiased predictors (BLUPs) for random instructor effects for each pair of outcomes. First-stage models include instructor, campus, year, and month fixed effects in addition to individual controls, section average controls, and zip code controls. Residuals are taken with respect to all of these variables other than instructor fixed effects. Individual controls include male, age, incoming GPA, incoming credits, indicator for repeat MTH208, number of times taking MTH208, 12 program dummies, and years since started program. Section average controls include section averages of these same characteristics plus total enrollment in section. Zip controls include the unemployment rate, median family income, percent of families below poverty line, and percent of adults with BA degree in zip code from 2004–7 ACS (plus missing zip). Students who did not enroll in MTH209 were assigned a zero (failing), and students who did not possess a test score for 208 or 209 were assigned the 10th percentile of the test score from their 208 section. Robust standard errors clustered by instructor in parentheses.

Appendix B: Final Exam Score Determination

For sections from July 2010 to March 2014, we have detailed information on student performance separately by course assignment or assessment, which includes everything from individual homework assignments to group exercises to exams. We use these data to obtain a final exam score for each student when available. Because the data do not have a single, clear code for the final exam component across all sections and instructors have the discretion to add additional final exam components, we use a decision rule to identify the "best" exam score for each student based on the text description of the assessment object.

Ideally, this measure would capture computer-administered tests, since instructors do not have discretion over these. We therefore define a quality measure, ranging from 1 (best) to 4 (worst), that indicates how clean we believe the identification of these test scores to be. Once a student in a certain section is assigned a test score, it is marked and not considered in later steps, so students are assigned a single quality measure and the assigned test score is of the highest quality available.

Group 1 consists of the computer-administered common assessments available to all UPX instructors. To identify these assessments, we flag strings that contain words or phrases associated with the computer testing regime (e.g., "Aleks," "MyMathLab," or "MML") as well as words or phrases indicating a final exam (e.g., "final exam," "final examination," "final test"). If a student has an assessment that meets these criteria, we use the score from this assessment as the student's final exam score.[29] Specifically, we use the fraction of test items answered correctly as our measure of student performance. Roughly 11 percent of student sections in our test score subsample have a final exam score with this highest level of quality for both MTH208 and MTH209 test scores.

Some students have a single assessment with a word or phrase indicating a final exam (e.g., "final exam," "final examination," "final test") but no explicit indication that the exam was from the standardized online system. If the assessment does not contain any additional words or phrases indicating that the test was developed by the instructor (e.g., "in class," "instructor generated"), we are reasonably confident that it refers to the standardized online system. Hence we use this assessment score as the student's final exam, but we consider these assessments as part of group 2 for the purpose of exam

---

29. In extremely rare cases (less than 4 percent of the sample), students will have more than one assessment that meets these criteria, in which case we sum the attained and maximal score for these components and calculate the percentage score. This is, in part, because for many cases, there was no grade component that could be clearly identified as the test score (e.g., a student may have "Aleks final exam: part 1" and "Aleks final exam: part 2"). About 3.75 percent of these cases have two assessments that meet the criteria. The maximum number of components for a student is five.

quality. Another 77 percent of student sections fall into this category for the MTH208 and MTH209 sections.

The third group looks at strings such as "test," "quiz," and "course exam." While quizzes and tests may sometimes refer to weekly refresher assessments, these strings identify final test scores reasonably well after having considered decision rules 1 and 2. About 9 percent of the student sections fall into this category for both section types. The fourth and final group selects a grade component as a final test score if the title includes both "class" and "final." Another 2 percent of the sample is assigned a test score of this quality for both the MTH208 and MTH209 sections.

References

Bettinger, E., L. Fox, S. Loeb, and E. Taylor. 2015. "Changing Distributions: How Online College Classes Alter Student and Professor Performance." Working paper, Stanford University.

Bettinger, E. P., and B. T. Long. 2005. "Do Faculty Serve as Role Models? The Impact of Instructor Gender on Female Students." *American Economic Review* 95 (2): 152–57.

———. 2010. "Does Cheaper Mean Better? The Impact of Using Adjunct Instructors on Student Outcomes." *Review of Economics and Statistics* 92 (3): 598–613.

Braga, M., M. Paccagnella, and M. Pellizzari. 2014. "The Academic and Labor Market Returns of University Professors." *IZA Discussion Papers*, no. 7902.

Brodaty, T., and M. Gurgand. 2016. "Good Peers or Good Teachers? Evidence from a French University." *Economics of Education Review* 54:62–78.

Carrell, S. E., and J. E. West. 2010. "Does Professor Quality Matter? Evidence from Random Assignment of Students to Professors." *Journal of Political Economy* 118 (3): 409–32.

Chetty, R., J. N. Friedman, and J. E. Rockoff. 2014. "Measuring the Impacts of Teachers I: Evaluating Bias in Teacher Value-Added Estimates." *American Economic Review* 104 (9): 2593–2632.

Cook, J. B., and R. K. Mansfield. 2015. "Task-Specific Experience and Task-Specific Talent: Decomposing the Productivity of High School Teachers." Working paper.

Ehrenberg, R. G. 2012. "American Higher Education in Transition." *Journal of Economic Perspectives* 26 (1): 193–216.

Ehrenberg, R. G., and L. Zhang. 2005. "Do Tenured and Tenure-track Faculty Matter?" *Journal of Human Resources* 40 (3): 647–59.

Fairlie, R. W., F. Hoffmann, and P. Oreopoulos. 2014. "A Community College Instructor like Me: Race and Ethnicity Interactions in the Classroom." *American Economic Review* 104 (8): 2567–91.

Figlio, D. N., M. O. Schapiro, and K. B. Soter. 2015. "Are Tenure Track Professors Better Teachers?" *Review of Economics and Statistics* 97 (4): 715–24.

Hoffmann, F., and P. Oreopoulos. 2009a. "Professor Qualities and Student Achievement." *Review of Economics and Statistics* 91 (1): 83–92.

———. 2009b. "A Professor like Me: The Influence of Instructor Gender on College Achievement." *Journal of Human Resources* 44 (2): 479–94.

Jackson, C. K., J. E. Rockoff, and D. O. Staiger. 2014. "Teacher Effects and Teacher-Related Policies." *Annual Review of Economics* 6:801–25.

Jacob, B. A., and L. Lefgren. 2008. "Can Principals Identify Effective Teachers? Evidence on Subjective Performance Evaluation in Education." *Journal of Labor Economics* 26 (1): 101–36.

Kane, T. J., J. E. Rockoff, and D. O. Staiger. 2008. "What Does Certification Tell Us about Teacher Effectiveness? Evidence from New York City." *Economics of Education Review* 27 (6): 615–31.

Morris, Jolene. 2016. "University of Phoenix, Online Campus Course Syllabus—Math 208 r3." Accessed October 26, 2016. http://www.jolenemorris.com /mathematics/Math208/CM/Week0/math_208_syllabus.htm.

Ost, B. 2014. "How Do Teachers Improve? The Relative Importance of Specific and General Human Capital." *American Economic Journal: Applied Economics* 6 (2): 127–51.

Papay, John P., and Matthew A. Kraft. 2015. "Productivity Returns to Experience in the Teacher Labor Market: Methodological Challenges and New Evidence on Long-Term Career Improvement." *Journal of Public Economics* 130:105–19.

Rivkin, S. G., E. A. Hanushek, and J. F. Kain. 2005. "Teachers, Schools, and Academic Achievement." *Econometrica* 73 (2): 417–58.

Rockoff, J. E. 2004. "The Impact of Individual Teachers on Student Achievement: Evidence from Panel Data." *American Economic Review* 94 (2): 247–52.

Rothstein, J. 2009. "Student Sorting and Bias in Value Added Estimation: Selection on Observables and Unobservables." *Education Finance and Policy* 4 (4): 537–71.

———. 2010. "Teacher Quality in Educational Production: Tracking, Decay, and Student Achievement." *Quarterly Journal of Economics* 125 (1): 175–214.

———. 2015. "Teacher Quality Policy When Supply Matters." *American Economic Review* 105 (1): 100–130.

8

The Competitive Effects of Online Education

David J. Deming, Michael Lovenheim,
and Richard Patterson

Online education is an increasingly important component of the US higher education landscape. In 2014, one in three college students attending degree-granting US institutions took at least one course online (Allen and Seaman 2015). Millions of students from all over the world also have enrolled in massive open online courses (MOOCs) offered in partnership with major research universities such as Harvard, MIT, and Stanford (Ho et al. 2014; McPherson and Bacow 2015; Waldrop 2014). By 2012, more than 6 percent of all US bachelor's degrees were awarded online (Deming et al. 2016). The rapid rise of online course offerings and degrees has led to predictions that competition from MOOCs and other online course offerings will lead to "disruptive innovation" in higher education (e.g., Christensen and Eyring 2011; Cowen and Tabarrok 2014). While there is a growing body of research examining student outcomes among those enrolling in online degree programs or courses (Bettinger et al. 2017; Deming et al. 2016), no prior work has estimated the impact of this change in higher education markets on brick-and-mortar schools.

The exuberance over MOOCs and other high-profile online offerings obscures the fact that most of the growth in online higher education has been

David J. Deming is professor of public policy at the Harvard Kennedy School, professor of education and economics at the Harvard Graduate School of Education, and a research associate of the National Bureau of Economic Research.

Michael Lovenheim is professor of economics, labor and industrial relations, and policy analysis and management at Cornell University and a research associate of the National Bureau of Economic Research.

Richard Patterson is assistant professor of economics in the Department of Social Sciences at the United States Military Academy.

For acknowledgments, sources of research support, and disclosure of the authors' material financial relationships, if any, please see http://www.nber.org/chapters/c13881.ack.

among the least selective institutions, especially for-profit colleges (Deming, Goldin, and Katz 2012). In 2013, selective institutions accounted for only about 2 percent of enrollment in fully online programs, compared to 33 percent in the for-profit sector (Deming et al. 2015).[1] Online for-profits spend very little per student and are viewed less favorably by employers than nonselective brick-and-mortar schools of all types (Deming et al. 2016).

For public institutions, the allure of online education lies in its potential to cut costs in a time of declining state support and tightening budgets (Bowen et al. 2014). Yet cost savings from larger classes and less student-faculty contact may cause instructional quality to suffer, and high-quality online courses are—at least at the time of writing—equally or even more expensive to develop and staff than in-person courses (McPherson and Bacow 2015).[2]

In this chapter, we ask whether online degree programs can improve educational productivity by exerting competitive pressure on traditional brick-and-mortar institutions. How might competition from online providers affect the market for higher education? In a well-functioning marketplace, the new availability of a cost-saving technology should increase efficiency, because colleges compete with each other to provide the highest quality education at the lowest price. The market for selective colleges is increasingly geographically integrated, and these colleges compete fiercely on the quality margin (Clotfelter 1999; Hoxby 1997, 2009). In contrast, the vast majority of students in nonselective colleges attend school close to their homes and in their home states. In 2013, 39.3 percent of students at selective colleges were from out of state, compared to just 13.8 percent of students in less-selective four-year schools and only 5.6 percent in community colleges.

In principle, local education markets can still be competitive. However, there are a few reasons to suspect that many are not. First, public colleges and universities are heavily subsidized by state and local governments and face political pressure to keep tuition low. Prices at public institutions are often set below marginal cost, which drives out private competitors who are not receiving such subsidies. Second, for political and historical reasons, public institutions are often located in communities that are not populous enough to support private competitors.

As a result of the uneven geographic dispersion of postsecondary schools and the high probability that students enrolling in nonselective schools attend close to home, nonselective public institutions in less-dense areas either are local monopoly providers of education or have considerable

---

1. We define selective institutions as those that received a rating of Most Competitive, Highly Competitive, or Very Competitive according to the 2009 Barron's Profile of American Colleges.

2. Several recent studies conducted by a wide variety of institutions find that online course-taking reduces student learning and lowers persistence through college (Figlio, Rush, and Yin 2013; Xu and Jaggars 2013; Hart, Friedmann, and Hill 2014; Streich 2014; Bettinger et al. 2017). Bowen et al. (2014) compare student performance in a fully online statistics course to a hybrid version across six different public research universities and find no difference in learning.

market power. Online education has the potential to disrupt these local monopolies by introducing competition from alternative providers that do not require students to leave home to attend. The impact of competition from online providers will depend on the degree of monopoly power held by incumbents as well as the extent to which students are willing to substitute online and in-person programs.

We analyze the impact of increases in prevalence and market share of online institutions on student outcomes and institutional behavior at traditional brick-and-mortar schools. Studying the impact of competitive pressure from online institutions on local education markets is inherently difficult for two reasons. First, competitive pressure is challenging to measure directly, especially since there are sparse data on online degree programs offered by traditional brick-and-mortar schools. Second, it is difficult to isolate the impact of competition from online institutions from other changes affecting the market for higher education, because online degree programs by their nature are available everywhere at the same time.

We address these challenges by exploiting a 2006 change in the federal regulation of online education called the 50 percent rule. As we discuss later, this regulatory change allowed institutions to specialize in the provision of online degrees and dramatically lowered barriers to entry into online education. Deming et al. (2015) show that the median price of an online degree dropped by 34 percent between 2006 and 2013, suggesting that online degree providers were competing with each other for students. While the regulatory change was national, we argue that it should affect local education markets differently depending on their level of competitiveness prior to 2006.

We measure competitiveness using the Herfindahl index, a standard measure of market concentration. High values of the Herfindahl index indicate that postsecondary enrollment is concentrated in a small number of institutions that are likely to enjoy monopoly power. We compare changes before and after 2006 in enrollment, prices, and other outcomes in markets with more or less market concentration using a generalized differences-in-differences framework. We define education "markets" as the metropolitan statistical areas (MSAs) or as counties if an area is not in an MSA. Finally, we calculate a Herfindahl index as of the year 2000, which predates the spread of online education.

Our results generally align with theoretical predictions of how schools should react to increased competition. We find that the impact of online competition on enrollment, prices, and educational resources is greater in markets where enrollment was more highly concentrated prior to 2006. A one-standard-deviation increase in the Herfindahl index is associated with a post-2006 enrollment decline of about 2 percent and an increase in per-student instructional expenditures of about 1.8 percent. The impacts on enrollment are largest among not-for-profit and for-profit private institutions. Finally, we show that the impacts of online competition are larger in smaller markets and are concentrated among less-selective institutions.

Online competition shifts resources toward instructional expenditures. Overall, a one-standard-deviation increase in the Herfindahl index post-2006 raises per-student instructional expenditures by 1.8 percent. This effect is largest in the public sector and among four-year schools. In the private and two-year sectors, there is no increase in per-student instructional spending, but these institutions do experience a decline in revenues per student. These declines likely are driven by enrollment decreases from increased online competition. Thus, two-year and private colleges experience a relative shift toward instructional expenditures, which are held constant in the face of declining overall resources.

Taken together, our results suggest that public and private institutions respond differently to online competition. We find little change in enrollment or resources for public institutions, but both enrollment and total resources decline in private institutions that compete with online degree programs. Schools in both sectors spend relatively more on instruction due to competition from online schools. The shifting of resources toward instruction may be a competitive response intended to stave off further enrollment losses. While we are unable to directly test why public and private institutions respond differently to competition, one possibility is that students perceive online options as closer substitutes for less-selective private schools than for public schools. The fact that public schools respond to online competition even when their enrollments do not substantially decline suggests an important role for competitive *pressure* in driving responses to online degree programs.

We examine the effect of online competition on tuition prices as well. Our tuition analysis is restricted to private schools because public school tuition is heavily subsidized and is unlikely to reflect market forces. Somewhat contrary to expectations, we find that online competition increases average tuition, particularly in the private four-year sector, and that it is associated with increased tuition dispersion, especially in the private two-year sector. One possible explanation is that tuition increases are a response to revenue losses associated with enrollment reductions from online competition. Additionally, most online institutions are for-profits that charge high prices and serve students who are heavily subsidized by federal Title IV financial aid. If students do not face the full cost of their education when making enrollment decisions, quality competition may be more salient than price competition.

A second approach we take to identifying the competitive effects of online education programs is to use the differential spread of internet availability across states (Goolsbee, Lovenheim, and Slemrod 2010). Since online enrollment requires access to the internet, competitive pressures from online schools should be greater in areas with more internet access. A drawback of this approach is that we only have comprehensive internet penetration data at the state level, which necessitates defining education markets in a more aggregated manner.[3]

Similar to the market concentration analysis, we adopt a difference-in-differences strategy to examine how postsecondary outcomes change in states with different post-2006 rates of internet penetration. Our findings are broadly consistent with those from the market power analysis: internet penetration growth post-2006 is associated with decreased log enrollment and higher per-student instructional expenditures.

Overall, our results suggest that there may be important general equilibrium effects of online degree programs on the market for higher education. Hoxby (1997) studies how declining transportation costs and increased sharing of information and standardized testing led to geographic integration of the market for higher education over the last several decades. Those changes were most consequential for elite colleges, which increasingly compete in a national market for students. This chapter fits into the broader literature on the industrial organization of higher education by studying the impact of a technological change—online education—on less-selective, mostly open-access postsecondary institutions. Like Hoxby (1997), our results suggest that the geographic integration of higher education markets may lead to efficiency gains as institutions compete with each other for students. However, these gains accrue predominantly to students attending traditional postsecondary institutions and need to be balanced with the worse outcomes associated with online educational options.

8.1   A Brief History of Online Education in the United States

Long before the internet, distance education took the form of correspondence courses that delivered lessons by mail, radio, and television. US colleges and universities such as University of Maryland University College (UMUC) and the University of Wisconsin-Extension have been offering correspondence courses in some form for nearly a hundred years.

Fully online degrees were developed in the mid-1990s, when dial-up internet started to become available for commercial use. Early examples of such programs include CALCampus and Western Governors University. The first postsecondary institution to open an online campus was the University of Phoenix, which enrolled more than 1,200 students in the 1994–95 academic year, according to data from the US Department of Education Integrated Postsecondary Education Data System (IPEDS).

---

3. Dettling, Goodman, and Smith (2018) examine the effect of high-speed internet on college application behavior using Federal Communications Commission data on the number of county-level broadband internet service providers. These data are only available through 2008 but allow substate variation. We have analyzed our models using these data, but with only two years of post-2006 observations, the estimates are imprecise. Furthermore, we show below that most of our results are driven by the 2009–13 period, which is missed by these data.

The for-profit sector moved relatively slowly into online education. By 2000, only a handful of for-profits had online degree programs at all. One reason was technological—in 2000 only 37 percent of Americans had internet connections at home, and only 3 percent had high-speed broadband access (Pew Charitable Trusts 2016). By 2005, more than 60 percent of Americans had internet access, and broadband access grew 11-fold to 33 percent.

Regulatory restrictions also played an important role in the growth of online degree programs. The Higher Education Act (HEA) of 1992 required that schools distributing federal Title IV aid have no more than 50 percent of total student course time spent in distance education (the 50 percent rule). The rule was interpreted broadly to include mail-in correspondence courses as well as online degree programs.

The 50 percent rule did not prevent schools from offering online degrees, but it did limit market entry by effectively requiring all institutions to enroll one student in person for every student enrolled online. Specialized online schools could not exist under the 50 percent rule. The 1998 HEA created the Distance Education Demonstration Program (DEDP), a pilot program that allowed waivers of the 50 percent rule for selected institutions. Notable participants included the University of Phoenix, Capella University, and Western Governors University. Online enrollment grew rapidly among DEDP participants between 1998 and 2005, and in February 2006, the Higher Education Reconciliation Act (HERA) eliminated the 50 percent rule.

These regulatory changes had a large impact on enrollments in online programs. IPEDS only began tracking online enrollment directly in 2013, but the data are collected at the campus branch level. This makes it possible to measure enrollment at individual branches of "chain" institutions with multiple campuses, such as the University of Phoenix. We estimate online enrollment using the method outlined in Deming, Goldin, and Katz (2012), which classifies a school campus as online if it has the word *online* in its name or if no more than 33 percent of the school's students are from one US state. This is a conservative measure of online enrollment because many schools offer online degree programs through their in-person branches (see Deming, Goldin, and Katz 2012 for more details). Figure 8.1 plots estimated yearly enrollment in online degree programs using this method and shows the significant rise in these types of programs in the early to mid-2000s.

Figure 8.1 further divides online enrollment into two categories: (1) campuses with a significant but not complete online presence and (2) campuses or entire institutions that are online only.[4] Between 2000 and 2006, online

---

4. The first category includes central branches of "chain" for-profit institutions where online students from across the country are likely to be assigned. For example, in 2009 DeVry University operated 26 campus branches across the United States. The Illinois branch had an enrollment of 24,624, which was more than three times larger than the next largest branch and about 40 percent of total enrollment in DeVry. While some of these students were enrolled in

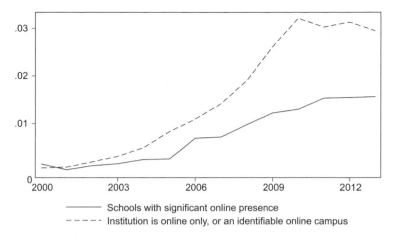

0   2000   2003   2006   2009   2012

———— Schools with significant online presence
– – – – Institution is online only, or an identifiable online campus

Fig. 8.1   Increasing specialization of online degree programs: Share of total US enrollment in online degree programs by year
Source: Integrated Postsecondary Education Data System (IPEDS).

institutions grew from essentially zero to about 1.75 percent of all US postsecondary enrollments. This growth was modestly larger for specialized online campuses.

In the four years following the end of the 50 percent rule, online schools grew from 1.75 to 4.5 percent of all US enrollment. Online-only campuses and institutions accounted for about 2.1 percentage points of this increase, or about 75 percent of the growth in online enrollment over the 2006–10 period. Moreover, the number of institutions satisfying our definition of *online* grew from 13 in 2004 to 24 in 2006 to 39 in 2010. These trends suggest that the market for online education grew rapidly and became significantly more competitive after 2006.

8.2   How Might Online Degrees Affect Higher Education Markets?

Online institutions affect local education markets by increasing competitive pressure. Students who previously had only a limited set of choices (or perhaps no choice at all) now can choose to enroll in online institutions instead. This increase in the number of options available to students means that local colleges and universities no longer have monopoly power and must compete for students. Thus, the impact of online institutions should be proportional both to the amount of prior market power of local institutions

the in-person Illinois branch, most were enrolled online. In contrast, University of Phoenix has a separate online campus that enrolled more than 300,000 students—about 77 percent of total University of Phoenix enrollment—in 2009. Other schools, such as Ashford University and Capella University, have only a single campus branch at which nearly everyone is enrolled online.

and to the substitutability between local nonselective schools and online degree programs.

We focus on the impact of increased competitive pressure from online schools on enrollment and resource allocation among traditional post-secondary institutions. While no prior work has examined this question, the topic relates closely to existing research on the competitive effects of K–12 school choice. A sizable body of research examines how school choice policies affect resource levels and distribution in traditional public schools (Cook 2018; Hoxby 2000, 2003; Jackson 2012). While these chapters find that elementary and secondary schools respond to competitive pressures by changing educational inputs, the direction and magnitude of effects tend to vary.

Competition in the postsecondary market has many similarities to competition in the elementary and secondary markets, although it is different in three important ways. First, postsecondary schools charge tuition. Thus, unlike with K–12 school choice, there is a price mechanism that can act to clear the market. Of course, most colleges and universities receive substantial state subsidies, and financial aid weakens the relationship between posted tuition and what students actually pay, but the fact that postsecondary schools—and in particular, private schools—can compete over prices differentiates this setting from choice in K–12 markets.

Second, institutions of higher education have broader purposes than K–12 schools. An elementary or secondary school's main objective is to increase student learning in a small set of academic subjects. Colleges and universities also aim to increase student learning, but they focus on a wider variety of subjects. Moreover, they aim to produce knowledge in the form of research. Higher education markets therefore are more horizontally differentiated than their K–12 counterparts. Colleges with different objectives and different student bodies are unlikely to compete with each other. This is a key reason we focus on nonselective schools, which offer a relatively homogenous product in a standard fee-for-service model (Hoxby 2014).

Third, nonattendance is usually not an option in the K–12 setting. In contrast, since people are not required to attend college, market entry of online degree programs might increase total postsecondary enrollment. This could happen through a direct effect of increasing access to college but also indirectly: if competition increases the quality of education offerings, more students might be pulled into higher education.

The structure of higher education markets gives rise to several predictions, which we test empirically below. Our first prediction is that the impact of competition from online degree programs on enrollment will be greater in markets where enrollment is more concentrated in a small number of institutions. This is because in the absence of outside competitors, local institutions with monopoly power will generally be providing a lower-quality education for the price.

Our second prediction is that online degree programs should increase price competition and reduce economic rents for schools with monopoly power. Given that prices at public institutions are only weakly market driven at best, we might expect price competition to be most important for private institutions. If institutions compete primarily over price, then the introduction of a common (online) option should lead to a decline in the variance of tuition prices across local education markets. Again, this effect should be larger for private institutions.

Finally, we might also expect competitive pressure to lead to changes in institutional resource allocation, such as increased spending on instruction and/or student support services. The predicted effects for tuition and resources are linked: schools can compete on both prices and quality, but they might not do so equally. If competition is mainly over quality, the level and variance of tuition prices actually could increase. This might occur in an environment where tuition is subsidized by financial aid, making the actual prices faced by prospective students less salient. Thus, how postsecondary schools will respond to heightened competition is determined in part by the factors over which they compete.

8.3   Data

8.3.1   Main Analysis Data

Our main source of institutional data for this study is IPEDS, which contains institution-level information on enrollment, posted tuition prices, revenues, expenditures, and educational resources for all US postsecondary institutions that distribute federal Title IV financial aid (Pell Grants and Stafford Loans). We collected IPEDS data at the institution-year level for years 1990–2013.[5] Our analysis is mostly restricted to the years 2000–2013, which provides several years in which online degree program prevalence was low and also insulates us from biases related to many changes in how IPEDS measures core variables of interest in the 1990s. Using 2000 as our base year allows us to obtain market concentrations that are not affected by online degree programs but that are recent enough to accurately reflect market power in later years.

It is important to distinguish selective from nonselective institutions in our context because selective schools are much more geographically integrated, which means they have considerably less geographic market power (Hoxby 2009, 2014). In 2000, 44.3 percent of first-time freshmen in selective four-year institutions were from out of state, compared to only 15.2 percent in less-selective four-year public schools and 7.5 percent in community col-

---

5. We refer to school years by the calendar year of the spring term. For example, we refer to school year 2012–13 as 2013.

leges. Additionally, most online programs are open enrollment—very few practice selective admissions.[6] As a result, schools that have selective admissions policies are unlikely to be in direct competition with online degree programs. We therefore focus on less selective and nonselective institutions that serve highly local markets, which we define as any institution that has a rating of Most Competitive, Highly Competitive, or Very Competitive according to the 2009 Barron's Profile of American Colleges.

The main variables of interest in this study are enrollment, in-state tuition charges, per-student revenues, total expenditures per student, and instructional expenditures per student. The IPEDS revenue and expenditure data contain outliers that are likely to reflect measurement error and that can cause undue influence on mean estimates. We therefore winsorize these variables by cutting the top and bottom 1 percent of revenues, expenditures, and instructional expenditures per student.[7] Table 8.1 shows means and standard deviations of the outcome variables we employ in this study, both overall and by institution type. The means generally conform to expectations, with four-year and private institutions having higher per-student revenues and expenditures than their public and two-year counterparts. Furthermore, public institutions are much larger and charge lower tuition than private colleges and universities. Because we focus on nonselective institutions, our sample is composed of 8,782 schools, about one-third of which are public and a little over half of which are four-year.

8.3.2 Measuring Market Concentration

There is little reason to expect that the distribution of public institutions across metropolitan areas reflects a competitive equilibrium. While private colleges may enter markets endogenously in response to potential profit opportunities, the location of public institutions largely reflects historical and political factors. There has been almost no new entry of public colleges or universities in the United States over the last 25 years. Many public institutions are located in nonurban areas that would not otherwise support a market for higher education—for example, in 2013, 18 percent of nonselective public enrollment was in nonurban areas, compared to only 8 percent for private nonselective institutions.

The uneven distribution of colleges and universities across areas in the United States drives heterogeneity in the competitive effects of online postsecondary programs. To measure local market power, we first define a postsecondary market as the MSA in which a school is located. If a school is not located in an MSA, we define the market as the county. This definition

---

6. In our data, only one online-only institution reports practicing selective admissions—Grand Canyon University.

7. Winsorizing the data in this way has little impact on the log estimates but does affect the level estimates as expected. Results using the full sample are available from the authors upon request.

Table 8.1   Descriptive statistics of analysis variables

Variable	Full sample	Public institutions	Private institutions	Four-year institutions	Two-year institutions
Nonselective Herfindahl index	0.312 (0.309)	0.453 (0.363)	0.249 (0.257)	0.284 (0.292)	0.327 (0.316)
Public Herfindahl index	0.404 (0.322)	0.539 (0.355)	0.342 (0.286)	0.370 (0.308)	0.423 (0.329)
Private Herfindahl index	0.290 (0.294)	0.376 (0.332)	0.261 (0.274)	0.285 (0.298)	0.293 (0.292)
No public Herfindahl index	0.013 (0.115)		0.019 (0.137)	0.023 (0.151)	0.008 (0.087)
No private Herfindahl index	0.024 (0.154)	0.078 (0.268)		0.014 (0.119)	0.030 (0.170)
Total enrollment	2,337 (5,669)	5,769 (7,465)	816 (3,763)	3,292 (7,170)	1,799 (4,528)
Log total enrollment	6.218 (1.847)	7.719 (1.728)	5.553 (1.470)	6.994 (1.583)	5.782 (1.842)
In-state tuition	11,064 (7,658)	4,161 (2,848)	14,384 (7,001)	13,959 (8,318)	9,694 (6,915)
Log in-state tuition	9.018 (0.866)	8.094 (0.742)	9.463 (0.487)	9.342 (0.680)	8.865 (0.902)
Revenues per student	18,058 (19,167)	15,227 (20,347)	19,332 (18,470)	23,126 (21,834)	15,057 (16,686)
Expenditures per student	16,359 (16,469)	13,302 (17,204)	17,737 (15,936)	21,132 (18,531)	13,516 (14,373)
Instructional expenditures per student	6,062 (5,933)	5,512 (6,146)	6,310 (5,818)	7,112 (6,326)	5,437 (5,593)
Number of institutions	8,782	2,176	6,606	3,077	5,705
Number of observations	88,249	27,090	61,159	28,679	50,788

Source: 2000–2013 IPEDS data as described in the text. All Herfindahl indices are for nonselective schools, which are those with an admissions profile below "Very Competitive" in the 2009 Barron's Profile of American Colleges. Each cell shows the mean for each variable with the standard deviation directly following in parentheses.

presumes that students have more options in cities and can easily move across counties within the city to enroll. In less-urban areas, the local schooling option is typically the community college or the nonselective four-year school located in one's county.

As stated earlier in the chapter, our measure of market concentration is the Herfindahl index of enrollment shares. The Herfindahl index is a measure of the extent to which enrollment is spread out evenly among many postsecondary schools or whether it is concentrated in one or only a couple of schools. It is preferable to raw counts of the number of different types of schools because it takes into account the size of enrollment at each local college; a small school affects local competition less than a larger one. Formally, the Herfindahl index is the sum of squared enrollment shares across colleges within a market:

$$H_j = \sum_{i=1}^{N_j} E_{ij}^2,$$

where E_{ij} is the enrollment share in institution i in market j and N_j is the total number of postsecondary institutions in market j; $H \in [0,1]$, with values closer to 1 indicating less competition (i.e., more concentrated enrollment).

We calculate Herfindahl indices using 2000 enrollment data for all nonselective schools in a market as well as separately by level (two-year, four-year) and control (public, private). Thus H_j is a fixed characteristic of the market that does not change over time. Table 8.1 provides means of Herfindahl indices. The mean Herfindahl index value is about 0.31. However, the standard deviation is also about 0.31, suggesting that there is significant variation in college concentration across markets.[8] Private schools on average have less market power, with a mean Herfindahl index of 0.29. Table 8.1 also shows that for a small number of local markets, sector-specific Herfindahl indices cannot be calculated because there was no school of that type in the market in 2000.

Table 8.1 includes tabulations separately for public and private institutions as well as for two-year and four-year schools. Public institutions and community colleges tend to be located in markets in which there is more market power.[9] Across school types, there is in general much less competition from public institutions than from private institutions. This probably reflects endogenous decisions by private institutions to enter markets based on the supply of potential students. We examine below whether there are heterogeneous effects of online competition across the different types of sector-specific market concentration.

Figures 8.2 and 8.3 show the geographic distribution of nonselective market shares by MSA and by county, respectively. In the cases where the counties in figure 8.3 overlap with an MSA in figure 8.2, the MSA is the relevant market. The different shading in figure 8.2 corresponds to quartiles of the Herfindahl index. For counties, more than 40 percent have a Herfindahl index of one. We therefore split counties into terciles of the distribution with an index value less than one and then a category with only single-school counties. As expected, there is much higher market concentration when markets are defined as counties rather than MSAs. The main conclusions from these figures are that there is considerable variation in local market power

---

8. The US Department of Justice considers a market to be highly concentrated when the Herfindahl index is higher than 0.26, which illustrates the high level of market power in the nonselective higher education market. Appendix figure 8.A1 contains Herfindahl index distributions and highlights the large amount of variation across areas in the amount of market concentration: many areas have a Herfindahl index below 0.1, while a substantial number have an index above 0.25.

9. Appendix figure 8.A1 shows the distribution of the nonselective Herfindahl index for public and private institutions. While the modes of the distributions are similar, there is a much larger mass of public institutions with considerable market power.

Fig. 8.2   Herfindahl indices of nonselective school market share by city
Source: Authors' calculations from 2000 IPEDS. Nonselective schools are those with an admissions profile below "Very Competitive" in the 2009 Barron's Profile of American Colleges.

Fig. 8.3   Herfindahl indices of nonselective school market share by county
Source: Authors' calculations from 2000 IPEDS. Nonselective schools are those with an admissions profile below "Very Competitive" in the 2009 Barron's Profile of American Colleges.

across space and that there is little geographic clustering of market power. Thus our market power measures are not simply picking up unobserved aspects of higher education markets that are correlated with geographic region or state.

Figures 8.2 and 8.3 also demonstrate that many areas of the country are characterized by a high degree of nonselective market power. Among MSAs, the top quartile has a Herfindahl index above 0.68, and among counties, it is 0.94. In contrast, the bottom quartile of the distribution has little market power, especially among MSAs. Thus, there is much geographic variation in the scope for online postsecondary options to have competitive effects on local higher education markets.

8.3.3   Measuring Internet Penetration Rates

Internet penetration rates are calculated at the state-year level using the Current Population Survey (CPS). Beginning in 1989, the CPS has included

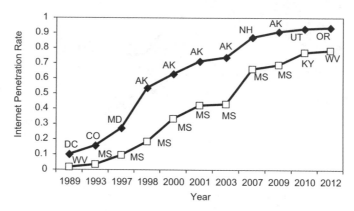

Fig. 8.4   Internet penetration rates
Source: 1989, 1993, 1997, 1998, 2000, 2001, 2003, 2007, 2009, 2010 CPS data as described in the text. The state listed next to each data point shows the state with the highest (diamond) and lowest (square) internet penetration rate in that year.

questions in various forms about internet access and usage. These questions were asked in 1989, 1993, 1997, 1998, 2000, 2001, 2003, 2007, 2009, 2010, and 2012. We follow the approach developed in Goolsbee, Lovenheim, and Slemrod (2010) to construct a state-year panel of internet access rates that accounts for the fact that the wording of the questions changes over time. In 1989 and 1993, a respondent is defined as having internet access if he or she reports having email or a computer with a modem. In the 1997–2003 surveys, we code respondents as having internet access if they respond that they have access to the internet at home, school, or work. Post-2003, the CPS directly asks if respondents have internet access. Between survey years, state-level internet penetration rates are linearly interpolated.

Figure 8.4 contains trends in internet penetration rates between 1989 and 2012 for the highest and lowest internet penetration states in each year. The maximum and minimum states change over time, so the figure also shows which state constitutes each observation. Internet access generally trends upward strongly over this period, but it does so unevenly across states. There hence is significant cross-state variation in the time pattern of internet access. Below, we explore whether this time pattern is related to postsecondary outcomes among nonselective institutions in a state and in particular whether changes in internet penetration rates have differential impacts after 2006, when the supply of online enrollment options increased.

8.4   Empirical Strategy

We first examine how postsecondary outcomes change after 2006 as a function of 2000 market concentrations in a difference-in-difference setting.

In particular, we estimate the following regressions at the institution-year level:

(1) $\qquad Y_{ismt} = \alpha + \beta_1(H_m \times POST_t^{2006}) + \beta_2 X_{imt} + \delta_i + \theta_{st} + \varepsilon_{ismt}$,

where i indexes institutions, s indexes state, m indexes market (county or MSA) and t indexes year. The variable H_m is the nonselective market Herfindahl index in 2000. We control for time-varying characteristics of markets, such as the market-year unemployment rate, total population, poverty rate, proportion that is black, proportion that is Hispanic, proportion that are veterans, and proportion that is male, and our models also include institution fixed effects (δ_i) and state-by-year fixed effects (θ_{st}). Note that the main effect of H_m is absorbed by the institution fixed effects, since institutions do not move across markets. Standard errors are clustered at the market level throughout.

The coefficient of interest in this equation is β_1, which shows how the relationship between market power (as measured by the Herfindahl index) and postsecondary outcomes changes in 2006 when online programs became more prevalent. Similar to any difference-in-difference design, this approach embeds two main assumptions: (1) schools in markets with different levels of market power would have exhibited similar trends absent the rise of online programs and (2) there are no shocks or policies that occur after 2006 that differentially affect markets with different values of H_m.

We provide evidence of the validity of the first assumption by estimating event studies of the following form:

(2) $\qquad Y_{ismt} = \alpha + \sum_{j=2000}^{2013} \gamma_j H_m \times I(t = j) + \beta_2 X_{imt} + \delta_i + \theta_{st} + \varepsilon_{ismt}$.

This model estimates a separate coefficient on H_m in every year, and the coefficients $\gamma_{2000} - \gamma_{2005}$ provide evidence of whether there are differential pre-2006 trends as a function of 2000 market share. Note that our model does not necessarily predict a sharp break in 2006, since online schools were growing in prevalence prior to 2006. However, the 2006 regulatory change sped up the rate of entry of online programs. We therefore expect a shift in how 2000 market shares relate to postsecondary outcomes after 2006, although the exact timing is unclear. Furthermore, there are likely to be some "pretreatment" trends that reflect the rise of online programs prior to 2006.

The second assumption is much more difficult to test. We control for market-year-level observable characteristics to account for any compositional changes across areas that may be correlated with 2000 market shares. Our estimates also include state-by-year fixed effects that account for any state-specific postsecondary policies or state-specific shocks. Additionally, we estimate models using selective colleges and universities, as they may face similar unobserved shocks but should not be affected by online competition. Because we cannot perfectly test the assumptions underlying our preferred approach, we implement a second empirical strategy that uses differences in internet penetration rate changes across states. While this approach relies on assumptions about the exogeneity of internet penetration rate changes, these assumptions differ substantially from those needed to justify our preferred approach. To the extent that the estimates from both methods are similar, this alternate approach provides support for our results.

We estimate difference-in-difference models that examine how the relationship between internet penetration rates in state s and year t (I_{st}) changes in 2006:

$$(3) \quad Y_{ismt} = \alpha + \beta_1(I_{st} \times POST_t^{2006}) + \beta_2 X_{imt} + \beta_3 I_{st} + \delta_i + \theta_t + \varepsilon_{imt}.$$

Note that I_{st} varies over time within states. The identifying variation in this model thus comes both from changes in the relationship between internet penetration rates and postsecondary outcomes in 2006 and from changes in internet penetration rates within states. The main assumption underlying this model is that the only reason the relationship between I_{st} and the outcomes changes in 2006 is because of the growth of online education. We also need to assume that there are no shocks or other policies that occur in 2006 that are correlated with I_{st}. Because I_{st} and H_m are not highly correlated—the correlation coefficient between the Herfindahl index and the growth in internet penetration between 2000 and 2012 is -0.05—it is highly unlikely that any unobserved shock that would bias the first approach would also bias the second approach in the same direction.

8.5   Results

8.5.1   Enrollment

Table 8.2 shows estimates from equation (1) of the impact of post-2006 online competition on enrollment. Panel A presents results in levels, and panel B shows the natural log of enrollment. Because of the large variance in enrollment, we prefer the log estimates. However, we present both for completeness. Column 1 presents pooled results for all nonselective colleges. Columns 2 and 3 present results for public and private enrollment (including both not-for-profit and for-profit institutions), while columns 4 and 5 split by four-year and two-year colleges, respectively.

We find consistent evidence across specifications that less-competitive markets experienced relative declines in enrollment after the expansion of online degree programs. A one-standard-deviation increase in market concentration (0.31, as measured by the Herfindahl index) leads to a decline in post-2006 enrollment of about 2 percent. We find larger impacts for private institutions; a one-standard-deviation increase in market concentration reduces post-2006 enrollment by 2.5 percent. Public schools in panel A

Table 8.2   **The effect of online competition on traditional school enrollment**

Independent variable	All nonselective	Public	Private	4-year	2-year
	Panel A: Total enrollment				
Nonselective H-index	−356.0***	−730.4***	−489.3***	−467.0*	−185.6***
× Post-2006	(113.0)	(121.7)	(179.3)	(258.2)	(45.2)
Observations	88,169	27,075	61,094	31,747	56,422
R^2	0.048	0.276	0.036	0.075	0.103
	Panel B: Log Total Enrollment				
Nonselective H-index	−0.064***	−0.002	−0.080***	−0.062**	−0.059***
× Post-2006	(0.017)	(0.019)	(0.031)	(0.027)	(0.020)
Observations	88,169	27,075	61,094	31,747	56,422
R^2	0.130	0.232	0.130	0.144	0.137

Source: Authors' calculations as described in the text using 2000–2013 IPEDS data. Each column in each panel comes from a separate regression that controls for market-year unemployment rate, total population, poverty rate, proportion black, proportion Hispanic, proportion veterans, and proportion male. All estimates also include state-by-year fixed effects and institution fixed effects. Herfindahl (H-) indices are for nonselective schools, which are those with an admissions profile below "Very Competitive" in the 2009 Barron's Profile of American Colleges. Standard errors clustered at the market (MSA/county) level are in parentheses; *** indicates statistical significance at the 1 percent level, ** indicates significance at the 5 percent level, and * indicates significance at the 10 percent level.

show evidence of a sizable and statistically significant decline in enrollment, but the results in panel B indicate these results are not robust to measuring enrollment in logs. This is likely because of the existence of some very large public schools, which have an undue influence on the estimates in panel A. We thus conclude that enrollment in public schools does not respond to competitive pressures overall. The last two columns show that effects are similar in percentage terms for four-year and two-year schools; a one-standard-deviation increase in the Herfindahl index leads to an enrollment reduction of about 2 percent after 2006.

Figure 8.5 presents estimates of equation (2) graphically, following the less-restrictive specification in equation (2). Note that we have excluded 2005 in these results, which essentially normalizes all estimates to be relative to this pretreatment year. All event study estimates that follow use this convention. When we allow the impacts of market concentration to vary by year, we find a borderline significant decline of about 4 percent in log enrollment for private institutions in 2007, exactly one year after the end of the 50 percent rule. The coefficients remain negative in nearly every year from 2007 to 2013. In contrast, we find no statistically significant impact on log enrollment at public institutions for any year after 2006, which is consistent with the evidence in panel B of table 8.2.

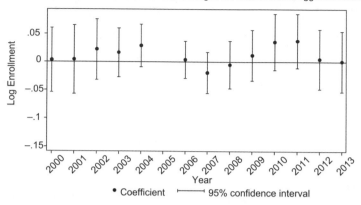

Non-Selective Market Concentration and Changes in Public School Logged Enrollment

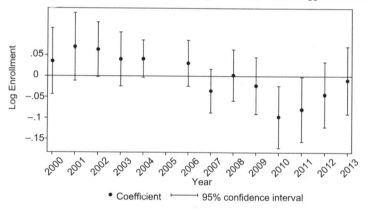

Non-Selective Market Concentration and Changes in Private School Logged Enrollment

Fig. 8.5   The effect of online competition on traditional school enrollment: Event study estimates by school type

Source: Authors' estimation of equation (2) using 2000–2013 IPEDS data as described in the text. Each point is an estimate of γ_j, and the bars extending from each point show the 95 percent confidence interval calculated from standard errors that are clustered at the market (MSA/county) level. γ_{2005} is set to zero, so all estimates are relative to that year. The regression controls for market-year unemployment rate, total population, poverty rate, proportion black, proportion Hispanic, proportion veterans, and proportion male. All estimates also include state-by-year fixed effects and institution fixed effects. Herfindahl (H-) indices are for nonselective schools, which are those with an admissions profile below "Very Competitive" in the 2009 Barron's Profile of American Colleges.

8.5.2   Tuition

In section 8.2, we predicted that competition from online degree programs would cause price convergence across local education markets. Figure 8.6 presents some initial evidence on this question by plotting the enrollment-weighted coefficient of variation (the standard deviation divided by the mean) for tuition in public and private nonselective colleges between 1990

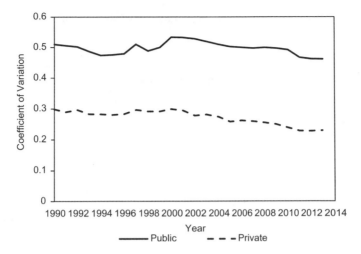

Fig. 8.6   Cross-market coefficient of variation in in-state posted tuition

Source: 1990–2013 IPEDS. The coefficient of variation is the cross-market (MSA/county) standard deviation divided by the year-specific mean. Tuition is only for nonselective schools, which are those with an admissions profile below "Very Competitive" in the 2009 Barron's Profile of American Colleges.

and 2013. Figure 8.6 shows that variation in tuition at private nonselective institutions held steady throughout the 1990s but started to decline in the early 2000s. In contrast, there is little change in the variance of tuition at public institutions over this period.

While time series evidence is suggestive, in table 8.3 we present estimates of equation (1) with tuition as the outcome in order to more closely link any tuition changes with underlying market shares. Because public tuition is not primarily determined by market competition, we focus on private institutions. Column 1 presents results for all private schools, while columns 2 and 3 focus on private four-year and two-year institutions, respectively.

Surprisingly, we find little evidence that competition from online institutions lowers tuition in more-concentrated markets. The coefficients in column 1 are positive but are not statistically significant at even the 10 percent level. They suggest a small positive effect on average tuition of about 0.5 percent for a one-standard-deviation increase in the Herfindahl index. There is a negative but not significant effect for private two-year schools in column 3 that is very small in absolute value, while the results in column 2 actually imply *increases* in private four-year tuition in more-concentrated markets. Figure 8.7 shows event study estimates for nonselective private schools. These results show that private tuition increases as a function of the 2000 market share after 2006, with all the increases coming after 2009. Furthermore, there is little evidence of pre-2006 differential trends in tuition that would lead to a bias in our estimates.

Table 8.3   The effect of online competition on in-state posted tuition among private institutions

Independent variable	All private	Private 4-year	Private 2-year
Panel A: Tuition levels			
Nonselective H-index × Post-2006	267.9	860.7***	−264.6
	(182.7)	(278.6)	(242.3)
School-year observations	53,744	18,780	34,964
Unique schools	5,977	4,345	1,971
R^2	0.254	0.254	0.320
Panel B: Log tuition			
Nonselective H-index × Post-2006	0.0169	0.0354***	−0.006
	(0.0118)	(0.0136)	(0.0181)
School-year observations	53,731	18,775	34,956
Unique schools	5,971	1,968	4,342
R^2	0.318	0.360	0.329
Panel C: Tuition coefficient of variation			
Nonselective H-index × Post-2006	0.036***	0.0069	0.046***
	(0.010)	(0.012)	(0.015)
School-year observations	53,744	18,780	34,964
Unique schools	5,977	4,345	1,971
R^2	0.034	0.098	0.185

Source: Authors' calculations as described in the text using 2000–2013 IPEDS data. Each column in each panel comes from a separate regression that controls for market-year unemployment rate, total population, poverty rate, proportion black, proportion Hispanic, proportion veterans, and proportion male. All estimates include state-by-year fixed effects and institution fixed effects. The coefficient of variation is the absolute deviation from the national year-specific mean divided by the national year-specific mean. Herfindahl (H-) indices are for nonselective schools, which are those with an admissions profile below "Very Competitive" in the 2009 Barron's Profile of American Colleges. Standard errors clustered at the market (MSA/county) level are in parentheses; *** indicates statistical significance at the 1 percent level, ** indicates significance at the 5 percent level, and * indicates significance at the 10 percent level.

What could explain the positive effect on private-sector tuition? One explanation is that the enrollment declines in table 8.2 forced private colleges to charge more to cover their fixed costs. In other words, private schools might be forced to raise tuition in order to make up for the loss in resources associated with declining enrollment. Another explanation is that price competition is not particularly strong in higher education markets where enrollment is heavily subsidized by federal Pell Grant and Stafford Loan dollars, and thus price is not very salient to consumers. This suggests that schools will compete over other features, such as resources. While these explanations are not mutually exclusive, we lack the ability to distinguish them in the data.

Panel C shows the impact of online competition on market-level variation in tuition prices. The dependent variable is the absolute difference between the institution's posted tuition and the national average tuition divided by

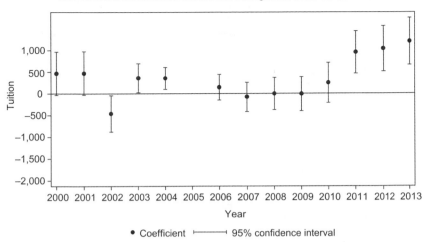

Fig. 8.7   The effect of online competition on traditional private school tuition: Event study estimates

Source: Authors' estimation of equation (2) using 2000–2013 IPEDS data as described in the text. Each point is an estimate of $\gamma\gamma_{jj}$, and the bars extending from each point show the 95 percent confidence interval calculated from standard errors that are clustered at the market (MSA/county) level. γ_{2005} is set to zero, so all estimates are relative to that year. The regression controls for market-year unemployment rate, total population, poverty rate, proportion black, proportion Hispanic, proportion veterans, and proportion male. All estimates also include state-by-year fixed effects and institution fixed effects. Herfindahl (H-) indices are for nonselective schools, which are those with an admissions profile below "Very Competitive" in the 2009 Barron's Profile of American Colleges.

the national average tuition. Thus the estimates yield the effect of increased competition on the coefficient of variation (the standard deviation divided by the mean). Interestingly, the estimates indicate an *increase* in price dispersion post-2006 as a function of 2000 market share. These estimates are driven by private two-year schools, where a one-standard-deviation increase in the Herfindahl index leads to a 1.4 percentage point increase in the coefficient of variation. Again, this evidence suggests that schools likely are not competing over posted prices, which is sensible given the sizable subsidies offered to students through the financial aid system.[10] Indeed, if prices are difficult for students to observe, higher competition could cause an increase in posted prices that are driven by university expansions in educational resources.

10. It is possible that these schools are competing over net price with institutional aid. However, nonselective schools in general and two-year schools in particular tend to offer little institutional aid.

Table 8.4   The effect of online competition on traditional school resources

Dependent variable form	Independent variable	All nonselective	Public	Private	4-year	2-year
Panel A: Total expenditures per student						
Level	Nonselective H-index	−328.9	1,620	−564.0	1,094*	−383.1
	× Post-2006	(576.3)	(1,036)	(766.5)	(659.8)	(794.4)
Log	Nonselective H-index	−0.041**	−0.010	−0.045	0.015	−0.056**
	× Post-2006	(0.017)	(0.024)	(0.027)	(0.019)	(0.024)
Panel B: Instructional expenditures per student						
Level	Nonselective H-index	−155.6	740.7**	−151.7	456.8**	−284.2
	× Post-2006	(210.0)	(364.6)	(269.0)	(197.5)	(304.0)
Log	Nonselective H-index	0.059***	0.060*	−0.008	0.101***	0.037
	× Post-2006	(0.022)	(0.033)	(0.031)	(0.022)	(0.032)
Panel C: Total revenues per student						
Level	Nonselective H-index	−1,185*	1,953	−1,982**	−117.3	−941.9
	× Post-2006	(703.3)	(1,298)	(884.1)	(928.6)	(999.3)
Log	Noselective H-index	−0.055***	−0.015	−0.074***	−0.015	0.064***
	× Post-2006	(0.016)	(0.024)	(0.027)	(0.022)	(0.022)

Source: Authors' calculations as described in the text using 2000–2013 IPEDS data. Each cell comes from a separate regression that controls for market-year unemployment rate, total population, poverty rate, proportion black, proportion Hispanic, proportion veterans, and proportion male. All estimates also include state-by-year fixed effects and institution fixed effects. Herfindahl (H-) indices are for nonselective schools, which are those with an admissions profile below "Very Competitive" in the 2009 Barron's Profile of American Colleges. Total expenditure per student, instructional expenditures per student, and total revenues per student are top and bottom coded (or winsorized) at the 99th and 1st percentiles to address measurement issues generated by extreme outliers. Standard errors clustered at the market (MSA/county) level are in parentheses; *** indicates statistical significance at the 1 percent level, ** indicates significance at the 5 percent level, and * indicates significance at the 10 percent level.

8.5.3 Spending

Table 8.4 presents estimates of equation (1) where the outcomes are expenditures (panel A), instructional expenditures (panel B), and revenues (panel C) per student. Given the enrollment declines shown in table 8.2, there can be a mechanical positive effect on per-student expenditures if expenditures react slowly to enrollment changes or if expenditures are nonlinear with enrollment. However, we view it as unlikely that all the resource changes we document are due to enrollment effects.

As in table 8.2, we show results for all nonselective schools as well as separately for public and private institutions and for two-year and four-year institutions. Because there is a lot of variation in expenditures, these estimates are necessarily noisier than those discussed above. But we find evidence that expenditures per student increased more after 2006 in more-concentrated markets. The impacts are largest for instructional expenditures—a one-standard-deviation increase in market share leads to an increase in instructional expenditures per student of about 1.8 percent. As shown in table 8.1,

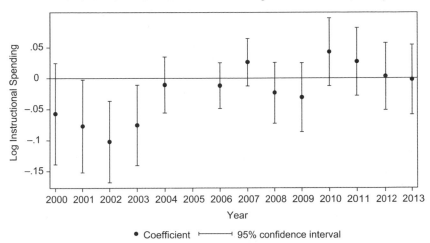

Fig. 8.8   The effect of online competition on traditional school resources: Event
study estimates

Source: Authors' estimation of equation (2) using 2000–2013 IPEDS data as described in the
text. Each point is an estimate of $\gamma\gamma_{ij}$, and the bars extending from each point show the 95 percent confidence interval calculated from standard errors clustered at the market (MSA/
county) level. γ_{2005} is set to zero, so all estimates are relative to that year. The regression controls for market-year unemployment rate, total population, poverty rate, proportion black,
proportion Hispanic, proportion veterans, and proportion male. All estimates also include
state-by-year fixed effects and institution fixed effects. Herfindahl (H-) indices are for nonselective schools, which are those with an admissions profile below "Very Competitive" in the
2009 Barron's Profile of American Colleges.

there is significant variance associated with these outcomes, so we favor
the log model; we focus on these, although we present both for interested
readers.

The impact on instructional expenditures is largest for four-year schools
(3.1 percent for a one-standard-deviation increase in the Herfindahl index)
and for public schools (1.9 percent for a one-standard-deviation increase
in the Herfindahl index). We find no statistically significant impact of market concentration on instructional spending in two-year schools or private
schools.

Figure 8.8 shows event studies for instructional expenditures per student.
The estimates are imprecise, but there is some evidence of an increase in
per-student instructional spending after 2006, most of which occurs after
2009. However, the pretrend for this outcome actually begins around 2004.
One possible explanation is that schools increased instructional spending in
anticipation of increased competition from online schools.

The results for overall spending per student are consistent with those for
instructional spending but are less precise. The one exception is that we see

a reduction in overall spending due to increased competition among all non-selective schools, which is driven by the private sector. Panel C shows that the expenditure declines in the private sector that we document are driven in large part by changes in per-student revenues. Both private and two-year schools experience significant declines in revenues due to heightened competitive pressures.

Private schools are heavily reliant on tuition funding. Table 8.2 shows that these institutions experience sizable declines in enrollment when there is increased competition. We also find—in table 8.3—that they increase tuition in response to online competition. However, table 8.4 shows that these tuition increases do not fully offset the impact of declining enrollment on per-student revenues.

Comparing the revenue changes to the expenditure changes, one possible explanation is that while private and two-year schools are shifting resources toward instruction, they nonetheless face increasingly binding financial constraints that reduce the total amount of resources available to them. The result is that these institutions are able to hold instructional expenditures per student relatively constant in the face of declining total resources. Despite the fact that revenues decline, there is a relative shift to instructional expenditures in the private and two-year sectors.

In contrast, there is no impact on per-student revenue in public schools and four-year schools. This could be because state appropriations counteract reductions in tuition revenue from enrollment declines in the four-year sector (we do not see a consistent enrollment effect in the public sector). It also is the case that four-year schools tend to be less reliant on tuition revenues, which reduces their exposure to revenue losses when enrollment declines. Instructional expenditures per student rise considerably, which suggests that public schools may respond to threats from online competitors by increasing the breadth of course offerings, lowering class sizes, or increasing instructional expenses. Unfortunately, the IPEDS data do not allow us to examine more specific categories of instructional spending.

8.5.4   Heterogeneity in Market Power across Sectors and by County Size

Throughout the analysis, we have characterized competition using non-selective enrollment concentrations. This aggregation may miss important heterogeneity in market power across sectors. As table 8.1 shows, private colleges tend to have less market power than public colleges. If institutions in these sectors compete within but not across sectors, our aggregation of all enrollments will miss important aspects of how competition operates. In table 8.5, we present results from a model similar to equation (1) but where we control separately for how the private Herfindahl index and the public Herfindahl index interacted with a post-2006 indicator. We also separately control for the interaction of post-2006 indicators and indicators for

Table 8.5   **The effect of online competition on traditional schools using sector-specific market share measures**

Independent variable	All nonselective	Public	Private
	Panel A: Log enrollment		
Public H-index	−0.00206	0.0103	0.0587**
	(0.0162)	(0.0199)	(0.0271)
Private H-index	−0.0608***	−0.0205	−0.1297***
	(0.0168)	(0.0184)	(0.0279)
	Panel B: Log expenditures per student		
Public H-index	−0.0494***	−0.0214	−0.0514***
	(0.0171)	(0.0260)	(0.250)
Private H-index	0.0093	0.0288	−0.0026
	(0.0178)	(0.0223)	(0.0261)
	Panel C: Log instructional expenditures per student		
Public H-index	0.0290	0.0600*	−0.0531*
	(0.0217)	(0.0358)	(0.0279)
Private H-index	0.0043	0.0039	0.0228
	(0.0219)	(0.0278)	(0.0294)

Source: Authors' calculations as described in the text using 2000 2013 IPEDS data. Each column in each panel comes from a separate regression that controls for market-year unemployment rate, total population, poverty rate, proportion black, proportion Hispanic, proportion veterans, and proportion male. All estimates also include state-by-year fixed effects and institution fixed effects. Herfindahl (H-) indices are for nonselective schools, which are those with an admissions profile below "Very Competitive" in the 2009 Barron's Profile of American Colleges. Standard errors clustered at the market (MSA/county) level are in parentheses: *** indicates statistical significance at the 1 percent level, ** indicates significance at the 5 percent level, and * indicates significance at the 10 percent level.

whether the market is missing each Herfindahl index. This occurs when the market does not have a school of the given type in it in 2000.

Panel A shows log enrollment estimates; the results load completely on the private sector Herfindahl index. The enrollment effect on all nonselective schools is similar to the effect in table 8.2, at 1.8 percent for a one standard deviation change in the private Herfindahl index (0.29). Reassuringly, the market concentration of private institutions has a greater impact on private college enrollment.

While private enrollment responds to heightened competition in both the public and private sectors, the effects are in opposing directions: A one-standard-deviation increase in the public institution Herfindahl index leads to an *increase* in private college enrollment of about 1.7 percent, whereas a one-standard-deviation increase in the private institution Herfindahl index leads to a 3.8 percent *decline* in enrollment. In contrast, we find no evidence that increased public or private market concentration affects enrollment at public institutions after 2006.

In the last two panels of the table, we provide expenditure and instruc-

Table 8.6   The effect of online competition on traditional schools, by county size

Independent variable	Enrollment	Log enrollment	Log expenditures per student	Log instructional expenditures per student	Log revenues per student
	Panel A: Below-median population counties				
Nonselective H-index	−446.8*	−0.0472**	−0.0171	0.0623**	−0.0473*
× Post-2006	(246.3)	(0.0221)	(0.0267)	(0.0301)	(0.0250)
Observations	42,915	42,915	38,982	38,830	38,986
R^2	0.087	0.152	0.048	0.052	0.050
	Panel B: Above-median population counties				
Nonselective H-index	76.41	0.0274	−0.0101	−0.130	0.0320
× Post-2006	(202.4)	(0.0772)	(0.0734)	(0.0896)	(0.0791)
Observations	44,037	44,037	39,644	39,481	9,615
R^2	0.108	0.128	0.024	0.027	0.022

Source: Authors' calculations as described in the text using 2000–2013 IPEDS data. Each cell comes from a separate regression that controls for market-year unemployment rate, total population, poverty rate, proportion black, proportion Hispanic, proportion veterans, and proportion male. All estimates also include state-by-year fixed effects and institution fixed effects. Herfindahl (H-) indices are for nonselective schools, which are those with an admissions profile below "Very Competitive" in the 2009 Barron's Profile of American Colleges. Above- and below-median population counties determined by quantile of 19- to 23-year-old population as of 2000 in the CPS. Total expenditure per student, instructional expenditures per student, and total revenues per student are top and bottom coded (or winsorized) at the 99th and 1st percentiles to address measurement issues generated by extreme outliers. Standard errors clustered at the market (MSA/county) level are in parentheses; *** indicates statistical significance at the 1 percent level, ** indicates significance at the 5 percent level, and * indicates significance at the 10 percent level.

tional expenditure estimates overall and separately for the public and private sectors. In general, we find that expenditure and instructional expenditure at both public and private institutions are more responsive to competition among public schools, although the estimates are somewhat imprecise. Specifically, we find that per-student expenditure and instructional expenditure at private institutions decline with public-school market concentration after 2006, while public per-student instructional expenditure increases with public-school market concentration. Private college market concentration does not affect public or private institutional expenditures.

Cities and counties vary widely in both geographic size and population. Metro areas tend to have higher concentrations of postsecondary options than do nonmetropolitan counties in our sample, and so the effect of increased competition from online options might be particularly strong in lower-population areas. We test for such heterogeneity in table 8.6, which splits the sample by the median number of 19- to 23-year-olds in the 2000 CPS.[11] The effects of competition from online options are concentrated in

11. Another way to examine the role of population in our estimates would be to exclude the market-year population control. However, the institutional fixed effects absorb any fixed

Table 8.7   **The effect of online competition on selective postsecondary institutions**

Independent variable	Enrollment	Log enrollment	Log expenditures per student	Log instructional expenditures per student	Log revenues per student
Nonselective H-index × Post-2006	−93.48 (208.5)	−0.0225 (0.0152)	−0.0298 (0.0216)	−0.0255 (0.0277)	−0.0151 (0.0204)
Observations	6,418	6,418	6,333	6,333	6,262
R^2	0.340	0.369	0.331	0.307	0.380

Source: Authors' calculations as described in the text using 2000–2013 IPEDS data. The sample consists of institutions with an admissions profile of "Very Competitive" or higher in the 2009 Barron's Profile of American Colleges. Each cell comes from a separate regression that controls for market-year unemployment rate, total population, poverty rate, proportion black, proportion Hispanic, proportion veterans, and proportion male. All estimates also include state-by-year fixed effects and institution fixed effects. Herfindahl (H-) indices are for nonselective schools, which are those with an admissions profile below "Very Competitive" in the 2009 Barron's Profile of American Colleges. Total expenditure per student, instructional expenditures per student, and total revenues per student are top and bottom coded (or winsorized) at the 99th and 1st percentiles to address measurement issues generated by extreme outliers. Standard errors clustered at the market (MSA/county) level are in parentheses: *** indicates statistical significance at the 1 percent level, ** indicates significance at the 5 percent level, and * indicates significance at the 10 percent level.

below-median population counties. In these counties, the effects of competition mirror those from the sample overall: enrollment declines, instructional expenditures increase, and revenues decline. However, we find little evidence of a response in above-median population areas.[12] This heterogeneity is likely due to the fact that there already is a high degree of competition in larger markets, which mutes the competitive effects of online competition.

8.6   Robustness Checks

8.6.1   Estimates for Selective Institutions

Throughout the analysis, we have restricted attention to less-selective institutions, as they are most directly in competition with online postsecondary schools. As a specification check, we show results for "selective" colleges and universities that have a 2009 Barron's ranking of Very Competitive or higher. We expect online competition to have little impact on this higher education sector, and indeed that is what we find. Table 8.7 reports

---

characteristics of the markets they are in, including differences in population. As a result, examining heterogeneous treatment effects by area size is a more straightforward way to assess the role of population size.

12. We have examined similar heterogeneous effects separately for public/private and two-year/four-year schools as well. The results are very similar to those from table 8.6 in showing that the effects of online competition are concentrated in the lower-population counties. These results are excluded for parsimony but are available from the authors upon request.

Table 8.8   The effect of online competition on traditional schools' internet growth

Independent variable	Enrollment	Log enrollment	Expenditures per student	Instructional expenditures per student	Revenues per student
Internet rate	−2,368*	0.056	8,477	3,578	3,442
	(1,276)	(0.173)	(7,033)	(2,236)	(8,986)
Internet rate × Post-2006	64.91	−0.074	−1,675	−447.3	−3,681
	(543.7)	(0.151)	(3,421)	(1,231)	(4,396)

Source: Authors' calculations as described in the text using 2000–2013 IPEDS data. Each column comes from a separate regression that controls for state-year unemployment rate, total population, poverty rate, proportion black, proportion Hispanic, proportion veterans, and proportion male. All estimates include institution and year fixed effects. The estimation sample includes all nonselective schools, which are those with an admissions profile below "Very Competitive" in the 2009 Barron's Profile of American Colleges. Total expenditure per student, instructional expenditures per student, and total revenues per student are top and bottom coded (or winsorized) at the 99th and 1st percentiles to address measurement issues generated by extreme outliers. Standard errors clustered at the state level are in parentheses; *** indicates statistical significance at the 1 percent level, ** indicates significance at the 5 percent level, and * indicates significance at the 10 percent level.

the results from this robustness check: there is no statistically significant evidence of a change in enrollment or resources due to online competition among selective schools. Several of the coefficients are in the opposite direction from the nonselective results shown previously, and those that are in the same direction are attenuated. That we find no evidence of a response among more-selective institutions suggests we are identifying a causal effect of competition from the online sector rather than secular trends or shocks in postsecondary outcomes that are correlated with the Herfindahl index and the relaxation of the 50 percent rule.

8.6.2   Results from Internet Penetration Variation

Finally, in table 8.8 we present results from a complementary identification strategy that exploits state-by-year variation in internet penetration, following equation (3). This identification strategy has considerably less power than our preferred approach, so we only show estimates for all nonselective schools. Despite the reduced statistical power, these results present supporting evidence that is important given the potentially strong assumptions underlying causal identification in equation (1).

The results in table 8.8 are qualitatively similar to those shown above. A 10 percentage point increase in the internet penetration rate post-2006 leads to a 0.7 percent reduction in nonselective enrollment and an increase of $1,587 per student in instructional expenditures. We also find positive coefficients on overall expenditures and revenues per student. Only the instructional expenditures effect is significant at even the 10 percent level. While imprecise, the fact that these results are broadly consistent with our baseline estimates suggests our conclusions are not being overly affected by biases driven by differential trends or shocks correlated with 2000 market shares and with the timing of federal guidelines supporting online postsecondary options.

8.7   Conclusion

In this chapter, we study the impact of increased competition from online degree programs on traditional postsecondary institutions. Following a regulatory change that increased the market entry of and enrollment in online institutions after 2006, local schools in less-competitive markets experienced relative declines in enrollment. The impacts on enrollment were concentrated among less-selective private institutions that are likely to be online schools' closest competitors. We also find that institutions responded to competitive pressure by increasing instructional spending, a broad proxy for quality. These impacts are driven by public institutions, suggesting that they also felt pressure to improve quality in response to online competition. In contrast, we find no evidence that increased competition lowered prices for in-person degree programs, perhaps because federal Title IV subsidies weaken price competition in higher education.

Our results show the importance of thinking broadly about the impact of online degree programs on US higher education. Several recent studies have found that online courses and degree programs lead to less learning, lower degree completion rates, and worse labor market outcomes. However, our findings suggest that online education can be an important driver of innovation and productivity in US higher education even if (at least at the time of writing) online institutions are producing a lower-quality product. Our results provide preliminary evidence that the threat of "disruption" from online education may cause traditionally sluggish and unresponsive institutions to improve quality or risk losing students. Another direct benefit—unexamined in this chapter—is the impact of online schools on access to higher education for students who do not live near a traditional campus or who must enroll during irregular hours. While we are still in the early days, online degrees are likely to be a disruptive force in the market for US higher education, and so they remain an important topic for future work.

Appendix

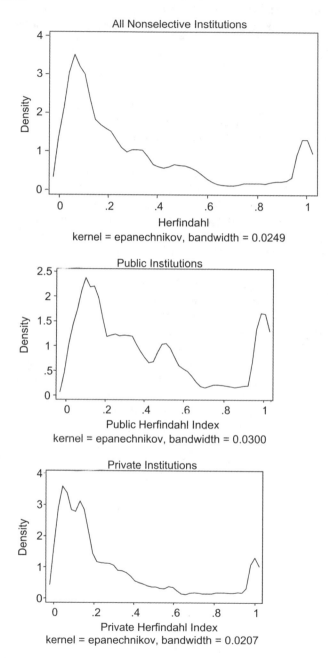

Fig. 8A.1   Distribution of Herfindahl indices

References

Allen, I. Elaine, and Jeff Seaman. 2015. *Grade Level: Tracking Online Education in the United States.* Accessed March 10, 2015. Babson Park, MA: Babson Survey Research Group.

Bettinger, Eric, Lindsay Fox, Susanna Loeb, and Eric Taylor. 2017. "Virtual Classrooms: How Online College Courses Affect Student Success." *American Economic Review* 107 (9): 2855–75.

Bowen, William G., Matthew M. Chingos, Kelly A. Lack, and Thomas I. Nygren. 2014. "Interactive Learning Online at Public Universities: Evidence from a Six-Campus Randomized Trial." *Journal of Policy Analysis and Management* 33 (1): 94–111.

Christensen, Clayton M., and Henry J. Eyring. 2011. *The Innovative University: Changing the DNA of Higher Education from the Inside Out.* Hoboken: John Wiley and Sons.

Clotfelter, Charles T. 1999. "The Familiar but Curious Economics of Higher Education: Introduction to a Symposium." *Journal of Economic Perspectives* 13:3–12.

Cook, Jason. 2018. "The Effect of Charter Competition on Unionized District Revenues and Resource Allocation." *Journal of Public Economics* 158 (February): 48–62.

Cowen, Tyler, and Alex Tabarrok. 2014. "The Industrial Organization of Online Education." *American Economic Review* 104 (5): 519–22.

Deming, David J., Claudia Goldin, and Lawrence F. Katz. 2012. "The For-Profit Postsecondary School Sector: Nimble Critters or Agile Predators?" *Journal of Economic Perspectives* 26 (1): 139–63.

Deming, David J., Claudia Goldin, Lawrence F. Katz, and Noam Yuchtman. 2015. "Can Online Learning Bend the Higher Education Cost Curve?" *American Economic Review* 105 (5): 496–501.

Deming, David J., Noam Yuchtman, Amira Abdulafi, Claudia Goldin, and Lawrence F. Katz. 2016. "The Value of Postsecondary Credentials in the Labor Market: An Experimental Study." *American Economic Review* 106 (3): 778–806.

Dettling, Lisa J., Sarena Goodman, and Jonathan Smith. 2018. "Every Little Bit Counts: The Impact of High-Speed Internet on the Transition to College." *Review of Economics and Statistics* 100 (2): 260–73.

Figlio, David, Mark Rush, and Lu Yin. 2013. "Is It Live or Is It Internet? Experimental Estimates of the Effects of Online Instruction on Student Learning." *Journal of Labor Economics* 31 (4): 763–84.

Goolsbee, Austan, Michael F. Lovenheim, and Joel Slemrod. 2010. "Playing with Fire: Cigarettes, Taxes and Competition from the Internet." *American Economic Journal: Economic Policy* 2 (1): 131–54.

Hart, Cassandra, Elizabeth Friedmann, and Michael Hill. 2014. "Online Course-Taking and Student Outcomes in California Community Colleges." Paper presented at conference of the Association for Public Policy Analysis and Management.

Ho, Andrew Dean, Justin Reich, Sergiy O. Nesterko, Daniel Thomas Seaton, Tommy Mullaney, Jim Waldo, and Isaac Chuang. 2014. "HarvardX and MITx: The First Year of Open Online Courses, Fall 2012–Summer 2013." Working paper, Harvard University.

Hoxby, Caroline M. 1997. "How the Changing Market Structure of US Higher Education Explains College Tuition." NBER Working Paper no. 6323, Cambridge, MA.

———. 2000. "Does Competition among Public Schools Benefit Students and Tax-payers?" *American Economic Review* 90 (5): 1209–38.

———. 2003. "School Choice and School Productivity: Could School Choice Be a Tide That Lifts All Boats?" In *The Economics of School Choice*, edited by Caroline M. Hoxby, 287–342. Chicago: University of Chicago Press.

———. 2009. "The Changing Selectivity of American Colleges." *Journal of Economic Perspectives* 23 (4): 95–118.

———. 2014. "The Economics of Online Postsecondary Education: MOOCs, Non-selective Education, and Highly Selective Education." NBER Working Paper no. 19816, Cambridge, MA.

Jackson, C. Kirabo. 2012. "School Competition and Teacher Labor Markets: Evidence from Charter School Entry in North Carolina." *Journal of Public Economics* 96 (5–6): 431–48.

McPherson, Michael S., and Lawrence S. Bacow. 2015. "Online Higher Education: Beyond the Hype Cycle." *Journal of Economic Perspectives* 29 (4): 135–53.

Pew Charitable Trusts. 2016. "Broadband vs. Dial-Up Adoption over Time." Accessed May 15, 2016. http://www.pewinternet.org/data-trend/internet-use/connection-type/.

Streich, Francie E. 2014. "Online Education in Community Colleges: Access, School Success, and Labor-Market Outcomes." PhD diss., University of Michigan.

Waldrop, M. Mitchell. 2014. "Massive Open Online Courses, aka MOOCs, Transform Higher Education and Science." *Nature Magazine*, March 13, 1–5.

Xu, Di, and Shanna Smith Jaggars. 2013. "The Impact of Online Learning on Students' Course Outcomes: Evidence from a Large Community and Technical College System." *Economics of Education Review* 37 (December): 46–57.

9

Estimating the Productivity of Community Colleges in Paving the Road to Four-Year College Success

Scott E. Carrell and Michal Kurlaender

Community colleges are the primary point of access to higher education for many Americans. More than 40 percent of all undergraduates attend a community college (College Board 2014). In recent years, the federal government has focused heavily on community colleges as critical drivers in the effort to increase the supply of college graduates in the United States. Moreover, the push for free community colleges, proposed by the Obama administration and modeled after programs such as the Tennessee Promise,[1] has also captured the attention of policy makers and the public at large.

Despite a relatively rich literature on the community college pathway, the research base on the quality differences between these institutions has been decidedly thin. The distinct mission and open-access nature of community colleges and the diverse goals of the students they serve make it difficult to assess differences in quality across campuses. Many suggest it is difficult to identify which outcomes should actually be measured (Bailey et al. 2006). Nevertheless, strengthening outcomes at community colleges has been a large part of the national conversation about higher education account-

Scott E. Carrell is professor of economics and the faculty athletics representative at the University of California, Davis, and a research associate of the National Bureau of Economic Research.

Michal Kurlaender is a professor and chancellor's fellow at the University of California, Davis, School of Education.

We thank the California Community College Chancellor's Office, the California State University Chancellor's Office, and the California Department of Education for their assistance with data access. Opinions reflect those of the authors and do not necessarily reflect those of the state agencies providing data. We thank Michel Grosz and Lester Lusher for their research assistance. For acknowledgments, sources of research support, and disclosure of the authors' material financial relationships, if any, please see http://www.nber.org/chapters/c13882.ack.

1. See the Tenness Promise home page: http://tennesseepromise.gov.

ability. Given the importance of the transfer pathway, it is critical to better understand the institutional determinants of transfer success. Although several papers have explored the potential quality differences across community colleges, to our knowledge, no paper has explored differences in institutional quality in the preparation for transfer by tracking students from the two-year to the four-year sector.

In this chapter, we investigate institutional differences in both the extensive and intensive margins of the transfer function across California's community college campuses. Specifically, we start with the extensive margin as in Kurlaender, Carrell, and Jackson (2016) by examining whether some community college campuses are significantly better (or worse) at producing students who transfer from the community college to a four-year college. Next, we examine the intensive margin of the transfer function by asking whether some community college campuses are better (or worse) at preparing students once they transfer to a bachelor of arts (BA) degree–granting institution. Importantly, due to the richness of our data set, we are able to adjust our estimates for a host of observed student differences and potential unobserved determinates that drive selection. Most notable is the fact that our student-level college outcomes are linked to California high school records, which include scores on 11th-grade math and English standardized tests. We are also able to control for unobservable differences that drive selection by controlling for four-year college fixed effects.

Additionally, we examine whether the community colleges, which are relatively more (or less) productive on the extensive margin of the transfer function, are also those colleges that are more (or less) productive on the intensive margin. Finally, we examine whether any observable characteristics of the community college are significantly correlated with transfer productivity.

The rest of the chapter is organized as follows: in section 9.1, we provide a brief background, reviewing some of the prior work on the transfer function and on community college quality; in section 9.2, we describe the setting, data, and methodological approach we employ for this analysis; in section 9.3, we describe the findings; in section 9.4, we discuss mechanisms; and in section 9.5, we conclude, providing a discussion of our findings and offering policy implications.

9.1   Background and Setting

The multiple missions and goals of community colleges have been well documented in the academic literature (Bailey, Jaggars, and Jenkins 2015; Brint and Karabel 1989 ; Dougherty 1994; Grubb 1991; Rosenbaum 2001). The majority of community college systems balance at least three goals: basic skills instruction, career-technical education programs, and baccalaureate transfer pathways. Rising tuition, admissions standards, and capacity constraints have limited access at many four-year universities, making community colleges the primary pathway to a baccalaureate degree for many students.

The transfer function is one of the most important and scrutinized indicators of community college success (Long and Kurlaender 2008; Melguizo, Kienzl, and Alfonso 2011). On the one hand, community colleges offer an open pathway to the BA to those for whom a four-year BA-granting institution may be out of reach (for financial, academic, or other reasons). However, the greater flexibility in enrollment afforded by community colleges (e.g., late entry, part time, combining employment with schooling) may be detrimental to a student's academic progress and lower his or her chances of transferring to a four-year college (Brint and Karabel 1989; Dougherty 1994; Grubb 1991).

Much has been written about who utilizes the transfer route from community colleges and about the individual determinants of transfer success. Several papers have concluded that those who transfer from a community college to a four-year college are of a higher social class, have higher academic preparation, are less likely to be minority, and are less likely to be female compared to the typical community college student (Adelman 2006; Dougherty 1987, 1994; Dougherty and Kienzl 2006; Gross and Goldhaber 2009; Grubb 1991; Lee and Frank 1990; Whitaker and Pascarella 1994). In fact, early work on the community college transfer route found that the socioeconomic status of the transfer group closely resembled the average social class of the original four-year college group (Dougherty 1994). Students' intent to transfer (Bradburn and Hurst 2001; Horn 2009), need for developmental courses (Bettinger and Long 2009), and course enrollment patterns while at community college (Doyle 2009; Roksa and Calcagno 2010) are also key predictors of community college transfer. Among those who do transfer to four-year institutions and complete their degrees, community college students attain similar if not the same educational and occupational rewards (Kane and Rouse 1999; Melguizo and Dowd 2008; Whitaker and Pascarella 1994).

Far less is known about institutional differences in transfer success—specifically, quality differences in the preparation community colleges offer students that transfer to BA-granting institutions. In a prior chapter, we investigated institutional quality differences among community colleges and found meaningful differences in student outcomes across California's community colleges. For example, after adjusting for differences in student inputs, our lower bound estimates show that going from the 10th to 90th percentile of campus quality is associated with a 3.68 (37.3 percent) increase in student transfer units earned, a 0.14 (20.8 percent) increase in the probability of persisting to year two at the community college, a 0.09 (42.2 percent) increase in the probability of transferring to a four-year college, and a 0.08 (26.6 percent) increase in the probability of completion of a two-year degree (Kurlaender, Carrell, and Jackson 2016).

Prior studies have explored quality differences across community colleges in the transfer function. Ehrenberg and Smith (2004) first examine differences across community colleges in New York using group data; their results indicate substantial variation in the probability of graduating with a four-year degree. They also highlight the importance of adjusting for student characteristics in academic preparation. Clotfelter and colleagues (2013) explore variation in success measures across North Carolina's 58 community colleges and find that conditional on student differences, colleges were largely indistinguishable from one another in degree receipt or transfer coursework, save for the differences between the very top and very bottom performing colleges (Clotfelter et al. 2013). Similarly, Cunha and Miller (2014) examine institutional differences in student outcomes across Texas's 30 traditional four-year public colleges. Their results show that controlling for student background characteristics (e.g., race, gender, free lunch, SAT score), the quality of high school attended, and application behavior significantly reduces the mean differences in average earned income, persistence, and graduation across four-year college campuses.

Several other researchers have also looked at the role of different institutional inputs as proxies for institutional quality. In particular, Stange (2012) exploits differences in instructional expenditures per student across community colleges and finds no impact on student attainment (degree receipt or transfer). Calcagno and colleagues (2008) identify several institutional characteristics that influence student outcomes: larger enrollment, more minority students, and more part-time faculty are associated with lower degree attainment and lower four-year transfer rates.

9.2   Research Design

9.2.1   Setting

California is home to the largest public higher education system in the nation. The 1960 Master Plan for Higher Education articulated the distinct functions of each of the state's three public postsecondary segments. The University of California (UC) is designated as the state's primary academic research institution and is reserved for the top one-eighth of the state's graduating high school class. The California State University (CSU) is intended primarily to serve the top one-third of California's high school graduating class in undergraduate training as well as graduate training through the master's degree, focusing mainly on professional training such as teacher education. Finally, the California Community Colleges (CCC) are meant to provide subbaccalaureate instruction for students through the first two years of undergraduate education (lower division) as well as vocational instruction, remedial instruction, English-as-a-second-language courses, adult noncredit instruction, community service courses, and workforce training services.

Although the vision of the Master Plan and its legacy have been heavily debated among scholars and policy makers, the result is that the state has invested heavily in its postsecondary schooling systems, and today, 84 percent of California postsecondary students attend a public two-year or four-year college. In addition to building coherence across the state's public higher education institutions, the Master Plan is also often applauded for strengthening the importance of universal access to postsecondary schooling through the community colleges. Two-thirds of all college students attend a community college in California; in 2015 the community college system served more than 2.1 million students across 113 colleges, representing 20 percent of the nation's community college students. Students enrolled at community colleges represent enormous diversity in their backgrounds and educational goals; however, the vast majority of community college enrollees intend to transfer to a four-year BA-granting institution.

A central component of California's Master Plan is the articulation of transfer pathways from the community colleges to the state's BA-granting institutions through specific general education coursework. This was recently strengthened through California's Senate Bill 1440, known as the Student Transfer Achievement Reform Act, which further reinforced articulation between the CCC and the CSU. The legislation required the community colleges to collaborate with the CSU to develop specific associate degrees for transfer based on specified general education and lower-division coursework at the community colleges that would translate to junior standing at the CSU upon transfer. The primary goal of the legislation was to reduce unnecessary course-taking and shorten the time to achieve a degree.

The architects of the Master Plan envisioned an efficient process for students who start their postsecondary schooling at a community college to obtain a baccalaureate degree. Researchers, higher education leaders, and state policy makers alike have discussed and debated the community college transfer function for more than half a century. Many of these discussions have focused on the importance of the transfer pathway for ensuring access, given capacity constraints at four-year institutions (Bohn, Reyes, and Johnson 2013). However, to date, we know very little about how institutions fare in meeting their transfer function role.

The CCC Chancellor's Office calculates transfer rates for first-time freshmen enrolled at community colleges based on two criteria: (1) 12 units earned and (2) attempt of a transfer-level math or English course. Based on this definition, the transfer rates within five years of entry at a CCC are about 41 percent system-wide and vary widely from college to college.[2] Other estimates are much lower and suggest that only 26 percent (Sengupta and Jepsen 2006) or even 18 percent (Shulock and Moore 2007) succeed in transferring to a

---

2. Calculations based on Transfer Rate Study of California Community College (2005–6 report), available at http://www.cccco.edu/Portals/4/TRIS/research/reports/transfer_report .pdf.

four-year university or earn an associate's degree within six years. Horn and Lew (2007) compare CCC transfer rates across different denominators that define transfer seeking and find very similar rates. Transfer rates also vary considerably by race/ethnicity. The raw gap in transfer rates between Hispanics and whites is 11.8 percentage points and between African Americans and whites is 7.7 percentage points (California Community Colleges Chancellor's Office 2011). National statistics—albeit somewhat dated—on the racial/ethnic gaps in transfer rates among BA-intending students who are enrolled in 12 or more credit hours note only 5 percentage points between whites and African Americans and no difference between whites and Hispanics (Bradburn and Hurst 2001).

The community college students in California who do successfully transfer to a four-year college overwhelmingly (about 80 percent) enroll at one of the campuses of the CSU system. The 23-campus CSU system is the largest public four-year higher education system in the country, educating about 1 in 10 California high school graduates and roughly 5.5 percent of the undergraduates enrolled in public four-year colleges in the entire nation.[3] The CSU system enrolls the majority of CCC transfer students. Among those who transfer, nearly 90 percent apply to only one CSU, and 80 percent enroll in the CSU closest to their community college (home).

California is an ideal state in which to investigate institutional differences at community colleges because of the large number of institutions present. Moreover, articulation between the public two-year and broad-access four-year colleges offers a unique opportunity to explore the transfer route more directly. California's public two-year and four-year colleges are situated in urban, suburban, and rural areas of the state, and their students come from public high schools that are among both the best and the worst in the nation. Thus the diversity of California's community college population reflects the student populations of other states in the United States and the mainstream public two-year colleges that educate them. As such, we believe that other states can learn important lessons from California's public postsecondary institutions.

9.2.2   Data

To explore institutional differences between community colleges in their transfer role as well as BA completion, we constructed two administrative data sets that linked cohorts of California high school juniors to both the CCC and the CSU campus they attended. These data were provided by the CCC Chancellor's Office, the CSU Chancellor's Office, and the California Department of Education.

First, to examine the extensive margin of the transfer function (the prob-

---

3. This calculation is based on a published CSU enrollment of 437,000 students (http://www
.calstate.edu/pa/2013Facts/documents/facts2013.pdf) and enrollment of 7.9 million students
in public four-year colleges nationwide in 2007 (http://nces.ed.gov/pubs2013/2013008.pdf).

ability of transferring to a four-year college), we linked all transcript and completion data for four first-time freshmen fall-semester cohorts (2004–8), ages 17–19, enrolled at a CCC with the census of California 11th-grade students with standardized test score data. The match, performed on name and birth date, high school attended, and cohort, initially captured 69 percent of first-time freshmen, ages 17–19, enrolled at a CCC (consistent with similar studies conducted by the CCC Chancellor's Office matched to K–12 data).[4]

We restrict the sample for our study to first-time freshmen at the community college who are of traditional age. We built cohorts of students who started in the summer or fall within one year of graduating high school, who attempted more than two courses (six units) in their first year, and who had complete high school test and demographic information. This sample contains 389,187 students across 108 CCC campuses.[5]

Second, to examine the intensive margin of the transfer function (how well students perform after transferring to a four-year college), we linked transcript-level records of four cohorts (2005–8) of CSU students who had transferred from a CCC to their California high school records provided by the California Department of Education. Similar to the community college data match, we linked the data on name, birth date, and gender. Using these identifiers, we were able to successfully match 70 percent of all CSU transfers. Importantly, these data from the CSU system record whether the student transferred from a CCC and from which campus specifically. Additionally, these data include information on academic performance (grade point average [GPA]), persistence at the CSU, graduation, and time to degree.

9.2.3   Measures

To examine institutional differences across community colleges in transfer and BA completion, we use multiple outcome measures. First, we start with the extensive margin by examining the probability that a student transfers from a CCC to *any* four-year college. Using National Student Clearinghouse data provided by the CCC Chancellor's office and linked to his or her own data records, we are able to tell whether a student transferred to a four-year college at any point after attending a CCC. As shown in table 9.1, 27 percent of first-time freshmen at a CCC eventually transfer to a four-year school.

---

4. Our match rates may be the result of several considerations. First, the name match occurred on the first three letters of a student's first name and last name, leading to many duplicates. Students may have entered different names or birth dates at the community college. Students may have omitted information at either system. Second, the denominator may also be too high; not all community college students attended California high schools. Finally, students who did attend a California high school but did not take the 11th-grade standardized tests were not included in the high school data.

5. We excluded the three campuses that use the quarter system as well as three adult education campuses. Summer students were only allowed in the sample if they took enough units in their first year to guarantee that they also took units in the fall.

Table 9.1   Sample descriptive statistics by student

Variable	Mean	SD	Min.	Max.	Observations
CC outcomes					
Ever Transfer	0.27	0.44	0	1	389,187
transfer to CSU	0.14	0.43	0	1	389,187
Transfer to UC	0.04	0.34	0	1	389,187
CSU outcomes					
First-term GPA	2.78	0.88	0	4	66,427
Persist to year 2	0.95	0.23	0	1	66,427
Graduate with BA	0.71	0.46	0	1	66,427
Time to degree (TTD; years)	3.14	1.21	1	9	46,378
TTD <= 2 years	0.34	0.47	0	1	46,378
TTD <= 3 years	0.71	0.45	0	1	46,378
Covariates					389,187
English test score	333.65	55.7	150	600	389,187
Math test score	291.64	48.98	150	600	389,187
Asian	0.08	0.27	0	1	389,187
Pacific Islander	0.01	0.08	0	1	389,187
Filipino	0.05	0.21	0	1	389,187
Hispanic	0.39	0.49	0	1	389,187
Black	0.07	0.25	0	1	389,187
White	0.40	0.49	0	1	389,187
Did not state race	0.01	0.08	0	1	389,187
Female	0.50	0.50	0	1	389,187
Eligible for subsidized lunch	0.32	0.47	0	1	389,187
Parent income < $24K	0.11	0.32	0	1	66,427
Parent income $24K–$36K	0.09	0.28	0	1	66,427
Parent income $36K–$48K	0.07	0.25	0	1	66,427
Parent income $48K–$60K	0.07	0.25	0	1	66,427
Parent income 60K–$72K	0.07	0.25	0	1	66,427
Parent income >$72K	0.27	0.44	0	1	66,427
Parent income missing	0.33	0.47	0	1	66,427
High school API	707.91	79.00	272.00	987.00	254,865

Notes: Variables with 389,287 observations come from the California Community College datafile, while variables with 66,427 observations come from the CSU datafile.

We then split this outcome by whether the student transferred to a CSU campus or a UC campus.

To examine the intensive margin of the transfer function, we next focus on what happens to students once they transfer to the CSU. We focus on the CSU because 52 percent of students in our sample who transferred to a BA-granting institution transferred to one of the 23 CSU campuses, while only 15 percent transferred to one of the nine UC campuses. Specifically, we measure first-term GPA, persistence rates to year two, BA degree completion, and time to degree as measured by the probability of graduating within two or three years of transfer. Tables 9.1 and 9.2 show summary statistics for these key outcome measures at the individual and college levels. The average transfer student earns a 2.78 GPA during his or her first term at the CSU

Table 9.2   **Sample descriptive statistics by community college**

Variable	Mean	SD	Min.	Max.
Outcomes				
Ever transfer	0.25	0.08	0.06	0.43
Transfer to CSU	0.12	0.05	0.01	0.22
Transfer to UC	0.04	0.03	0.00	0.16
CSU outcomes				
First-term GPA	2.74	0.17	2.22	3.12
Persist to year 2	0.93	0.04	0.67	1.00
Graduate with BA	0.68	0.09	0.29	0.81
Time to degree (TTD; years)	3.20	0.24	2.67	4.05
TTD <= 2 years	0.32	0.09	0.00	0.55
TTD <= 3 years	0.69	0.09	0.25	0.86
Covariates				
English test score (std.)	−0.05	0.27	−0.79	0.56
Math test score (std.)	−0.04	0.25	−0.72	0.44
Asian	0.07	0.07	0	0.37
Pacific Islander	0.01	0.01	0	0.05
Filipino	0.04	0.05	0	0.27
Hispanic	0.37	0.2	0.06	0.91
Black	0.08	0.11	0.01	0.69
White	0.41	0.22	0.01	0.85
Did not state race	0.01	0.01	0	0.05
Female	0.5	0.04	0.39	0.65
Eligible for subsidized lunch	0.34	0.16	0.07	0.73
Parent income < $24K	0.11	0.08	0	0.41
Parent income $24K–$36K	0.09	0.04	0	0.17
Parent income $36K–$48K	0.07	0.03	0	0.27
Parent income $48K–$60K	0.07	0.05	0	0.50
Parent income $60K–$72K	0.07	0.02	0	0.13
Parent income >$72K	0.27	0.10	0	0.46
Parent income missing	0.33	0.08	0	0.66
High school API	703.26	45.03	588.34	799.11
Community college characteristics (n = 102)				
Tenured to adjunct faculty ratio	0.94	0.37	0.24	2.53
Female to male faculty ratio	0.96	0.20	0.55	2.00
Faculty to student ratio	56.47	23.55	16.21	160.02
Support staff to student ratio	3.26	2.34	0.00	12.30
Faculty years of experience	5.10	0.83	2.49	7.61
Distance to the nearest CSU (miles)	19.42	25.12	0.89	159.52
Student Population (1,000s)	8.62	5.46	1.93	28.87
Fraction vocational education degrees/certificates	51.33	13.81	6.35	82.51

(on a 0- to 4-point scale). A vast majority of transfer students persist to the second year at CSU, with persistence rates greater than 90 percent in our sample. Graduation rates among transfer students are relatively high at 71 percent. Finally, the average time to degree in our sample is just over three years, while 34 percent and 71 percent of students graduate within two and three years of transfer, respectively.

Our data are unique in that we have the ability to connect a student's performance and outcomes at the community college and CSU with their high school data. As community colleges are open access, students do not submit transcripts from their high school and have not necessarily taken college entrance exams such as the SAT or ACT to enter. As a result, community colleges often know very little about their students' prior educational backgrounds. Researchers interested in understanding the community college population often face the same constraints (Ehrenberg and Smith 2004). Examining the outcomes of community colleges without considering the educational backgrounds of the students enrolling in a college may confound college effects with students' self-selection. Likewise, students who transfer to the CSU are also not required to take the ACT or SAT.

To address these selection issues, we are able to adjust our estimates of quality by first including important background information about a student's high school academic performance. We measure a student's performance on the 11th-grade English and mathematics California State Tests (CSTs).[6] We are also able to determine which math course a student took in 11th grade. In addition, we measure race/ethnicity, gender, and parental income.[7] To account for high school quality, we include the Academic Performance Index (API) of the high school attended (California's school accountability metric). Importantly, as students are enrolling in community college, they are asked about their goals for attending community college. Students can pick from an extensive list of 15 choices, including to transfer with an associate's degree, transfer without an associate's degree, gain a vocation certification, discover interests, improve basic skills, undecided, and others. We include students' self-reported goals as an additional covariate for their postsecondary degree intentions. Lastly, we add additional controls for college by year-level means of our individual characteristics (11th-grade CST math and English scores, race/ethnicity, gender, parental income, API, and student goal). Table 9.1 includes descriptive statistics on all our measures at the individual level, and table 9.2 includes descriptive statistics at the college level.[8]

---

6. We include CST scaled scores, which are approximately normally distributed across the state.

7. Our community college data set contains information regarding whether the student was eligible for free or reduced-priced lunch. Our CSU data file contains self-reported parental income measures.

8. Unlike the four-year-college quality literature, we do not account for students' college choice set, since most community college students enroll in the schools closest to where they attended high school. Using nationally representative data, Stange (2012) finds that in contrast to four-year college students, community college students do not appear to travel farther in search of higher-quality campuses, and importantly, "conditional on attending a school other than the closest one, there does not appear to be a relationship between student characteristics, school characteristics, and distance traveled among community college students" (Stange 2012, 81).

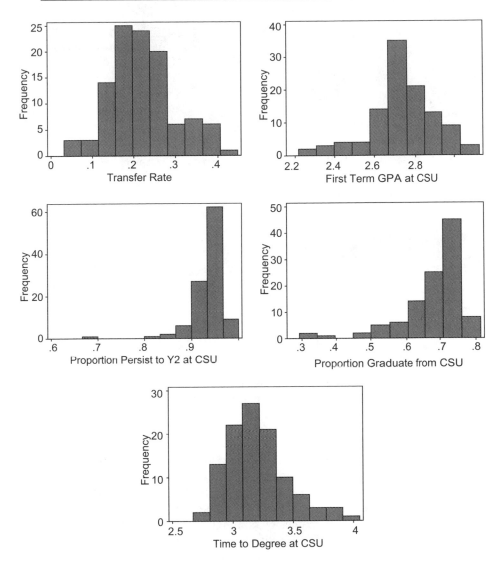

Fig. 9.1   Distribution of outcomes by community college
Source: Author's calculations based on data from CSU and CCCO Chancellor's Offices.

9.2.4   Empirical Methods

We begin by visually examining the raw outcome measures across the community colleges in our sample. Figure 9.1 presents the distribution of the proportion who transfer from a CCC, first-term GPA at CSU, proportion persisting to year two at the CSU, proportions completing a BA, and time to degree across the 108 community colleges. This figure shows consider-

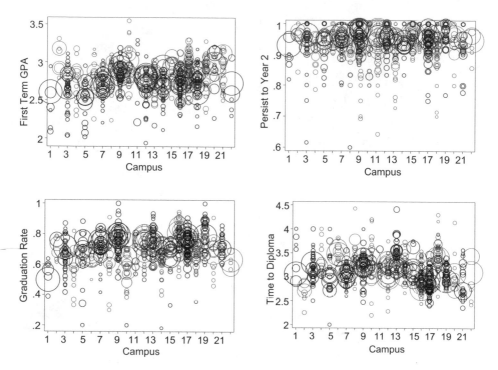

Fig. 9.2   Distribution of outcomes by community college and CSU
Source: Author's calculations based on data from CSU and CCCO Chancellor's Offices.

able variation across community college campuses in four of the five outcomes. The one exception is persistence to year two at the CSU, where a vast majority (95 percent) of students persists to year two. To further examine the amount of variation in the four posttransfer CSU outcomes (first-term GPA, persistence, graduation, and time to degree), in figure 9.2, we plot the variation in these outcomes by community college campus and CSU campus. Each CSU (receiving institution) is plotted along the *X*-axis with the corresponding sending community colleges plotted by size. These figures show two important facts. First, within each of the 23 CSU campuses, students transfer from many different community colleges. Specifically, the average CSU campus in our sample period received transfer students from 79 different CCCs. Second, there is considerable variation in the average outcomes across these community colleges from which the students transfer within each CSU campus.

Although there appears to be considerable variation in average outcomes within CSUs and across CCCs, we note that our figures are unadjusted by student inputs. Therefore, to motivate the importance of accounting for student inputs, we next plot each outcome against students' 11th-grade math

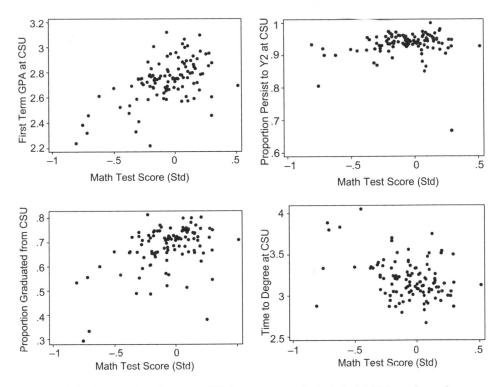

Fig. 9.3   Scatterplot of average CSU outcomes against students' 11th-grade math test scores

Source: Author's calculations based on data from CSU and CCCO Chancellor's Offices.

test scores at the college level (figure 9.3). From these simple scatterplots, it is clear that higher average student test scores are associated with better average CSU outcomes among transfer students, save for persistence. We also note that there is considerable variation in the average outcomes for students with similar high school test scores across the community colleges.

To examine whether there are significant causal differences in the extensive transfer margin (i.e., the probability of transfer) across community college campuses, we start by estimating the following linear random effects model as in Kurlaender, Carrell, and Jackson (2016):

(1) $Y_{iscty} = \beta_0 + \beta_1 x_i + \beta_2 \bar{x}_{cy} + \beta_3 w_s + \lambda_t + \phi_y + \zeta_c + \varepsilon_{iscty}$,

where Y_{iscty} is our outcome variable of interest (transfer to any four-year institutions, transfer to a CSU, or transfer to a UC) for individual i, from high school s, who is a first-time freshman enrolled at community college c, in term t in year y; x_i is a vector of individual-level characteristics (race/ethnicity, gender, parental education, and 11th-grade math and English language arts test scores), $\bar{x}_{cy}$ is community college by cohort means of x_i, and w_s is a measure of the quality of the high school attended (California's API score)[9] for each individual. Finally, ε_{iscty} is the individual-level error term.

The main parameter of interest is the community college random effect, ζ_c.[10] We estimate $\hat{\zeta}_c$ using an empirical Bayes shrinkage estimator to adjust for reliability. The empirical Bayes estimates are best linear unbiased predictors (BLUPs) of each community college's value added, which takes into account the variance (signal to noise) and the number of observations (students) at each college campus. Estimates of ζ_c with a higher variance and a fewer number of observations are shrunk toward zero (Rabe-Hesketh and Skrondal 2008).

The empirical Bayes technique is commonly used in measuring the quality of hospitals (Dimick, Staiger, and Birkmeyer 2010), schools or neighborhoods (Altonji and Mansfield 2014), and teachers (Carrell and West 2010; Kane, Rockoff, and Staiger 2008). In particular, we use methodologies similar to those recently used in the literature to rank hospital quality, which shows the importance of adjusting mortality rates for patient risk (Parker et al. 2006) and statistical reliability (caseload size; Dimick, Staiger, and Birkmeyer 2010). In our context, we similarly adjust our college rankings for "student risk" (student preparation, high school quality, and unobserved determinants of selection) as well as potential noise in our estimates driven by differences in campus size and student population.

Next, to examine whether there are significant differences in the intensive transfer margin (i.e., how well students perform after transfer) across the community college campuses, we estimate a slightly modified linear random effects model to account for selection into the CSU:

$$(2) \quad Y_{isctyu} = \beta_0 + \beta_1 x_i + \beta_2 \bar{x}_{cy} + \beta_3 w_s + \lambda_t + \phi_y + \zeta_c + \sigma_u + \varepsilon_{isctyu},$$

where Y_{isctyu} are the posttransfer outcome variables of interest (first-term GPA, persistence, graduation, and time to degree) for individual i, from high school s, who is a first-time freshman enrolled at community college c, in term t in year y at CSU campus u. All other variables in the model are the same as in equation (1), and σ_u are CSU campus fixed effects. Importantly, the CSU fixed effects control for all unobserved (fixed) variation at the CSU campus level—for example, professor experience and teaching quality, level of support services, and other unobservable differences across

---

9. The API is a measure of California schools' academic performance and growth. It is the chief component of California's Public Schools Accountability Act, passed in 1999. API is composed of schools' state standardized test scores and results on the California High School Exit Exam; scores range from a low of 200 to a high of 1000.

10. We use a random-effects model instead of a fixed-effects model due to the efficiency (minimum variance) of the random-effects model. However, our findings are qualitatively similar when using a fixed-effects framework; for our main results in table 9.3, the correlations between the fixed- and random-effects estimates range between 0.983 and 0.991.

the CSU campuses that influence posttransfer outcomes. Importantly, the CSU fixed effects also control for individual unobservable differences that drive selection and choice.

9.3   Results

9.3.1   Extensive Margin Transfer Outcomes

We start by examining whether there are significant differences across community colleges in the probability of transferring to a four-year college, as in Kurlaender, Carrell, and Jackson (2016). To do so, we examine whether there is significant variation in our estimates of $\hat{\zeta}_c$s for our three transfer outcomes of interest. Table 9.3 presents the results of the estimated standard deviation, σ_{ζ}, in our college effects for various specifications of equation (1). High values of σ_{ζ} indicate there is significant variation in the probability of transferring across community college campuses, while low values of σ_{ζ} would indicate that there is little difference in student transfer outcomes across campuses.

In specification 1, we start with the most naive estimates, where we include only year and term indicator variables. Results show that a one-standard-deviation change in campus quality is associated with a 0.072 percentage point increase in the probability of transfer. This effect is quite large, representing a 27 percent increase from the mean in the probability of transfer. However, these unadjusted estimates are analogous to comparing simple

Table 9.3   Standard deviations in random effects: Community college outcomes

		SD of random effects estimates		
Specification	Controls	Transfer	Transfer to CSU	Transfer to UC
(1)	Year/term	0.072	0.040	0.029
		[0.063, 0.082]	[0.035, 0.046]	[0.025, 0.033]
(2)	Test scores	0.054	0.034	0.023
		[0.047, 0.062]	[0.030, 0.040]	[0.020, 0.026]
(3)	Demographics	0.047	0.031	0.022
		[0.041, 0.054]	[0.027, 0.036]	[0.019, 0.025]
(4)	Goal	0.044	0.029	0.021
		[0.038, 0.050]	[0.025, 0.033]	[0.019, 0.025]
(5)	School API	0.039	0.027	0.021
		[0.034, 0.045]	[0.023, 0.031]	[0.018, 0.024]
(6)	College means	0.041	0.026	0.019
		[0.035, 0.047]	[0.022, 0.031]	[0.016, 0.022]
# of community colleges		108	108	108

Notes: Each cell represents the standard deviation of the community college random effects; 95 percent confidence intervals in brackets.

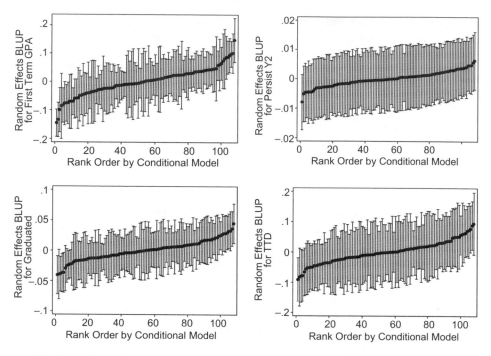

Fig. 9.3   Scatterplot of average CSU outcomes against students' 11th-grade math test scores

Source: Author's calculations based on data from CSU and CCCO Chancellor's Offices.

means in student transfer rates across college campuses and likely overstate the true value added of college campuses.

To adjust our estimates for differences in student-level inputs, in specifications 2–4 of table 9.3, we sequentially adjust our estimates of $\hat{\zeta}_c$ for a host of student-level covariates. This procedure is similar to the hospital quality literature that calculates risk-adjusted mortality rates (Dimick, Staiger, and Birkmeyer 2010). Importantly, starting in specification 2, we include scores from the 11th-grade California State Test (CST). Doing so likely removes a significant amount of potential bias in our estimates, as the teacher-quality literature has previously shown that teacher value-added estimates are unbiased when conditioned on prior-year test scores (Kane, Rockoff, and Staiger 2008). In specification 3, we add individual-level demographic characteristics (race/ethnicity, gender, and parental income level). In specification 4, we control for the student's goal for attending community college. In specification 5, we add California's API scores for each student's high school to control for differences in high school quality.

Results in specifications 2–5 indicate that even after controlling for student-level observable characteristics, there is considerable variation in transfer rates across California's community colleges. For specification 5, a one-standard-deviation increase in community college quality is associated with a 0.039 percentage point (14.4 percent) increase in the probability of transferring to a four-year college.

In specification 6, we add campus by cohort means of our various individual demographic variables to address concerns with selection on unobservables (Altonji, Elder, and Taber 2005), as suggested by Altonji and Mansfield (2014), and to control for differences in peer quality, which has been shown to affect transfer outcomes (Smith and Stange 2016). Doing so likely provides a *lower bound* of the estimated variance in the campus quality effects.[11] In this fully specified model, our estimate remains substantively unchanged with a one-standard-deviation increase in campus quality associated with a 0.041 percentage point (15.2 percent) increase in the probability of transferring.

In columns 2 and 3, we present results when we split the outcome by whether the student transferred to a CSU campus or a UC campus. Results show substantially higher variation across community college campuses in the probability of transferring to a CSU compared to a UC. Specifically, in our fully specified model, one standard deviation in the community college effect is associated with a 2.7 percentage point increase in the probability of transferring to a CSU and a 1.8 percentage point increase in the probability of transferring to a UC.

9.3.2 Intensive Margin Transfer Outcomes

The previous results show significant variation across community college campuses in the probability of transferring to a BA-granting institution. However, a natural follow-up question is whether some campuses produce students who perform better once they transfer. This question is analogous to the recent teacher-quality literature that examines how teachers affect both contemporaneous academic achievement as well as longer-term outcomes, such as later academic performance and labor market outcomes (Carrell and West 2010; Chetty et al. 2014). To answer this question, we next present results for our intensive margin outcomes that measure first-term GPA at the CSU, persistence to year two at the CSU, BA degree receipt, and time to degree as measured by the probability of graduating within two or three years at the CSU. As previously discussed, to overcome selection issues in college choice, we include CSU fixed effects in all our specifications, with results presented in table 9.4.

Analogous to our previously presented results, we start with a naive model that includes only year and term effects as well as CSU campus fixed effects. We then sequentially add control variables to the model. While the addition

---

11. Altonji and Mansfield (2014) show that, under reasonable assumptions, controlling for group means of individual-level characteristics "also controls for *all* of the across-group variation in the unobservable individual characteristics." This procedure provides a lower bound of the school-quality effects because school quality is likely an unobservable that drives individual selection.

Table 9.4   Standard deviations in random effects: CSU outcomes

		SD of random effects estimates				
Specification	Controls	First-term GPA	Persist to year 2	Graduate with BA	TTD <=2 years	TTD <=3 years
(1)	Year/term	0.122	0.011	0.039	0.041	0.036
		[0.103, 0.145]	[0.008, 0.015]	[0.031, 0.048]	[0.033, 0.050]	[0.028, 0.044]
(2)	Test scores	0.105	0.011	0.038	0.040	0.036
		[0.088, 0.126]	[0.008, 0.014]	[0.030, 0.047]	[0.032, 0.050]	[0.028, 0.045]
(3)	Demographics	0.088	0.010	0.034	0.035	0.030
		[0.072, 0.106]	[0.007, 0.014]	[0.027, 0.042]	[0.027, 0.044]	[0.023, 0.038]
(4)	School API	0.085	0.010	0.031	0.033	0.028
		[0.070, 0.104]	[0.007, 0.014]	[0.024, 0.040]	[0.026, 0.043]	[0.021, 0.036]
(5)	College means	0.066	0.009	0.025	0.028	0.023
		[0.054, 0.082]	[0.006, 0.013]	[0.019, 0.033]	[0.022, 0.037]	[0.017, 0.031]
# of community colleges		108	108	108	108	108

Notes: Each cell represents the standard deviation of the community college random effects. All specifications include CSU fixed effects; 95 percent confidence intervals in brackets.

of control variables reduces the variation in the campus effects, significant variations in outcomes across community college campuses persist. Results for the fully specified model (specification 5) show that a one-standard-deviation increase in community college campus quality is associated with a 0.066 (2.3 percent) increase in first-term GPA at the CSU, a 0.009 percentage point (1 percent) increase in the probability of persisting to year two, a 0.025 percentage point (3.6 percent) increase in the probability of BA completion, a 0.028 percentage point (8.2 percent) increase in the probability of graduating within two years of transfer, and a 2.3 percentage point (3.2 percent) increase in the probability of graduating within three years of transfer.

9.4   Mechanisms

Understanding why some colleges are more successful than others in the transfer function (or in other outcomes) is of critical importance and has captured the attention of higher education leaders in discussions about college quality, prompted in part by the US Department of Education's College Scorecard.[12] Although there are many factors that may influence productivity, we explore this question by regressing the community college campus effects (BLUPs) that we estimate in tables 9.3 and 9.4 on observable characteristics of the community college. Specifically, we explore whether the following attributes at the community college are correlated with college effectiveness: (1) tenured-to-adjunct faculty ratio, (2) female-to-male faculty ratio, (3) faculty-to-student ratio, (4) support staff-to-student ratio,

12. See https://collegescorecard.ed.gov.

(5) faculty experience, (6) distance to the nearest CSU, (7) school size, and (8) the fraction of degrees or certificates conferred that are vocational (career technical) education.[13]

Although we cannot claim the causality of the estimates, results show suggestive evidence that community colleges that are closer to a CSU, are larger in size, have more female faculty, and have a smaller fraction of students pursuing vocational education degrees are associated with better student transfer outcomes (table 9.5).

For example, a one-mile increase in the distance to the CSU is correlated with a –0.02 percentage point decrease in the probability of graduation ($p = 0.052$); however, distance is not correlated with our other outcomes. Likewise, a 1,000 student (0.18 standard deviations) increase in the size of the community college is associated with significant increases in first-term GPA (0.37 grade points), persistence to year two (0.03 percentage points), and graduating with a BA (0.08 percentage points).

As previously discussed, community colleges often have multiple missions. As such, it is not surprising that we find a negative correlation between our campus effect measuring the probability of transfer and the fraction of degrees and certificates conferred that are vocational. Specifically, we find that a 1 percentage point increase in the fraction of vocationally oriented degrees/certificates awarded is associated with a nearly 9 percentage point decrease in the probability of transferring.

Finally, faculty characteristics appear to be potentially related to student outcomes. Although imprecisely estimated, results show that a 0.10 point increase in the female-to-male faculty ratio is associated with a 0.42 increase in GPA ($p = 0.14$) and a 0.016 percentage point increase in the probability of graduating within two years of transfer ($p = 0.17$). Several experimental and quasi-experimental studies have explored specific faculty characteristics and institutional practices and programs and their impact on persistence and degree attainment. Studies exploring faculty characteristics have shown that professor gender, race/ethnicity, rank, education, and experience can significantly influence course performance, choice of major, and graduation (Carrell, Page, and West 2010; Carrell and West 2010; Fairlie, Hoffman, and Oreopoulos 2013; Hoffman and Oreopoulos 2009). However, it is unclear exactly why professor characteristics are correlated with student achievement.

A natural follow-up question is whether the community colleges that are relatively successful (or unsuccessful) in having their students transfer to a four-year college are the same community colleges that produce students

---

13. We also examined financial indicators such as faculty salaries and institutional spending; however, these data were only available for a subset of our colleges (67 of 108). Within this subset of schools, we found no significant correlations between our estimated college effects and financial indicators.

Table 9.5 College random effects regressed on observable characteristics

Variable Specification	Transfer ever (1)	Transfer to CSU (2)	First-term GPA (3)	Persist to year 2 (4)	Graduate with BA (5)	TTD <=2 years (6)	TTD <=3 years (6)
Tenured to adjunct faculty ratio	-0.707	0.749	2.237	0.068	0.359	0.359	0.640
	(1.066)	(0.721)	(1.494)	(0.147)	(0.524)	(0.602)	(0.452)
Female to male faculty ratio	-0.553	0.106	3.806	0.373	0.618	1.563	0.935
	(2.049)	(1.386)	(2.872)	(0.283)	(1.006)	(1.157)	(0.869)
Faculty to student ratio	-0.024	-0.014	0.030	0.002	-0.005	0.006	-0.008
	(0.019)	(0.013)	(0.027)	(0.003)	(0.009)	(0.011)	(0.008)
Support staff to student ratio	0.289	0.066	0.067	-0.014	-0.013	-0.109	0.063
	(0.184)	(0.125)	(0.258)	(0.025)	(0.091)	(0.104)	(0.078)
Average faculty years of experience at the college	-0.354	-0.089	-0.637	0.066	-0.180	-0.145	-0.106
	(0.519)	(0.351)	(0.727)	(0.072)	(0.255)	(0.293)	(0.220)
Distance to the nearest CSU (miles)	0.011	-0.014	0.023	0.000	-0.018**	0.006	0.007
	(0.018)	(0.012)	(0.025)	(0.002)	(0.009)	(0.010)	(0.008)
Student population (1,000s)	0.158*	0.028	0.404***	0.024**	0.082**	0.066	0.053
	(0.080)	(0.054)	(0.113)	(0.011)	(0.040)	(0.045)	(0.034)
Fraction vocational education degrees/certificates	-0.089***	-0.023	-0.042	0.009**	-0.006	-0.003	-0.018
	(0.030)	(0.020)	(0.042)	(0.004)	(0.015)	(0.017)	(0.013)
# of community colleges	102	102	102	102	102	102	102
R-squared	0.164	0.058	0.162	0.155	0.164	0.06	0.096

Notes: Each column represents a separate regression where the indicated community college random effects are regressed on observable characteristics of the community college. Random effects estimates were divided by 100 prior to running the regressions. ***, **, and * represent 0.01, 0.05, and 0.10 levels of significance, respectively.

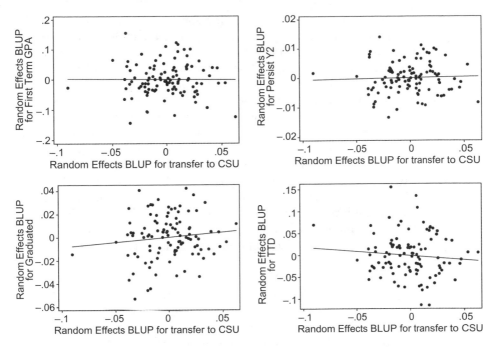

Fig. 9.5   Intensive transfer margin versus extensive transfer margin
Source: Author's calculations based on data from CSU and CCCO Chancellor's Offices.

who are relatively successful (or unsuccessful) at the four-year college after transferring. To explore this relationship, in figure 9.5, we plot each community college's extensive margin effects against their intensive margin effects.[14] The pattern of results suggests that there is a small positive relationship between the probability of transfer and student performance after transfer. That is, the community colleges that are more (or less) successful at producing students who transfer to a four-year college also produce students who tend to perform better (or worse) after transferring (in terms of GPA, graduation, and time to degree).

9.5   Conclusion

To our knowledge, this is the first study in the literature to examine how institutional differences across community colleges affect both the extensive and intensive margins of the transfer function. Results show there is significant variation in community college quality for both the probability of transfer and outcomes measuring how well students perform after transferring.

14. We plot the BLUPs of each community college's random effects.

Overall, our results show significant differences across community colleges in both the intensive and extensive margins of the transfer function. Specifically, after adjusting for observable student differences and unobservable factors that drive selection, we find that some community colleges are relatively more (or less) efficient in producing students who are more likely to transfer and to achieve at a higher level at their posttransfer institutions.

There is a small positive relationship between the extensive and intensive margin outcomes, indicating that the schools that are better at producing students who transfer also produce students who, on average, perform equally well or better at their four-year institutions posttransfer. We find some evidence that observable characteristics of the community colleges are correlated with transfer productivity. Specifically, larger community colleges, colleges closer to a CSU, and colleges with more female faculty are associated with a more positive transfer outcome. (In ongoing work, we also examine productivity by student type: academic preparation, income, and race.)

Of course, there may be a host of factors we don't observe that make some of these institutions more effective at the transfer function than others. The transfer process is complex, and navigating it successfully requires an understanding of the requirements to do so at two different institutions (i.e., the sending community college and the receiving CSU). Thus it is likely that colleges vary greatly in their ability to direct students along this pathway (e.g., through improved information, counseling, course articulation, or even scheduling). Moreover, colleges also vary in their implementation of state policies and programs aimed specifically at smoothing the transfer pathways. For example, as Baker (2016) shows, campus adoption of the Associate Degree for Transfer (an articulated a set of courses between community colleges and the CSU campuses), varied across the state's community college campuses. In addition, others have noted variation across colleges in the adoption of the Early Assessment Program (for student placement in remedial coursework; Friedmann, Kurlaender, and Van Ommeren 2016), in financial aid policies and procedures (Friedmann and Martorell 2017), and in the various components of the 2012 Student Success Act, which aims to improve completion and transfer outcomes at CCCs (Gordon 2017).

To date, much of the research on college quality has focused largely on more-selective four-year colleges and universities. Yet the increased policy focus on community colleges demands careful attention to quality differences among these open-access institutions, particularly in facilitating transfer and degree completion. In this chapter, we leverage rich administrative data from two of the largest public higher education systems to investigate institutional quality differences across community colleges in their efforts to prepare and pave the road for transfer students in pursuit of the BA.

References

Adelman, C. 2006. *The Toolbox Revisited*. Washington, DC: US Department of Education.

Altonji, Joseph G., Todd E. Elder, and Christopher R. Taber. 2005. "Selection on Observed and Unobserved Variables: Assessing the Effectiveness of Catholic Schools." *Journal of Political Economy* 113 (1): 151–84.

Altonji, Joseph, and Richard Mansfield. 2014. "Group-Average Observables as Controls for Sorting on Unobservables When Estimating Group Treatment Effects: The Case of School and Neighborhood Effects." NBER Working Paper no. 20781, Cambridge, MA.

Baker, Rachel. 2016. "The Effects of Structured Transfer Pathways in Community Colleges." *Educational Evaluation and Policy Analysis* 38 (4): 626–64.

Bailey, Thomas, Juan Carlos Calcagno, Davis Jenkins, Timothy Leinbach, and Gregory Kienzl. 2006. "Is Student-Right-to-Know All You Should Know? An Analysis of Community College Graduation Rates." *Research in Higher Education* 47 (5): 491–519.

Bailey, Thomas, Shaunna Jaggars, and Davis Jenkins. 2015. *Redesigning America's Community Colleges*. New York: Teacher's College.

Bettinger, Eric, and Bridget Terry Long. 2009. "Addressing the Needs of Underprepared Students in Higher Education: Does College Remediation Work?" *Journal of Human Resources* 44 (3): 736–71.

Bohn, Sara, Belinda Reyes, and Hans Johnson. 2013. *The Impact of Budget Cuts on California's Community Colleges*. Public Policy Institute of California. https://www.ppic.org/content/pubs/report/R_313SBR.pdf.

Bradburn, E. M., and D. G. Hurst. 2001. *Community College Transfer Rates to 4-Year Institutions Using Alternative Definitions of Transfer*. Washington, DC: US Department of Education, National Center for Education Statistics.

Brand, Jennie E., and Charles N. 2006. "Regression and Matching Estimates of the Effects of Elite College Attendance on Educational and Career Achievement." *Social Science Research* 35:749–70.

Brint, Steve, and Jerome Karabel. 1989. *The Diverted Dream: Community Colleges and the Promise of Educational Opportunity in America, 1900–1985*. New York: Oxford University Press.

Calcagno, Juan Carlos, Thomas Bailey, Davis Jenkins, Gregory Kienzl, and Timothy Leinbach. 2008. "Community College Student Success: What Institutional Characteristics Make a Difference?" *Economics of Education Review* 27:632–45.

California Community Colleges Chancellor's Office. "Data Resources." https://www.cccco.edu/About-Us/Chancellors-Office/Divisions/Digital-Innovation-and-Infrastructure/Research/Data-Sources-with-Documentation-Links.

Carrell, Scott E., Marianne E. Page, and James E. West, 2010. "Sex and Science: How Professor Gender Perpetuates the Gender Gap." *Quarterly Journal of Economics* 125 (3): 1101–44.

Carrell, Scott E., and James E. West. 2010. "Does Professor Quality Matter? Evidence from Random Assignment of Students to Professors." *Journal of Political Economy* 118 (3): 409–32.

Chetty, Raj, Nathanial Hendren, Patrick Kline, and Emmanuel Saez. 2014. "Where Is the Land of Opportunity? The Geography of Intergenerational Mobility in the United States." *Quarterly Journal of Economics* 129 (4): 1553–1623.

Clotfelter, Charles T., Helen F. Ladd, Clara G. Muschkin, and Jacob L. Vigdor.

2013. "Success in Community College: Do Institutions Differ?" *Research in Higher Education* 54:805–24.

Cunha, Jesse, and Trey Miller. 2013. "Measuring Value-Added in Higher Education: Possibilities and Limitations in the Use of Administrative Data." *Economics of Education Review* 42:64–77.

Dimick, Justin, Douglas Staiger, and John Birkmeyer. 2010. "Ranking Hospitals on Surgical Mortality: The Importance of Reliability Adjustment." *Health Services Research* 45 (6): 1614–29.

Dougherty, K. J. 1987. "The Effects of Community Colleges: Aid or Hindrance to Socioeconomic Attainment?" *Sociology of Education* 60 (2): 86–103.

———. 1994. *The Contradictory College: The Conflicting Origins, Impacts, and Futures of the Community College.* Albany: State University of New York Press.

Dougherty, K. J., and G. S. Kienzl. 2006. "It's Not Enough to Get through the Open Door: Inequalities by Social Background in Transfer from Community Colleges to Four-Year Colleges." *Teachers College Record* 108 (3): 452–87.

Doyle, William R. 2009. "The Effect of Community College Enrollment on Bachelor's Degree Completion." *Economics of Education Review* 28 (2): 199–206.

Ehrenberg, Ronald G., and Christopher L. Smith, 2004. "Analyzing the Success of Student Transitions from 2- to 4-Year Institutions within a State." *Economics of Education Review* 23:11–28.

Fairlie, Robert W., Florian Hoffmann, and Philip Oreopoulos. 2014. "A Community College Instructor like Me: Race and Ethnicity Interactions in the Classroom." *American Economic Review* 104 (8): 2567–91.

Friedmann, E., M. Kurlaender, and A. van Ommeren. 2016. "Addressing College Readiness Gaps at the College Door." *New Directions for Community Colleges* 176:45–52.

Friedmann, E., and F. Martorell. 2017. "Money Left on the Table: An Analysis of Financial Aid Receipt among Financially-Eligible Community College Students." Working paper presented at the Association of Public Policy and Management Conference, Chicago, November.

Goldhaber, Dan, Stephanie Liddle, Roddy Theobald, and Joe Walch. 2010. "Teacher Effectiveness and the Achievement of Washington's Students in Mathematics." Center for Education Data and Research, University of Washington. CEDR Working Paper 2010-06.

Gordon, L. 2017. "California 'Student Success' Initiative Slow to Increase Community College Completion Rates." *EdSource*, April 2.

Gross, Betheny, and Dan Goldhaber. 2009. "Community College Transfer and Articulation: Policies: Looking beneath the Surface." CRPE Working Paper 2009-1.

Grubb, W. Norton. 1991. "The Decline of Community College Transfer Rates: Evidence from National Longitudinal Surveys." *Journal of Higher Education* 62 (2): 194–222.

Hoffman, Florian, and Philip Oreopoulos. 2009. "Professor Qualities and Student Achievement." *Review of Economics and Statistics* 91 (2009): 83–92.

Horn, L., and S. Lew. 2007. *California Community College Transfer Rates: Who Is Counted Makes a Difference.* MPR research brief. http://mprinc.com/products /pdf/horn_ccc.pdf.

Horn, Laura. 2009. *On Track to Complete? A Taxonomy of Beginning Community College Students and Their Outcomes 3 Years after Enrolling: 2003–04 through 2006.* National Center for Educational Statistics Statistical Analysis Report. https://nces.ed.gov/pubs2009/2009152.pdf.

Kane, Thomas J., Jonah E. Rockoff, and Douglas O. Staiger. 2008. "What Does

Certification Tell Us about Teacher Effectiveness? Evidence from New York City." *Economics of Education Review* 27 (6): 615–31.

Kane, Thomas J., and Cecilia Elena Rouse. 1999. "The Community College: Educating Students at the Margin between College and Work." *Journal of Economic Perspectives* 13 (1): 63–84.

Kurlaender, Michal, Scott Carrell, and Jacob Jackson. 2016. "The Promises and Pitfalls of Measuring Community College Quality." *Russell Sage Foundation Journal of the Social Sciences* 2 (1): 174–90.

Lee, V., and K. Frank. 1990. "Students' Characteristics that Facilitate the Transfer from Two-Year to Four-Year Colleges." *Sociology of Education* 63 (3): 178–93.

Long, B. T., and M. Kurlaender. 2009. "Do Community Colleges Provide a Viable Pathway to Baccalaureate Degree?" *Educational Evaluation and Policy Analysis* 31 (1): 30–53.

Melguizo, T., and A. C. Dowd. 2008. "Baccalaureate Success of Transfers and Rising Four-Year College Juniors." *Teachers College Record* 111 (1): 55–89.

Melguizo, T., G. S. Kienzl, and M. Alfonso. 2011. "Comparing the Educational Attainment of Community College Transfer Students and Four-Year College Rising Juniors Using Propensity Score Matching Methods." *Journal of Higher Education* 82 (3): 265–91.

Parker, J. P., Z. Li, C. L. Damberg, B. Danielsen, and D. M. Carlisle. 2006. "Administrative versus Clinical Data for Coronary Artery Bypass Graft Surgery Report Cards: The View from California." *Medical Care* 44 (7): 687–95.

Rabe-Hesketh, Sophia, and Anders Skrondal. 2008. *Multilevel and Longitudinal Modeling Using Stata.* 2nd ed. College Station, TX: Stata Press.

Roksa, Josipa, and Juan Carlos Calcagno. 2010. "Catching Up in Community Colleges: Academic Preparation and Transfer to Four-Year Institutions." *Teachers College Record* 112:260–88.

Rosenbaum, James. 2001. *Beyond College for All: Career Paths for the Forgotten Half.* New York: Russell Sage Foundation.

Sengupta, Ria, and Christopher Jepsen. 2006. "California's Community College Students." *California Counts: Population Trends and Profiles* 8 (2): 1–24.

Shulock, Nancy, and Colleen Moore. 2007. *Rules of the Game: How State Policy Creates Barriers to Degree Completion and Impedes Student Success in the California Community Colleges.* Sacramento, CA: Institute for Higher Education and Leadership.

Smith, Jonathan, and Kevin Stange. 2016. "A New Measure of College Quality to Study the Effects of College Sector and Peers on Degree Attainment." *Education Finance and Policy* 11 (4): 369–403.

Stange, Kevin. 2012. "Ability Sorting and the Importance of College Quality to Student Achievement: Evidence from Community Colleges." *Education Finance and Policy* 7 (1): 74–105.

Whitaker, D., and E. Pascarella. 1994. "Two-Year College Attendance and Socioeconomic Attainment: Some Additional Evidence." *Journal of Higher Education* 65 (2): 194–210.

Contributors

Joseph G. Altonji
Department of Economics
Yale University
Box 208264
New Haven, CT 06520-8264

Scott E. Carrell
Department of Economics
University of California, Davis
One Shields Avenue
Davis, CA 95616

Paul N. Courant
Gerald R. Ford School of Public Policy
University of Michigan
Weill Hall
735 S. State Street #4126
Ann Arbor, MI 48109

Pieter De Vlieger
Department of Economics
University of Michigan
611 Tappan Avenue
Ann Arbor, MI 48109-1220

David J. Deming
Harvard Graduate School of
  Education
Gutman 411
Appian Way
Cambridge, MA 02138

Caroline M. Hoxby
Department of Economics
Stanford University
Landau Building, 579 Serra Mall
Stanford, CA 94305

Brian Jacob
Gerald R. Ford School of Public Policy
University of Michigan
735 South State Street
Ann Arbor, MI 48109

Michal Kurlaender
School of Education
University of California, Davis
One Shields Avenue
Davis, CA 95616

Michael Lovenheim
Department of Policy Analysis and
  Management
Cornell University
264 Ives Hall
Ithaca, NY 14853

Veronica Minaya
Community College Research Center
Teachers College, Columbia University
Box 174
525 West 120th Street
New York, NY 10027

Richard Patterson
Department of Social Sciences
United States Military Academy
607 Cullum Road
West Point, NY 10995

Evan Riehl
Department of Economics
Cornell University
266 Ives Hall
Ithaca, NY 14853

Juan E. Saavedra
Dornsife Center for Economic and
    Social Research
University of Southern California
635 Downey Way
Los Angeles, CA 90089

Judith Scott-Clayton
Teachers College
Columbia University
525 West 120th Street, Box 174
New York, NY 10027

Douglas Staiger
Department of Economics
Dartmouth College
HB6106, 301 Rockefeller Hall
Hanover, NH 03755-3514

Kevin Stange
Gerald R. Ford School of Public Policy
University of Michigan
5236 Weill Hall
735 South State Street
Ann Arbor, MI 48109

Sarah Turner
Department of Economics
University of Virginia
Monroe Hall, Room 237
248 McCormick Rd
Charlottesville, VA 22903

Miguel Urquiola
Department of Economics
Columbia University
1022 IAB, MC 3308
420 West 118th Street
New York, NY 10027

Seth D. Zimmerman
Booth School of Business
University of Chicago
5807 S. Woodlawn Avenue
Chicago, IL 60637

Author Index

Subject Index